uare

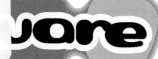

JUDITH PARK

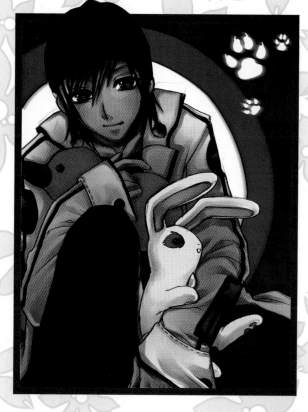

Yen Press

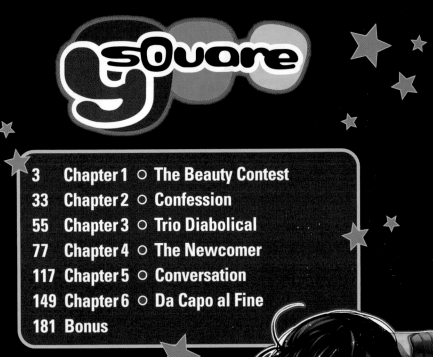

g square

Y SQUARE by Judith Park

Translation: Michael Waaler
Lettering: Logan Johnson

Text and illustrations copyright
© Judith Park / Carlsen Verlag GmbH, Hamburg 2005
Translation copyright © 2007 by Hachette Book Group USA, Inc.

Yen Press
Hachette Book Group USA
237 Park Avenue, New York, NY 10017

Visit our Web sites at www.HachetteBookGroupUSA.com
and www.YenPress.com.

Yen Press is a division of Hachette Book Group USA, Inc.
The Yen Press name and logo is a trademark of
Hachette Book Group USA, Inc.

First Edition: December 2007

The characters and events in this book are
fictitious. Any similarity to real persons, living
or dead, is coincidental and not intended by
the author.

10 9 8 7 6 5 4 3 2 1
BVG
Printed in the United
States of America

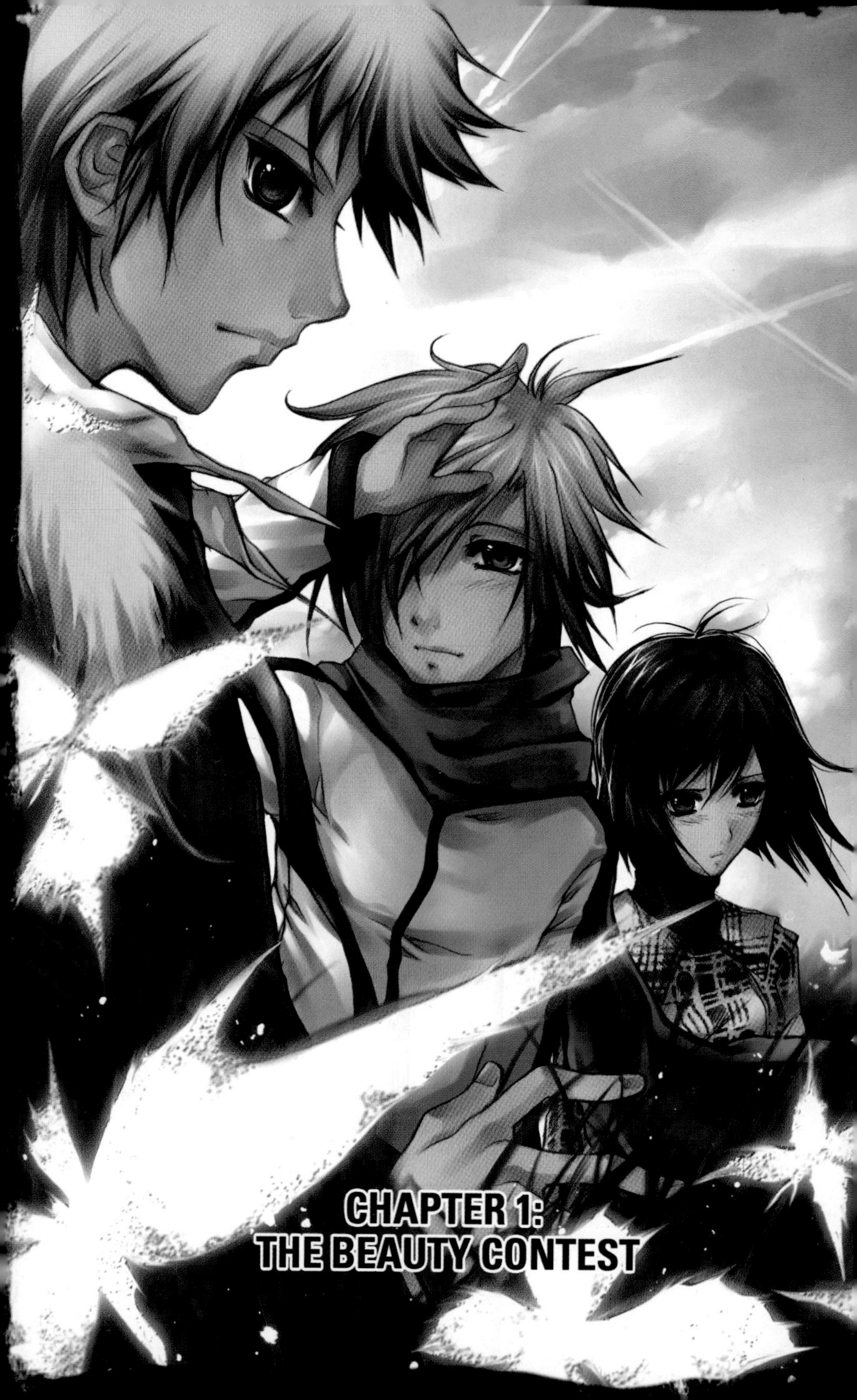
CHAPTER 1:
THE BEAUTY CONTEST

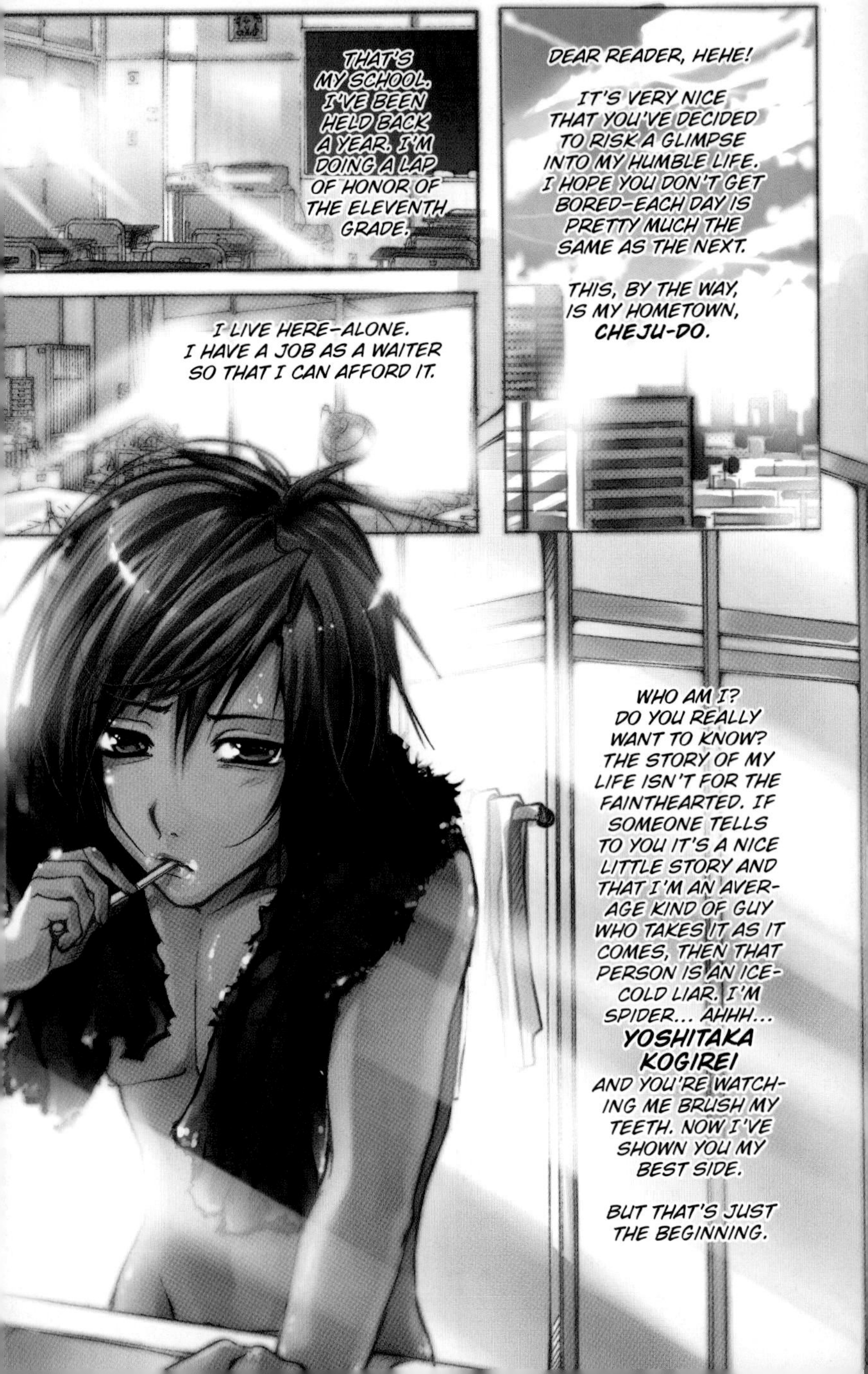
DEAR READER, HEHE!
IT'S VERY NICE THAT YOU'VE DECIDED TO RISK A GLIMPSE INTO MY HUMBLE LIFE. I HOPE YOU DON'T GET BORED–EACH DAY IS PRETTY MUCH THE SAME AS THE NEXT.
THIS, BY THE WAY, IS MY HOMETOWN, **CHEJU-DO**.
THAT'S MY SCHOOL. I'VE BEEN HELD BACK A YEAR. I'M DOING A LAP OF HONOR OF THE ELEVENTH GRADE.
I LIVE HERE–ALONE. I HAVE A JOB AS A WAITER SO THAT I CAN AFFORD IT.
WHO AM I? DO YOU REALLY WANT TO KNOW? THE STORY OF MY LIFE ISN'T FOR THE FAINTHEARTED. IF SOMEONE TELLS TO YOU IT'S A NICE LITTLE STORY AND THAT I'M AN AVERAGE KIND OF GUY WHO TAKES IT AS IT COMES, THEN THAT PERSON IS AN ICE-COLD LIAR. I'M SPIDER... AHHH... **YOSHITAKA KOGIREI** AND YOU'RE WATCHING ME BRUSH MY TEETH. NOW I'VE SHOWN YOU MY BEST SIDE.
BUT THAT'S JUST THE BEGINNING.

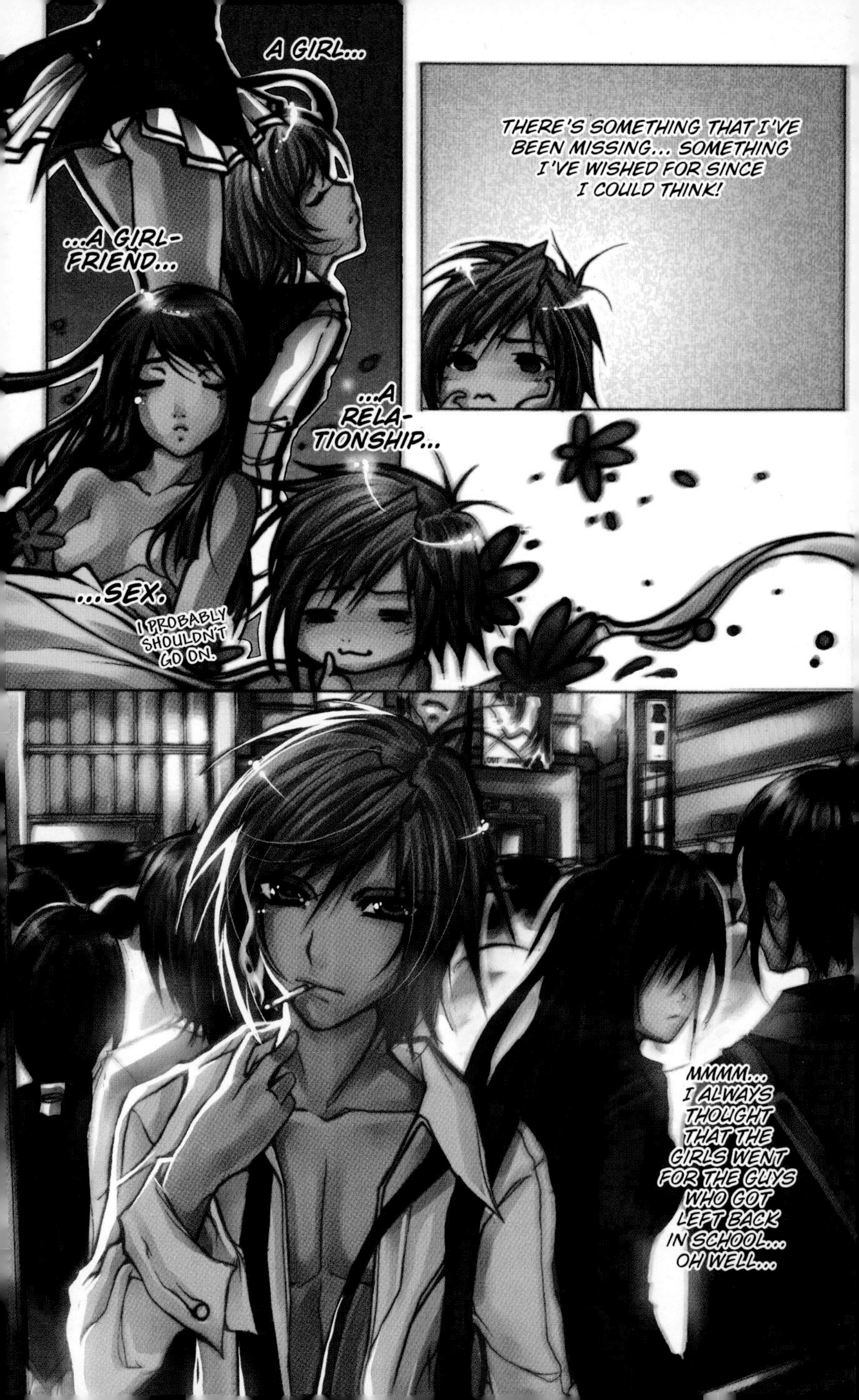
THERE'S SOMETHING THAT I'VE BEEN MISSING... SOMETHING I'VE WISHED FOR SINCE I COULD THINK!
A GIRL...
...A GIRL-FRIEND...
...A RELA-TIONSHIP...
...SEX.
I PROBABLY SHOULDN'T GO ON.
MMMM... I ALWAYS THOUGHT THAT THE GIRLS WENT FOR THE GUYS WHO GOT LEFT BACK IN SCHOOL... OH WELL...

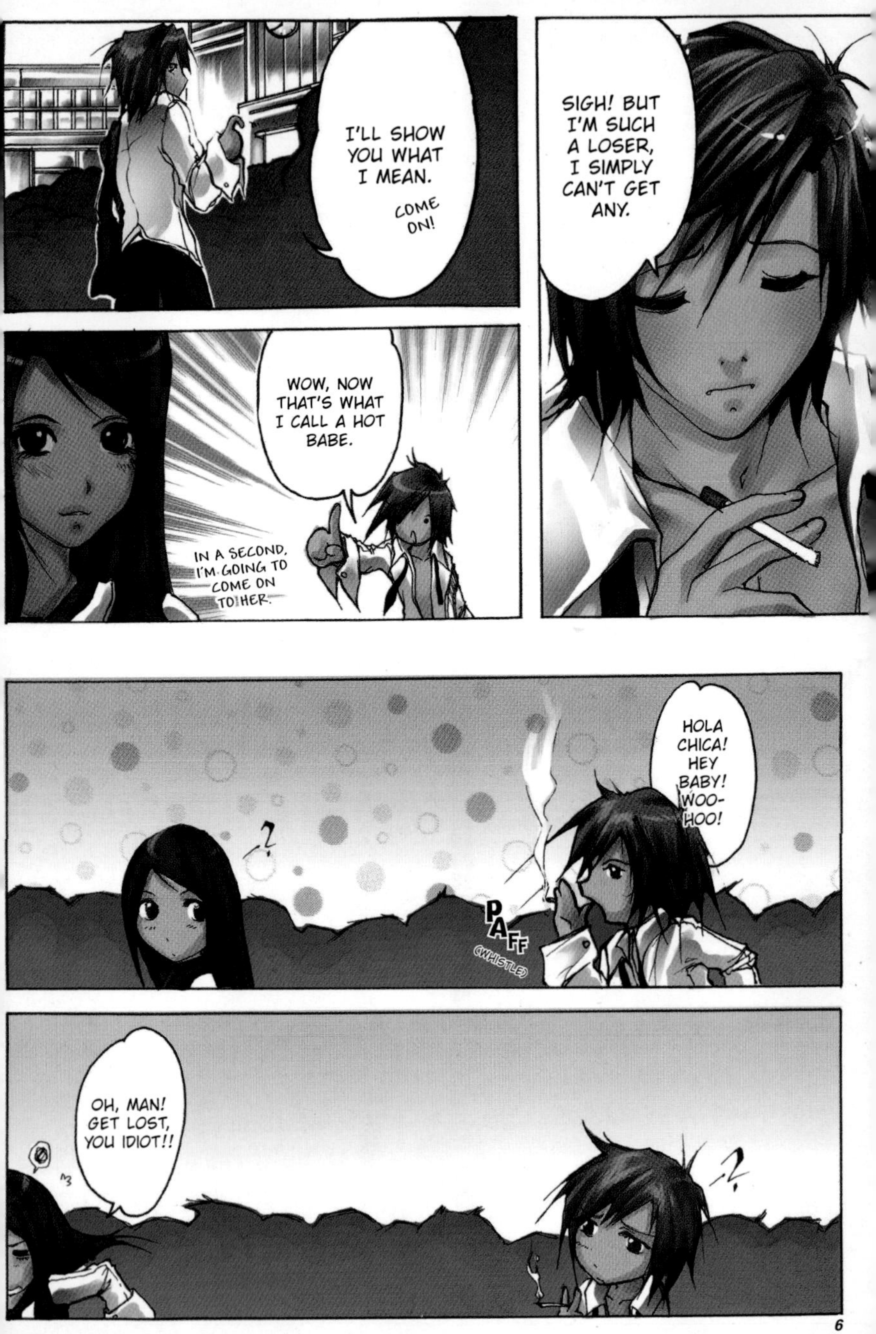
SIGH! BUT I'M SUCH A LOSER, I SIMPLY CAN'T GET ANY.
I'LL SHOW YOU WHAT I MEAN.
COME ON!
WOW, NOW THAT'S WHAT I CALL A HOT BABE.
IN A SECOND, I'M GOING TO COME ON TO HER.
HOLA CHICA! HEY BABY! WOO-HOO!
PAFF
(WHISTLE)
OH, MAN! GET LOST, YOU IDIOT!!

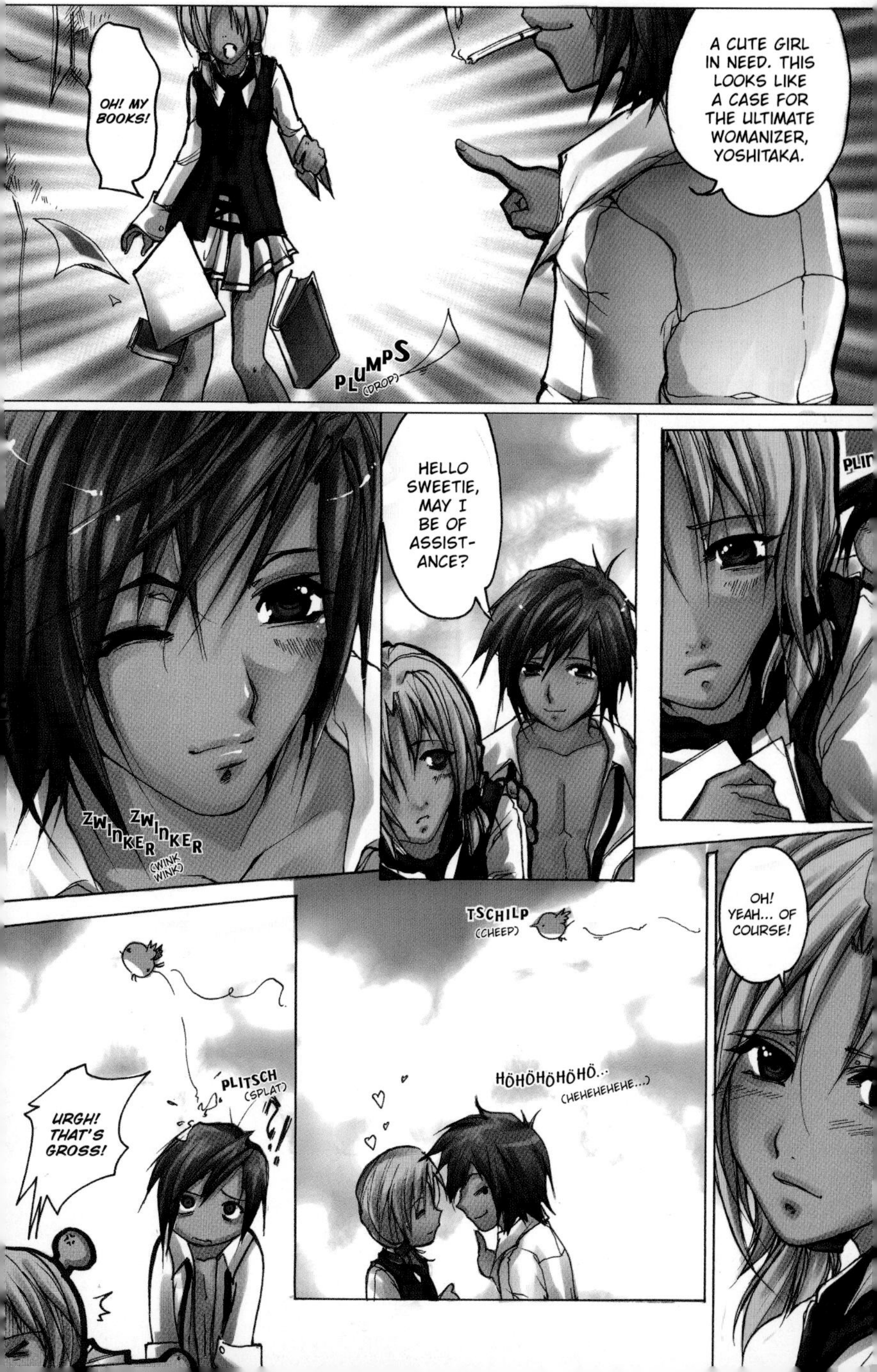
A CUTE GIRL IN NEED. THIS LOOKS LIKE A CASE FOR THE ULTIMATE WOMANIZER, YOSHITAKA.
OH! MY BOOKS!
PLUMPS
(DROP)
HELLO SWEETIE, MAY I BE OF ASSIST-ANCE?
ZWINKER ZWINKER
(WINK WINK)
OH! YEAH... OF COURSE!
TSCHILP
(CHEEP)
HÖHÖHÖHÖHÖ...
(HEHEHEHEHE...)
PLITSCH
(SPLAT)
URGH! THAT'S GROSS!

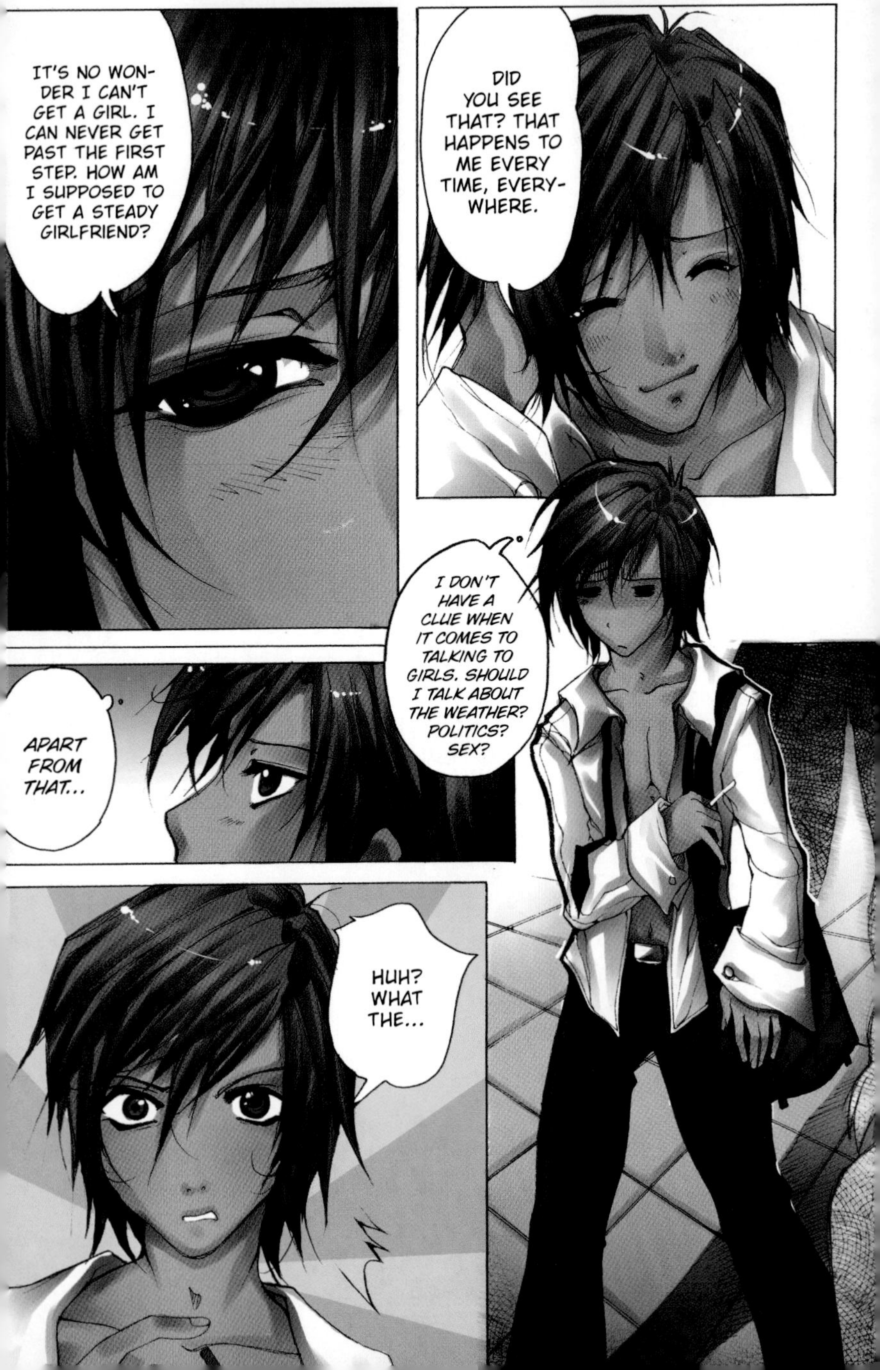
DID YOU SEE THAT? THAT HAPPENS TO ME EVERY TIME, EVERY-WHERE.
IT'S NO WON-DER I CAN'T GET A GIRL. I CAN NEVER GET PAST THE FIRST STEP. HOW AM I SUPPOSED TO GET A STEADY GIRLFRIEND?
I DON'T HAVE A CLUE WHEN IT COMES TO TALKING TO GIRLS. SHOULD I TALK ABOUT THE WEATHER? POLITICS? SEX?
APART FROM THAT...
HUH? WHAT THE...

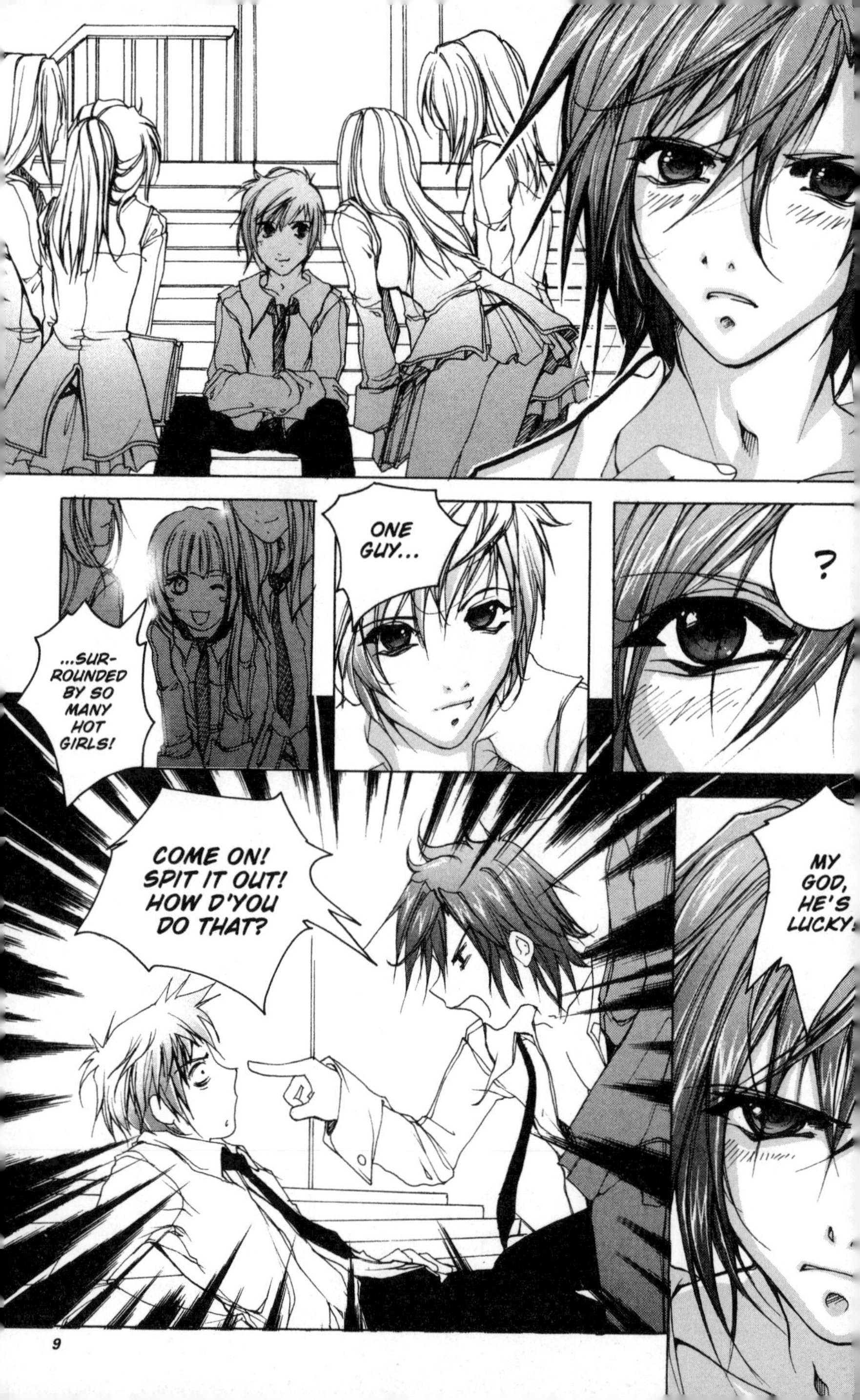
?
ONE GUY...
...SUR-ROUNDED BY SO MANY HOT GIRLS!
MY GOD, HE'S LUCKY.
COME ON! SPIT IT OUT! HOW D'YOU DO THAT?

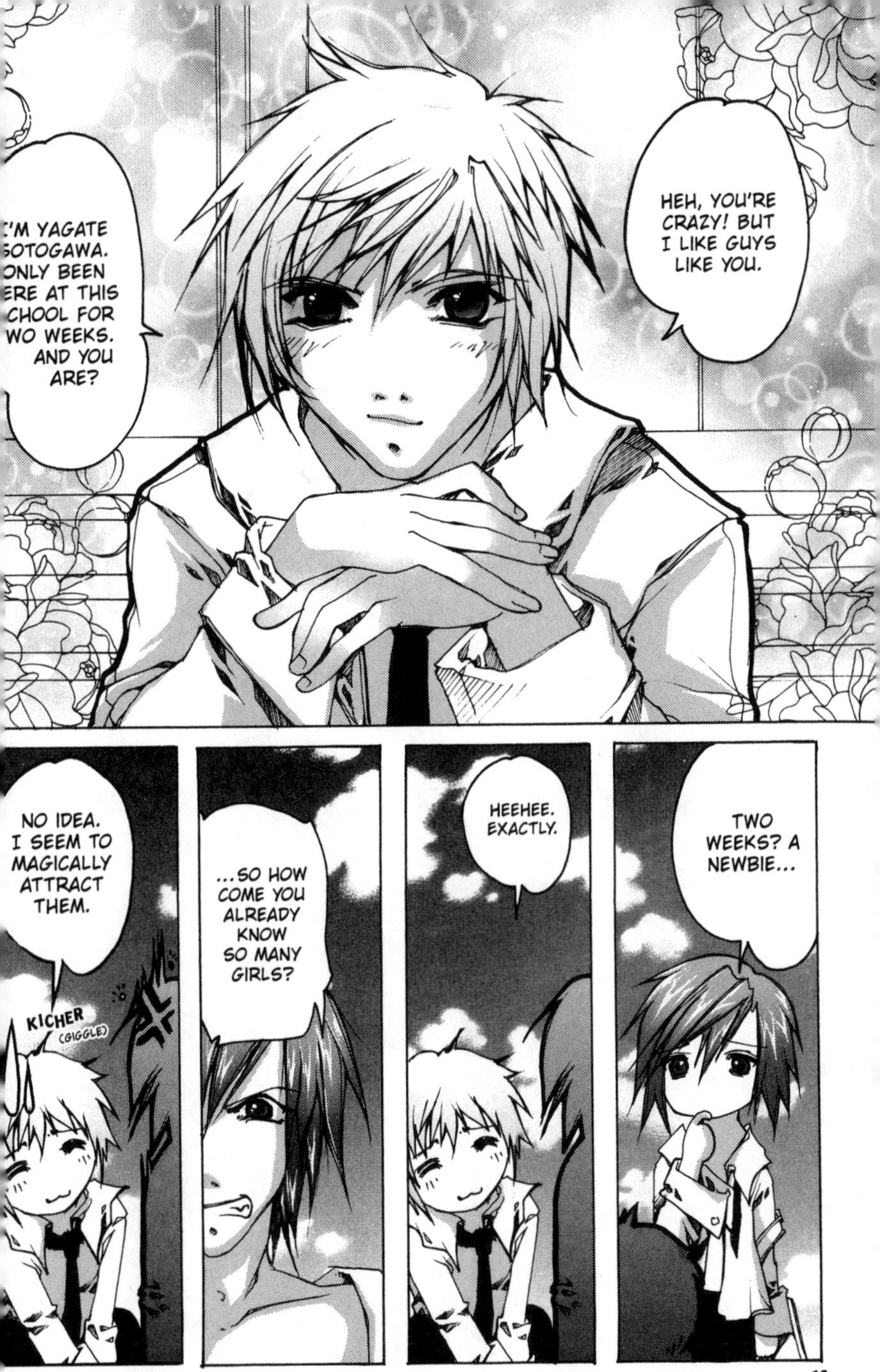
HEH, YOU'RE CRAZY! BUT I LIKE GUYS LIKE YOU.
I'M YAGATE SOTOGAWA. ONLY BEEN ERE AT THIS CHOOL FOR WO WEEKS. AND YOU ARE?
TWO WEEKS? A NEWBIE...
HEEHEE. EXACTLY.
...SO HOW COME YOU ALREADY KNOW SO MANY GIRLS?
NO IDEA. I SEEM TO MAGICALLY ATTRACT THEM.
KICHER
(GIGGLE)

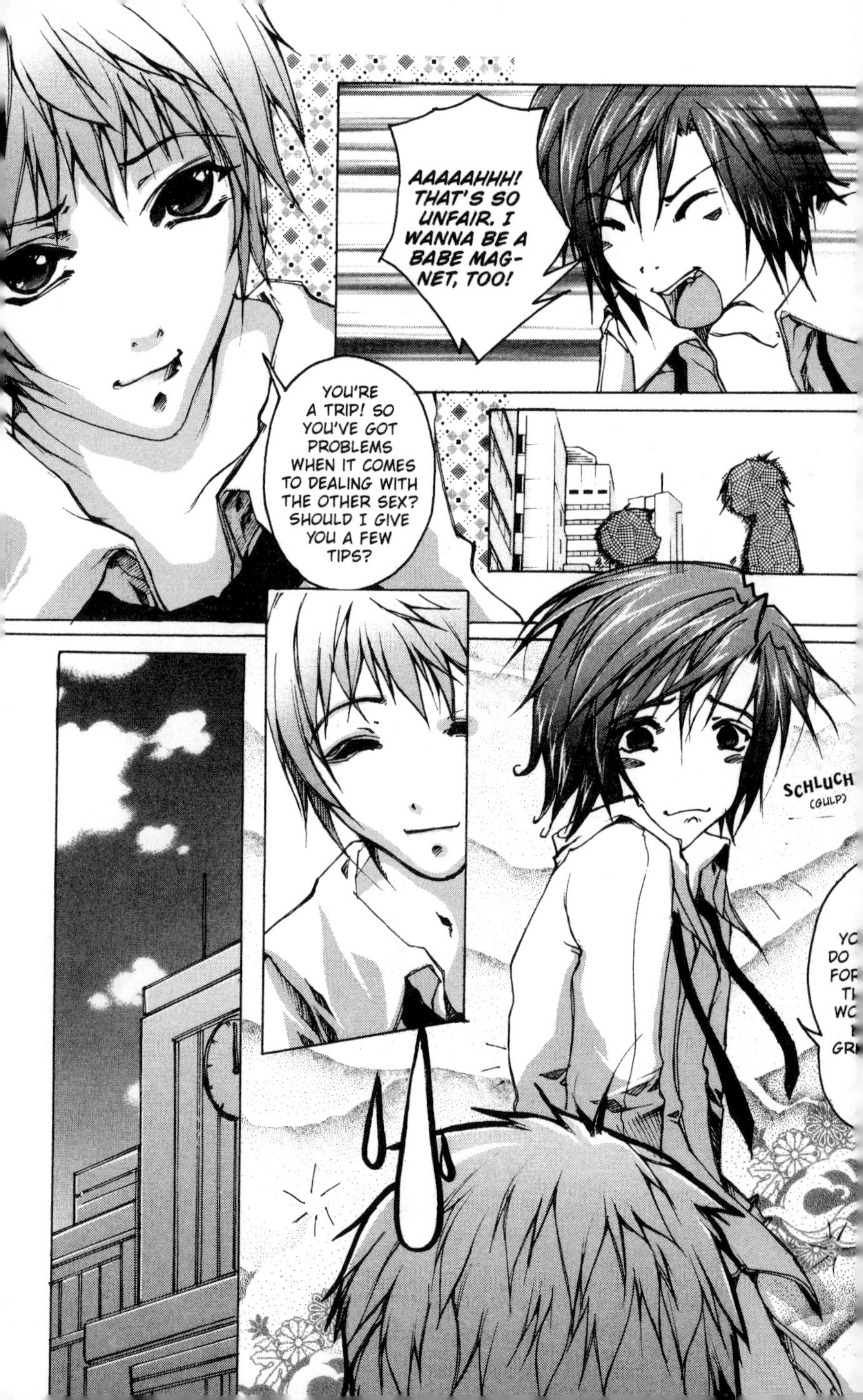
AAAAAHHH! THAT'S SO UNFAIR. I WANNA BE A BABE MAG-NET, TOO!
YOU'RE A TRIP! SO YOU'VE GOT PROBLEMS WHEN IT COMES TO DEALING WITH THE OTHER SEX? SHOULD I GIVE YOU A FEW TIPS?
SCHLUCH
(GULP)

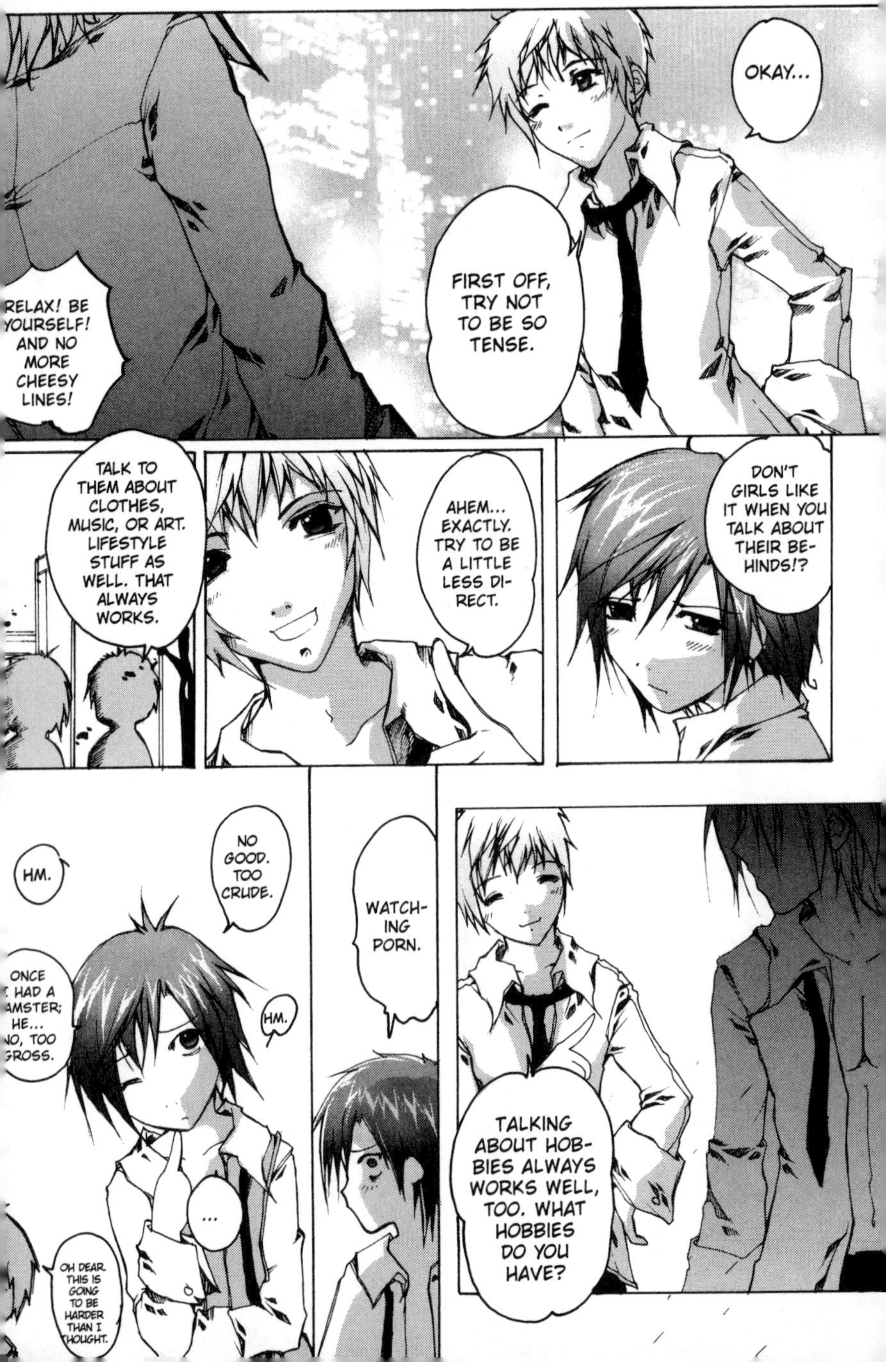
OKAY...
FIRST OFF, TRY NOT TO BE SO TENSE.
RELAX! BE YOURSELF! AND NO MORE CHEESY LINES!
DON'T GIRLS LIKE IT WHEN YOU TALK ABOUT THEIR BE-HINDS!?
AHEM... EXACTLY. TRY TO BE A LITTLE LESS DI-RECT.
TALK TO THEM ABOUT CLOTHES, MUSIC, OR ART. LIFESTYLE STUFF AS WELL. THAT ALWAYS WORKS.
TALKING ABOUT HOB-BIES ALWAYS WORKS WELL, TOO. WHAT HOBBIES DO YOU HAVE?
WATCH-ING PORN.
...
NO GOOD. TOO CRUDE.
HM.
HM.
ONCE I HAD A AMSTER; HE... O, TOO GROSS.
OH DEAR THIS IS GOING TO BE HARDER THAN I HOUGHT.

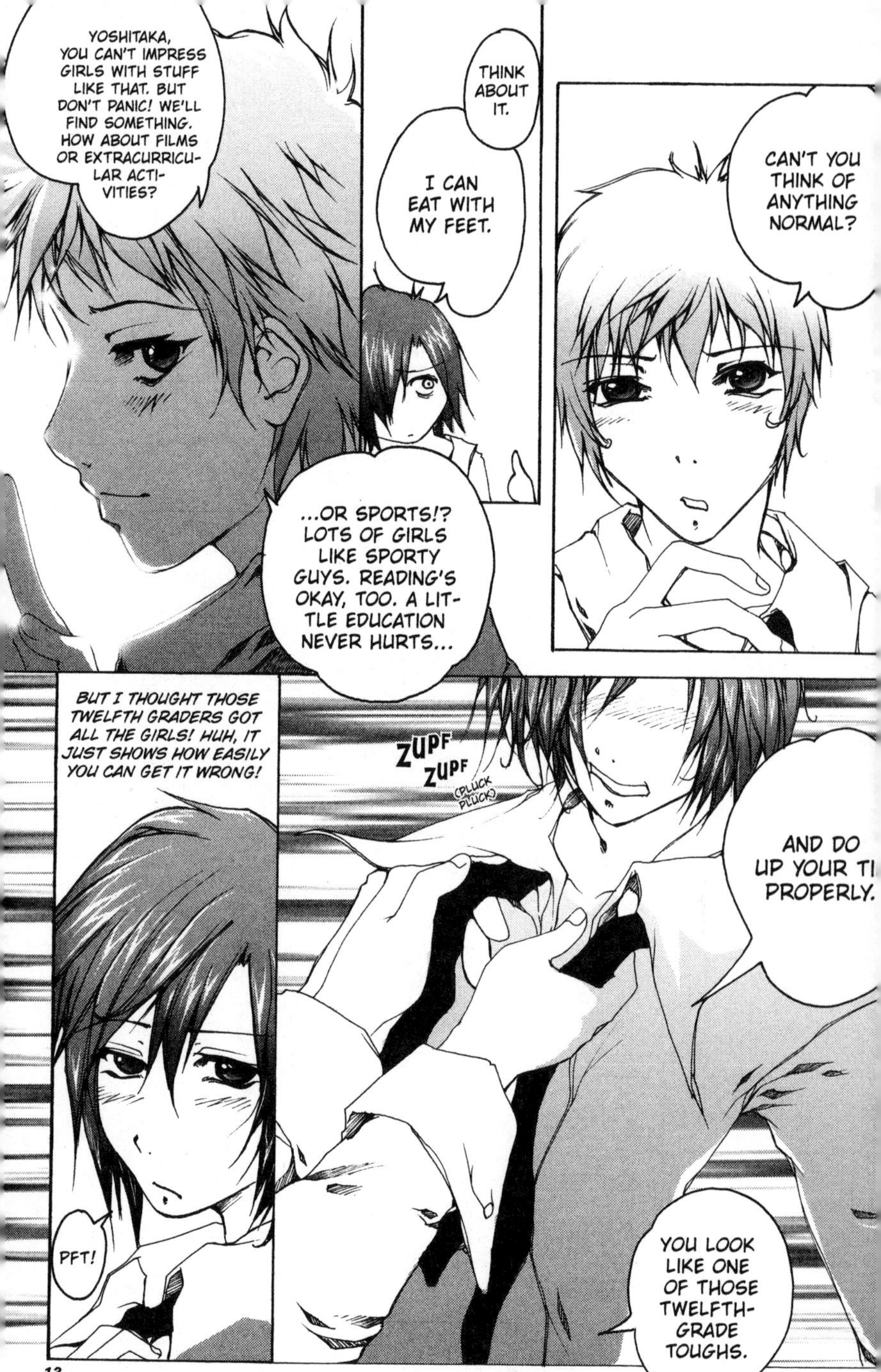
CAN'T YOU THINK OF ANYTHING NORMAL?
THINK ABOUT IT.
I CAN EAT WITH MY FEET.
YOSHITAKA, YOU CAN'T IMPRESS GIRLS WITH STUFF LIKE THAT. BUT DON'T PANIC! WE'LL FIND SOMETHING. HOW ABOUT FILMS OR EXTRACURRICU-LAR ACTI-VITIES?
...OR SPORTS!? LOTS OF GIRLS LIKE SPORTY GUYS. READING'S OKAY, TOO. A LIT-TLE EDUCATION NEVER HURTS...
AND DO UP YOUR TI PROPERLY.
ZUPF ZUPF
(PLUCK PLUCK)
YOU LOOK LIKE ONE OF THOSE TWELFTH-GRADE TOUGHS.
BUT I THOUGHT THOSE TWELFTH GRADERS GOT ALL THE GIRLS! HUH, IT JUST SHOWS HOW EASILY YOU CAN GET IT WRONG!
PFT!

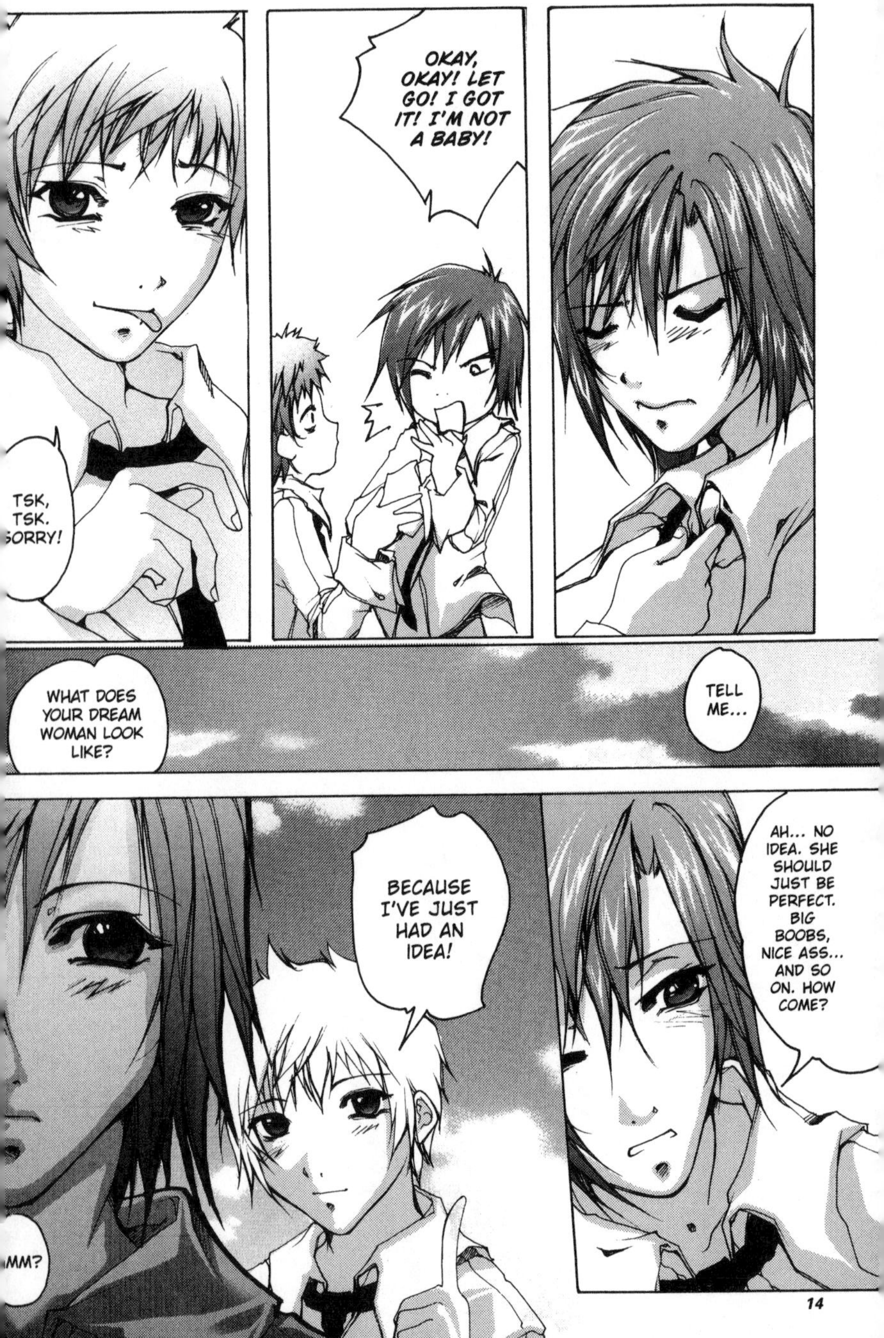
OKAY, OKAY! LET GO! I GOT IT! I'M NOT A BABY!
TSK, TSK. SORRY!
TELL ME...
WHAT DOES YOUR DREAM WOMAN LOOK LIKE?
AH... NO IDEA. SHE SHOULD JUST BE PERFECT. BIG BOOBS, NICE ASS... AND SO ON. HOW COME?
BECAUSE I'VE JUST HAD AN IDEA!
MM?

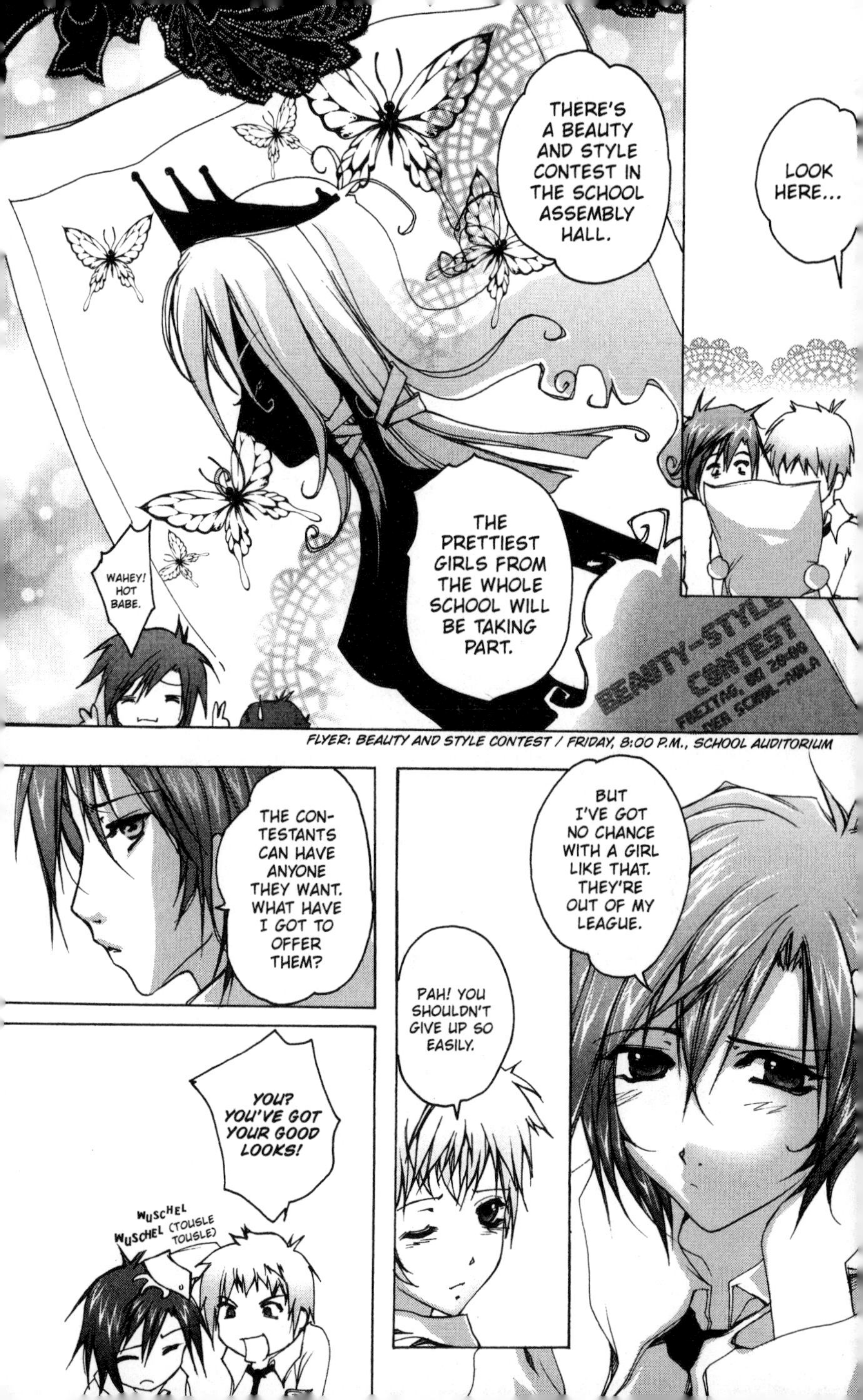
LOOK HERE...
THERE'S A BEAUTY AND STYLE CONTEST IN THE SCHOOL ASSEMBLY HALL.
THE PRETTIEST GIRLS FROM THE WHOLE SCHOOL WILL BE TAKING PART.
WAHEY! HOT BABE.
BEAUTY-STYLE CONTEST
FLYER: BEAUTY AND STYLE CONTEST / FRIDAY, 8:00 P.M., SCHOOL AUDITORIUM
BUT I'VE GOT NO CHANCE WITH A GIRL LIKE THAT. THEY'RE OUT OF MY LEAGUE.
PAH! YOU SHOULDN'T GIVE UP SO EASILY.
THE CON-TESTANTS CAN HAVE ANYONE THEY WANT. WHAT HAVE I GOT TO OFFER THEM?
YOU? YOU'VE GOT YOUR GOOD LOOKS!
WUSCHEL WUSCHEL (TOUSLE TOUSLE)

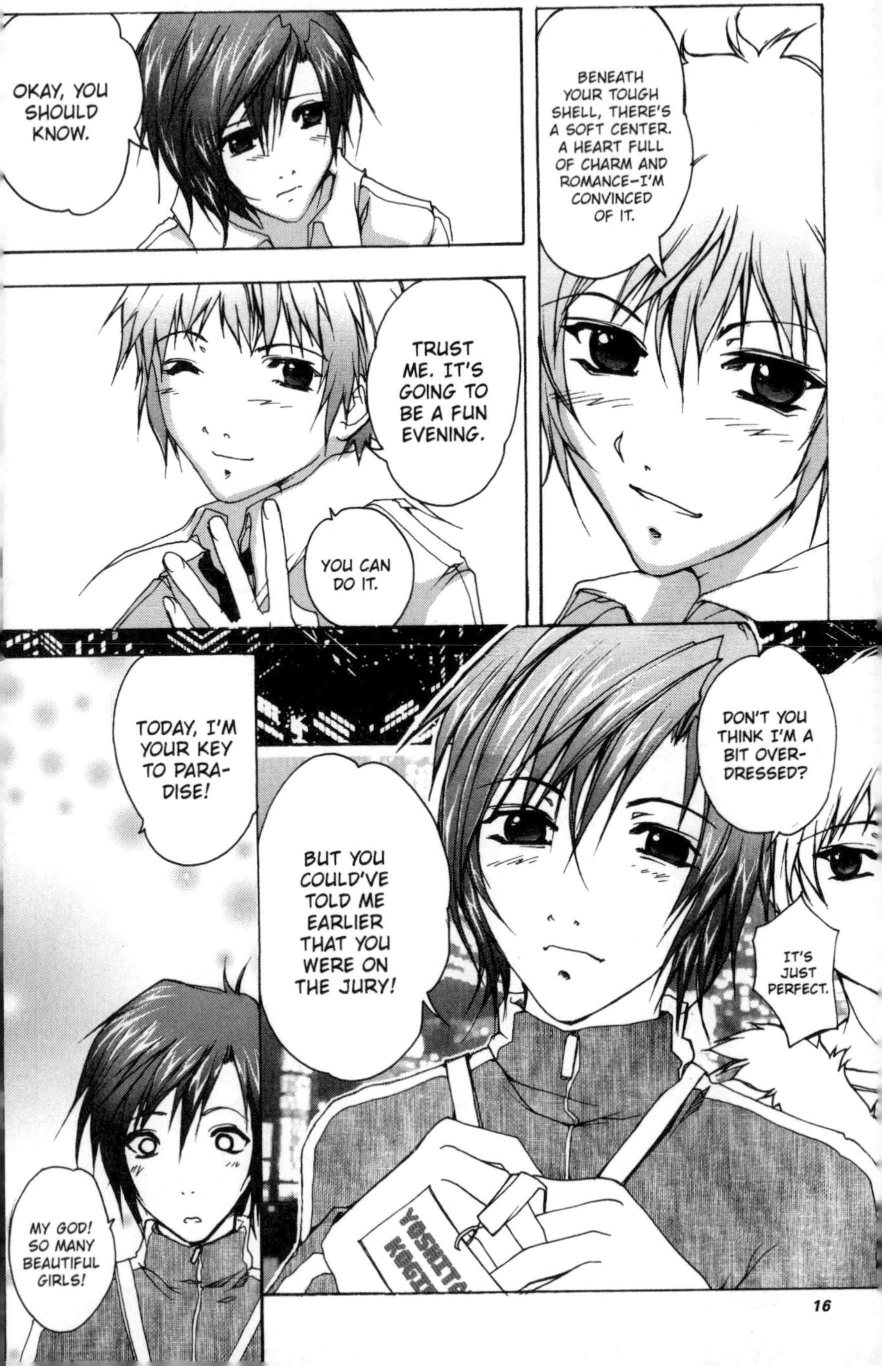
BENEATH YOUR TOUGH SHELL, THERE'S A SOFT CENTER. A HEART FULL OF CHARM AND ROMANCE–I'M CONVINCED OF IT.
OKAY, YOU SHOULD KNOW.
TRUST ME. IT'S GOING TO BE A FUN EVENING.
YOU CAN DO IT.
DON'T YOU THINK I'M A BIT OVER-DRESSED?
IT'S JUST PERFECT.
BUT YOU COULD'VE TOLD ME EARLIER THAT YOU WERE ON THE JURY!
TODAY, I'M YOUR KEY TO PARA-DISE!
MY GOD! SO MANY BEAUTIFUL GIRLS!

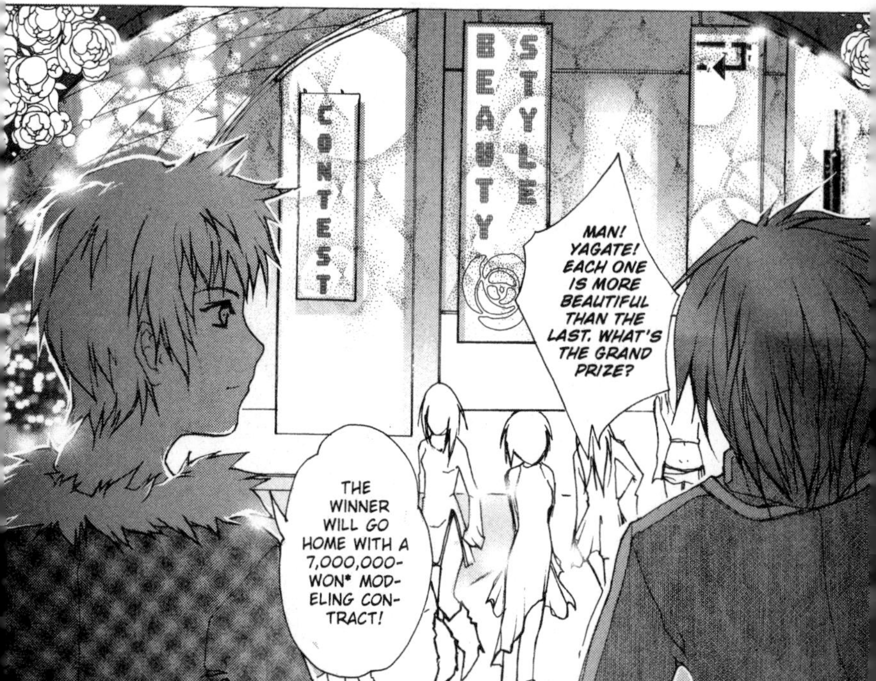
BEAUTY STYLE
CONTEST
MAN! YAGATE! EACH ONE IS MORE BEAUTIFUL THAN THE LAST. WHAT'S THE GRAND PRIZE?
THE WINNER WILL GO HOME WITH A 7,000,000-WON* MODELING CONTRACT!

*7,000,000 SOUTH KOREAN WON IS ROUGHLY $6,700.

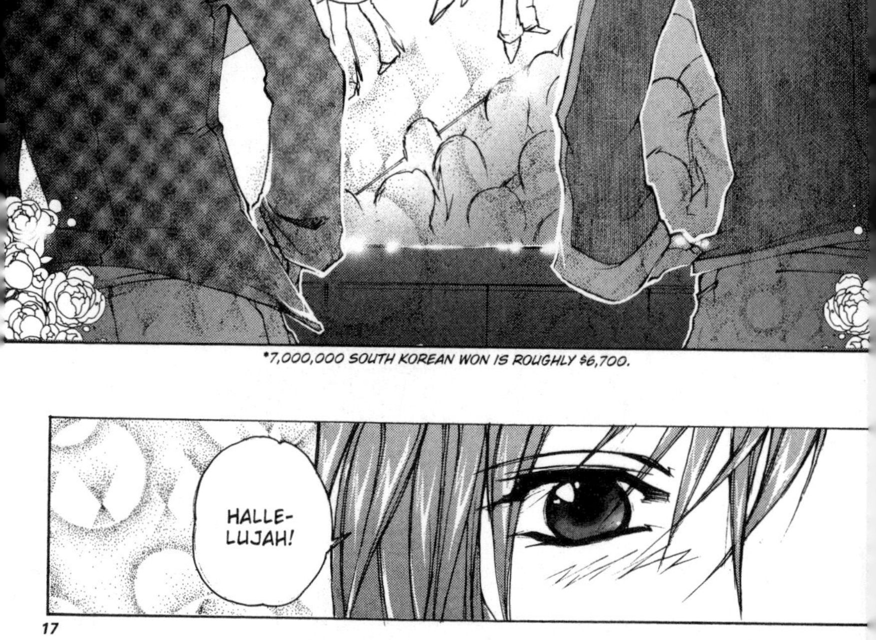
HALLELUJAH!

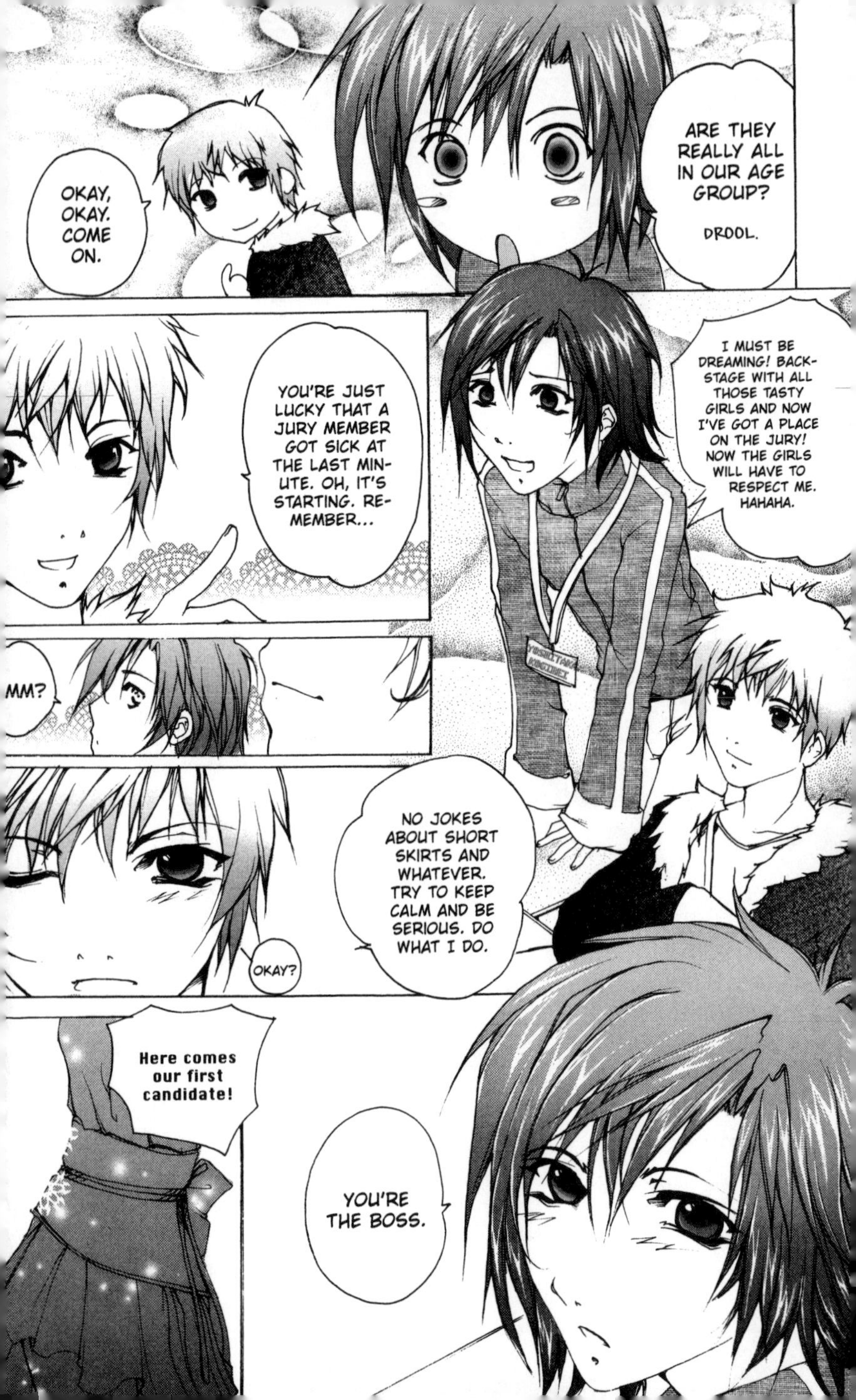

ARE THEY REALLY ALL IN OUR AGE GROUP?
DROOL.
OKAY, OKAY. COME ON.
I MUST BE DREAMING! BACKSTAGE WITH ALL THOSE TASTY GIRLS AND NOW I'VE GOT A PLACE ON THE JURY! NOW THE GIRLS WILL HAVE TO RESPECT ME. HAHAHA.
YOU'RE JUST LUCKY THAT A JURY MEMBER GOT SICK AT THE LAST MINUTE. OH, IT'S STARTING. REMEMBER...
MM?
NO JOKES ABOUT SHORT SKIRTS AND WHATEVER. TRY TO KEEP CALM AND BE SERIOUS. DO WHAT I DO.
OKAY?
YOU'RE THE BOSS.
Here comes our first candidate!

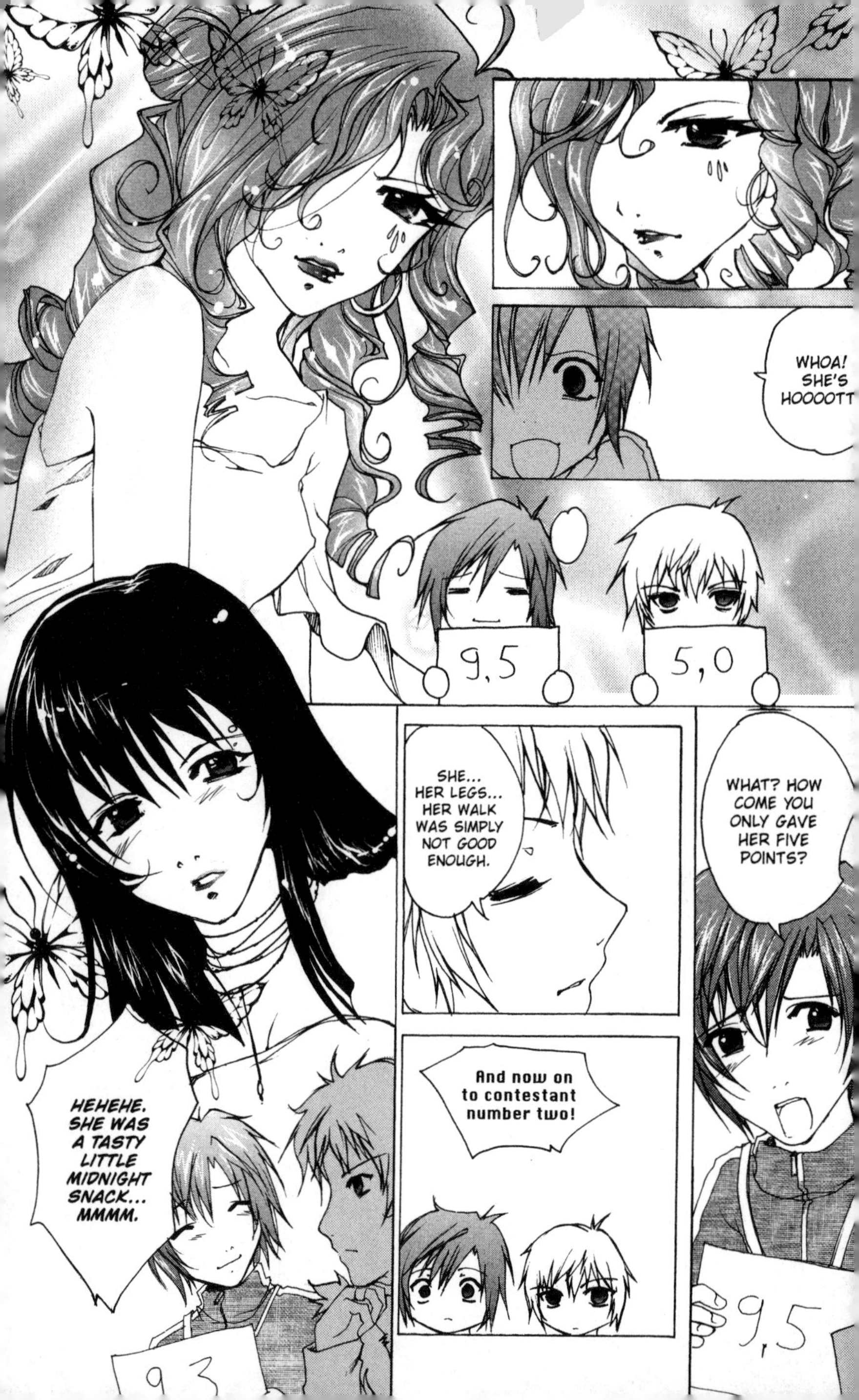

WHOA! SHE'S HOOOOTT
9,5
5,0
WHAT? HOW COME YOU ONLY GAVE HER FIVE POINTS?
9,5
SHE... HER LEGS... HER WALK WAS SIMPLY NOT GOOD ENOUGH.
And now on to contestant number two!
HEHEHE. SHE WAS A TASTY LITTLE MIDNIGHT SNACK... MMMM.

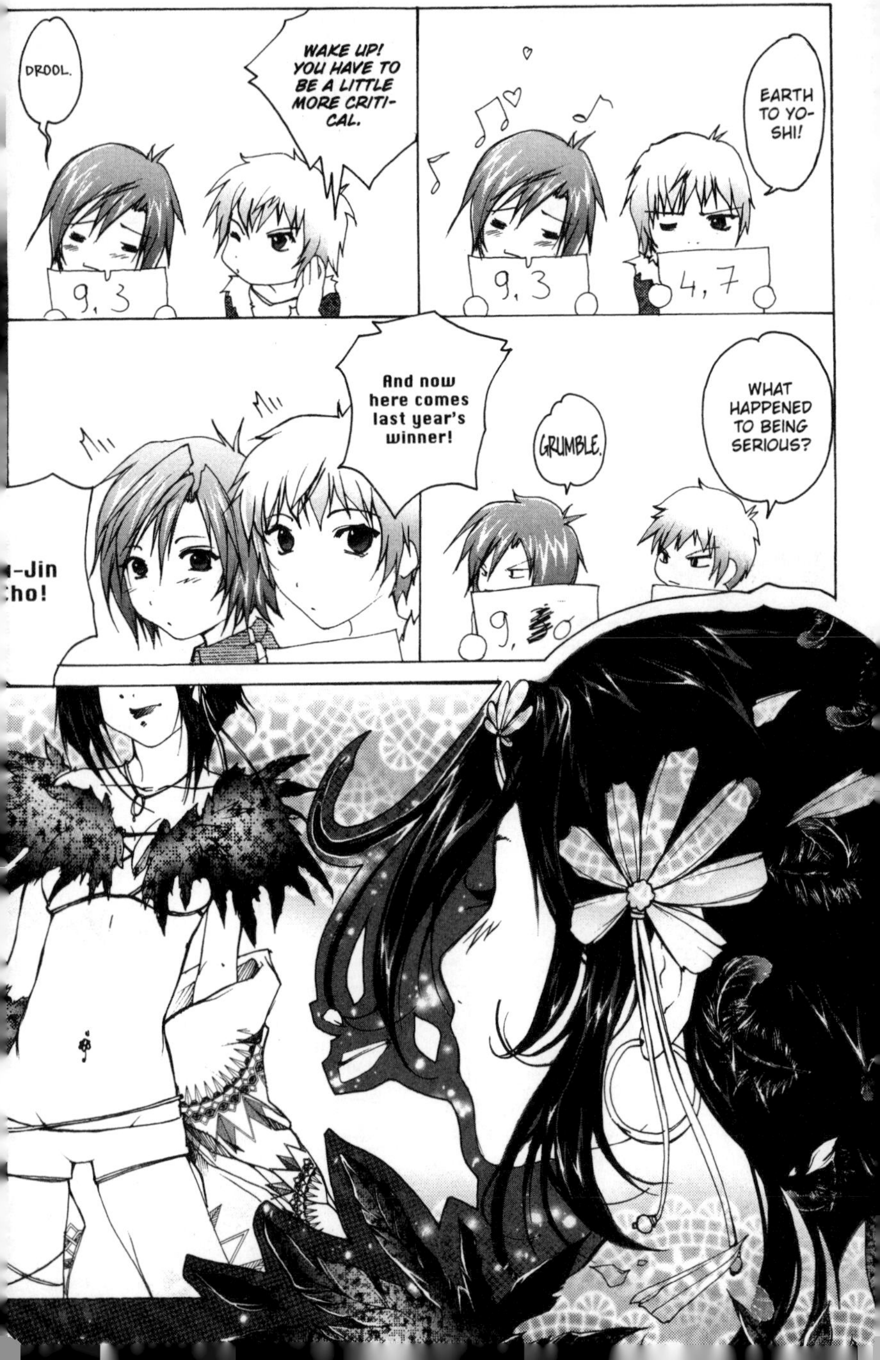
EARTH TO YO-SHI!
9, 3
4, 7
WAKE UP! YOU HAVE TO BE A LITTLE MORE CRITI-CAL.
DROOL.
9, 3
WHAT HAPPENED TO BEING SERIOUS?
GRUMBLE.
And now here comes last year's winner!
-Jin
ho!

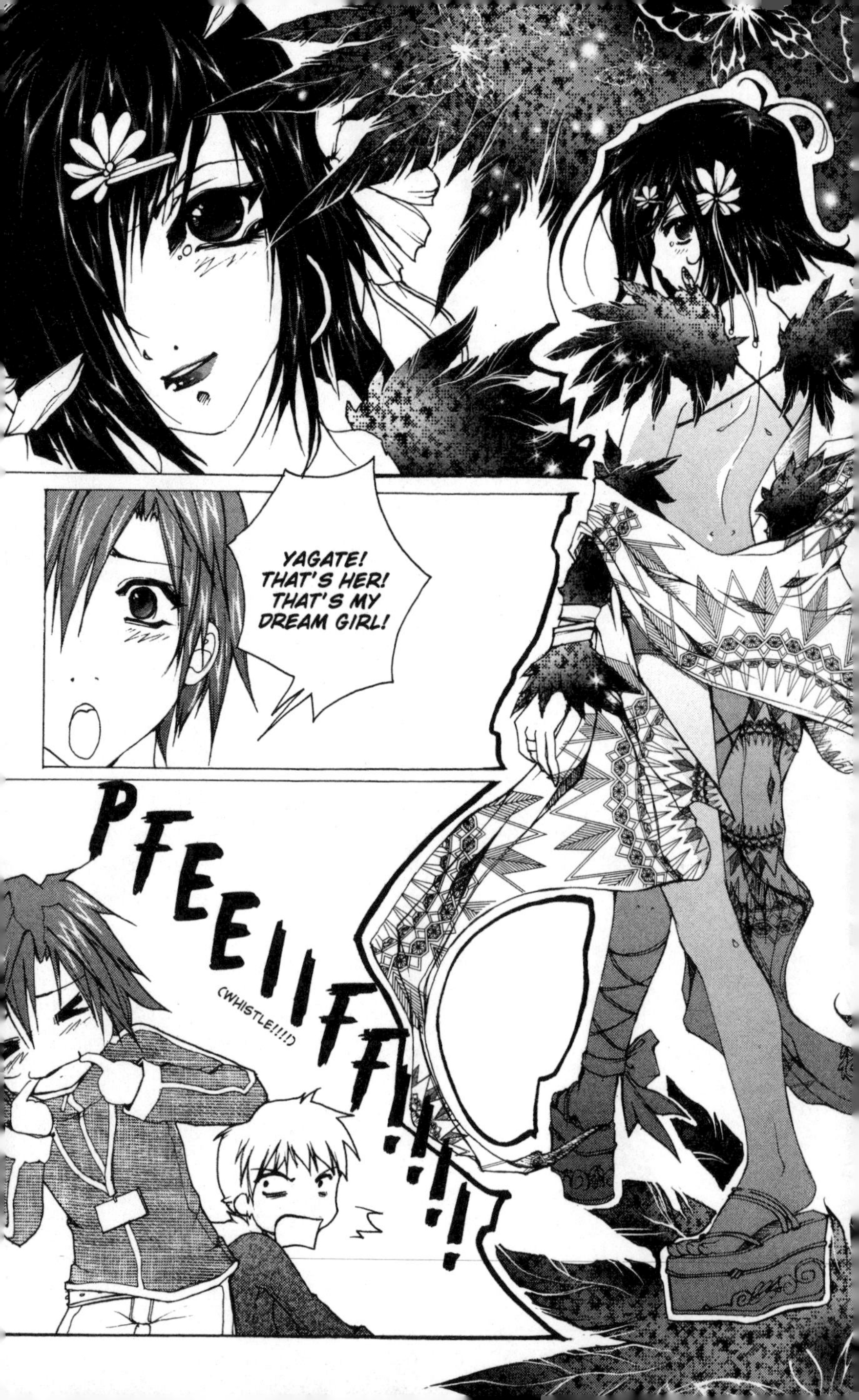
YAGATE! THAT'S HER! THAT'S MY DREAM GIRL!
PFEEIIFFT!!!!!
(WHISTLE!!!!)

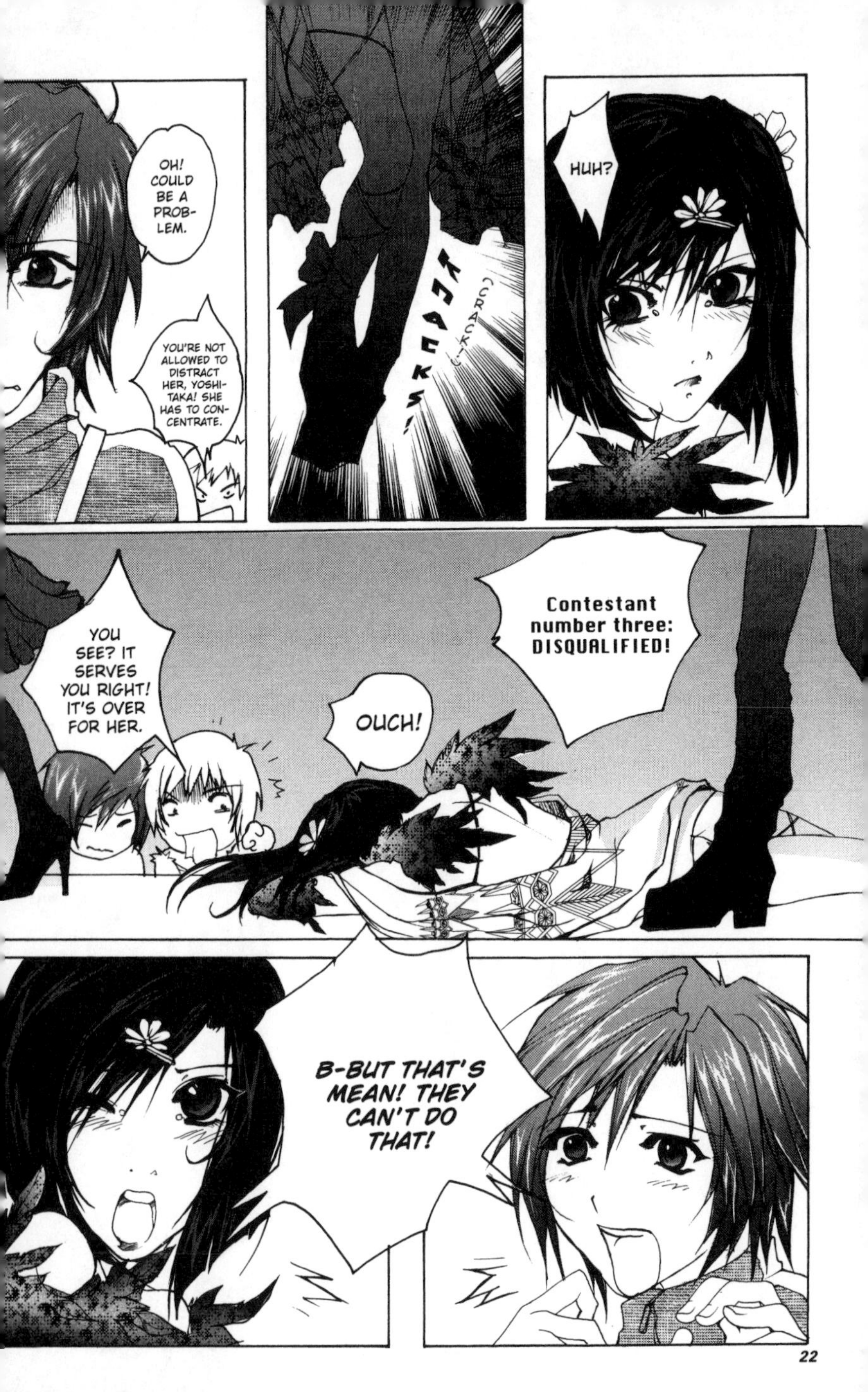
HUH?
KNACKS!
(CRACK!)
OH! COULD BE A PROBLEM.
YOU'RE NOT ALLOWED TO DISTRACT HER, YOSHITAKA! SHE HAS TO CONCENTRATE.
Contestant number three: DISQUALIFIED!
OUCH!
YOU SEE? IT SERVES YOU RIGHT! IT'S OVER FOR HER.
B-BUT THAT'S MEAN! THEY CAN'T DO THAT!

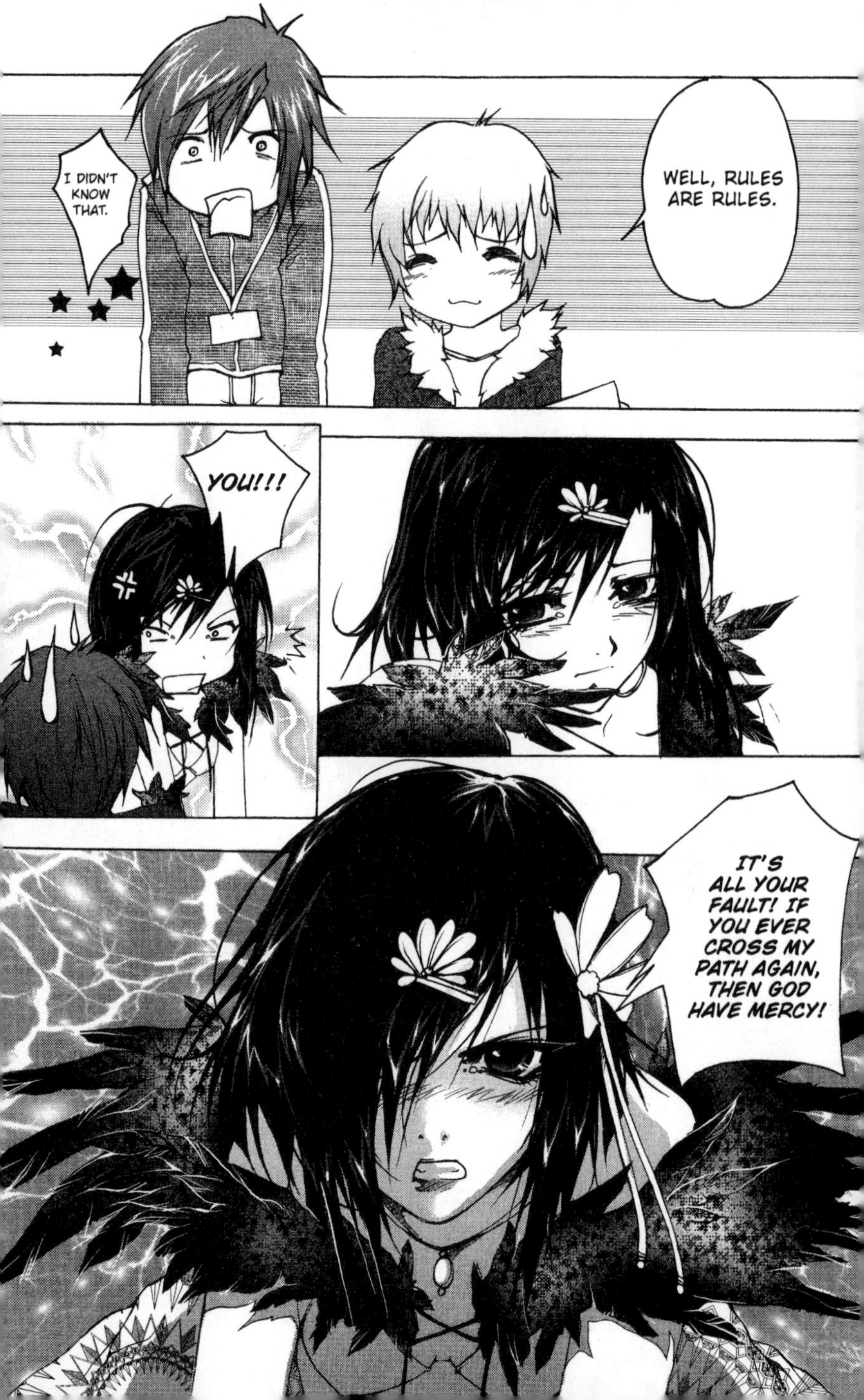
WELL, RULES ARE RULES.
I DIDN'T KNOW THAT.
YOU!!!
IT'S ALL YOUR FAULT! IF YOU EVER CROSS MY PATH AGAIN, THEN GOD HAVE MERCY!

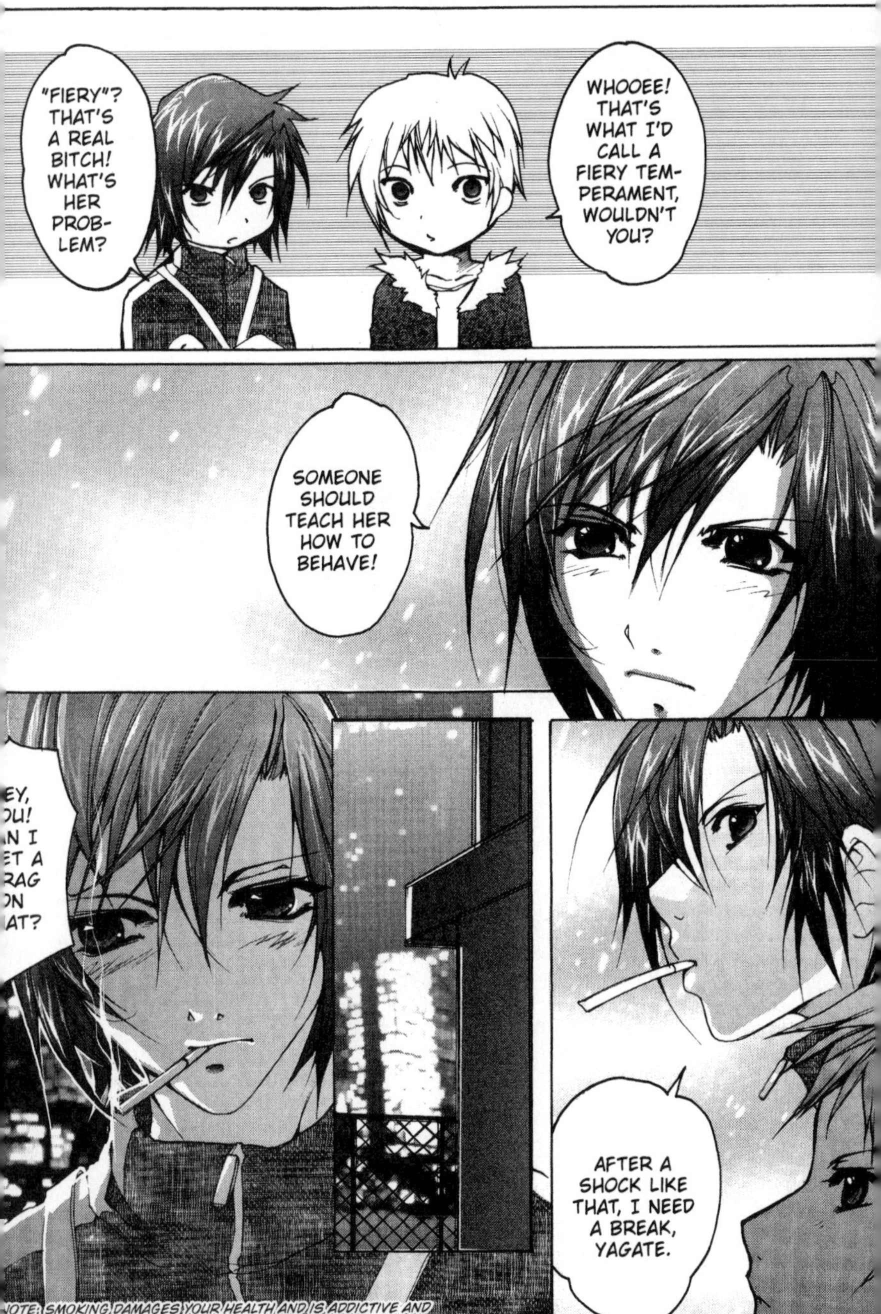
WHOOEE! THAT'S WHAT I'D CALL A FIERY TEMPERAMENT, WOULDN'T YOU?
"FIERY"? THAT'S A REAL BITCH! WHAT'S HER PROBLEM?
SOMEONE SHOULD TEACH HER HOW TO BEHAVE!
AFTER A SHOCK LIKE THAT, I NEED A BREAK, YAGATE.
EY, OU! N I ET A RAG ON AT?
NOTE: SMOKING DAMAGES YOUR HEALTH AND IS ADDICTIVE AND DISGUSTING. YOSHITAKA SHOULD GIVE IT UP AS SOON AS POSSIBLE.

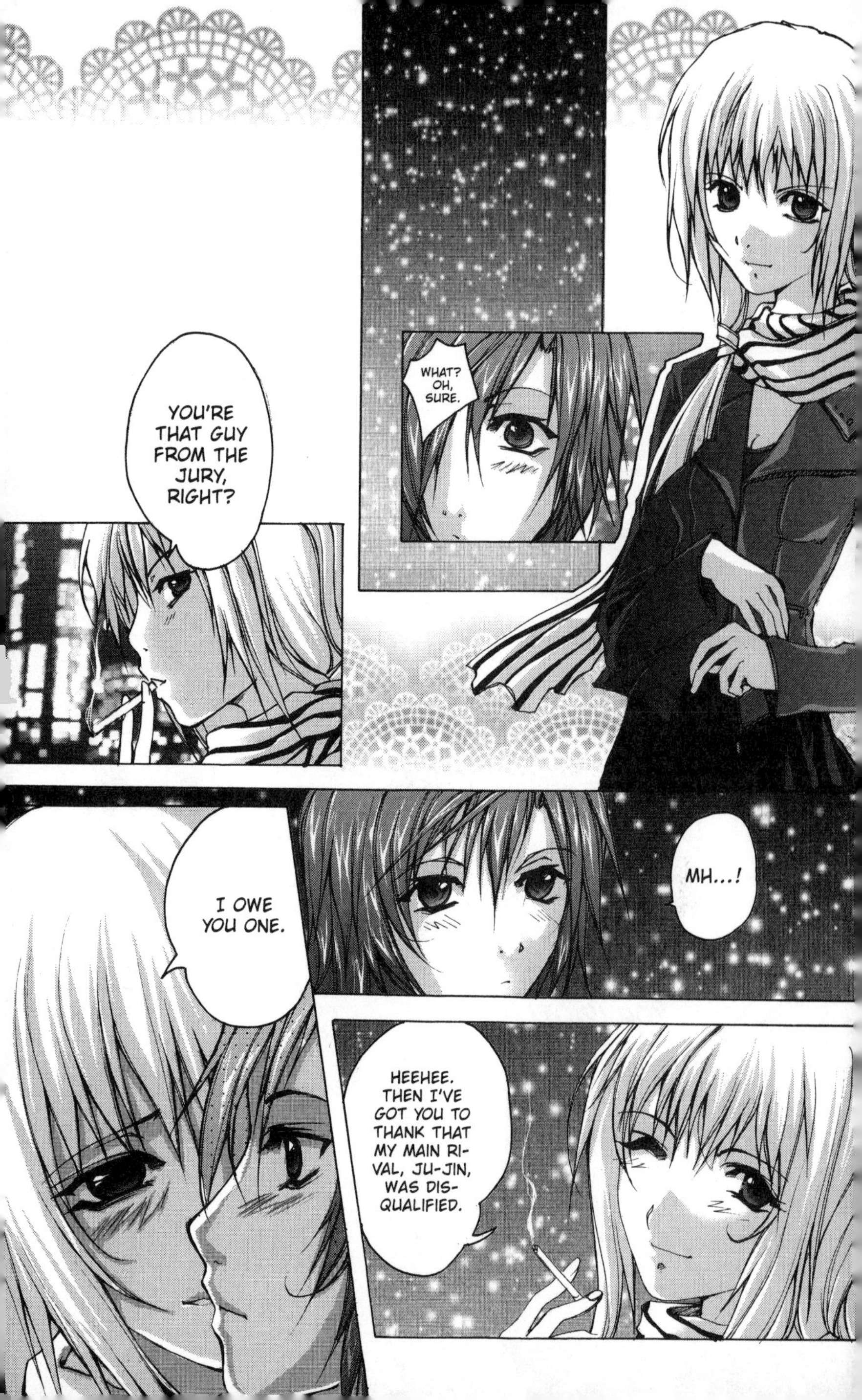
WHAT? OH, SURE.
YOU'RE THAT GUY FROM THE JURY, RIGHT?
MH...!
HEEHEE. THEN I'VE GOT YOU TO THANK THAT MY MAIN RI-VAL, JU-JIN, WAS DIS-QUALIFIED.
I OWE YOU ONE.

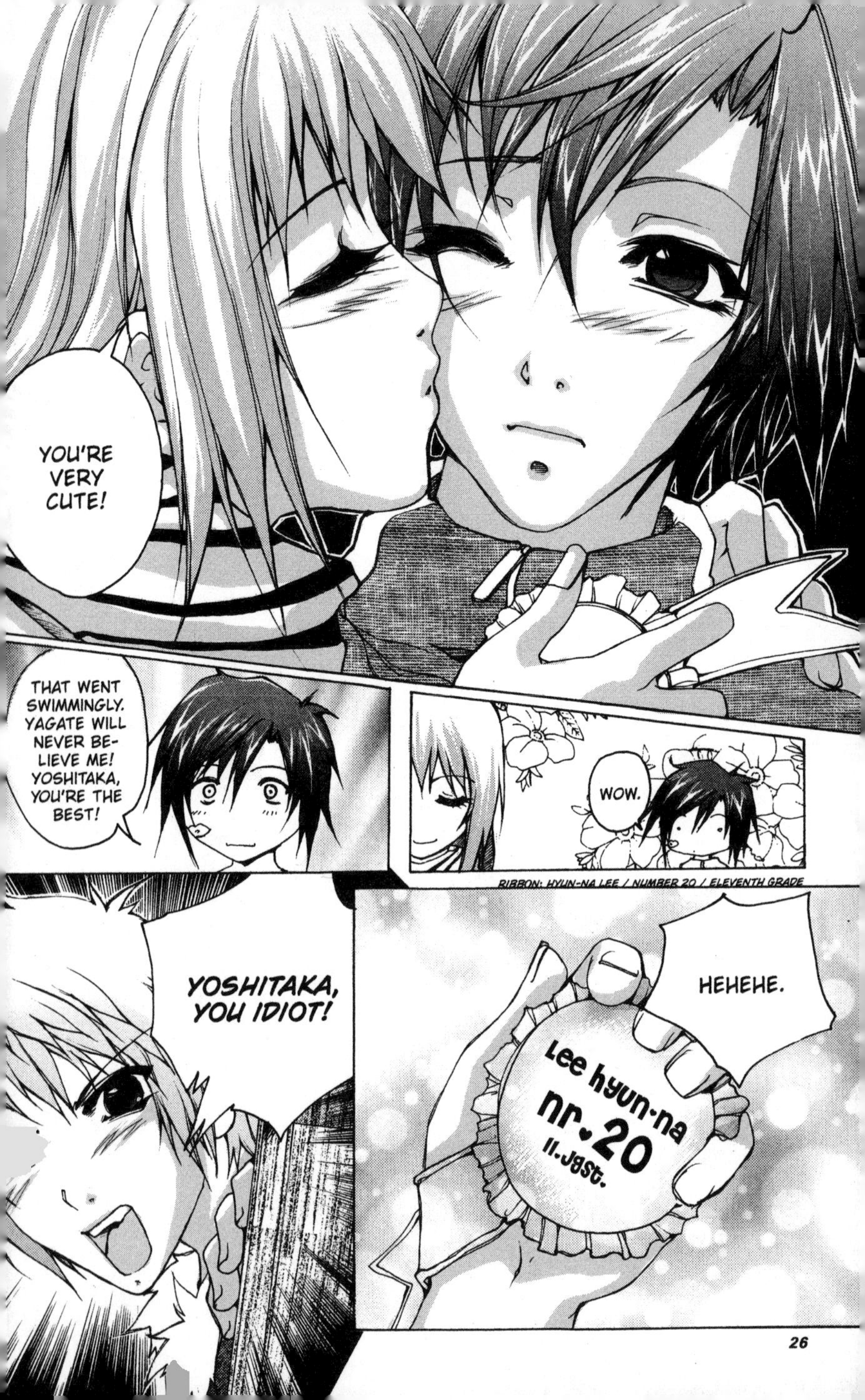
YOU'RE VERY CUTE!
WOW.
RIBBON: HYUN-NA LEE / NUMBER 20 / ELEVENTH GRADE
THAT WENT SWIMMINGLY. YAGATE WILL NEVER BE-LIEVE ME! YOSHITAKA, YOU'RE THE BEST!
HEHEHE.
Lee hyun-na nr.20 11.Jgst.
YOSHITAKA, YOU IDIOT!

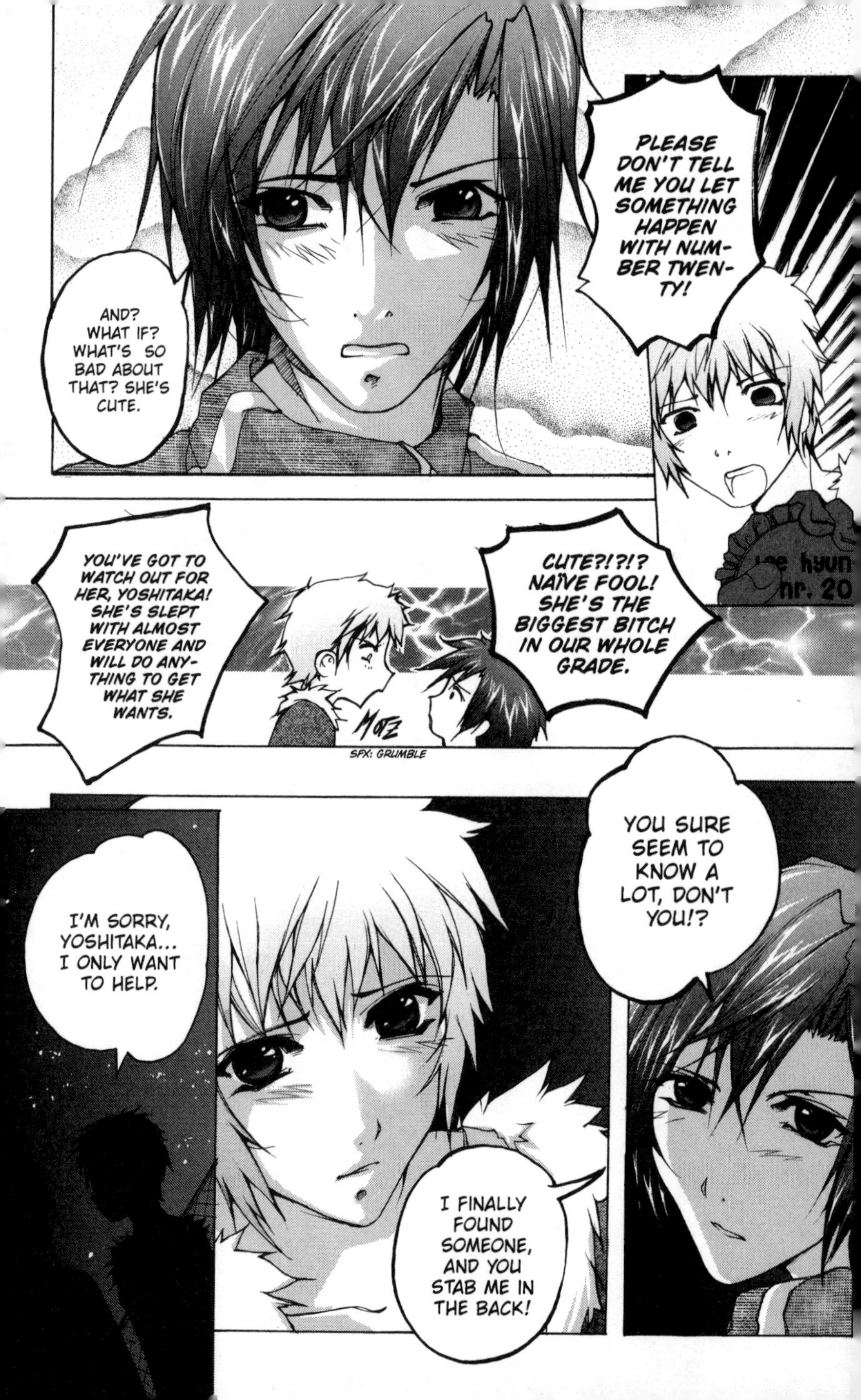
PLEASE DON'T TELL ME YOU LET SOMETHING HAPPEN WITH NUM-BER TWEN-TY!
hyun
nr. 20
AND? WHAT IF? WHAT'S SO BAD ABOUT THAT? SHE'S CUTE.
CUTE?!?!? NAÏVE FOOL! SHE'S THE BIGGEST BITCH IN OUR WHOLE GRADE.
YOU'VE GOT TO WATCH OUT FOR HER, YOSHITAKA! SHE'S SLEPT WITH ALMOST EVERYONE AND WILL DO ANY-THING TO GET WHAT SHE WANTS.
SFX: GRUMBLE
YOU SURE SEEM TO KNOW A LOT, DON'T YOU!?
I FINALLY FOUND SOMEONE, AND YOU STAB ME IN THE BACK!
I'M SORRY, YOSHITAKA... I ONLY WANT TO HELP.

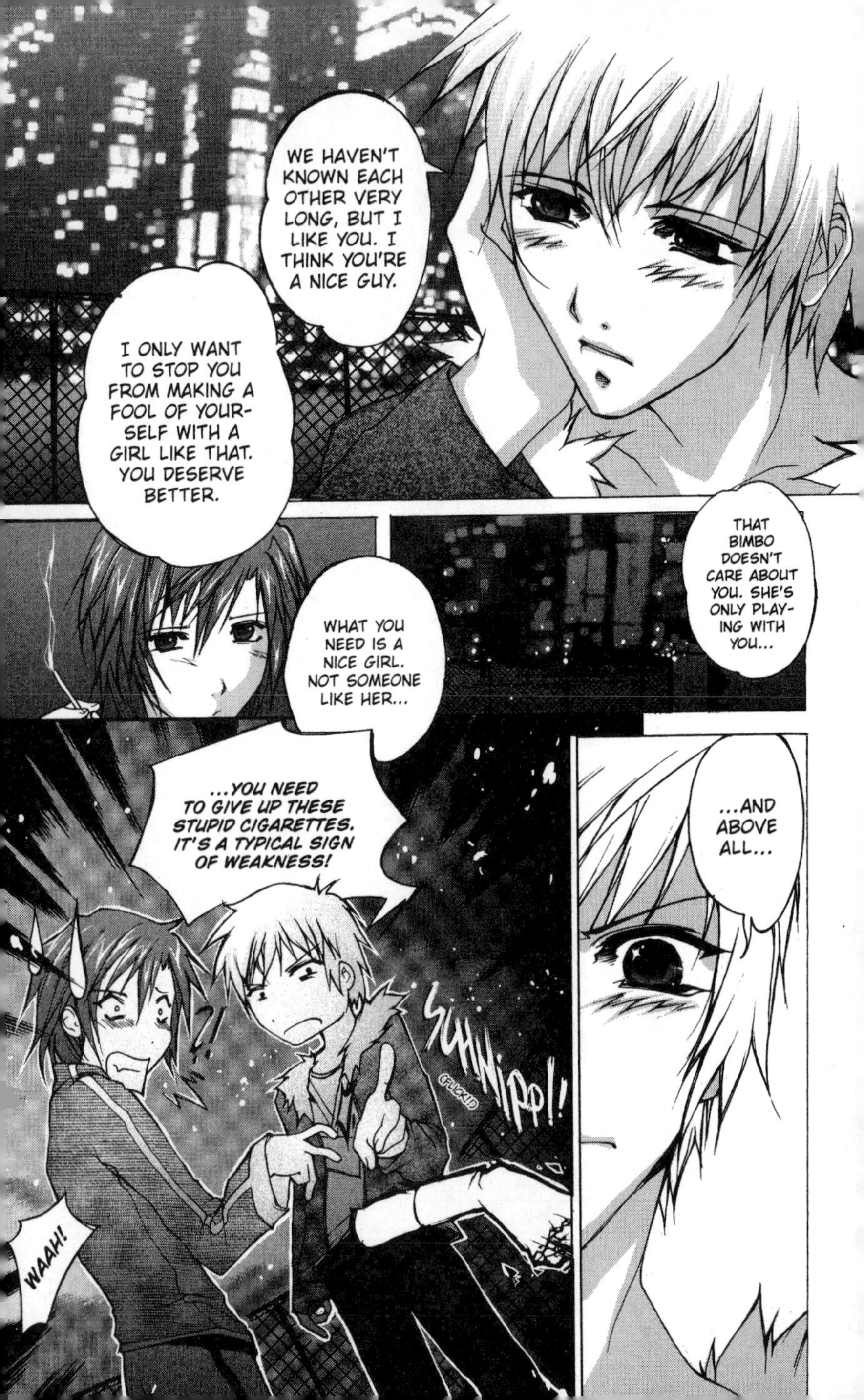
WE HAVEN'T KNOWN EACH OTHER VERY LONG, BUT I LIKE YOU. I THINK YOU'RE A NICE GUY.
I ONLY WANT TO STOP YOU FROM MAKING A FOOL OF YOUR-SELF WITH A GIRL LIKE THAT. YOU DESERVE BETTER.
THAT BIMBO DOESN'T CARE ABOUT YOU. SHE'S ONLY PLAY-ING WITH YOU...
WHAT YOU NEED IS A NICE GIRL. NOT SOMEONE LIKE HER...
...AND ABOVE ALL...
...YOU NEED TO GIVE UP THESE STUPID CIGARETTES. IT'S A TYPICAL SIGN OF WEAKNESS!
SCHNIPP!!
(FLICK!!)
WAAH!

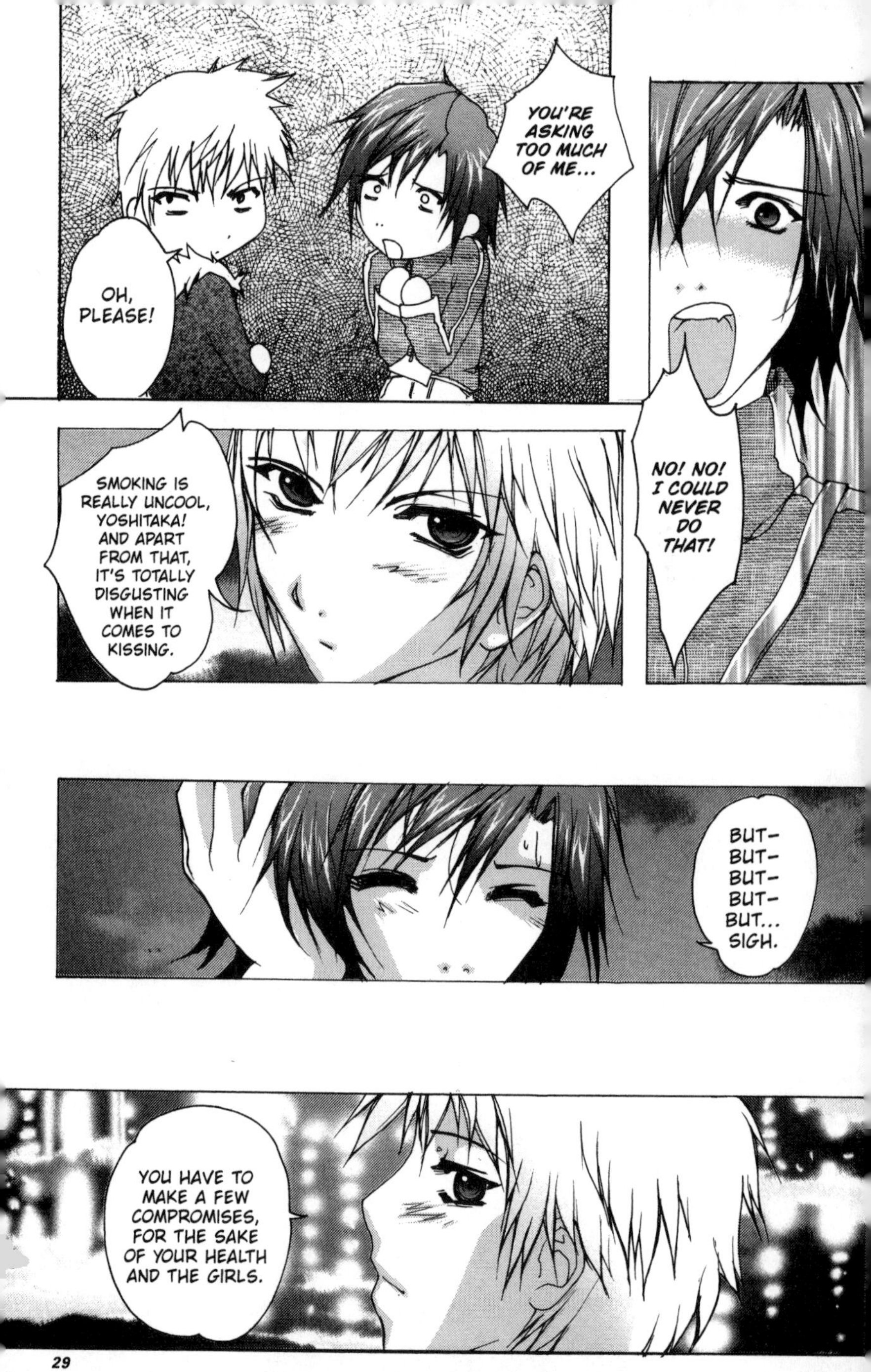
NO! NO! I COULD NEVER DO THAT!
YOU'RE ASKING TOO MUCH OF ME...
OH, PLEASE!
SMOKING IS REALLY UNCOOL, YOSHITAKA! AND APART FROM THAT, IT'S TOTALLY DISGUSTING WHEN IT COMES TO KISSING.
BUT-BUT-BUT-BUT-BUT... SIGH.
YOU HAVE TO MAKE A FEW COMPROMISES, FOR THE SAKE OF YOUR HEALTH AND THE GIRLS.

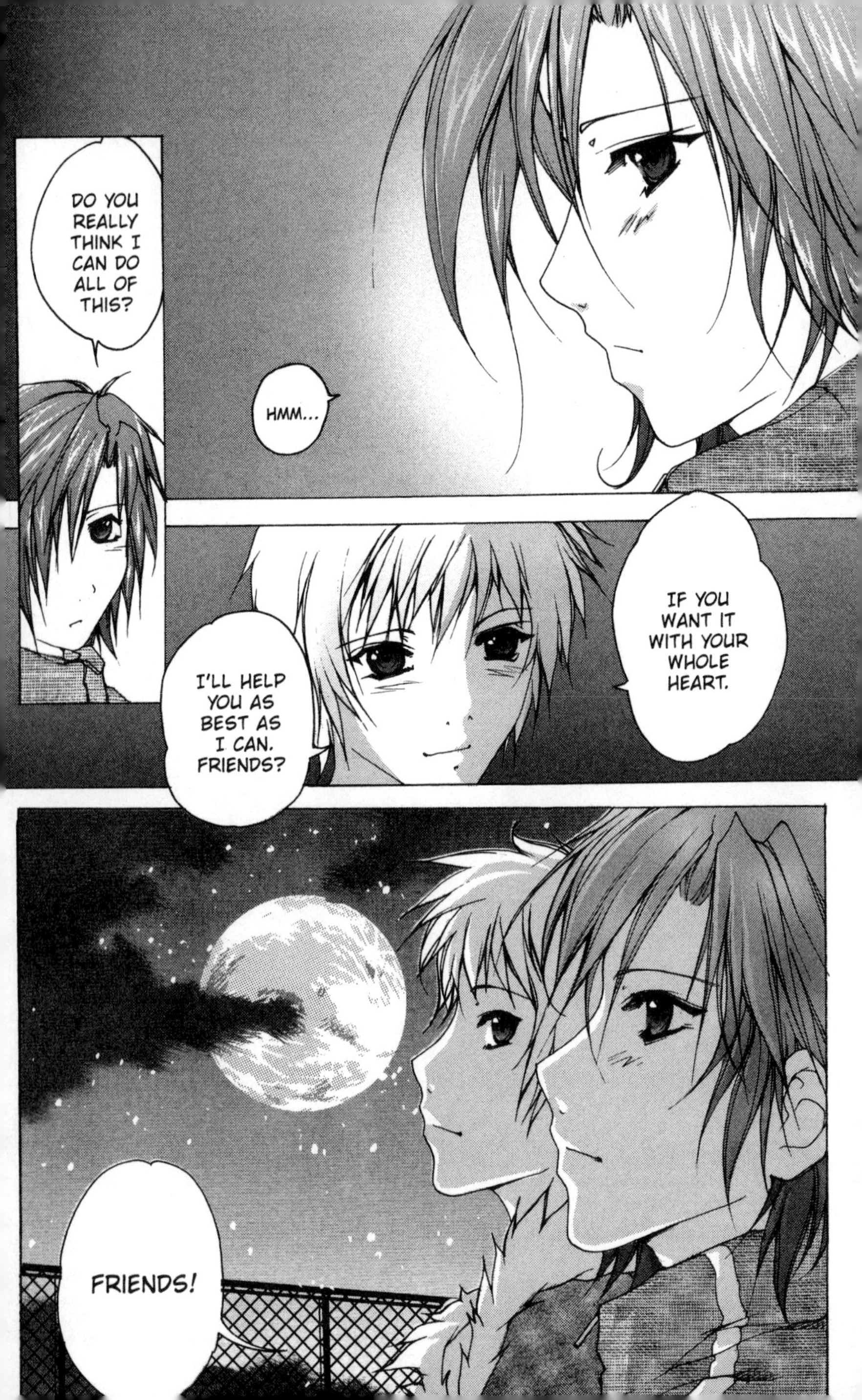
DO YOU REALLY THINK I CAN DO ALL OF THIS?
HMM...
IF YOU WANT IT WITH YOUR WHOLE HEART.
I'LL HELP YOU AS BEST AS I CAN. FRIENDS?
FRIENDS!

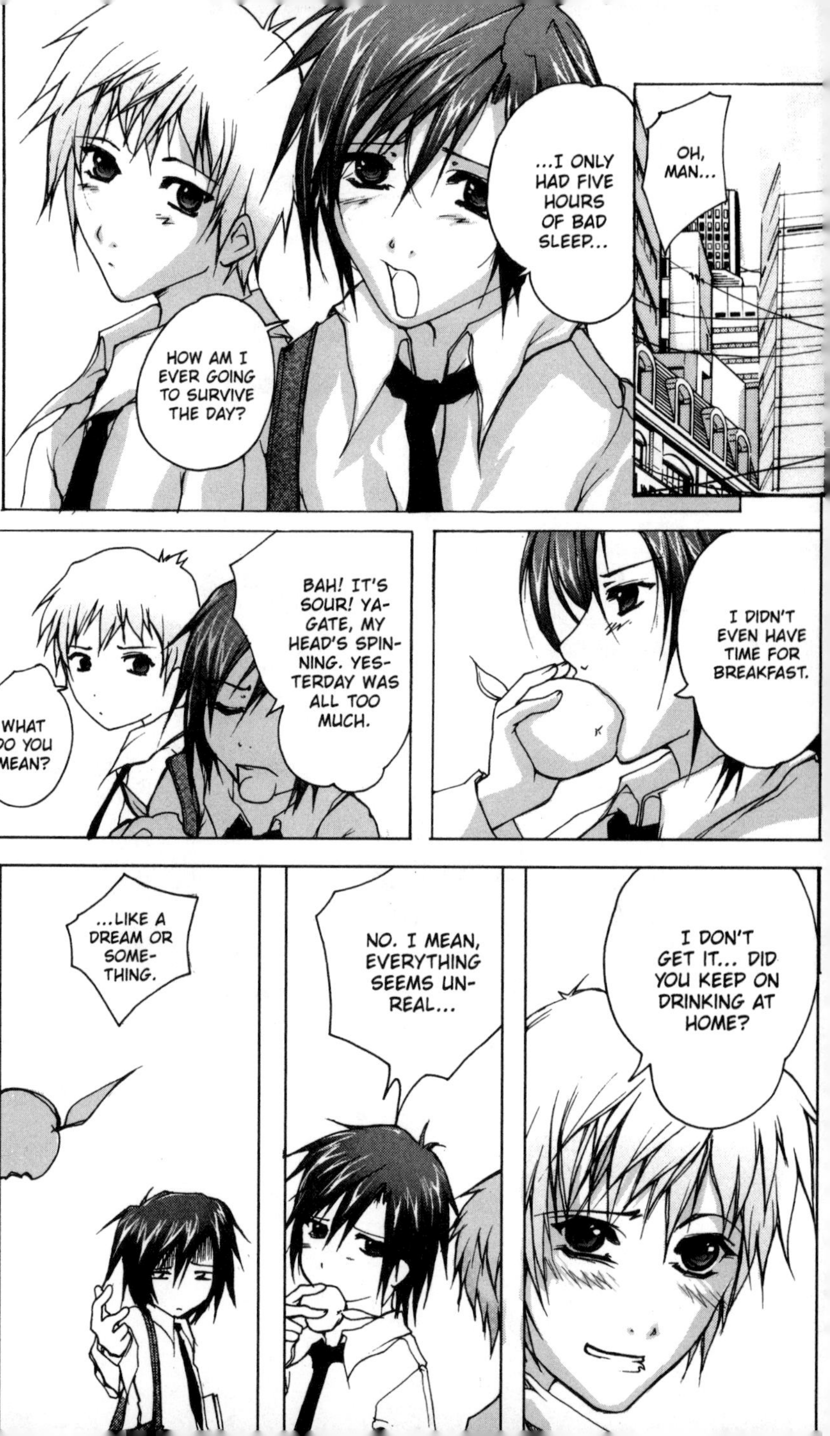
OH, MAN...
...I ONLY HAD FIVE HOURS OF BAD SLEEP...
HOW AM I EVER GOING TO SURVIVE THE DAY?
I DIDN'T EVEN HAVE TIME FOR BREAKFAST.
BAH! IT'S SOUR! YAGATE, MY HEAD'S SPINNING. YESTERDAY WAS ALL TOO MUCH.
WHAT DO YOU MEAN?
I DON'T GET IT... DID YOU KEEP ON DRINKING AT HOME?
NO. I MEAN, EVERYTHING SEEMS UNREAL...
...LIKE A DREAM OR SOMETHING.

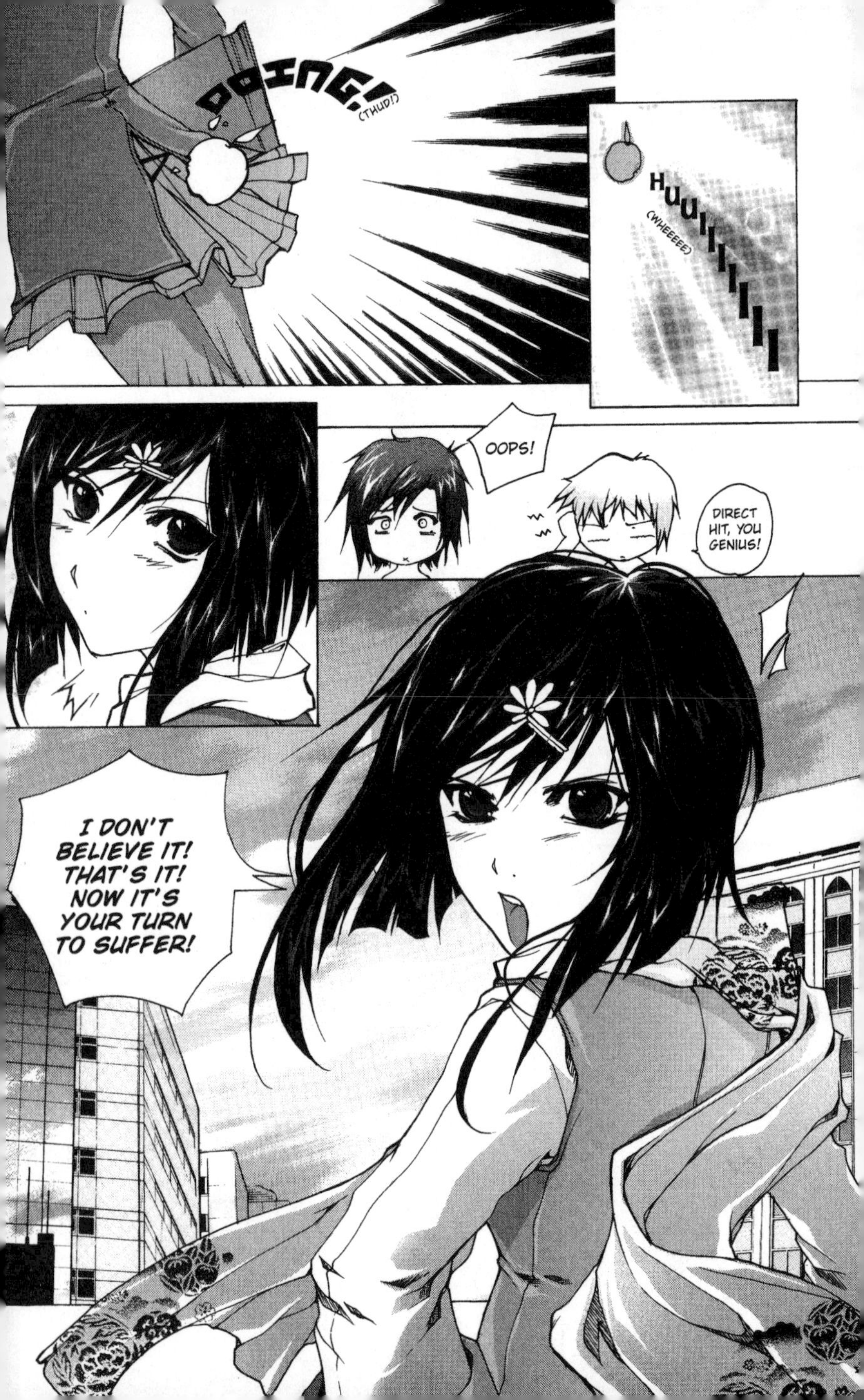
HUUIIIIIIII
(WHEEEEE)
DOING!
(THUD!)
OOPS!
DIRECT HIT, YOU GENIUS!
I DON'T BELIEVE IT! THAT'S IT! NOW IT'S YOUR TURN TO SUFFER!

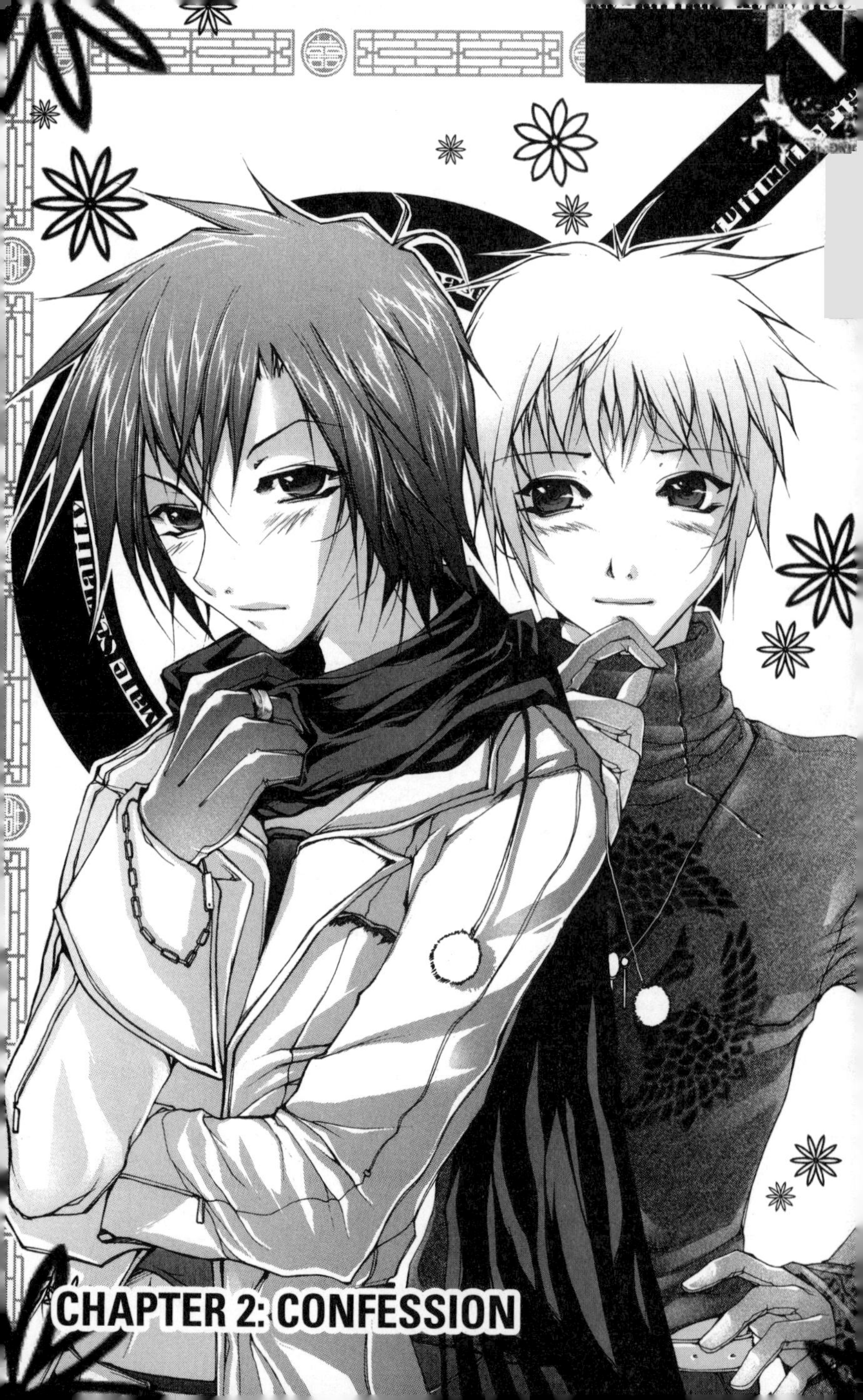

CHAPTER 2: CONFESSION

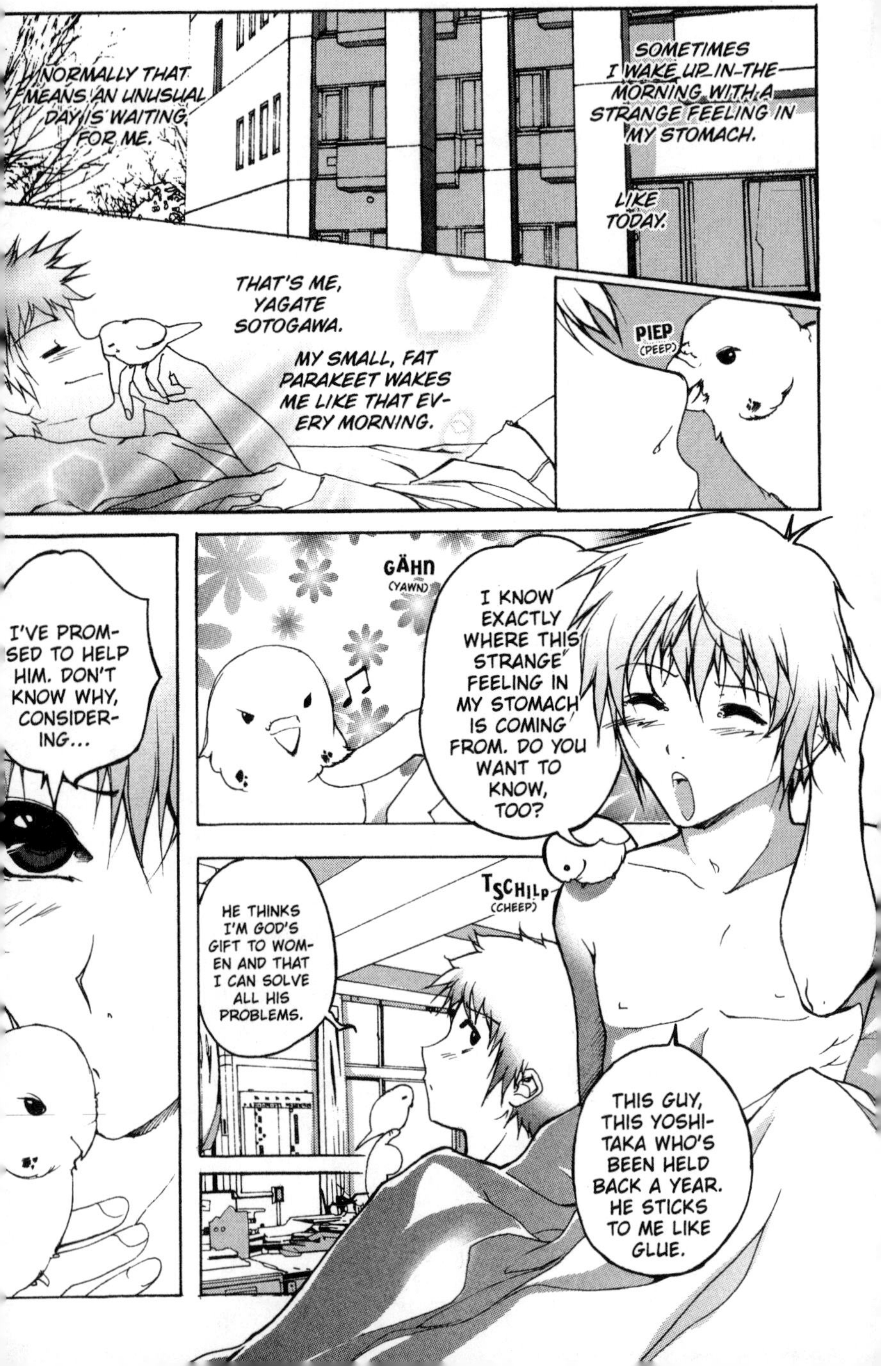
SOMETIMES I WAKE UP IN THE MORNING WITH A STRANGE FEELING IN MY STOMACH.
LIKE TODAY.
NORMALLY THAT MEANS AN UNUSUAL DAY IS WAITING FOR ME.
PIEP (PEEP)
THAT'S ME, YAGATE SOTOGAWA.
MY SMALL, FAT PARAKEET WAKES ME LIKE THAT EVERY MORNING.
GÄHN (YAWN)
I KNOW EXACTLY WHERE THIS STRANGE FEELING IN MY STOMACH IS COMING FROM. DO YOU WANT TO KNOW, TOO?
TSCHILP (CHEEP)
THIS GUY, THIS YOSHITAKA WHO'S BEEN HELD BACK A YEAR. HE STICKS TO ME LIKE GLUE.
HE THINKS I'M GOD'S GIFT TO WOMEN AND THAT I CAN SOLVE ALL HIS PROBLEMS.
I'VE PROMSED TO HELP HIM. DON'T KNOW WHY, CONSIDERING...

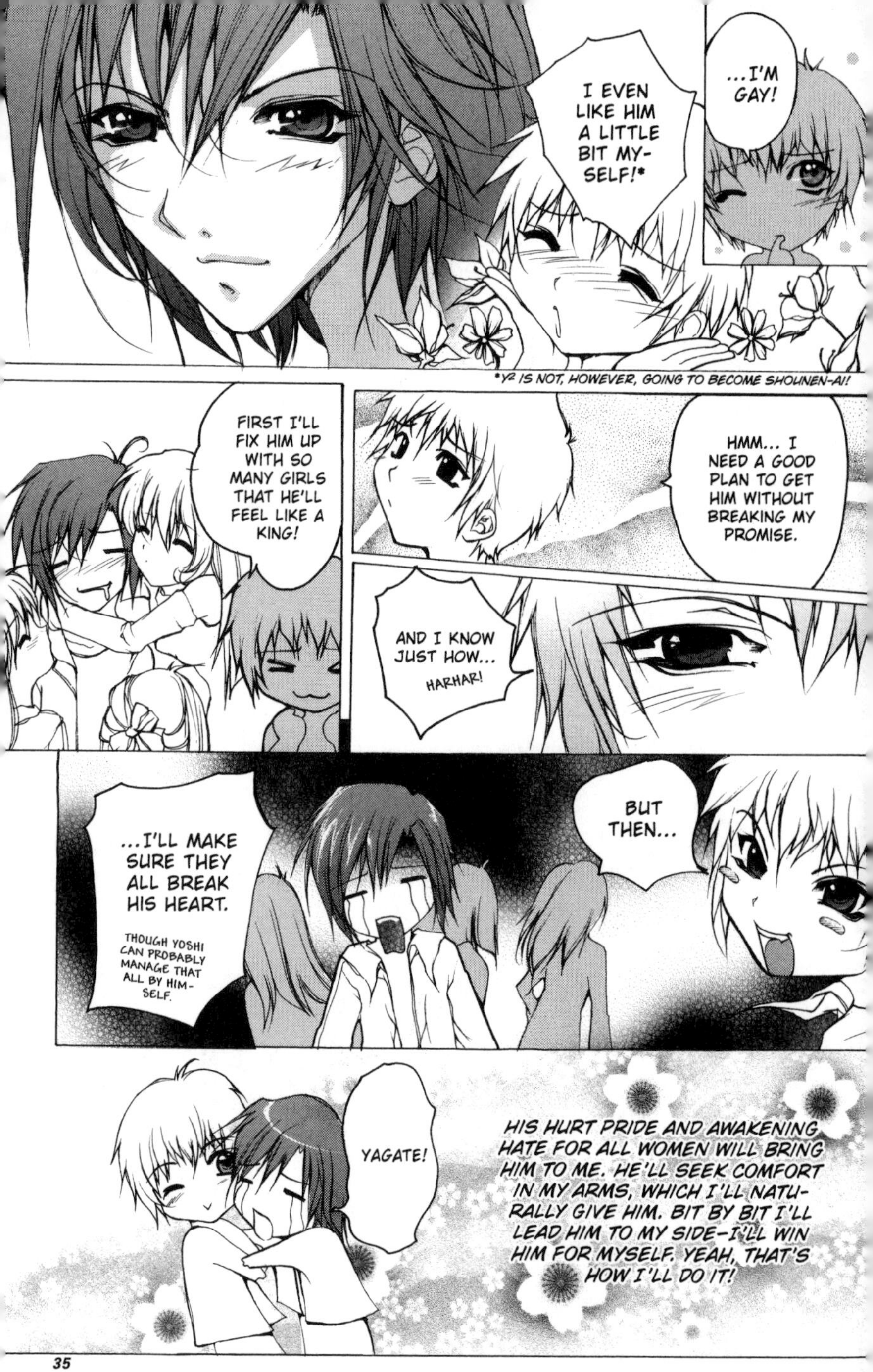

...I'M GAY!
I EVEN LIKE HIM A LITTLE BIT MY-SELF!*
*Y² IS NOT, HOWEVER, GOING TO BECOME SHOUNEN-AI!
HMM... I NEED A GOOD PLAN TO GET HIM WITHOUT BREAKING MY PROMISE.
AND I KNOW JUST HOW...
HARHAR!
FIRST I'LL FIX HIM UP WITH SO MANY GIRLS THAT HE'LL FEEL LIKE A KING!
BUT THEN...
...I'LL MAKE SURE THEY ALL BREAK HIS HEART.
THOUGH YOSHI CAN PROBABLY MANAGE THAT ALL BY HIM-SELF.
HIS HURT PRIDE AND AWAKENING HATE FOR ALL WOMEN WILL BRING HIM TO ME. HE'LL SEEK COMFORT IN MY ARMS, WHICH I'LL NATU-RALLY GIVE HIM. BIT BY BIT I'LL LEAD HIM TO MY SIDE–I'LL WIN HIM FOR MYSELF. YEAH, THAT'S HOW I'LL DO IT!
YAGATE!

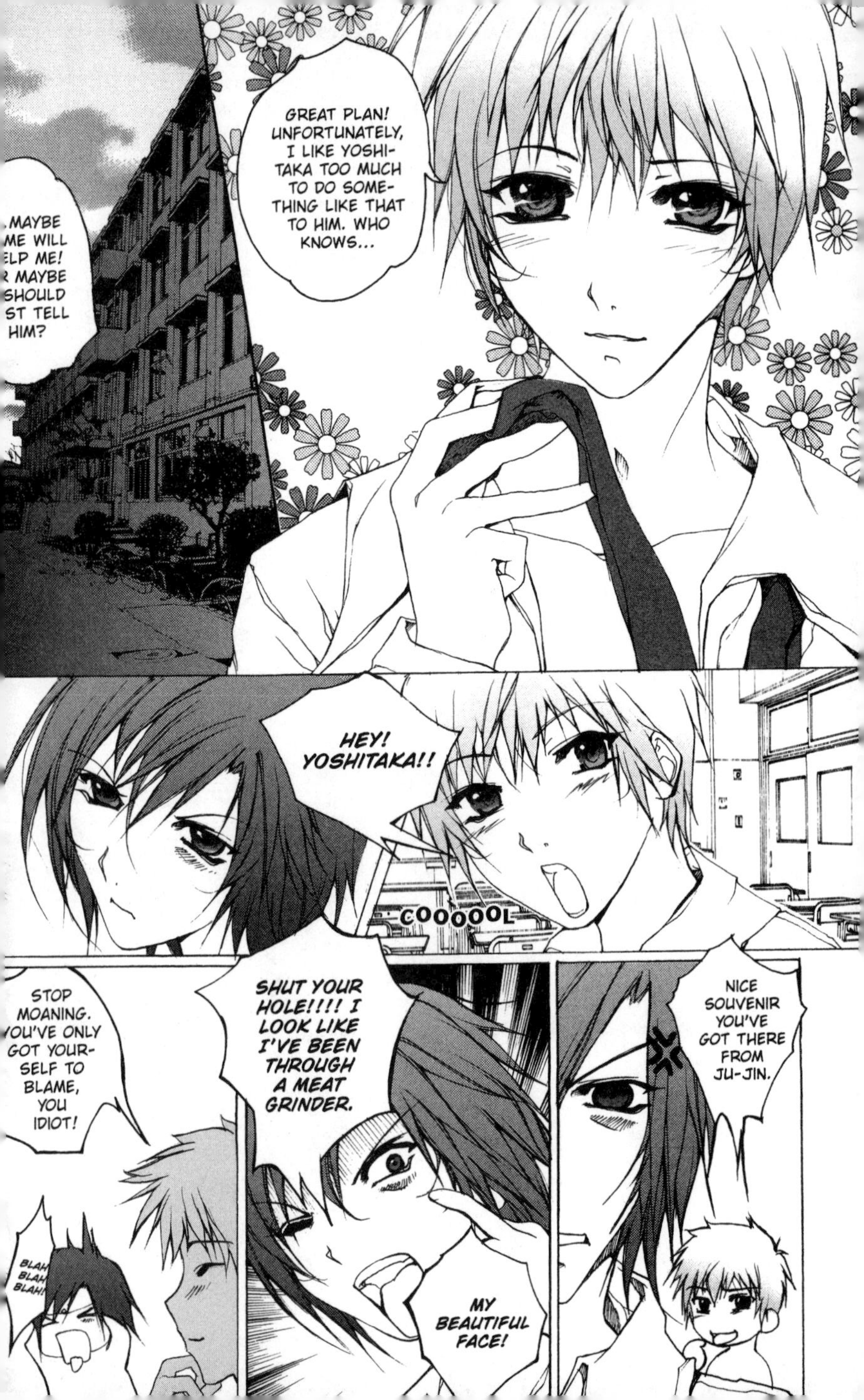
GREAT PLAN! UNFORTUNATELY, I LIKE YOSHI-TAKA TOO MUCH TO DO SOME-THING LIKE THAT TO HIM. WHO KNOWS...
MAYBE ME WILL LP ME! R MAYBE SHOULD ST TELL HIM?
HEY! YOSHITAKA!!
COOOOOL
NICE SOUVENIR YOU'VE GOT THERE FROM JU-JIN.
SHUT YOUR HOLE!!!! I LOOK LIKE I'VE BEEN THROUGH A MEAT GRINDER.
MY BEAUTIFUL FACE!
STOP MOANING. OU'VE ONLY GOT YOUR-SELF TO BLAME, YOU IDIOT!
BLAH BLAH BLAH

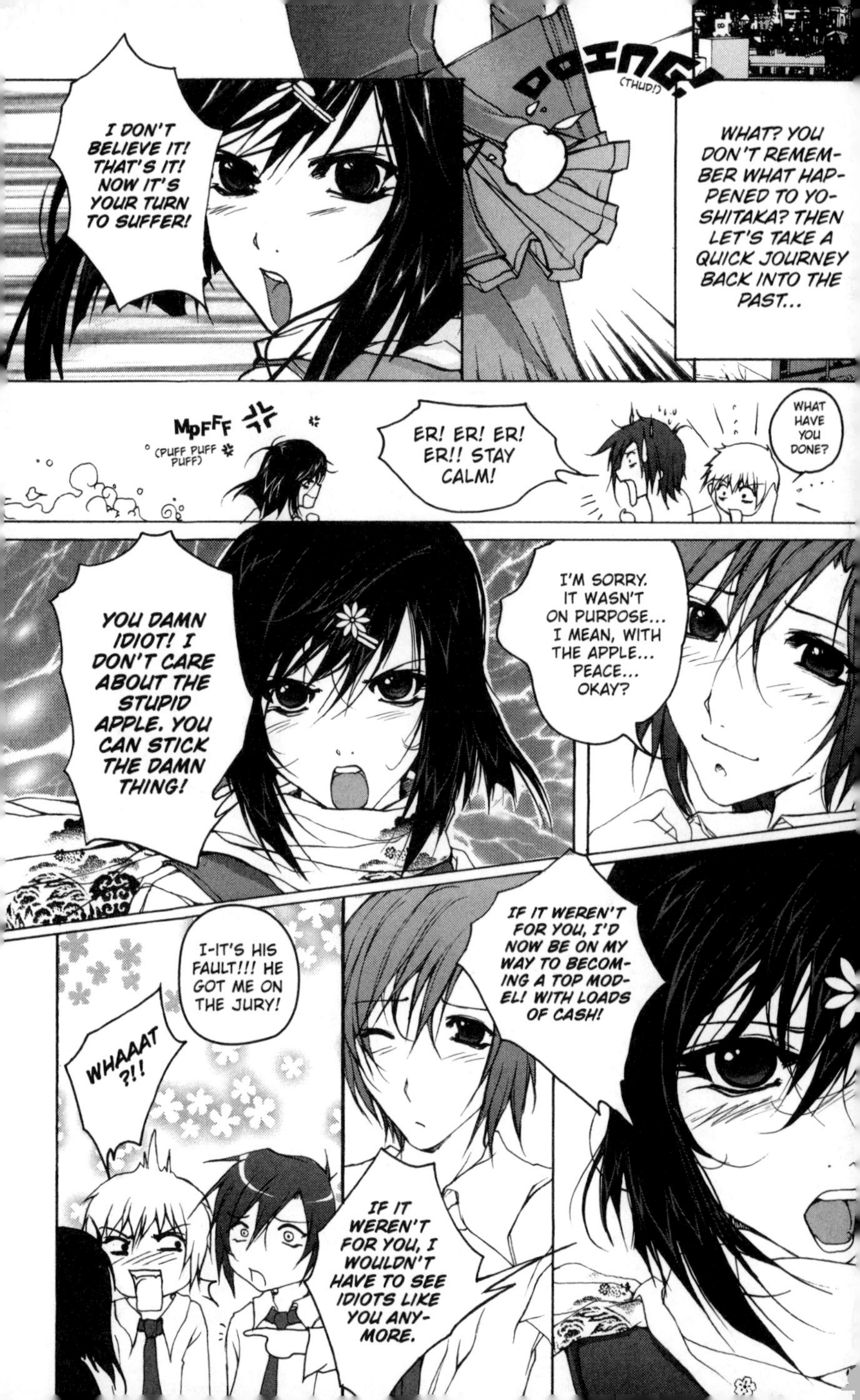
WHAT? YOU DON'T REMEMBER WHAT HAPPENED TO YOSHITAKA? THEN LET'S TAKE A QUICK JOURNEY BACK INTO THE PAST...
DOING
(THUD!)
I DON'T BELIEVE IT! THAT'S IT! NOW IT'S YOUR TURN TO SUFFER!
WHAT HAVE YOU DONE?
ER! ER! ER! ER!! STAY CALM!
MPFFF
(PUFF PUFF PUFF)
I'M SORRY. IT WASN'T ON PURPOSE... I MEAN, WITH THE APPLE... PEACE... OKAY?
YOU DAMN IDIOT! I DON'T CARE ABOUT THE STUPID APPLE. YOU CAN STICK THE DAMN THING!
IF IT WEREN'T FOR YOU, I'D NOW BE ON MY WAY TO BECOMING A TOP MODEL! WITH LOADS OF CASH!
IF IT WEREN'T FOR YOU, I WOULDN'T HAVE TO SEE IDIOTS LIKE YOU ANYMORE.
I-IT'S HIS FAULT!!! HE GOT ME ON THE JURY!
WHAAAT?!!

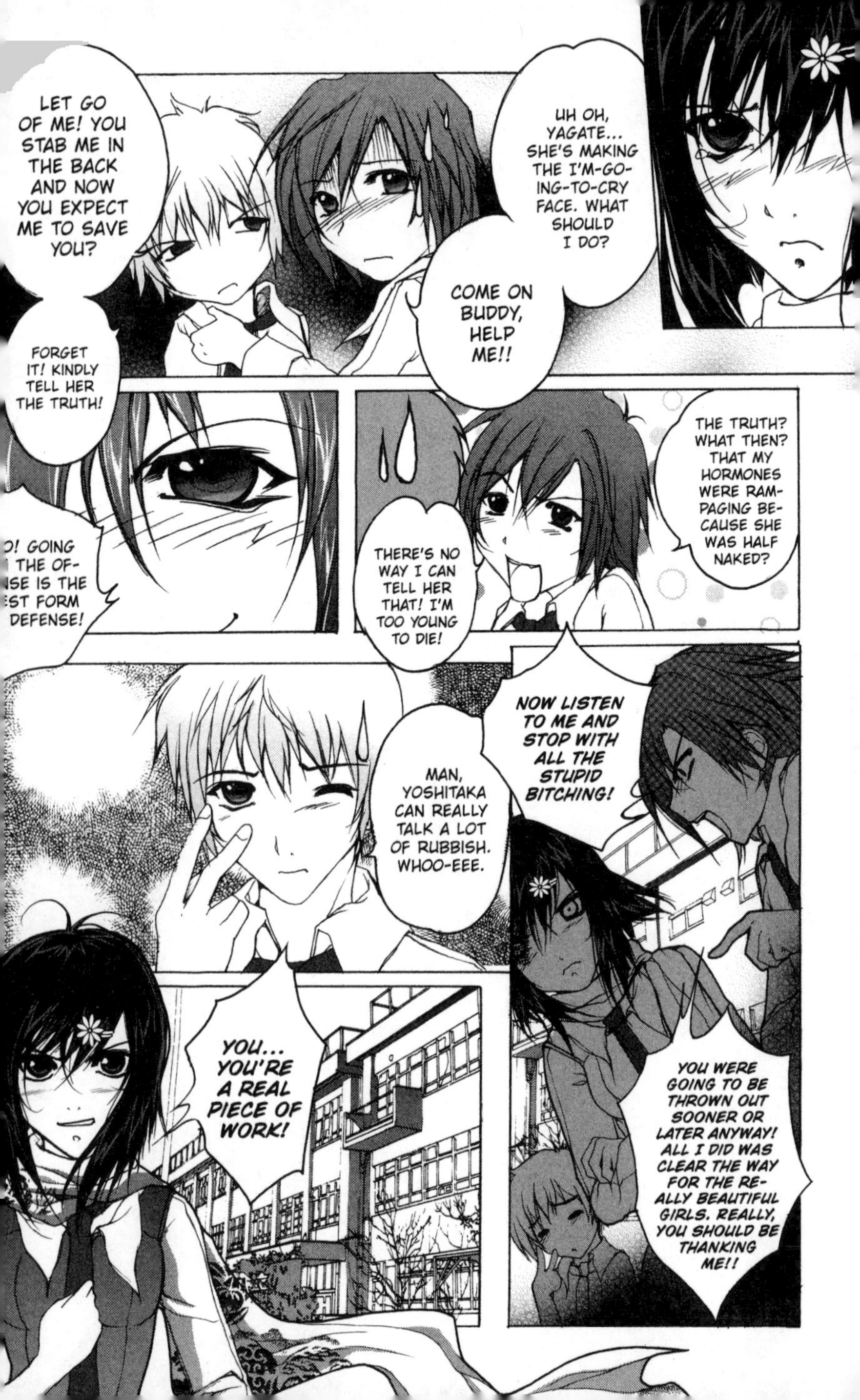
UH OH, YAGATE... SHE'S MAKING THE I'M-GOING-TO-CRY FACE. WHAT SHOULD I DO?
COME ON BUDDY, HELP ME!!
LET GO OF ME! YOU STAB ME IN THE BACK AND NOW YOU EXPECT ME TO SAVE YOU?
FORGET IT! KINDLY TELL HER THE TRUTH!
THE TRUTH? WHAT THEN? THAT MY HORMONES WERE RAMPAGING BECAUSE SHE WAS HALF NAKED?
THERE'S NO WAY I CAN TELL HER THAT! I'M TOO YOUNG TO DIE!
O! GOING THE OF- SE IS THE ST FORM DEFENSE!
NOW LISTEN TO ME AND STOP WITH ALL THE STUPID BITCHING!
YOU WERE GOING TO BE THROWN OUT SOONER OR LATER ANYWAY! ALL I DID WAS CLEAR THE WAY FOR THE REALLY BEAUTIFUL GIRLS. REALLY, YOU SHOULD BE THANKING ME!!
MAN, YOSHITAKA CAN REALLY TALK A LOT OF RUBBISH. WHOO-EEE.
YOU... YOU'RE A REAL PIECE OF WORK!

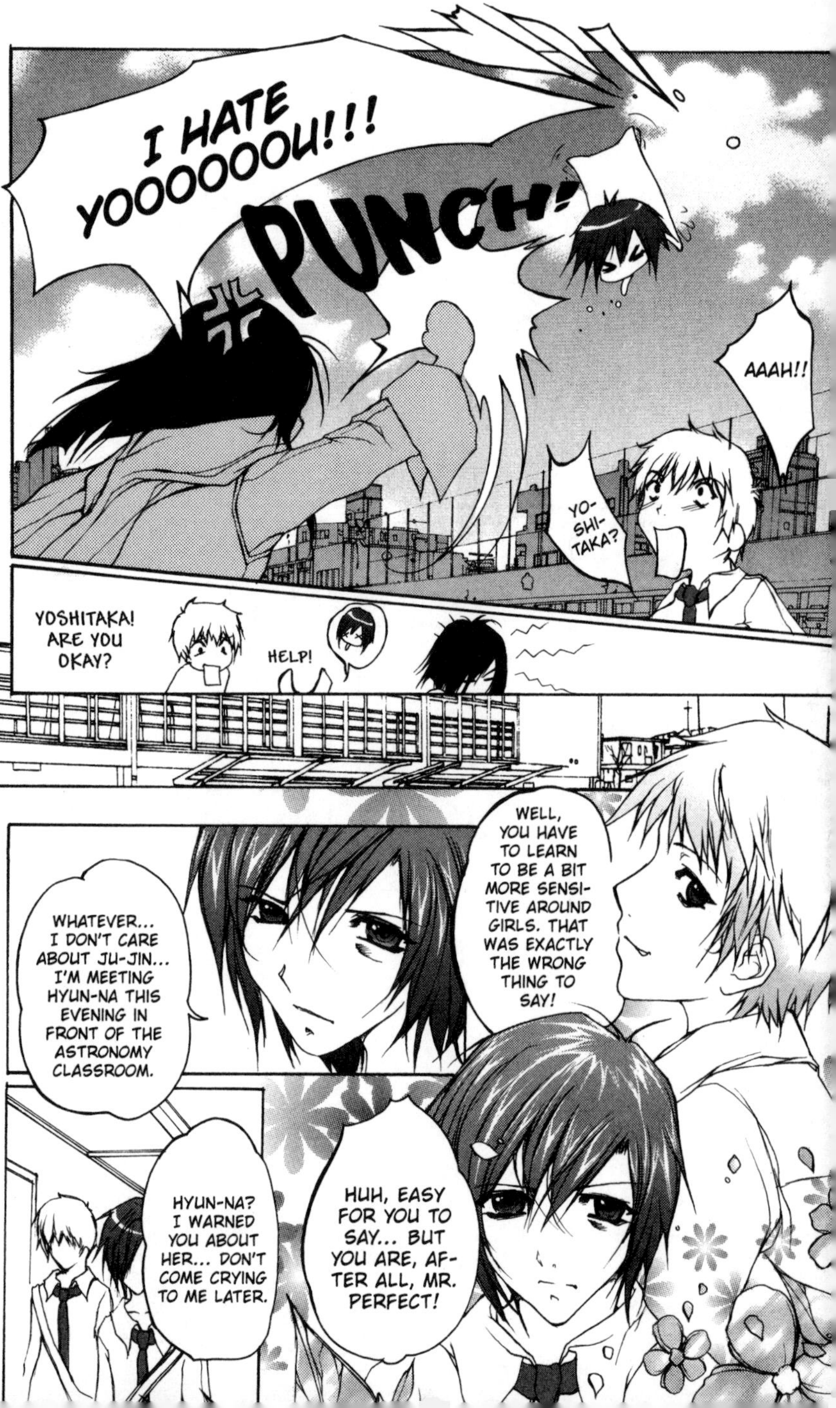
I HATE YOOOOOOU!!!
PUNCH!
AAAH!!
YO-SHI-TAKA?
YOSHITAKA! ARE YOU OKAY?
HELP!
WELL, YOU HAVE TO LEARN TO BE A BIT MORE SENSITIVE AROUND GIRLS. THAT WAS EXACTLY THE WRONG THING TO SAY!
WHATEVER... I DON'T CARE ABOUT JU-JIN... I'M MEETING HYUN-NA THIS EVENING IN FRONT OF THE ASTRONOMY CLASSROOM.
HUH, EASY FOR YOU TO SAY... BUT YOU ARE, AFTER ALL, MR. PERFECT!
HYUN-NA? I WARNED YOU ABOUT HER... DON'T COME CRYING TO ME LATER.

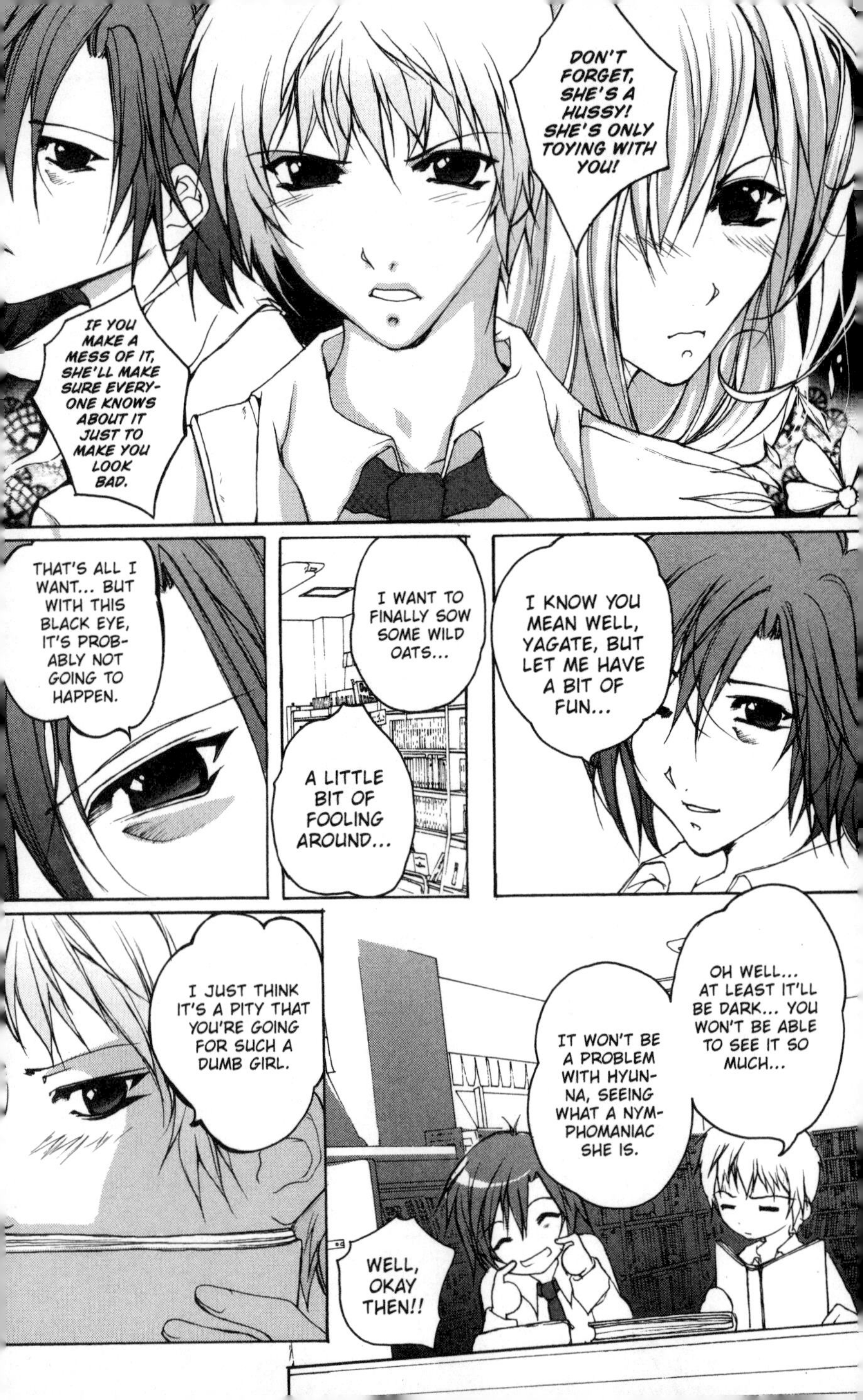

DON'T FORGET, SHE'S A HUSSY! SHE'S ONLY TOYING WITH YOU!
IF YOU MAKE A MESS OF IT, SHE'LL MAKE SURE EVERYONE KNOWS ABOUT IT JUST TO MAKE YOU LOOK BAD.
I KNOW YOU MEAN WELL, YAGATE, BUT LET ME HAVE A BIT OF FUN...
I WANT TO FINALLY SOW SOME WILD OATS...
A LITTLE BIT OF FOOLING AROUND...
THAT'S ALL I WANT... BUT WITH THIS BLACK EYE, IT'S PROBABLY NOT GOING TO HAPPEN.
OH WELL... AT LEAST IT'LL BE DARK... YOU WON'T BE ABLE TO SEE IT SO MUCH...
IT WON'T BE A PROBLEM WITH HYUNNA, SEEING WHAT A NYMPHOMANIAC SHE IS.
WELL, OKAY THEN!!
I JUST THINK IT'S A PITY THAT YOU'RE GOING FOR SUCH A DUMB GIRL.

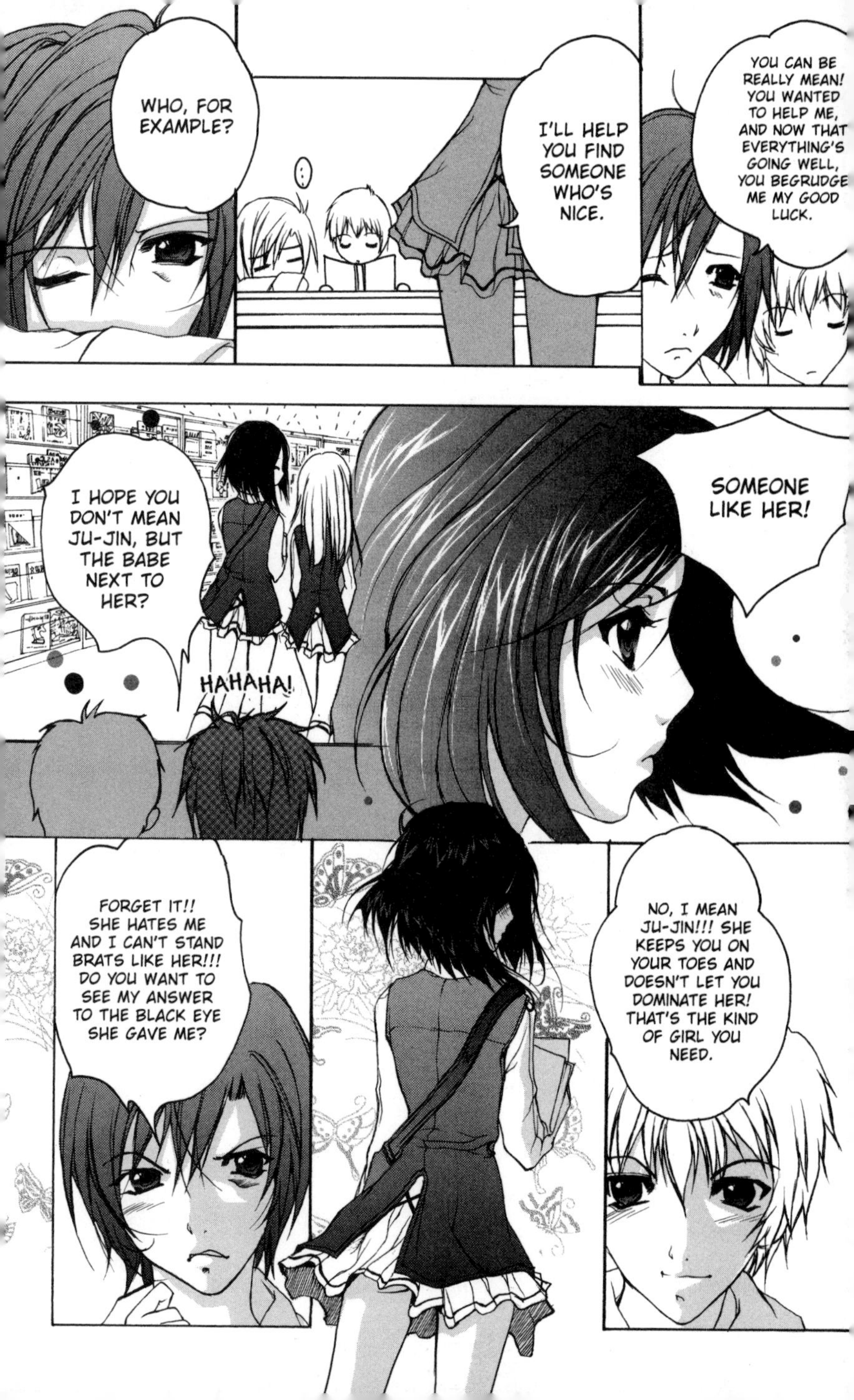

YOU CAN BE REALLY MEAN! YOU WANTED TO HELP ME, AND NOW THAT EVERYTHING'S GOING WELL, YOU BEGRUDGE ME MY GOOD LUCK.
I'LL HELP YOU FIND SOMEONE WHO'S NICE.
WHO, FOR EXAMPLE?
SOMEONE LIKE HER!
I HOPE YOU DON'T MEAN JU-JIN, BUT THE BABE NEXT TO HER?
HAHAHA!
NO, I MEAN JU-JIN!!! SHE KEEPS YOU ON YOUR TOES AND DOESN'T LET YOU DOMINATE HER! THAT'S THE KIND OF GIRL YOU NEED.
FORGET IT!! SHE HATES ME AND I CAN'T STAND BRATS LIKE HER!!! DO YOU WANT TO SEE MY ANSWER TO THE BLACK EYE SHE GAVE ME?

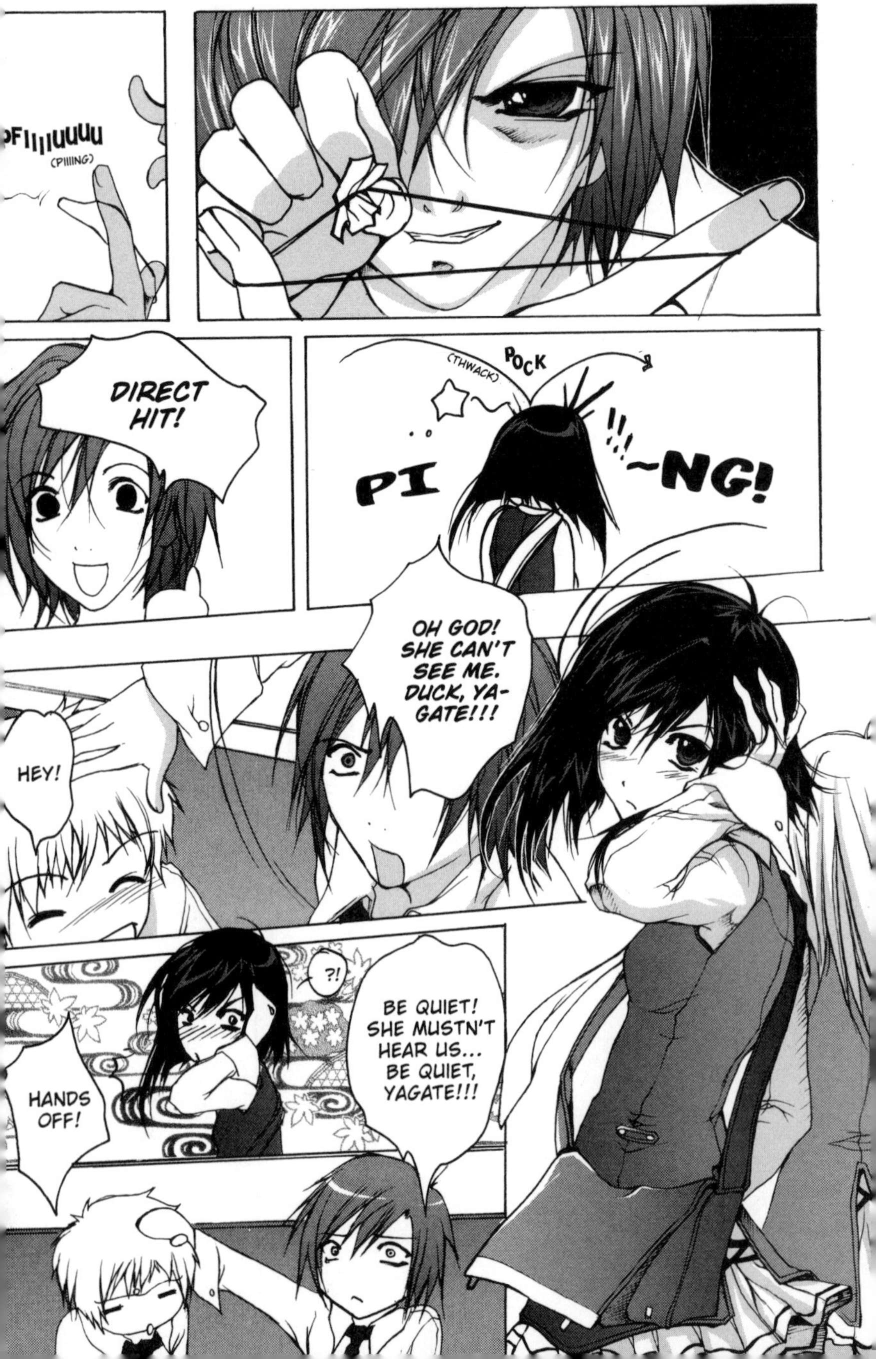
PFIIIIUUUU
(PIIIING)
POCK
(THWACK)
PI ~NG!
!!!
DIRECT HIT!
OH GOD! SHE CAN'T SEE ME. DUCK, YA-GATE!!!
HEY!
BE QUIET! SHE MUSTN'T HEAR US... BE QUIET, YAGATE!!!
?!
HANDS OFF!

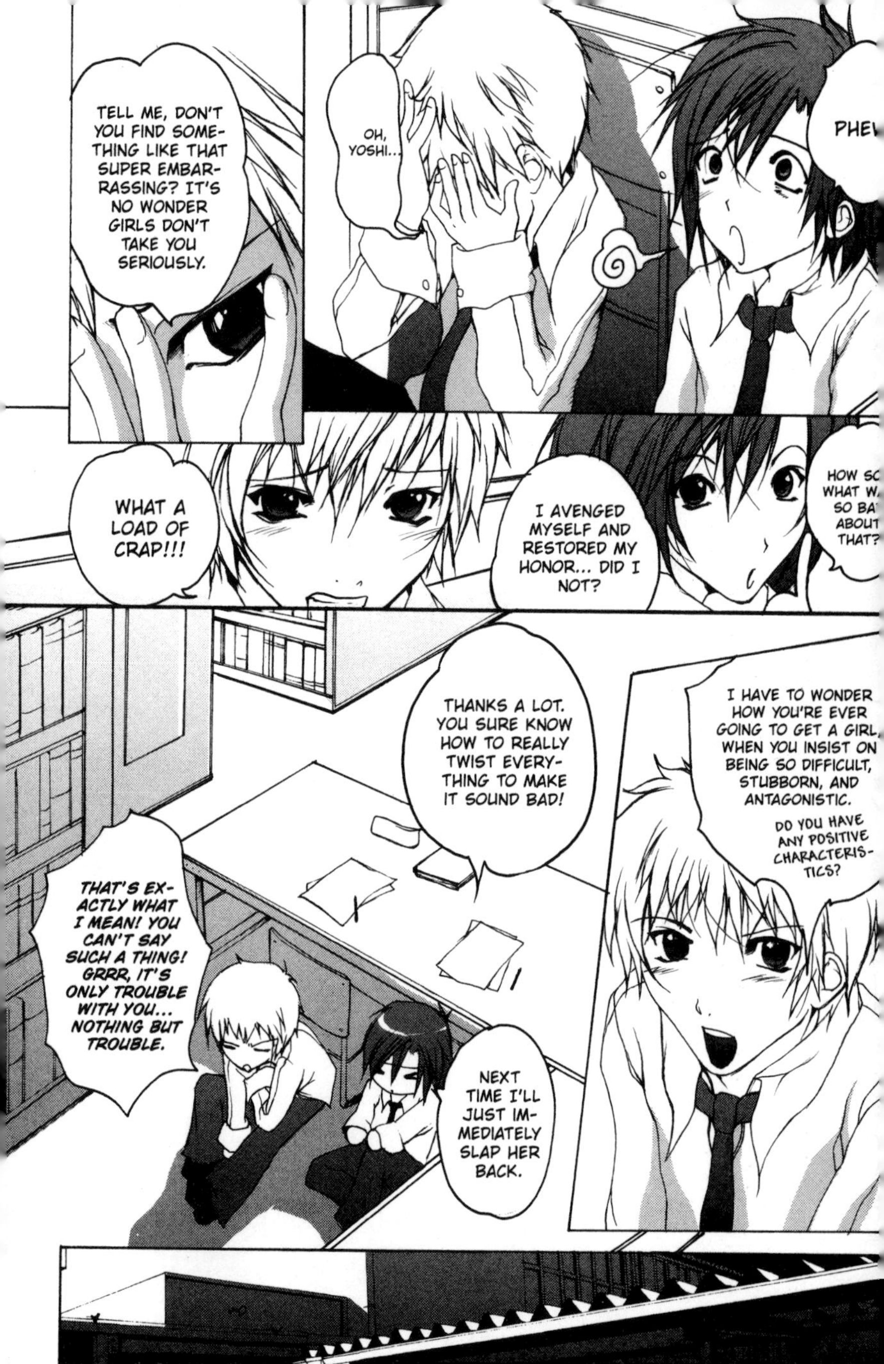
PHEW
OH, YOSHI...
TELL ME, DON'T YOU FIND SOMETHING LIKE THAT SUPER EMBARRASSING? IT'S NO WONDER GIRLS DON'T TAKE YOU SERIOUSLY.
HOW SO WHAT WA SO BA ABOUT THAT?
I AVENGED MYSELF AND RESTORED MY HONOR... DID I NOT?
WHAT A LOAD OF CRAP!!!
I HAVE TO WONDER HOW YOU'RE EVER GOING TO GET A GIRL, WHEN YOU INSIST ON BEING SO DIFFICULT, STUBBORN, AND ANTAGONISTIC.
DO YOU HAVE ANY POSITIVE CHARACTERISTICS?
THANKS A LOT. YOU SURE KNOW HOW TO REALLY TWIST EVERYTHING TO MAKE IT SOUND BAD!
THAT'S EXACTLY WHAT I MEAN! YOU CAN'T SAY SUCH A THING! GRRR, IT'S ONLY TROUBLE WITH YOU... NOTHING BUT TROUBLE.
NEXT TIME I'LL JUST IMMEDIATELY SLAP HER BACK.

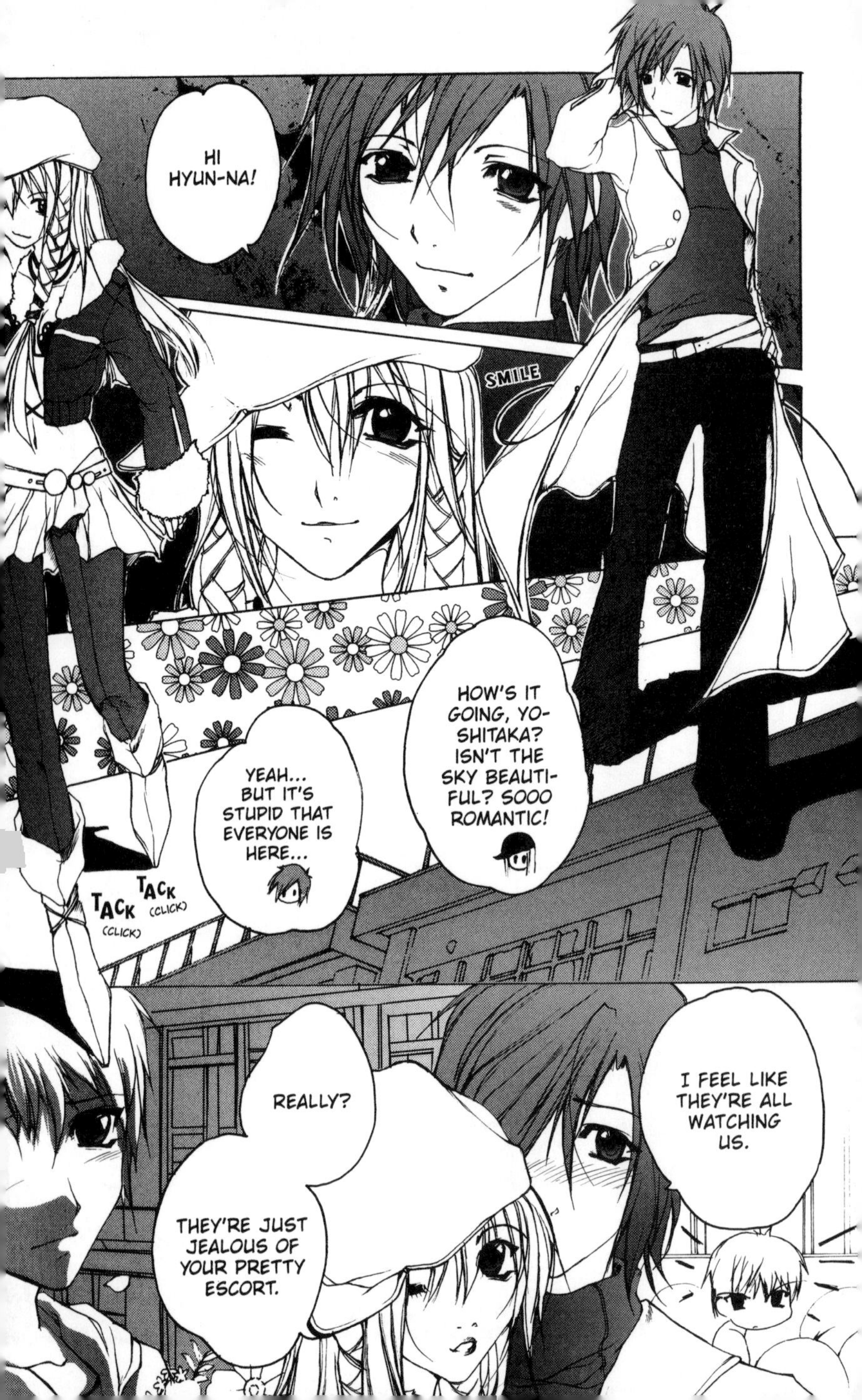
HI HYUN-NA!
SMILE
HOW'S IT GOING, YO-SHITAKA? ISN'T THE SKY BEAUTI-FUL? SOOO ROMANTIC!
YEAH... BUT IT'S STUPID THAT EVERYONE IS HERE...
TACK (CLICK)
TACK (CLICK)
I FEEL LIKE THEY'RE ALL WATCHING US.
REALLY?
THEY'RE JUST JEALOUS OF YOUR PRETTY ESCORT.

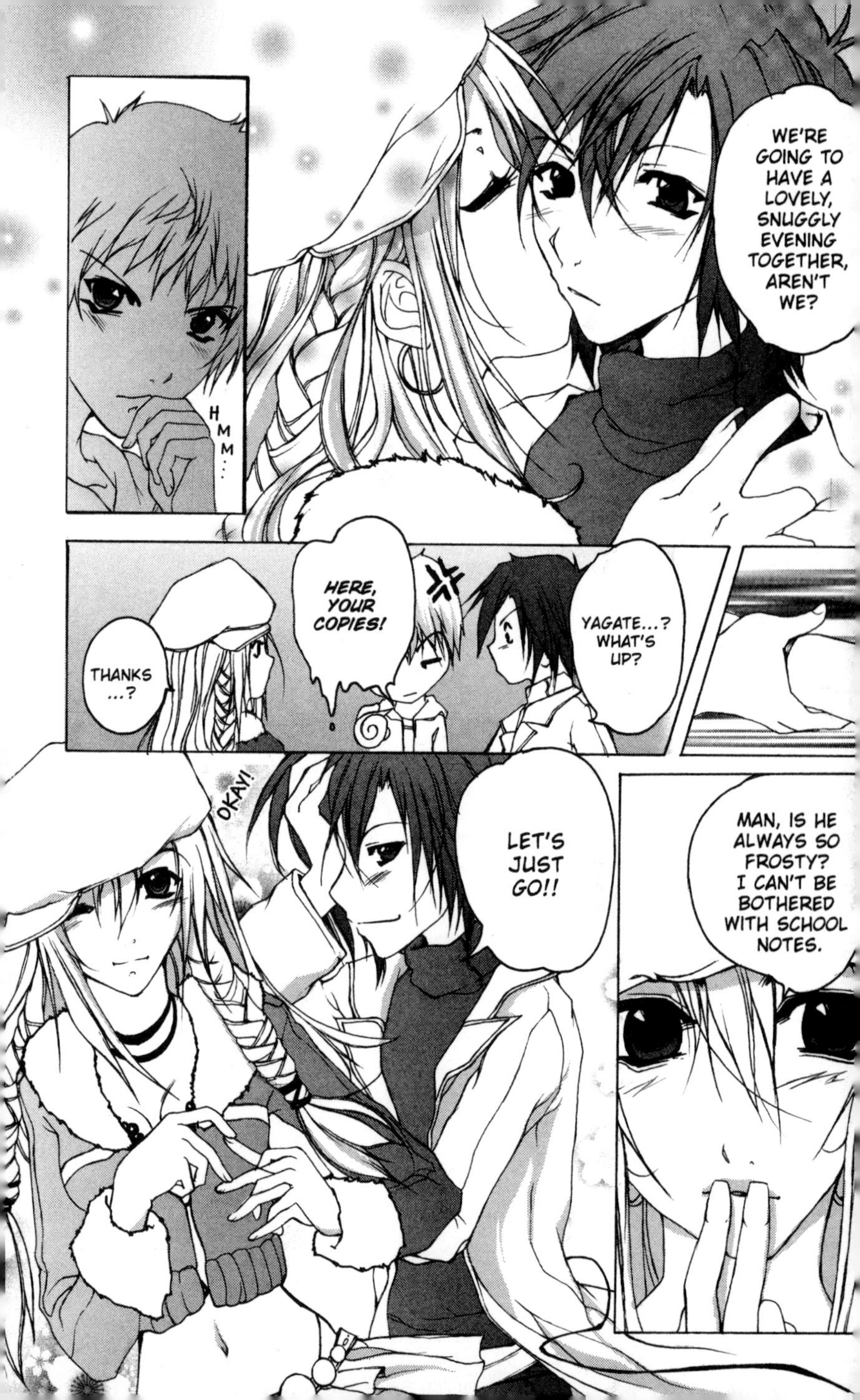
WE'RE GOING TO HAVE A LOVELY, SNUGGLY EVENING TOGETHER, AREN'T WE?
HMM...
YAGATE...? WHAT'S UP?
HERE, YOUR COPIES!
THANKS ...?
MAN, IS HE ALWAYS SO FROSTY? I CAN'T BE BOTHERED WITH SCHOOL NOTES.
LET'S JUST GO!!
OKAY!

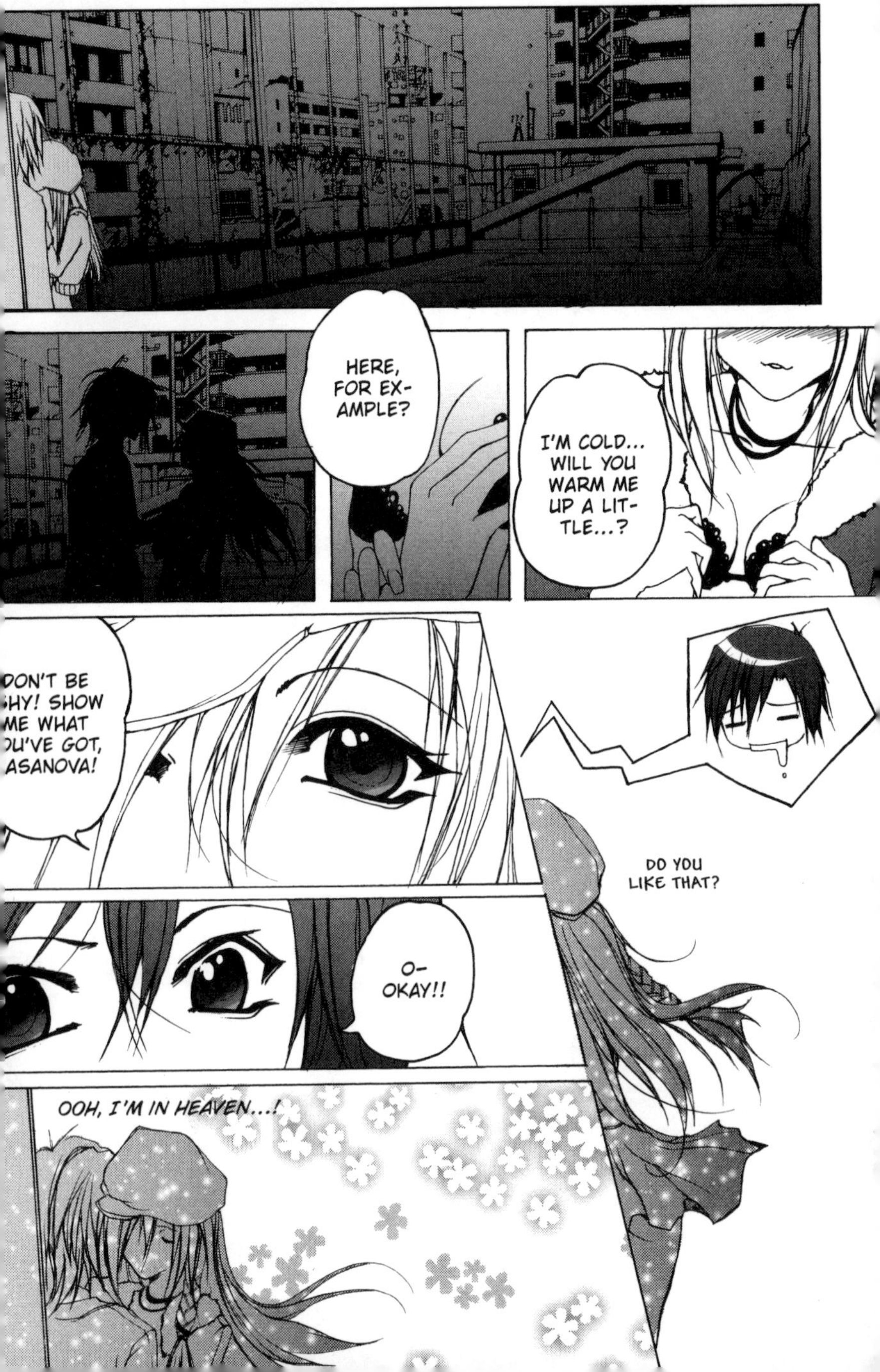
I'M COLD... WILL YOU WARM ME UP A LIT-TLE...?
HERE, FOR EX-AMPLE?
DO YOU LIKE THAT?
DON'T BE SHY! SHOW ME WHAT YOU'VE GOT, CASANOVA!
O-OKAY!!
OOH, I'M IN HEAVEN...!

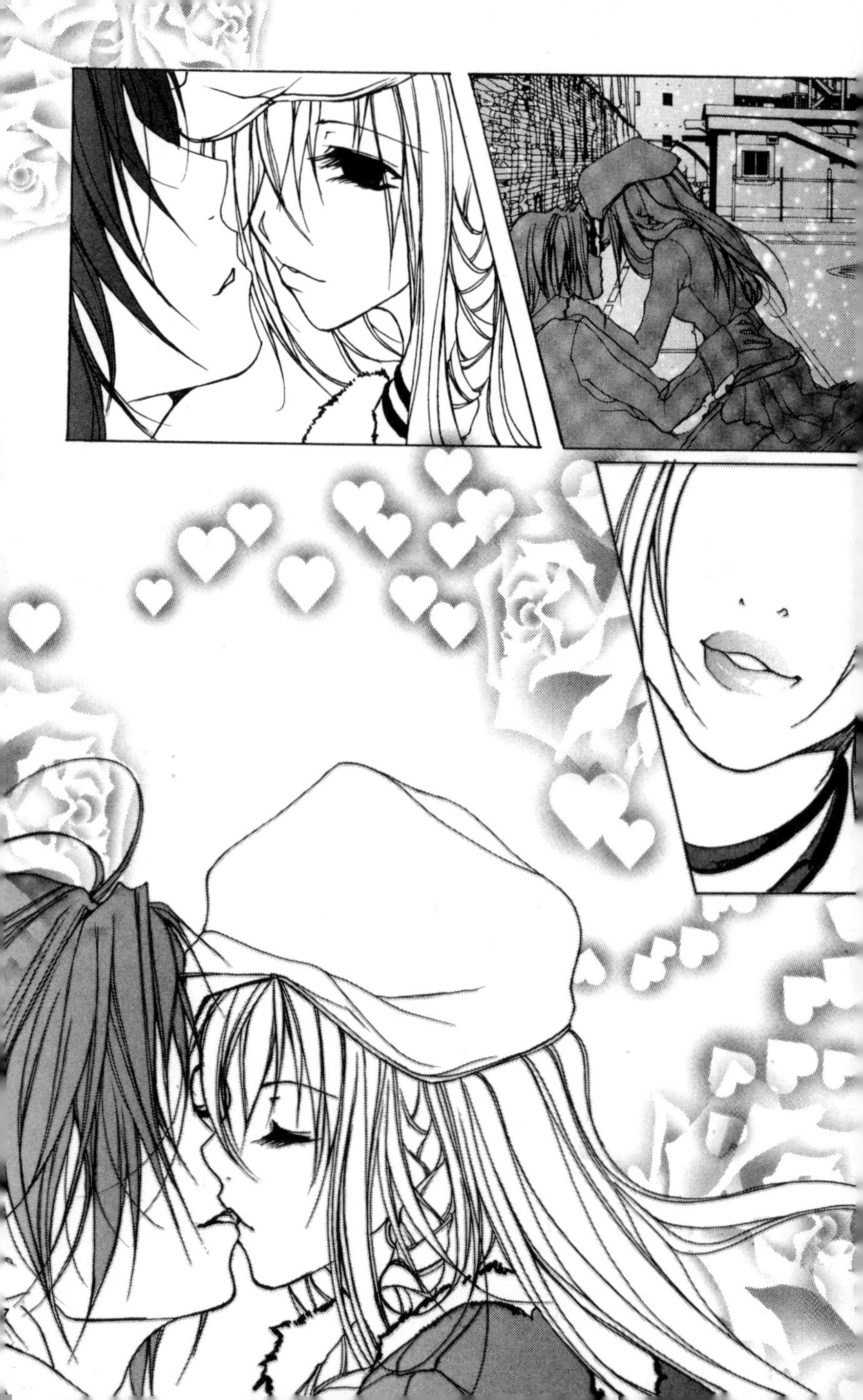

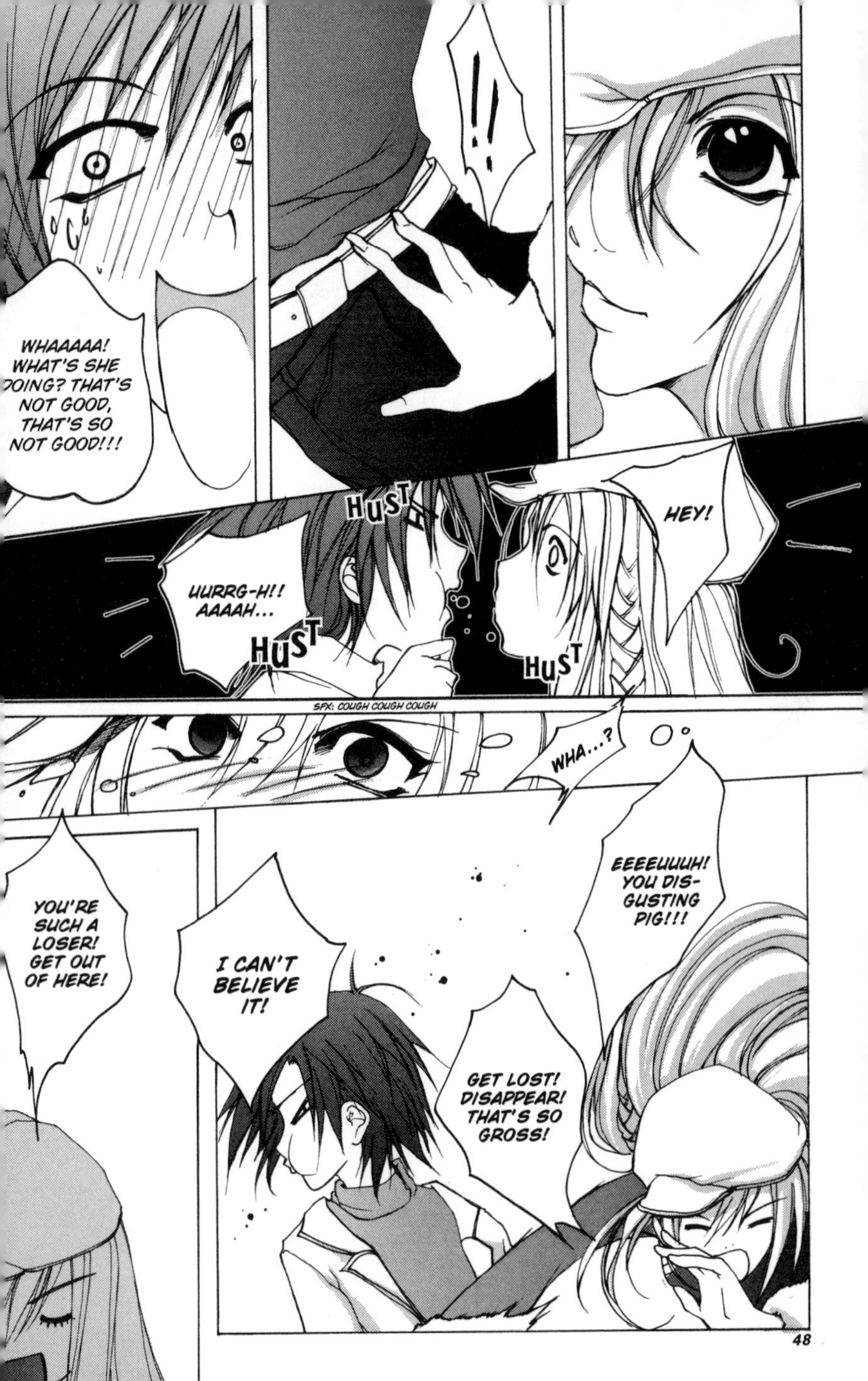
!!
WHAAAAA! WHAT'S SHE DOING? THAT'S NOT GOOD, THAT'S SO NOT GOOD!!!
HEY!
HUST
HUST
UURRG-H!! AAAAH...
HUST
SFX: COUGH COUGH COUGH
WHA...?
EEEEUUUH! YOU DIS-GUSTING PIG!!!
GET LOST! DISAPPEAR! THAT'S SO GROSS!
I CAN'T BELIEVE IT!
YOU'RE SUCH A LOSER! GET OUT OF HERE!

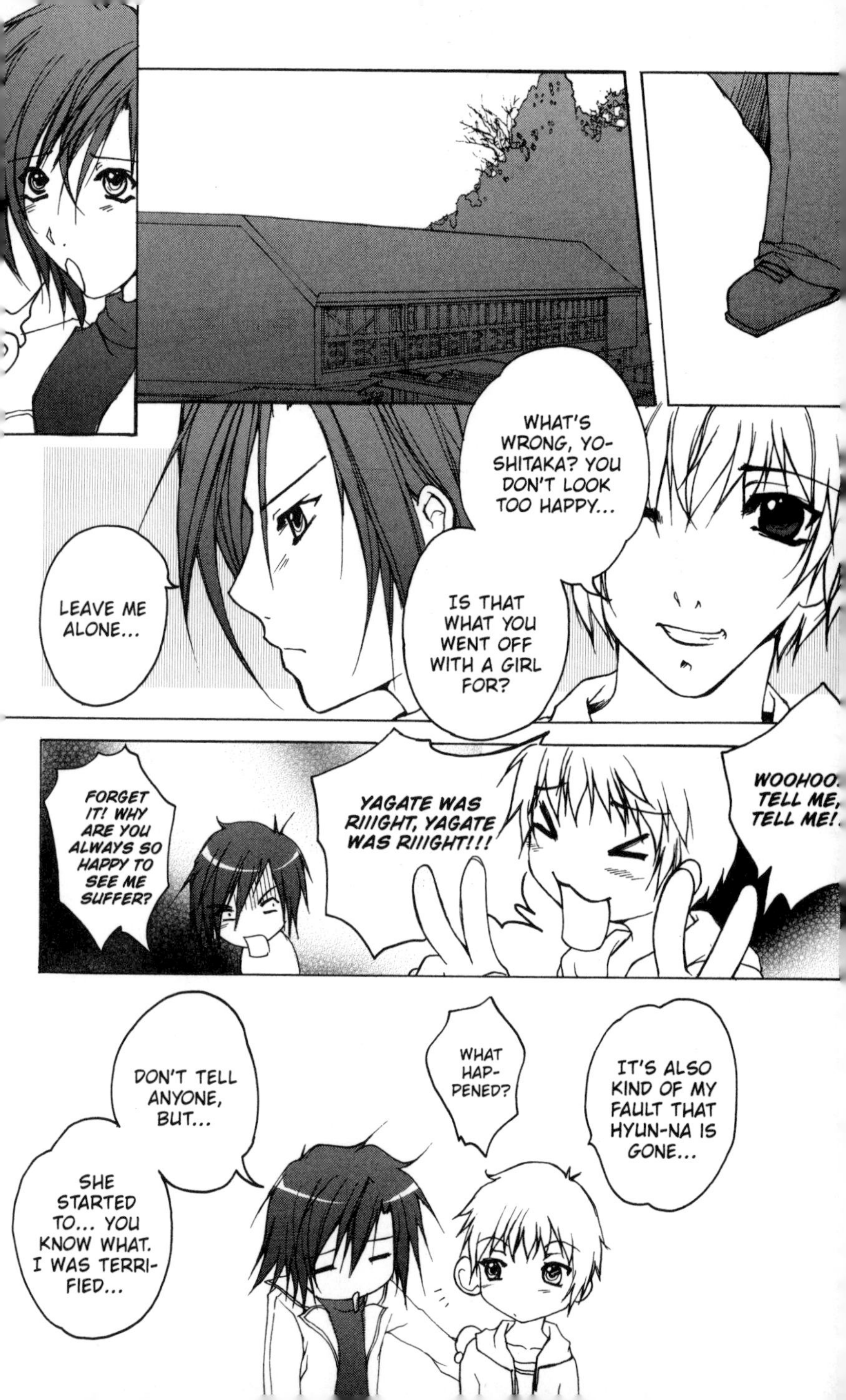
WHAT'S WRONG, YO-SHITAKA? YOU DON'T LOOK TOO HAPPY...
IS THAT WHAT YOU WENT OFF WITH A GIRL FOR?
LEAVE ME ALONE...
WOOHOO. TELL ME, TELL ME!
YAGATE WAS RIIIGHT, YAGATE WAS RIIIGHT!!!
FORGET IT! WHY ARE YOU ALWAYS SO HAPPY TO SEE ME SUFFER?
IT'S ALSO KIND OF MY FAULT THAT HYUN-NA IS GONE...
WHAT HAP-PENED?
DON'T TELL ANYONE, BUT...
SHE STARTED TO... YOU KNOW WHAT. I WAS TERRI-FIED...

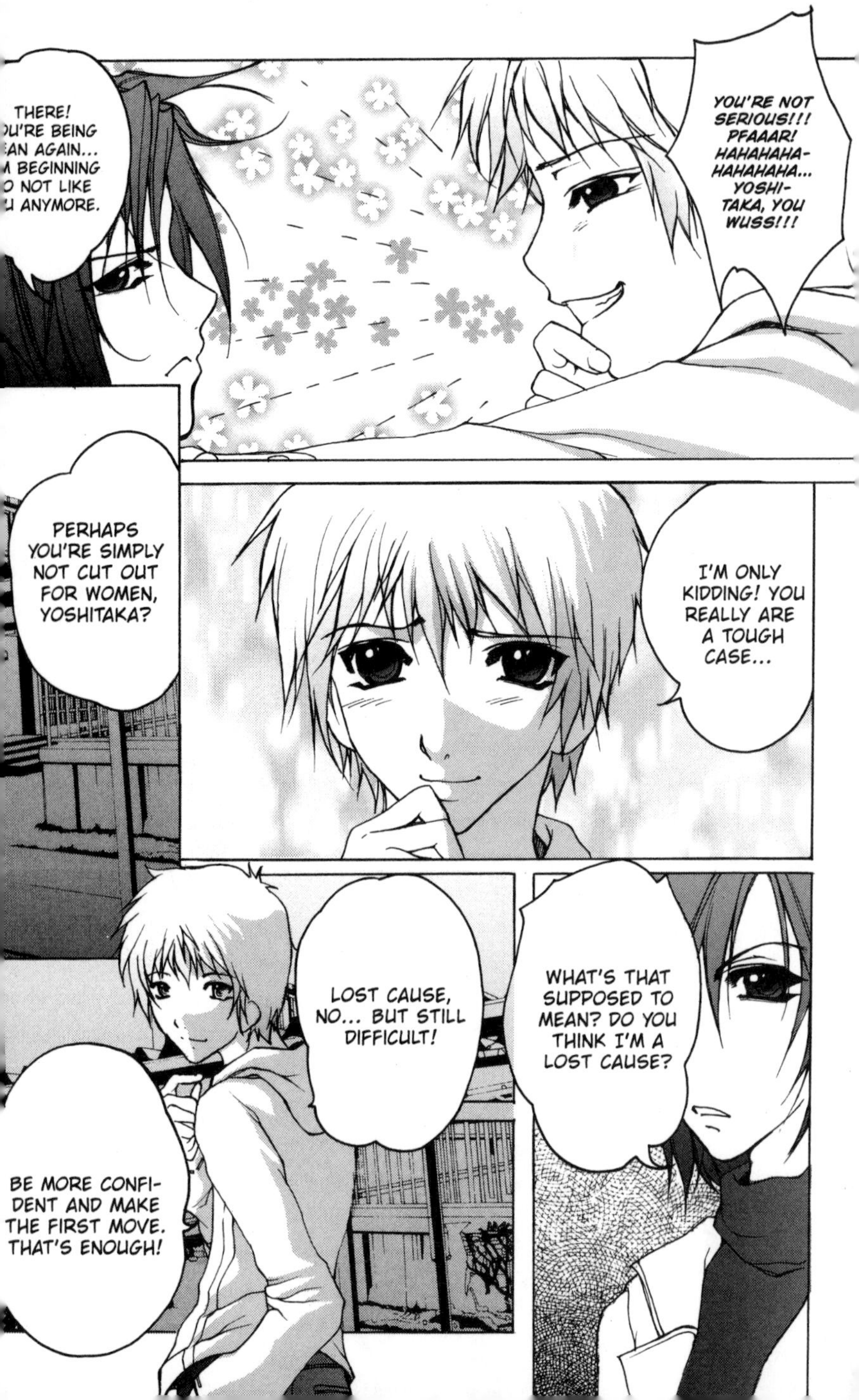
YOU'RE NOT SERIOUS!!! PFAAAR! HAHAHAHA-HAHAHAHA... YOSHI-TAKA, YOU WUSS!!!
THERE! OU'RE BEING EAN AGAIN... M BEGINNING O NOT LIKE U ANYMORE.
I'M ONLY KIDDING! YOU REALLY ARE A TOUGH CASE...
PERHAPS YOU'RE SIMPLY NOT CUT OUT FOR WOMEN, YOSHITAKA?
WHAT'S THAT SUPPOSED TO MEAN? DO YOU THINK I'M A LOST CAUSE?
LOST CAUSE, NO... BUT STILL DIFFICULT!
BE MORE CONFI-DENT AND MAKE THE FIRST MOVE. THAT'S ENOUGH!

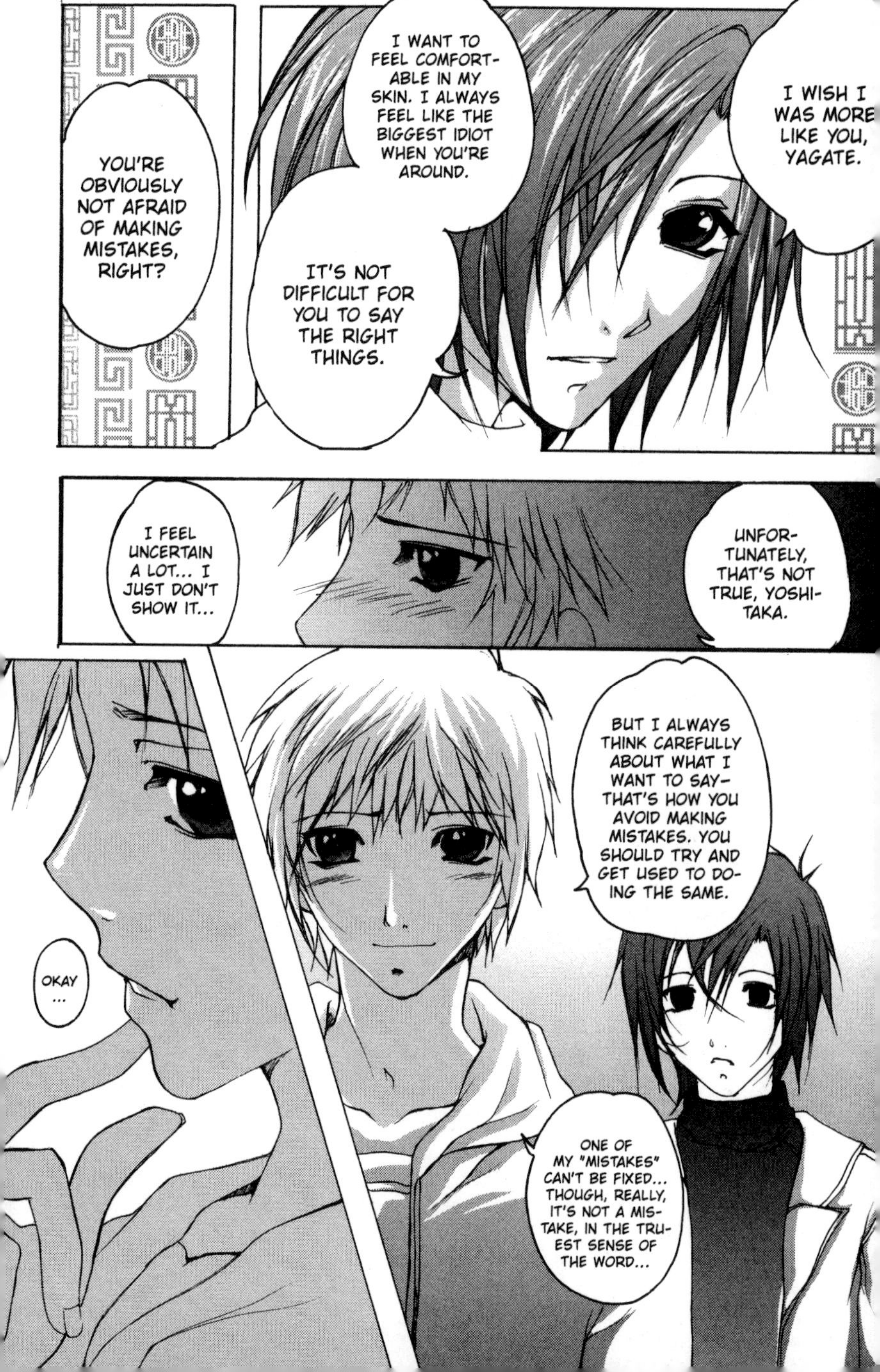

I WISH I WAS MORE LIKE YOU, YAGATE.
I WANT TO FEEL COMFORTABLE IN MY SKIN. I ALWAYS FEEL LIKE THE BIGGEST IDIOT WHEN YOU'RE AROUND.
IT'S NOT DIFFICULT FOR YOU TO SAY THE RIGHT THINGS.
YOU'RE OBVIOUSLY NOT AFRAID OF MAKING MISTAKES, RIGHT?
UNFORTUNATELY, THAT'S NOT TRUE, YOSHITAKA.
I FEEL UNCERTAIN A LOT... I JUST DON'T SHOW IT...
BUT I ALWAYS THINK CAREFULLY ABOUT WHAT I WANT TO SAY— THAT'S HOW YOU AVOID MAKING MISTAKES. YOU SHOULD TRY AND GET USED TO DOING THE SAME.
ONE OF MY "MISTAKES" CAN'T BE FIXED... THOUGH, REALLY, IT'S NOT A MISTAKE, IN THE TRUEST SENSE OF THE WORD...
OKAY ...

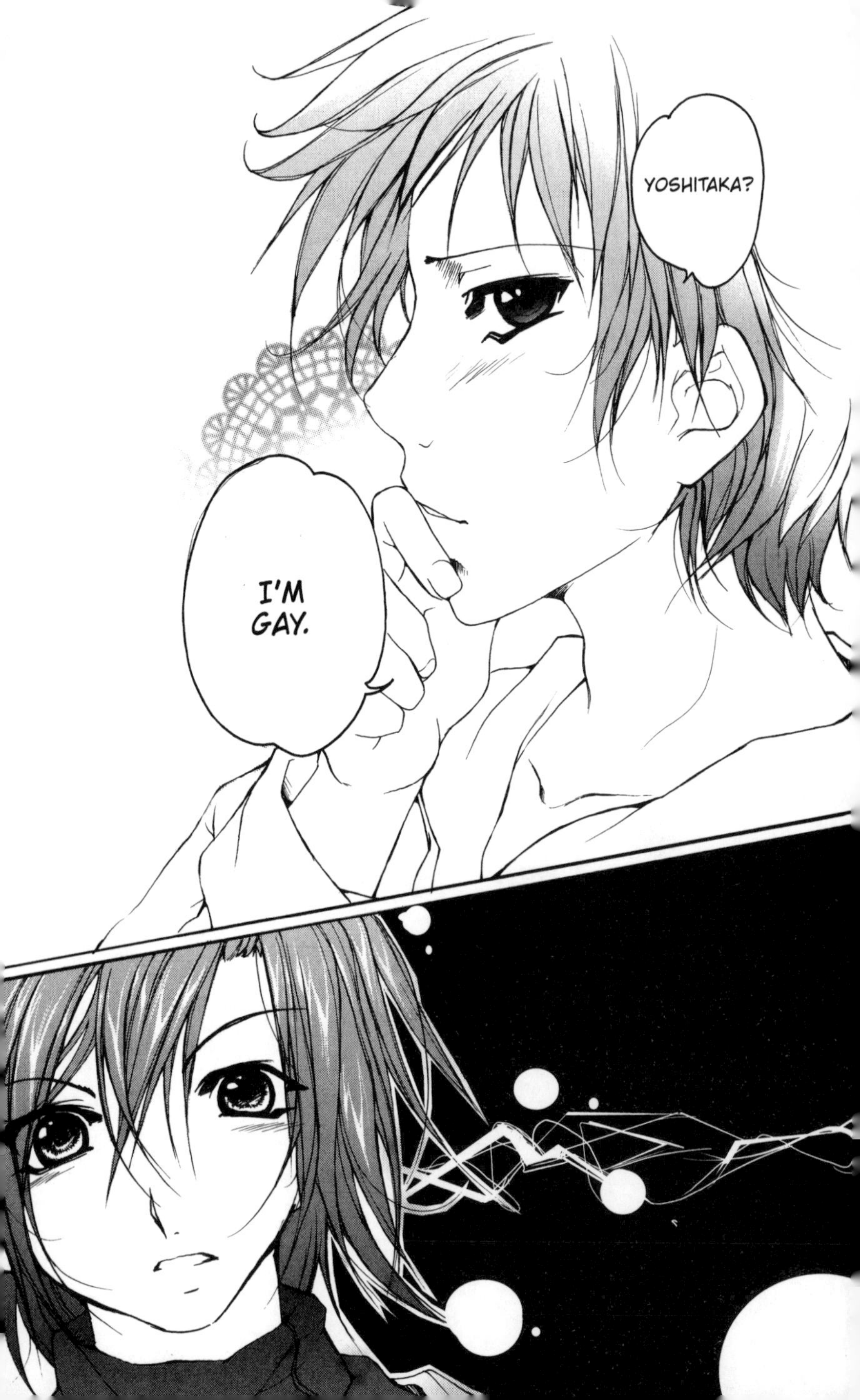
YOSHITAKA?
I'M GAY.

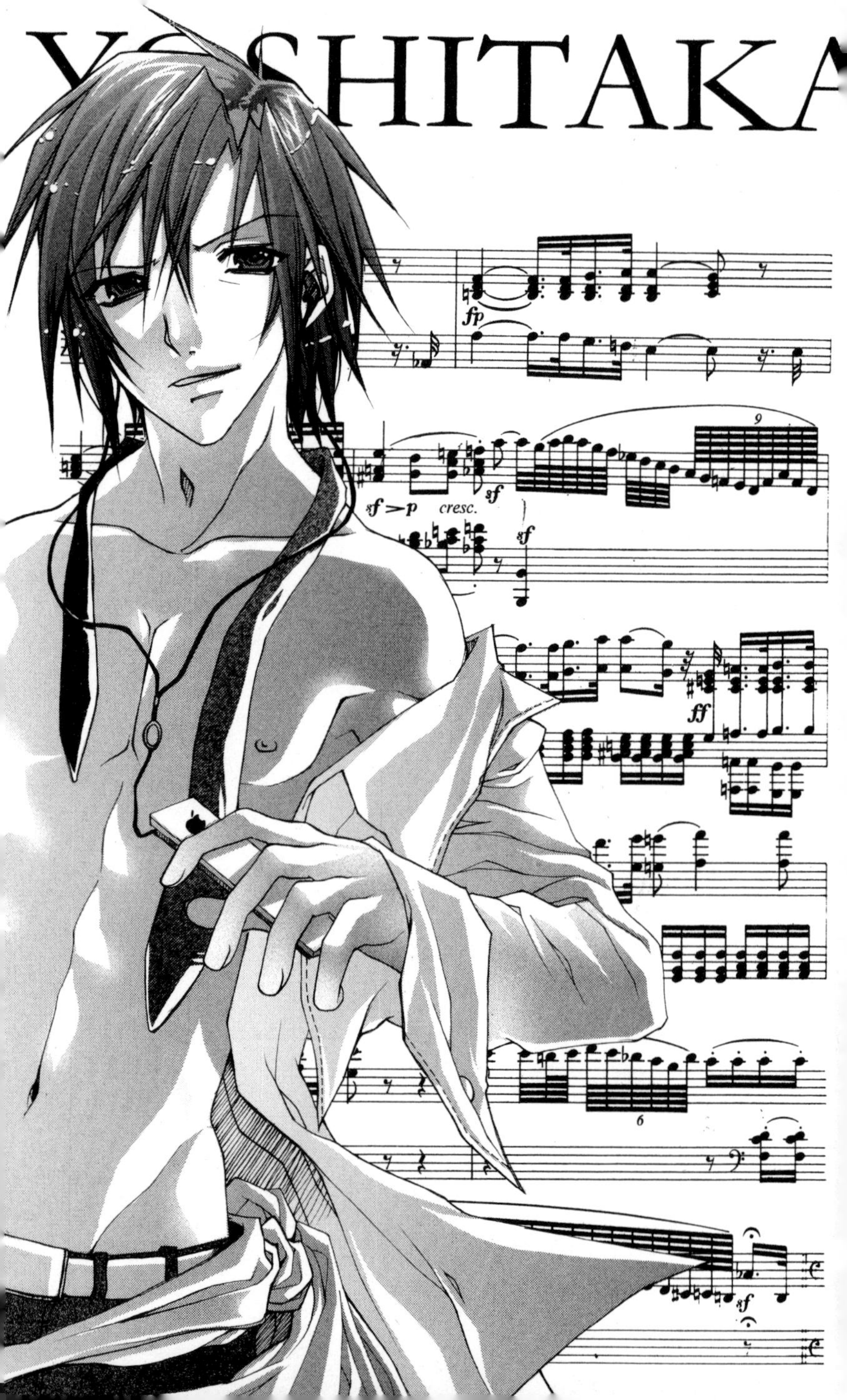
SHITAKA
fp
sf > p cresc.
sf
ff

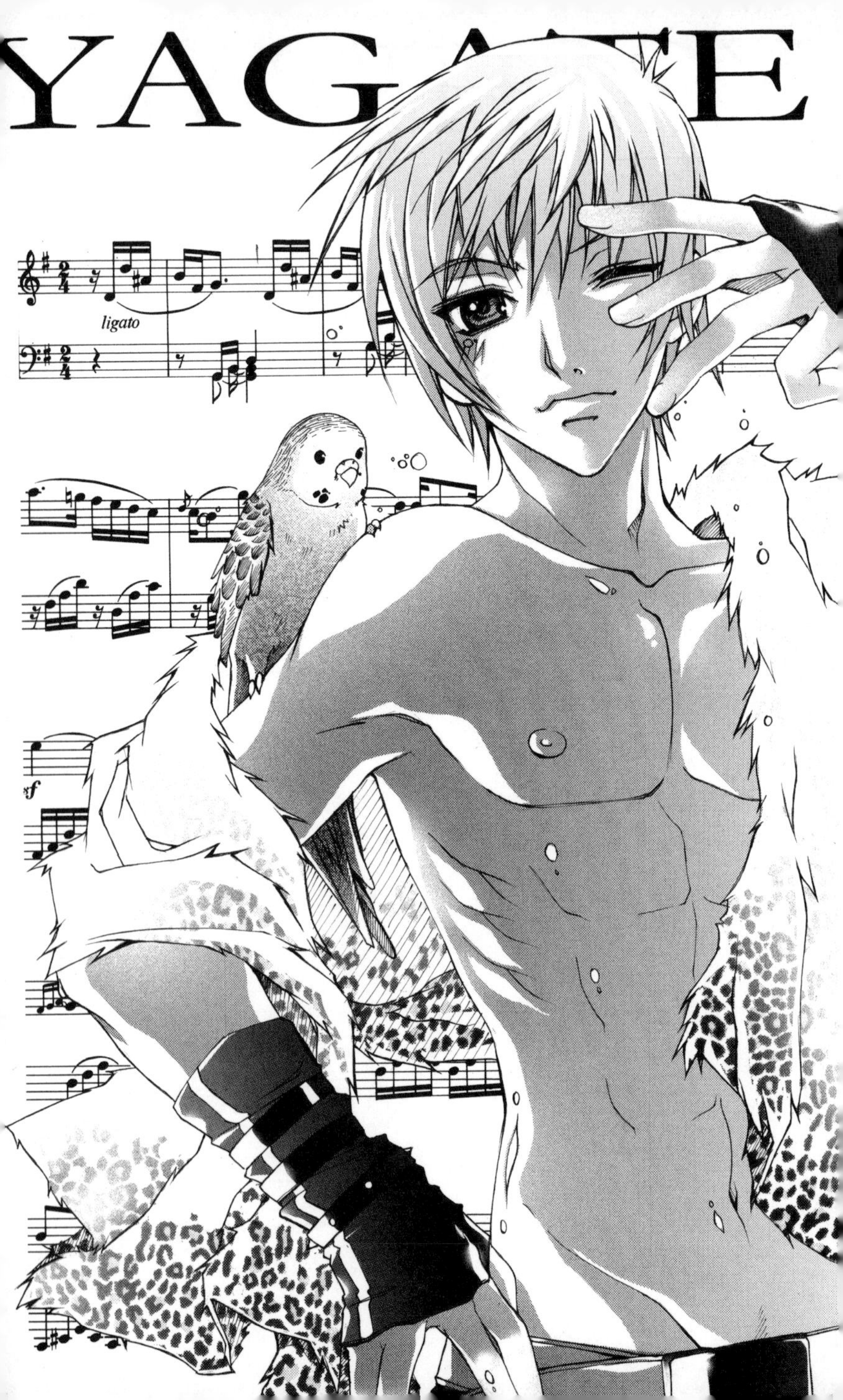
ligato
f

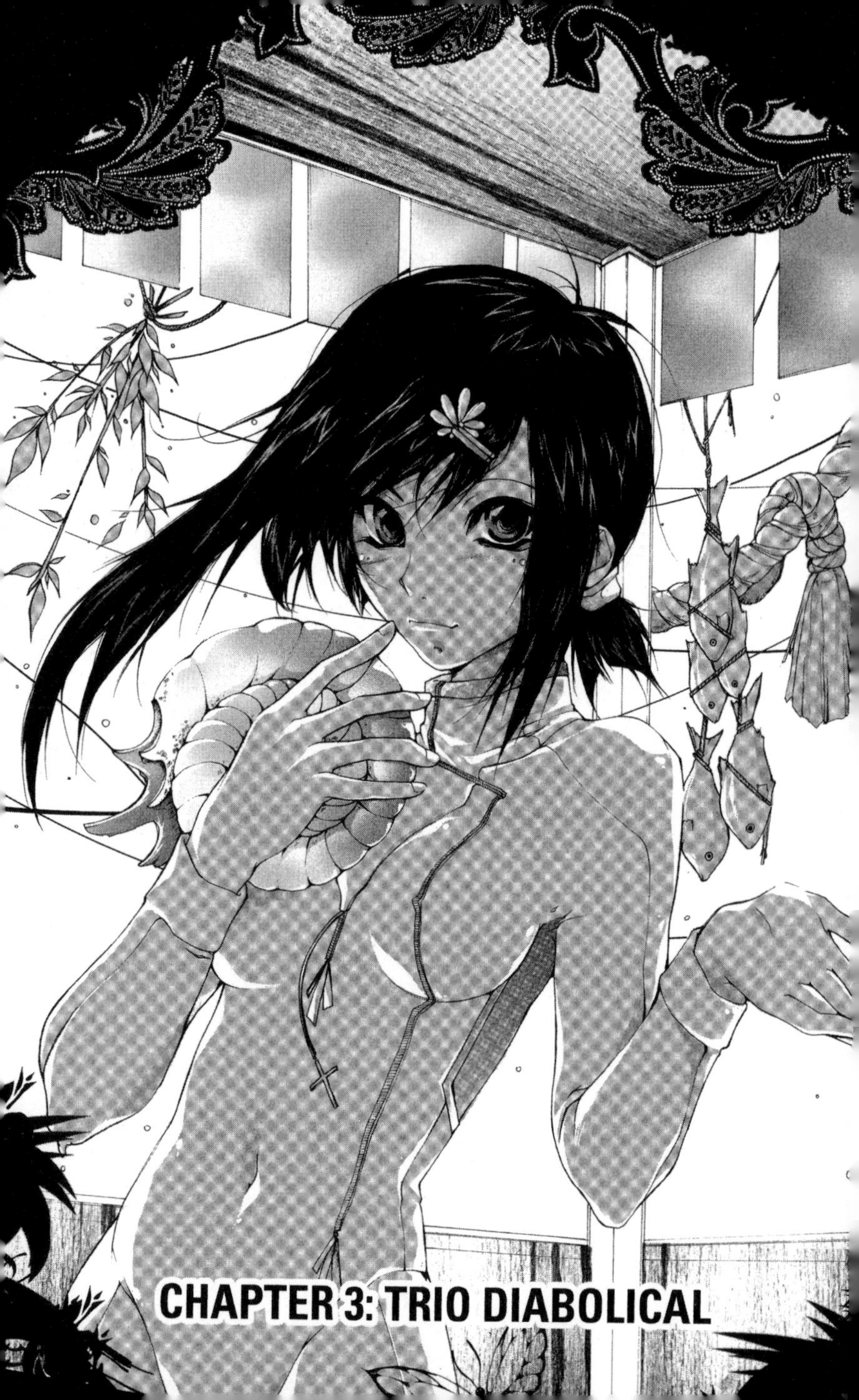
CHAPTER 3: TRIO DIABOLICAL

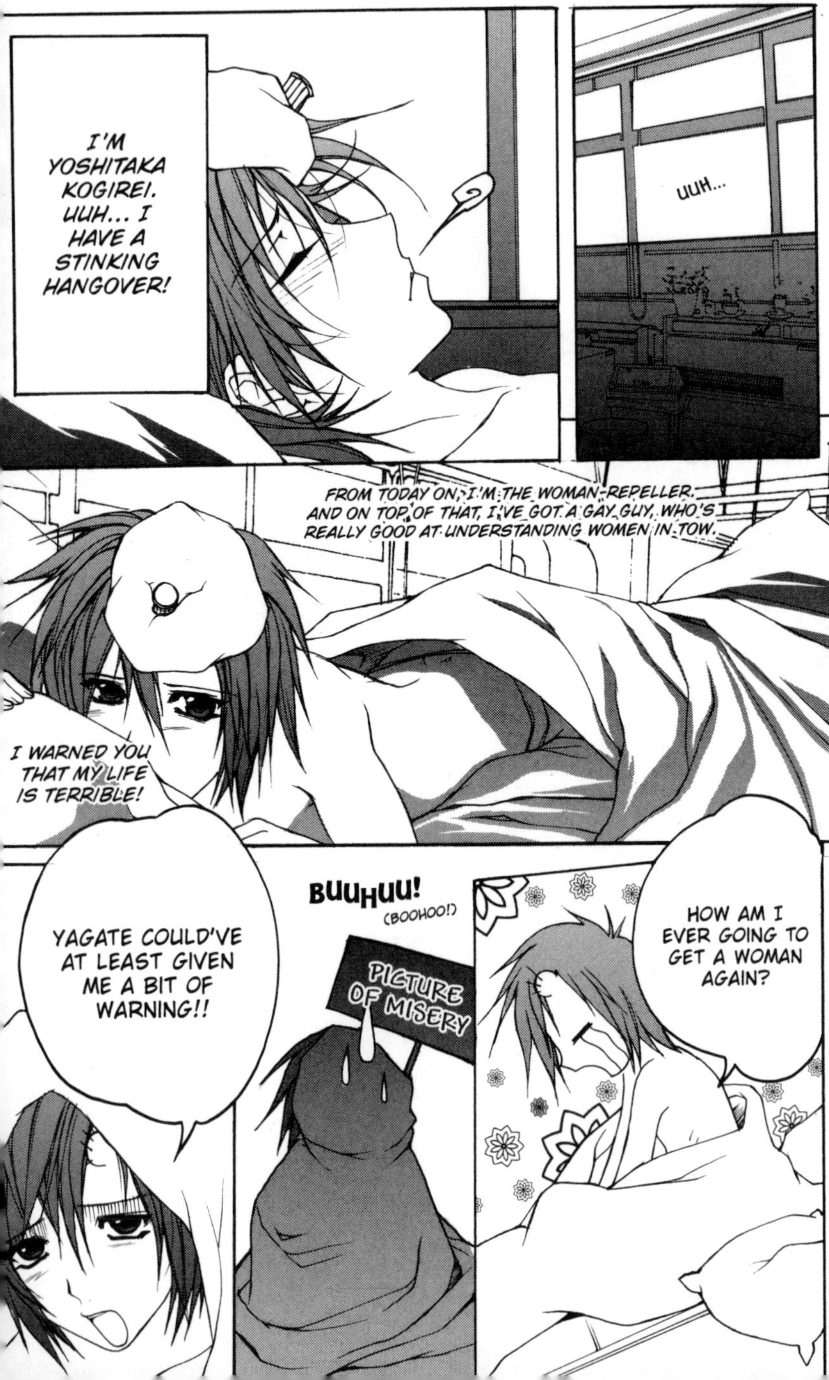
UUH...
I'M YOSHITAKA KOGIREI. UUH... I HAVE A STINKING HANGOVER!
FROM TODAY ON, I'M THE WOMAN-REPELLER. AND ON TOP OF THAT, I'VE GOT A GAY GUY, WHO'S REALLY GOOD AT UNDERSTANDING WOMEN IN TOW.
I WARNED YOU THAT MY LIFE IS TERRIBLE!
HOW AM I EVER GOING TO GET A WOMAN AGAIN?
BUUHUU!
(BOOHOO!)
PICTURE OF MISERY
YAGATE COULD'VE AT LEAST GIVEN ME A BIT OF WARNING!!

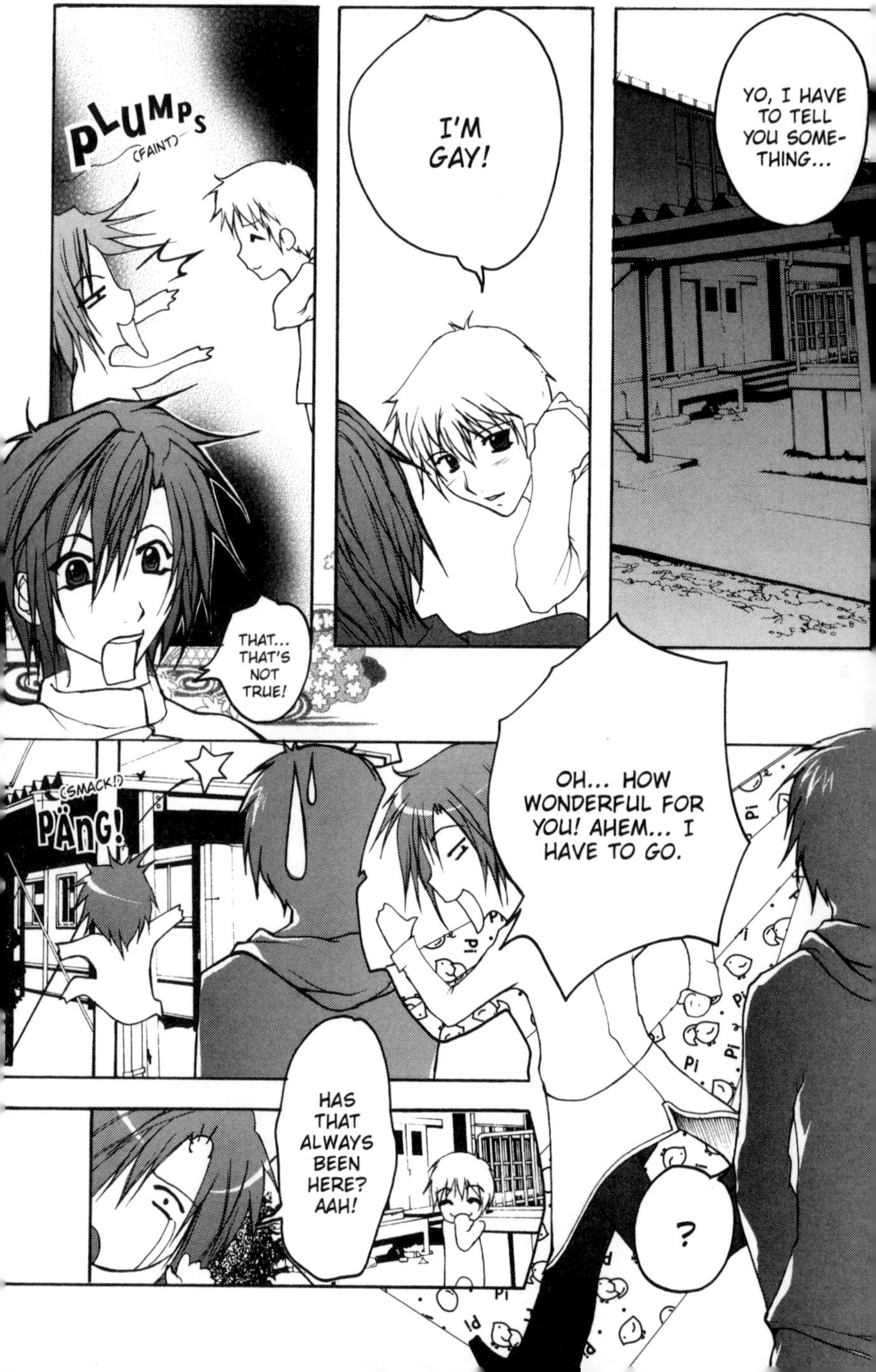
YO, I HAVE TO TELL YOU SOME-THING...
I'M GAY!
PLUMPS
(FAINT)
THAT... THAT'S NOT TRUE!
OH... HOW WONDERFUL FOR YOU! AHEM... I HAVE TO GO.
?
(SMACK!)
PÄNG!
HAS THAT ALWAYS BEEN HERE? AAH!

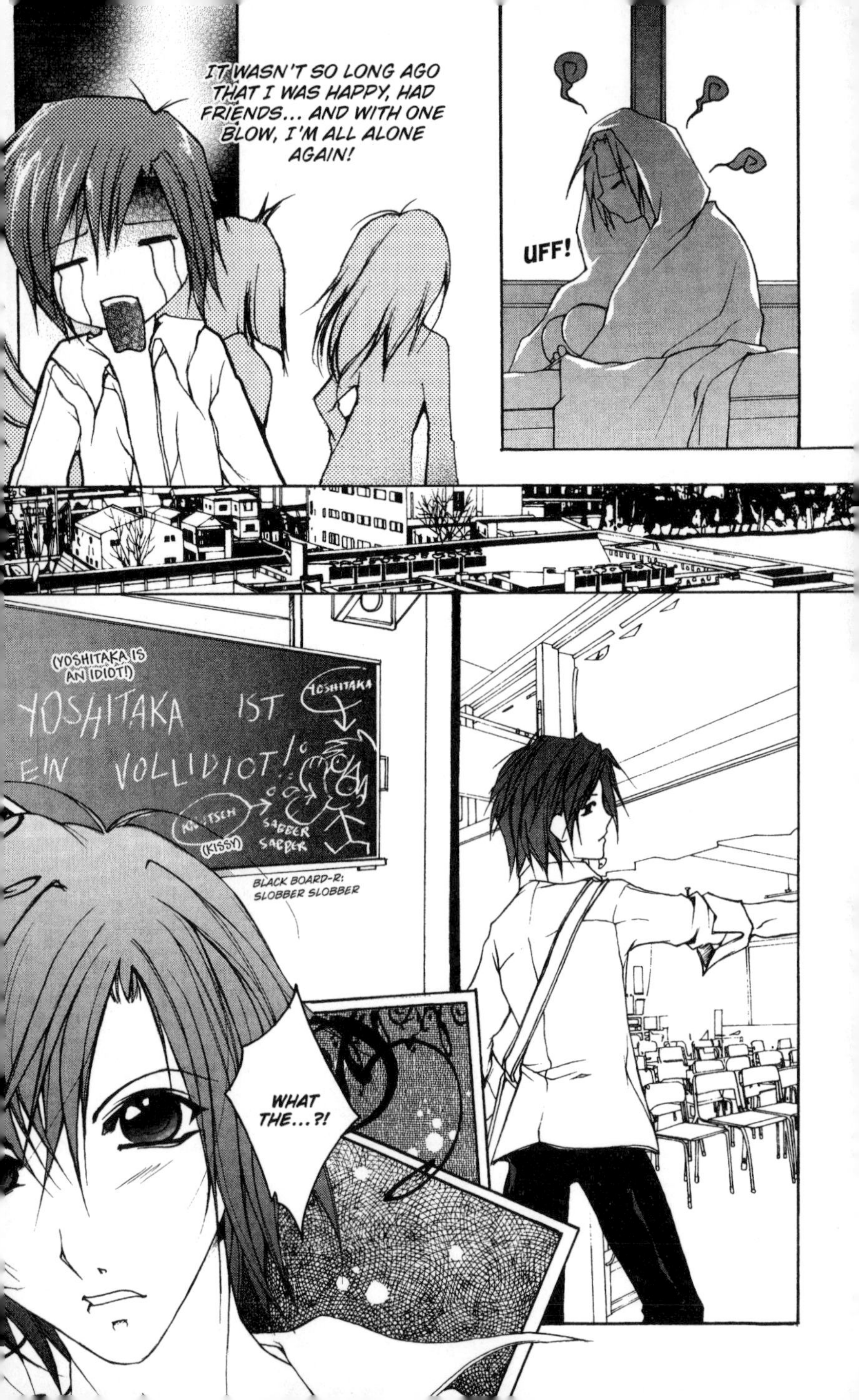
UFF!
IT WASN'T SO LONG AGO THAT I WAS HAPPY, HAD FRIENDS... AND WITH ONE BLOW, I'M ALL ALONE AGAIN!
(YOSHITAKA IS AN IDIOT!)
YOSHITAKA IST EIN VOLLIDIOT!
YOSHITAKA
(KISSY)
SABBER SABBER
BLACK BOARD-R: SLOBBER SLOBBER
WHAT THE...?!

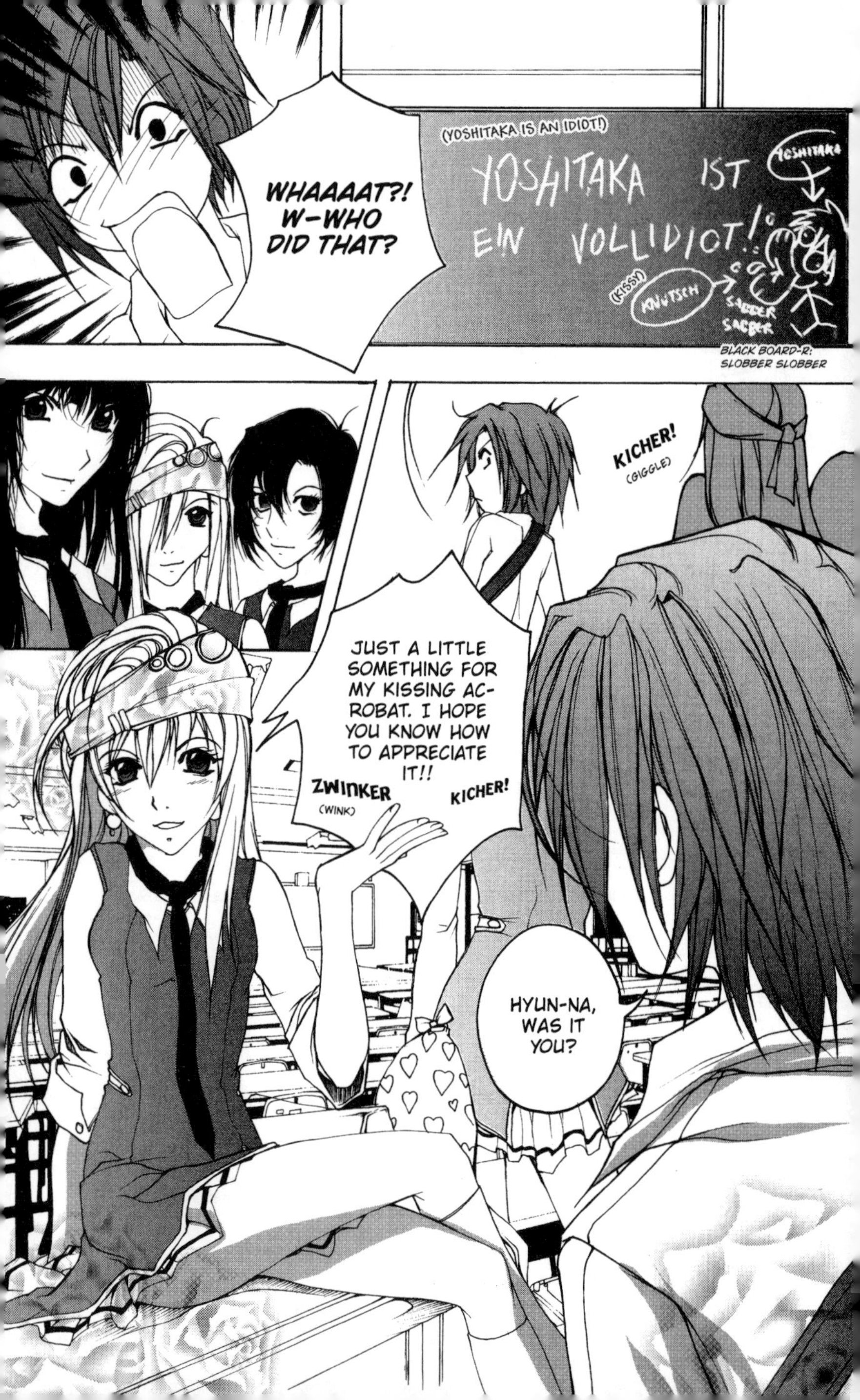
(YOSHITAKA IS AN IDIOT!)
YOSHITAKA IST EIN VOLLIDIOT!
YOSHITAKA
(KISSY)
KNUTSCH
SABBER SABBER
WHAAAAT?! W-WHO DID THAT?
BLACK BOARD-R: SLOBBER SLOBBER
KICHER!
(GIGGLE)
JUST A LITTLE SOMETHING FOR MY KISSING AC-ROBAT. I HOPE YOU KNOW HOW TO APPRECIATE IT!!
KICHER!
ZWINKER
(WINK)
HYUN-NA, WAS IT YOU?

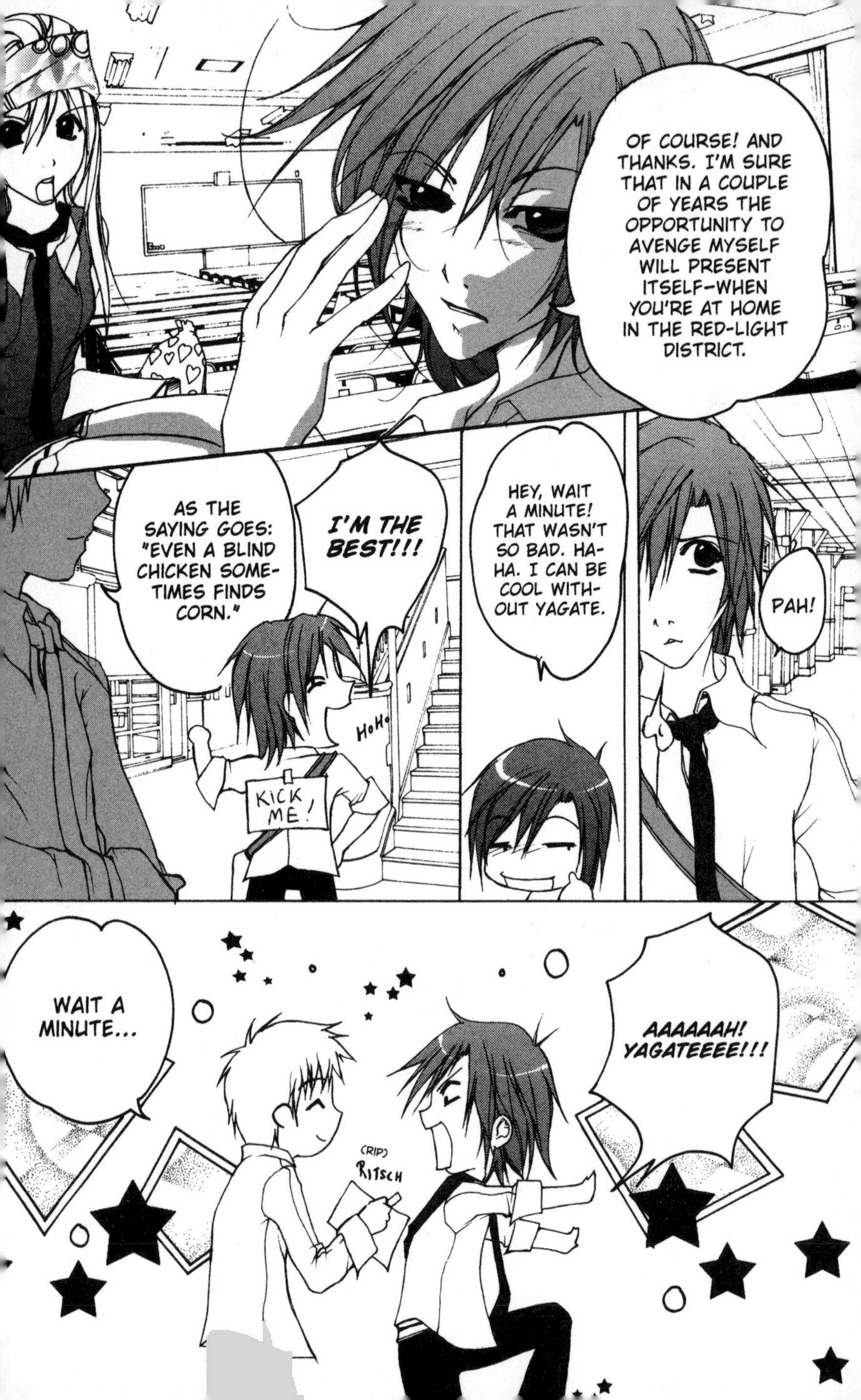
OF COURSE! AND THANKS. I'M SURE THAT IN A COUPLE OF YEARS THE OPPORTUNITY TO AVENGE MYSELF WILL PRESENT ITSELF—WHEN YOU'RE AT HOME IN THE RED-LIGHT DISTRICT.
PAH!
HEY, WAIT A MINUTE! THAT WASN'T SO BAD. HA-HA. I CAN BE COOL WITH-OUT YAGATE.
I'M THE BEST!!!
AS THE SAYING GOES: "EVEN A BLIND CHICKEN SOME-TIMES FINDS CORN."
HoHo
KICK ME!
AAAAAAH! YAGATEEEE!!!
WAIT A MINUTE...
(RIP) RITSCH

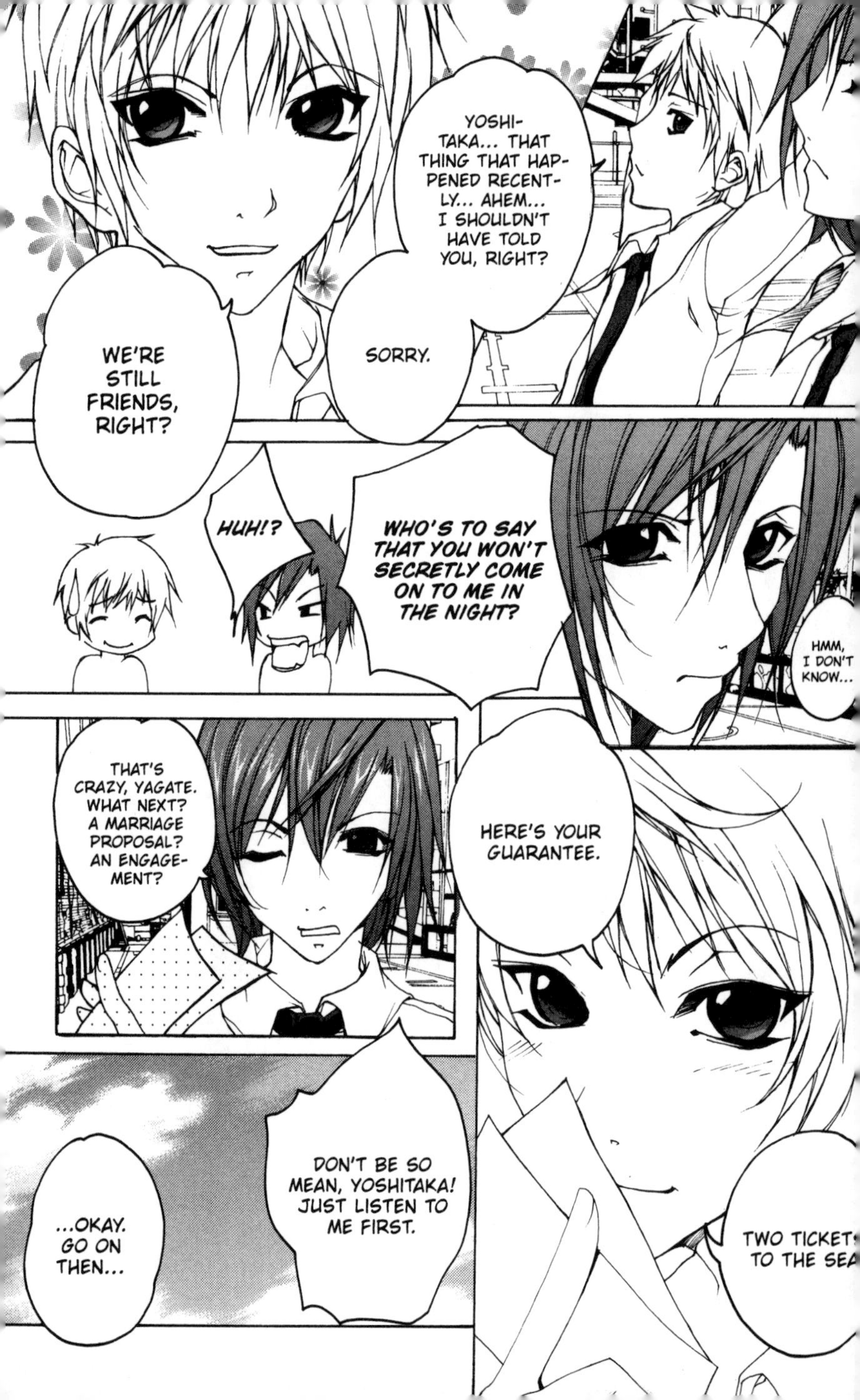

YOSHI-TAKA... THAT THING THAT HAP-PENED RECENT-LY... AHEM... I SHOULDN'T HAVE TOLD YOU, RIGHT?
SORRY.
WE'RE STILL FRIENDS, RIGHT?
HMM, I DON'T KNOW...
WHO'S TO SAY THAT YOU WON'T SECRETLY COME ON TO ME IN THE NIGHT?
HUH!?
HERE'S YOUR GUARANTEE.
TWO TICKET TO THE SEA
THAT'S CRAZY, YAGATE. WHAT NEXT? A MARRIAGE PROPOSAL? AN ENGAGE-MENT?
DON'T BE SO MEAN, YOSHITAKA! JUST LISTEN TO ME FIRST.
...OKAY. GO ON THEN...

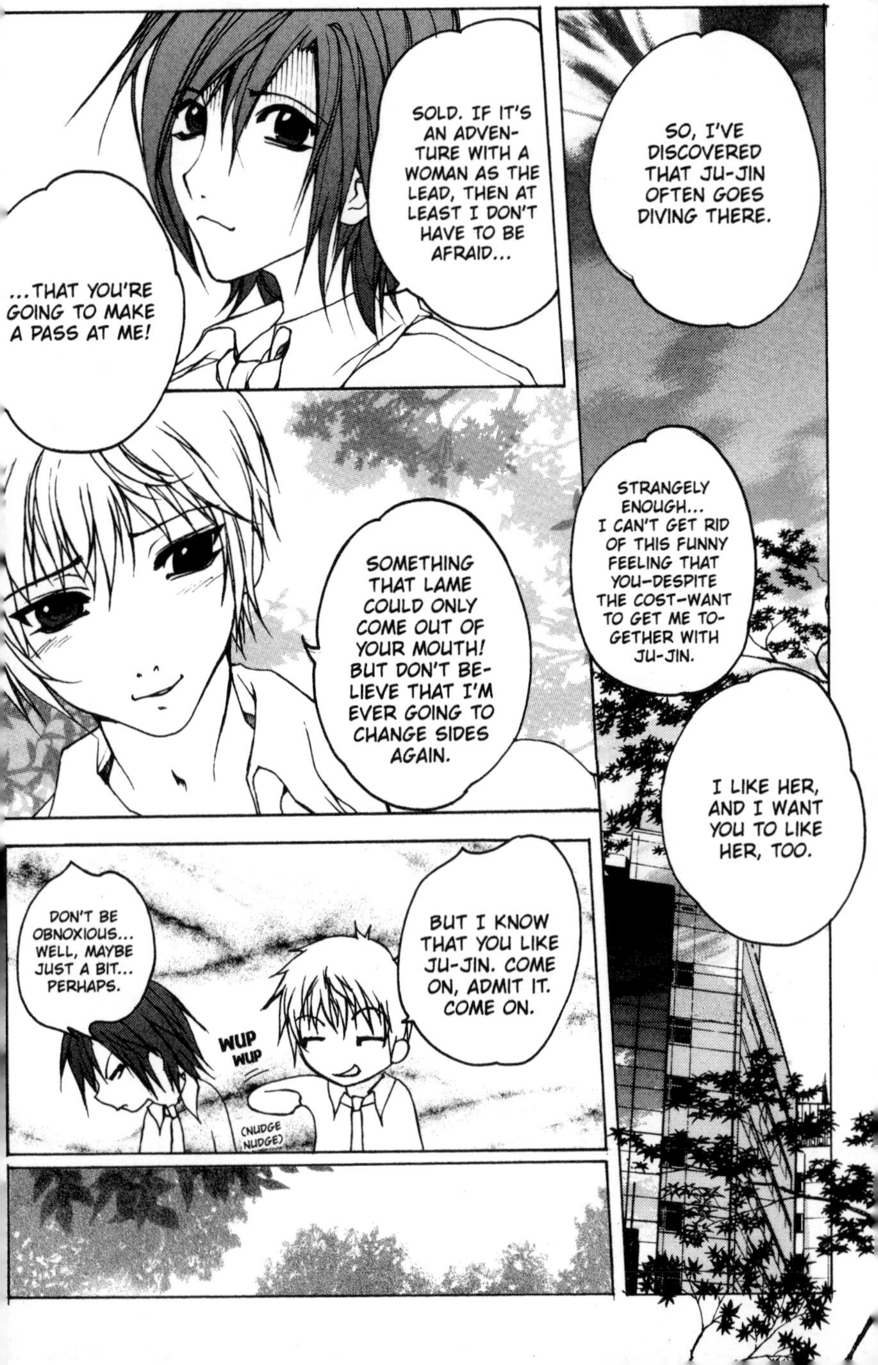
SO, I'VE DISCOVERED THAT JU-JIN OFTEN GOES DIVING THERE.
STRANGELY ENOUGH... I CAN'T GET RID OF THIS FUNNY FEELING THAT YOU–DESPITE THE COST–WANT TO GET ME TO-GETHER WITH JU-JIN.
I LIKE HER, AND I WANT YOU TO LIKE HER, TOO.
SOLD. IF IT'S AN ADVEN-TURE WITH A WOMAN AS THE LEAD, THEN AT LEAST I DON'T HAVE TO BE AFRAID...
...THAT YOU'RE GOING TO MAKE A PASS AT ME!
SOMETHING THAT LAME COULD ONLY COME OUT OF YOUR MOUTH! BUT DON'T BE-LIEVE THAT I'M EVER GOING TO CHANGE SIDES AGAIN.
BUT I KNOW THAT YOU LIKE JU-JIN. COME ON, ADMIT IT. COME ON.
WUP WUP
(NUDGE NUDGE)
DON'T BE OBNOXIOUS... WELL, MAYBE JUST A BIT... PERHAPS.

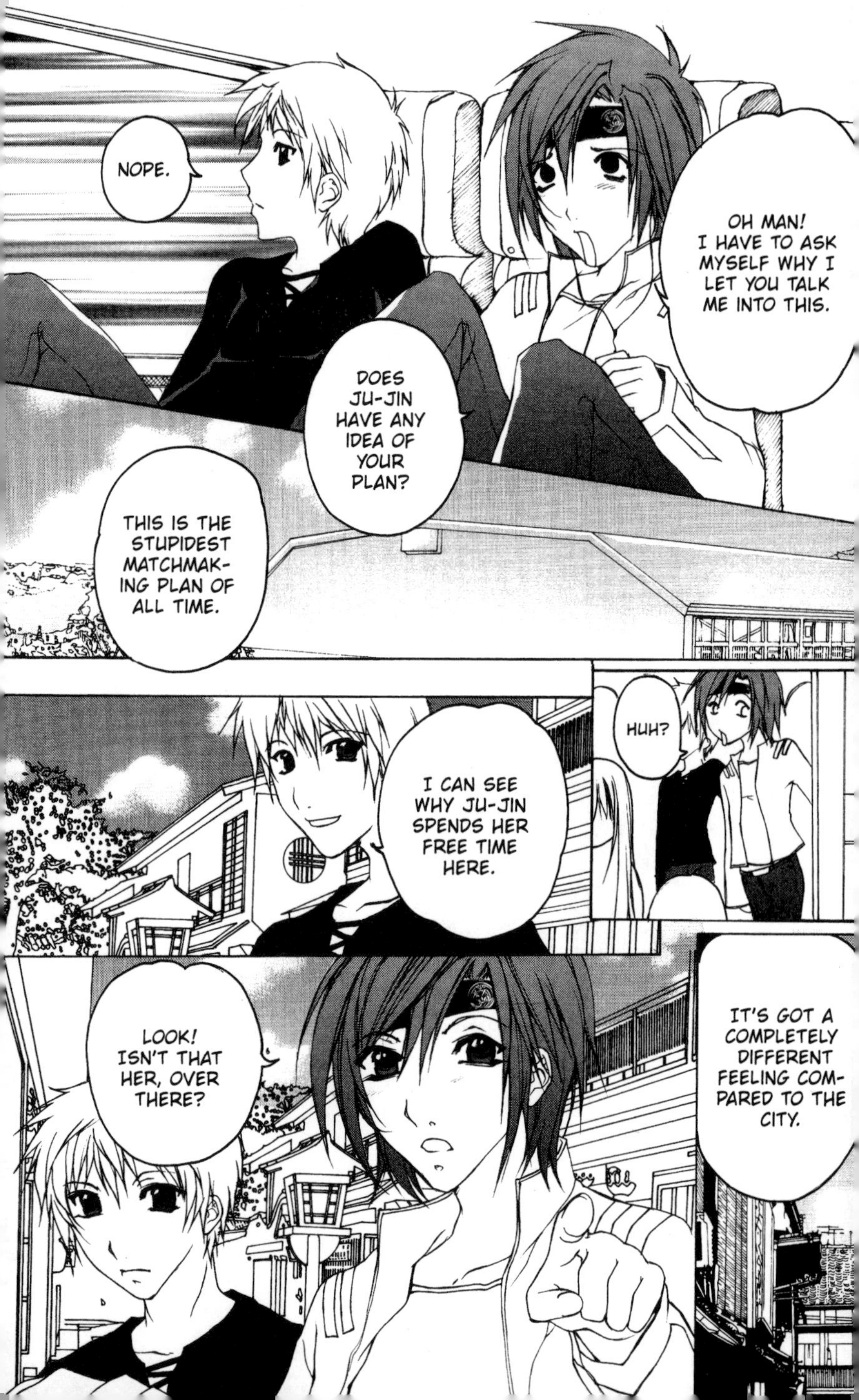

OH MAN! I HAVE TO ASK MYSELF WHY I LET YOU TALK ME INTO THIS.
DOES JU-JIN HAVE ANY IDEA OF YOUR PLAN?
NOPE.
THIS IS THE STUPIDEST MATCHMAK-ING PLAN OF ALL TIME.
HUH?
I CAN SEE WHY JU-JIN SPENDS HER FREE TIME HERE.
IT'S GOT A COMPLETELY DIFFERENT FEELING COM-PARED TO THE CITY.
LOOK! ISN'T THAT HER, OVER THERE?

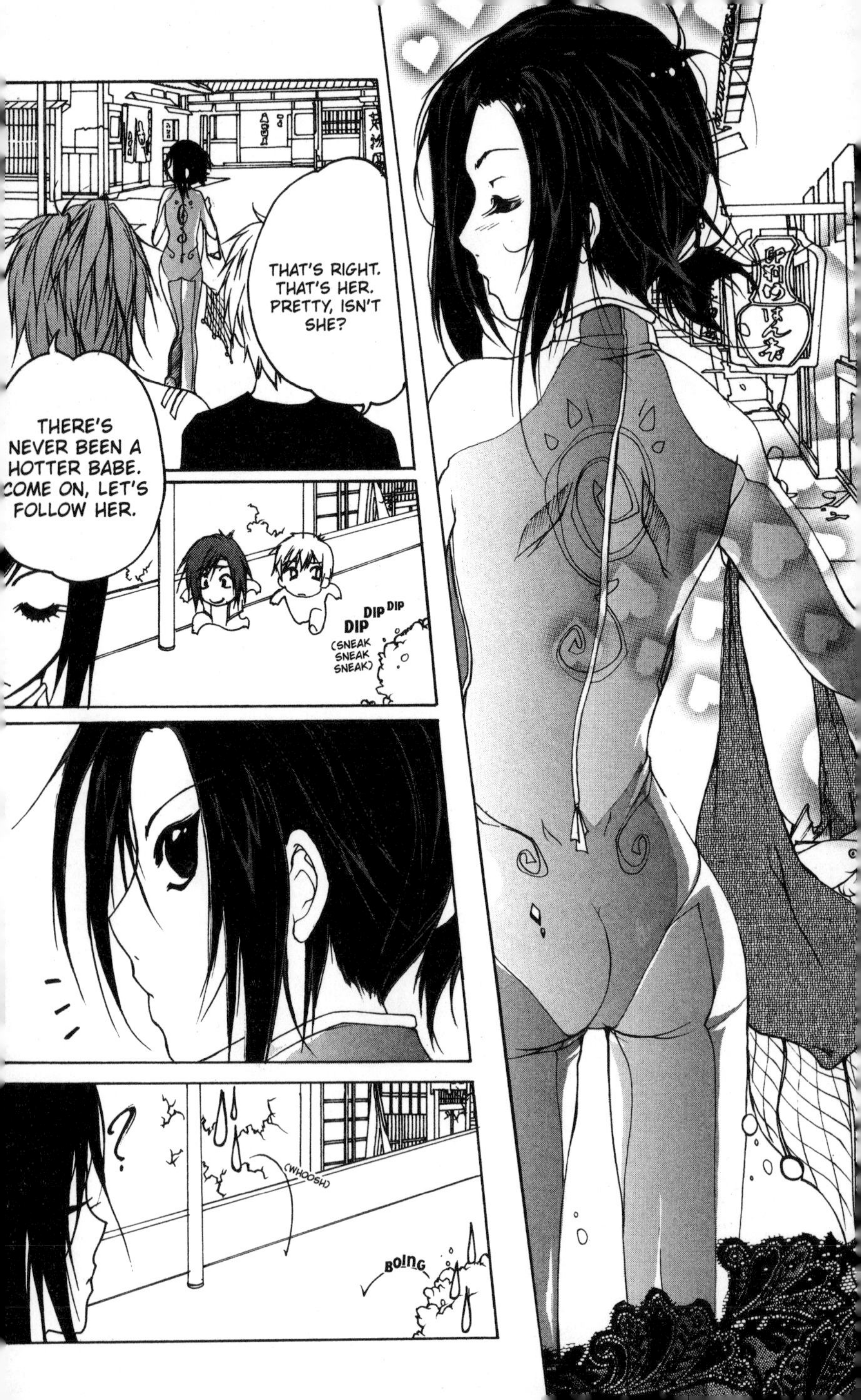
THAT'S RIGHT. THAT'S HER. PRETTY, ISN'T SHE?
THERE'S NEVER BEEN A HOTTER BABE. COME ON, LET'S FOLLOW HER.
DIP DIP DIP
(SNEAK SNEAK SNEAK)
?
(WHOOSH)
BOING

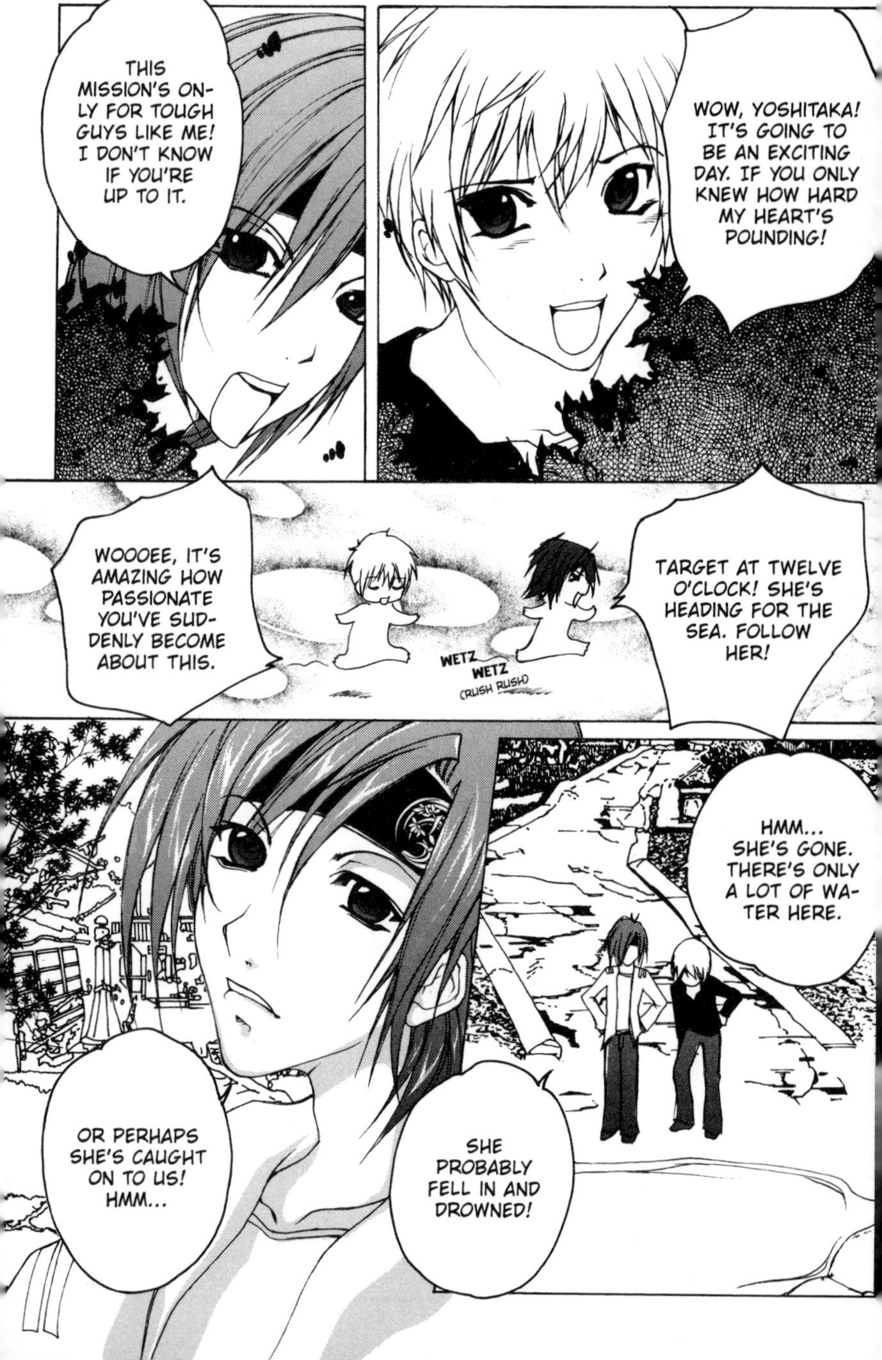
WOW, YOSHITAKA! IT'S GOING TO BE AN EXCITING DAY. IF YOU ONLY KNEW HOW HARD MY HEART'S POUNDING!
THIS MISSION'S ON-LY FOR TOUGH GUYS LIKE ME! I DON'T KNOW IF YOU'RE UP TO IT.
TARGET AT TWELVE O'CLOCK! SHE'S HEADING FOR THE SEA. FOLLOW HER!
WOOOEE, IT'S AMAZING HOW PASSIONATE YOU'VE SUD-DENLY BECOME ABOUT THIS.
WETZ WETZ
(RUSH RUSH)
HMM... SHE'S GONE. THERE'S ONLY A LOT OF WA-TER HERE.
SHE PROBABLY FELL IN AND DROWNED!
OR PERHAPS SHE'S CAUGHT ON TO US! HMM...

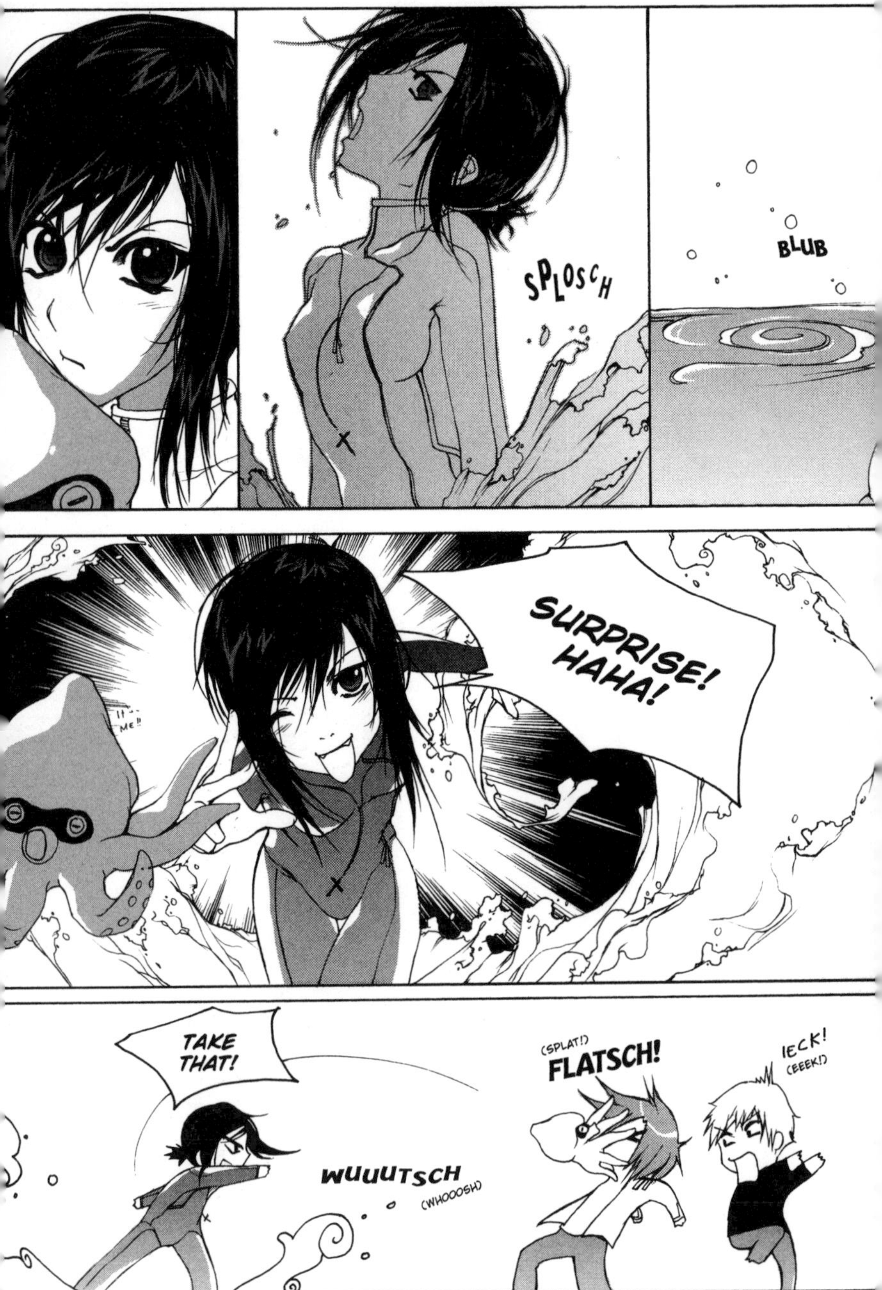
BLUB
SPLOSCH
SURPRISE! HAHA!
It... ME!!
IECK!
(EEEK!)
FLATSCH!
(SPLAT!)
WUUUTSCH
(WHOOOSH)
TAKE THAT!

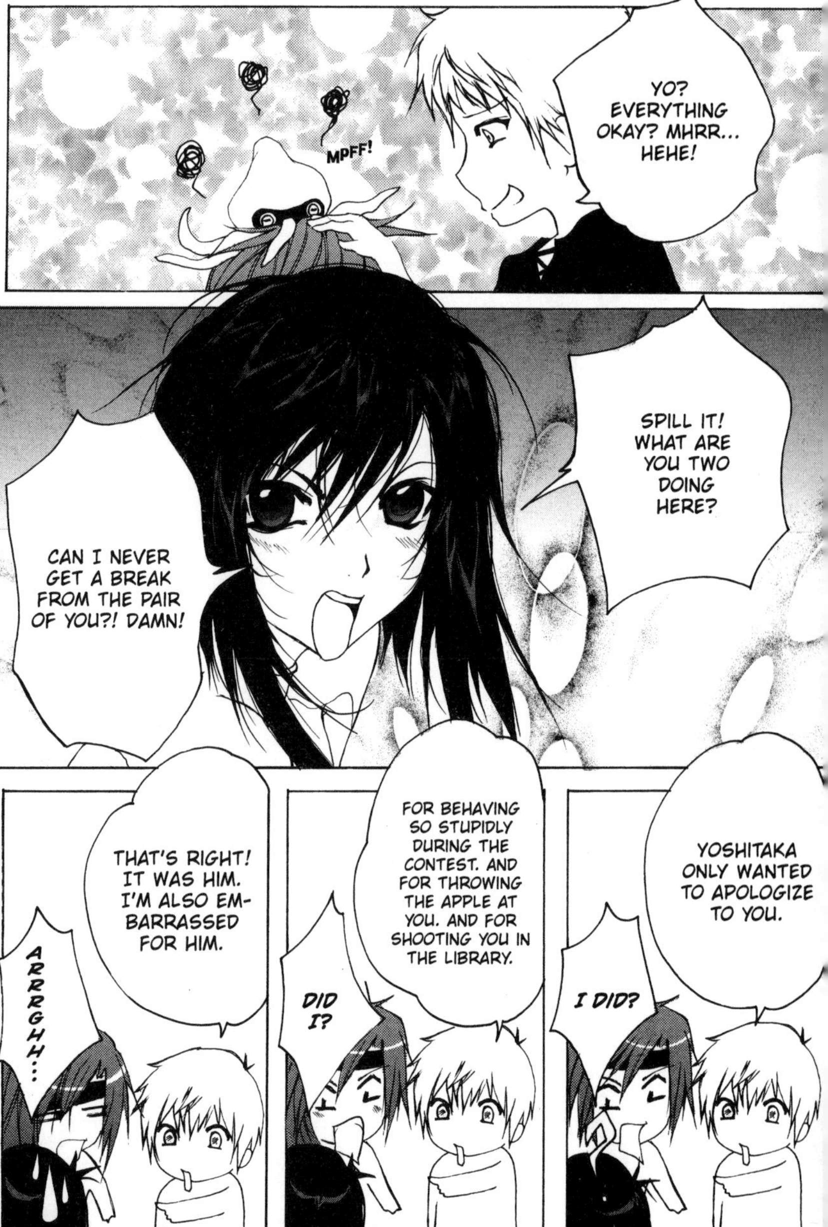
YO? EVERYTHING OKAY? MHRR... HEHE!
MPFF!
SPILL IT! WHAT ARE YOU TWO DOING HERE?
CAN I NEVER GET A BREAK FROM THE PAIR OF YOU?! DAMN!
YOSHITAKA ONLY WANTED TO APOLOGIZE TO YOU.
I DID?
FOR BEHAVING SO STUPIDLY DURING THE CONTEST. AND FOR THROWING THE APPLE AT YOU. AND FOR SHOOTING YOU IN THE LIBRARY.
DID I?
THAT'S RIGHT! IT WAS HIM. I'M ALSO EM-BARRASSED FOR HIM.
ARRRGHH...

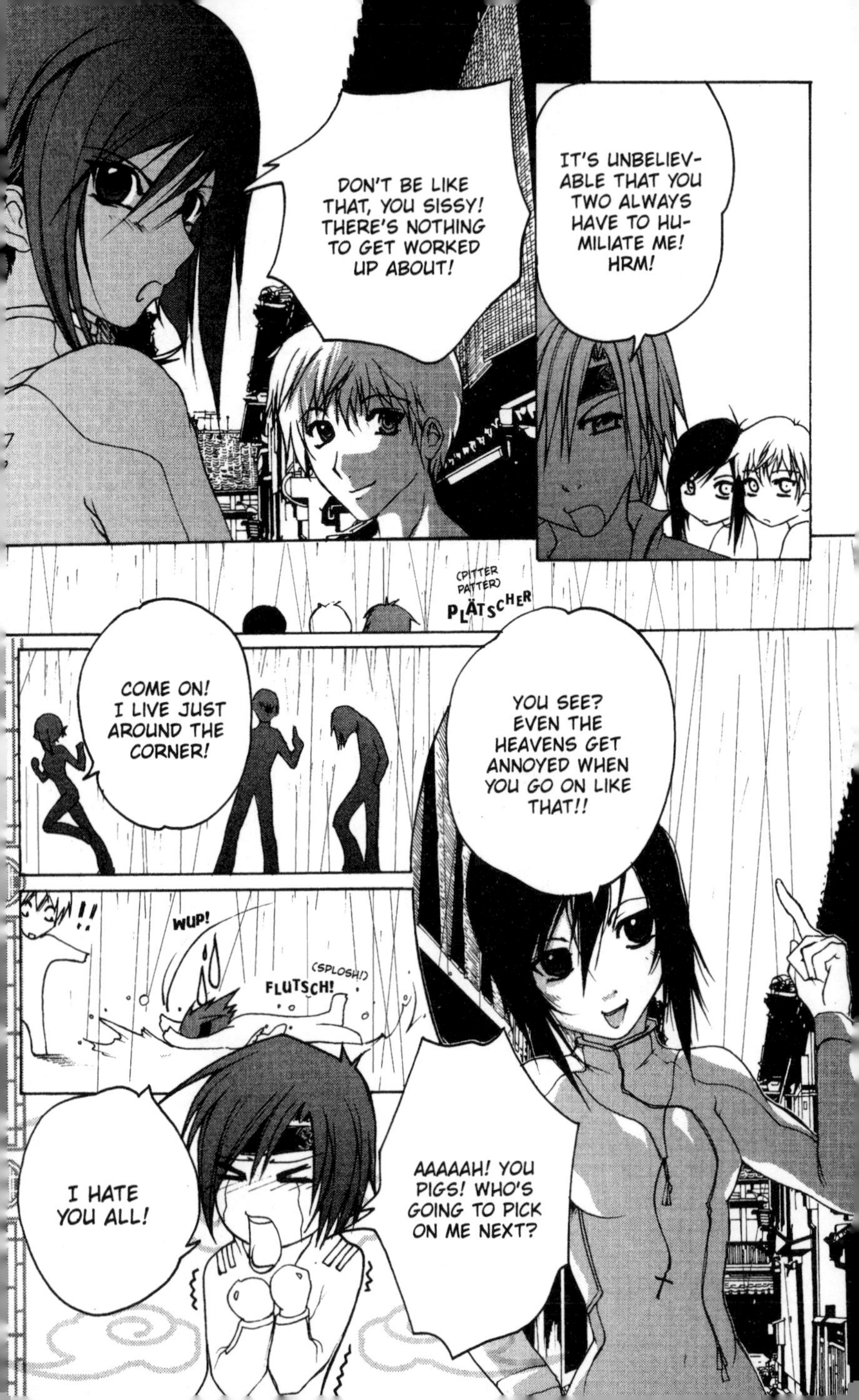

IT'S UNBELIEVABLE THAT YOU TWO ALWAYS HAVE TO HUMILIATE ME! HRM!
DON'T BE LIKE THAT, YOU SISSY! THERE'S NOTHING TO GET WORKED UP ABOUT!
PLÄTSCHER
(PITTER PATTER)
YOU SEE? EVEN THE HEAVENS GET ANNOYED WHEN YOU GO ON LIKE THAT!!
COME ON! I LIVE JUST AROUND THE CORNER!
!!
WUP!
FLUTSCH!
(SPLOSH!)
AAAAAH! YOU PIGS! WHO'S GOING TO PICK ON ME NEXT?
I HATE YOU ALL!

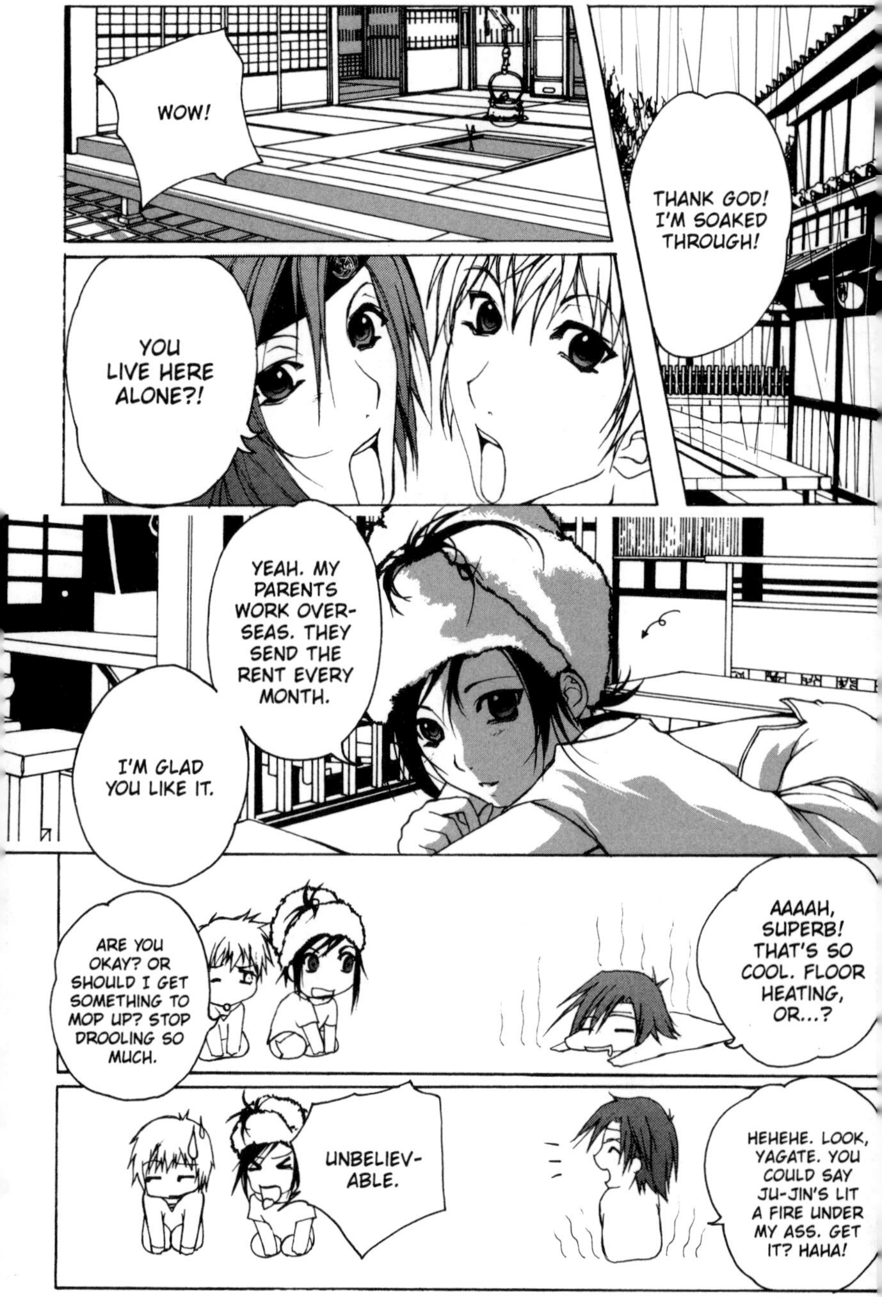
THANK GOD! I'M SOAKED THROUGH!
WOW!
YOU LIVE HERE ALONE?!
YEAH. MY PARENTS WORK OVER-SEAS. THEY SEND THE RENT EVERY MONTH.
I'M GLAD YOU LIKE IT.
AAAAH, SUPERB! THAT'S SO COOL. FLOOR HEATING, OR...?
ARE YOU OKAY? OR SHOULD I GET SOMETHING TO MOP UP? STOP DROOLING SO MUCH.
HEHEHE. LOOK, YAGATE. YOU COULD SAY JU-JIN'S LIT A FIRE UNDER MY ASS. GET IT? HAHA!
UNBELIEV-ABLE.

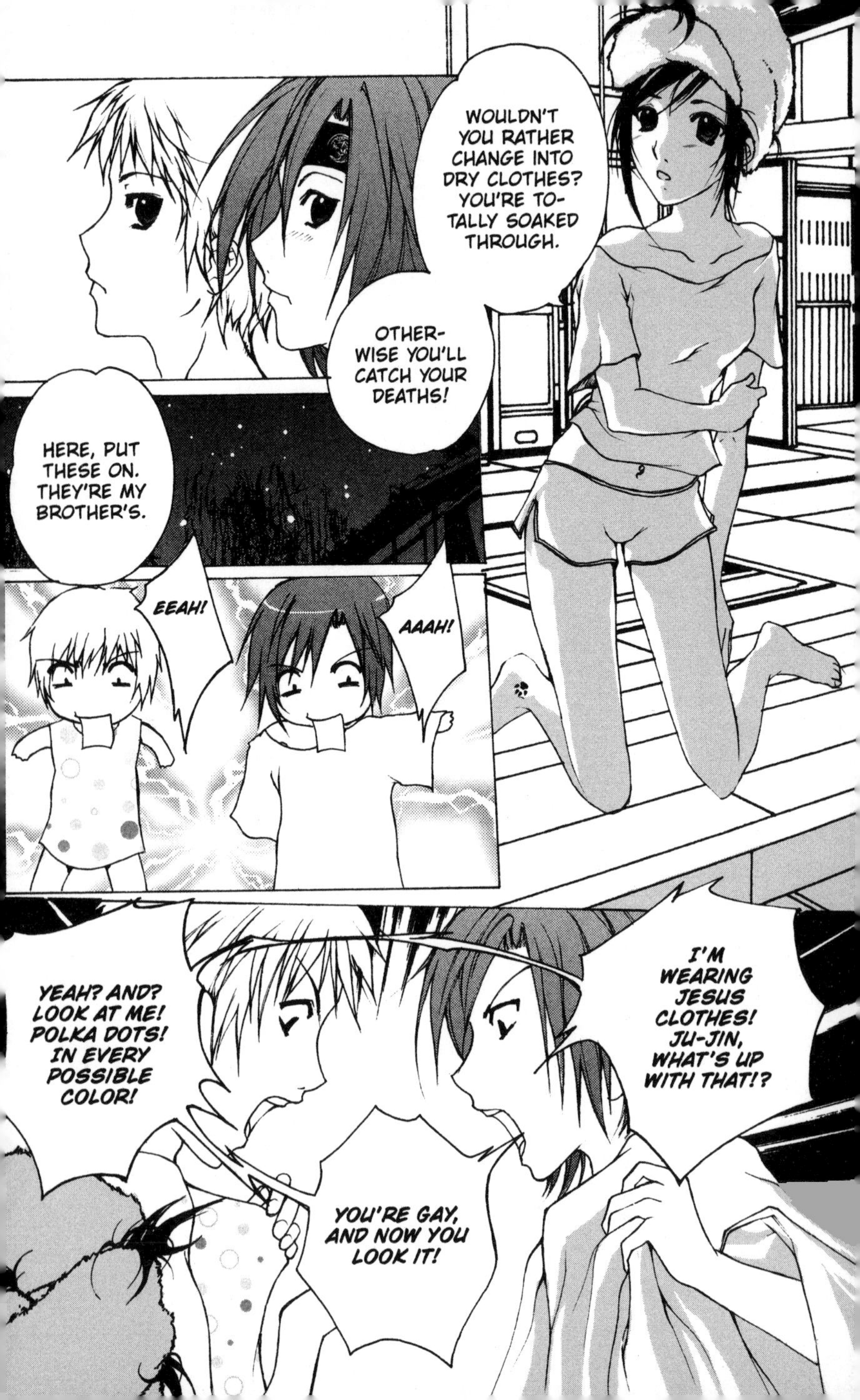
WOULDN'T YOU RATHER CHANGE INTO DRY CLOTHES? YOU'RE TO-TALLY SOAKED THROUGH.
OTHER-WISE YOU'LL CATCH YOUR DEATHS!
HERE, PUT THESE ON. THEY'RE MY BROTHER'S.
AAAH!
EEAH!
I'M WEARING JESUS CLOTHES! JU-JIN, WHAT'S UP WITH THAT!?
YEAH? AND? LOOK AT ME! POLKA DOTS! IN EVERY POSSIBLE COLOR!
YOU'RE GAY, AND NOW YOU LOOK IT!

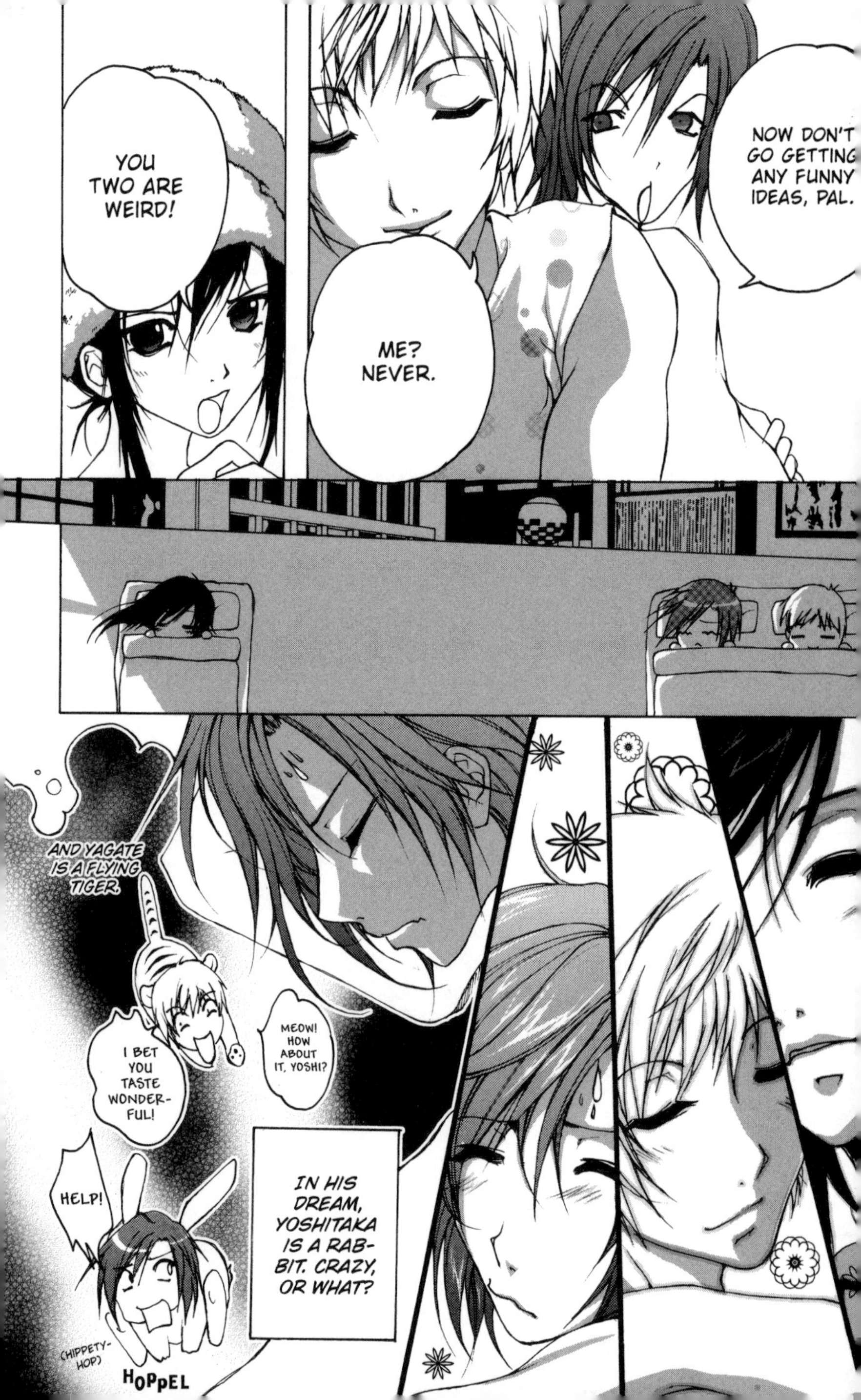
NOW DON'T GO GETTING ANY FUNNY IDEAS, PAL.
ME? NEVER.
YOU TWO ARE WEIRD!
IN HIS DREAM, YOSHITAKA IS A RAB-BIT. CRAZY, OR WHAT?
AND YAGATE IS A FLYING TIGER.
MEOW! HOW ABOUT IT, YOSHI?
I BET YOU TASTE WONDER-FUL!
HELP!
(HIPPETY-HOP)
HOPPEL

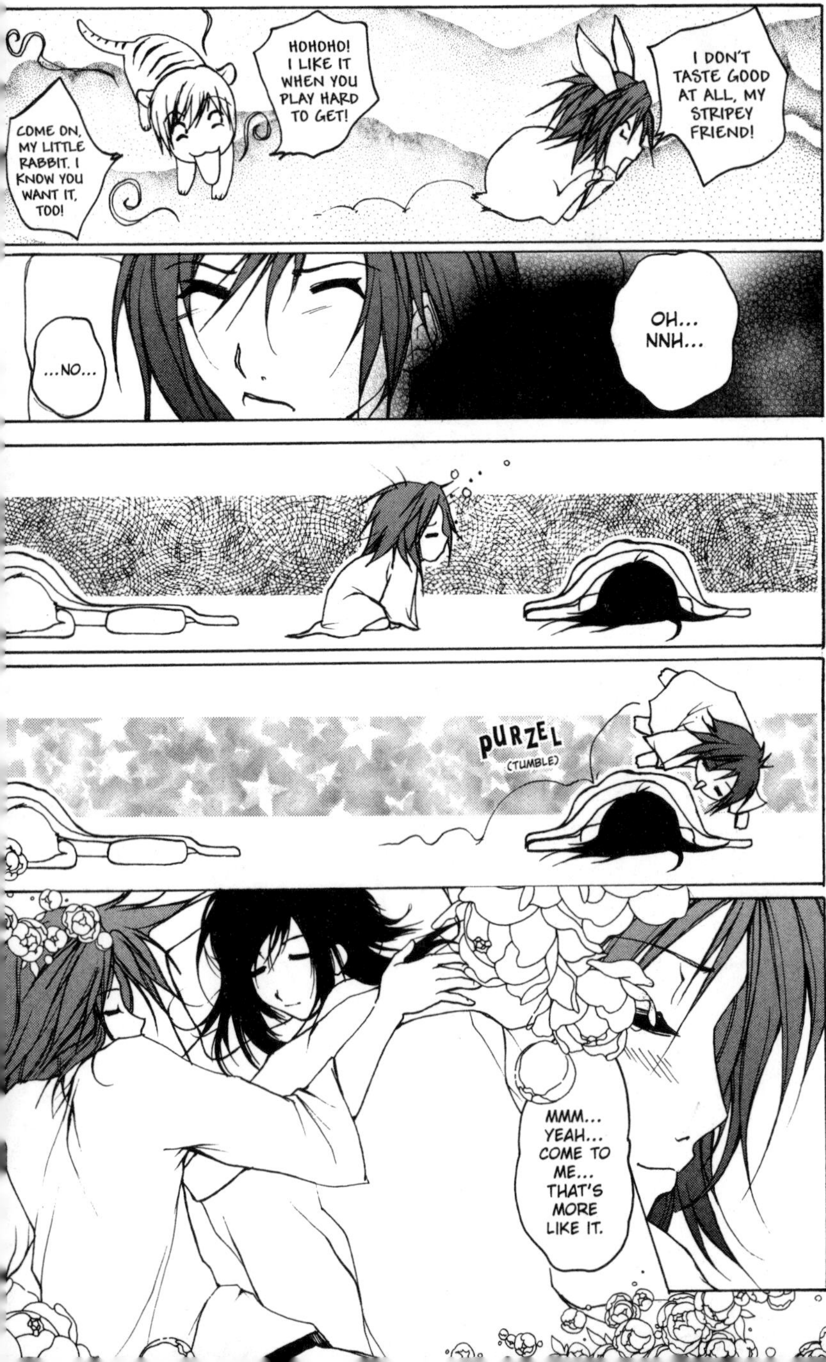
I DON'T TASTE GOOD AT ALL, MY STRIPEY FRIEND!
HOHOHO! I LIKE IT WHEN YOU PLAY HARD TO GET!
COME ON, MY LITTLE RABBIT. I KNOW YOU WANT IT, TOO!
OH... NNH...
...NO...
PURZEL
(TUMBLE)
MMM... YEAH... COME TO ME... THAT'S MORE LIKE IT.

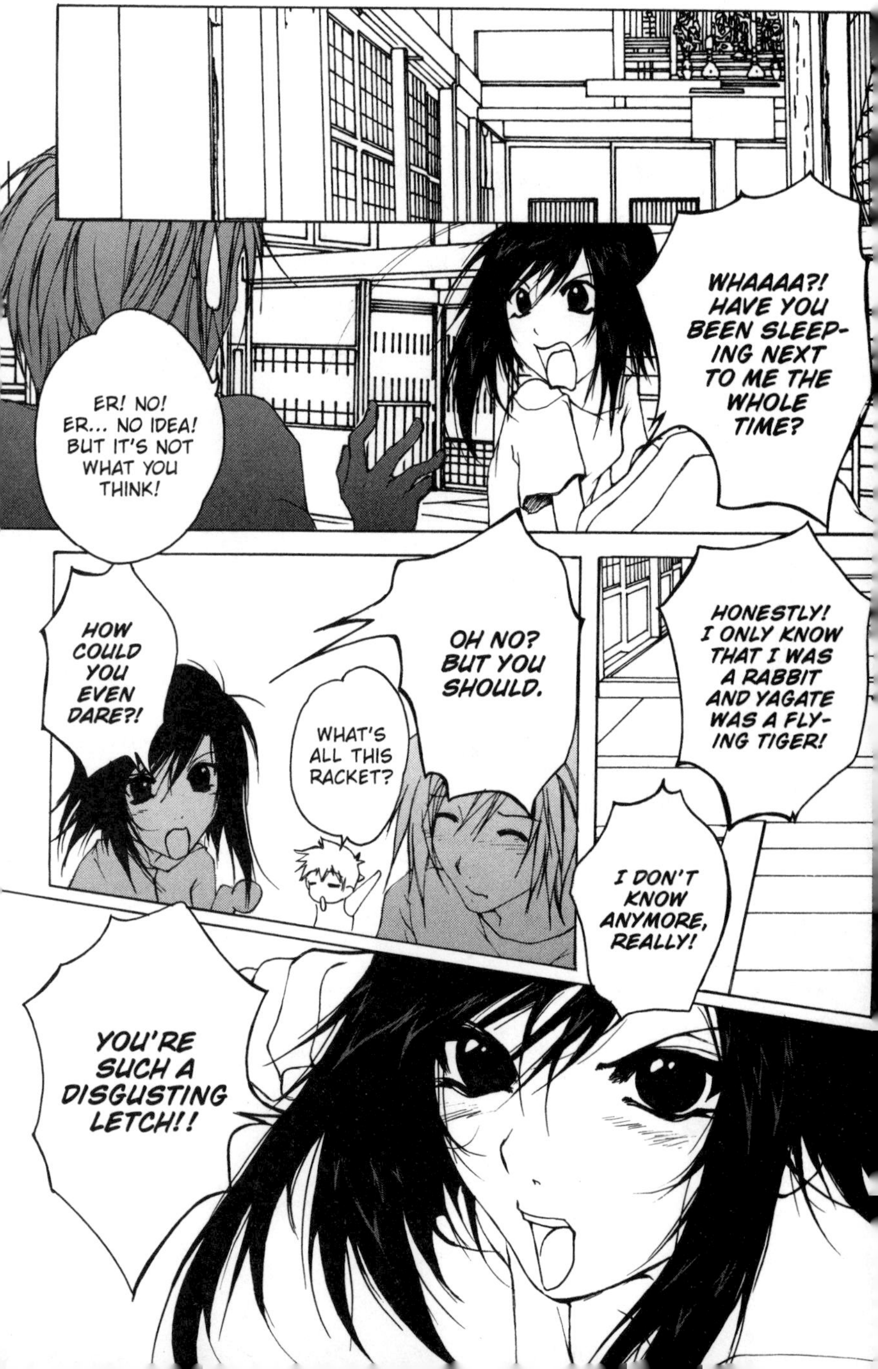
WHAAAA?! HAVE YOU BEEN SLEEP-ING NEXT TO ME THE WHOLE TIME?
ER! NO! ER... NO IDEA! BUT IT'S NOT WHAT YOU THINK!
HONESTLY! I ONLY KNOW THAT I WAS A RABBIT AND YAGATE WAS A FLY-ING TIGER!
I DON'T KNOW ANYMORE, REALLY!
OH NO? BUT YOU SHOULD.
WHAT'S ALL THIS RACKET?
HOW COULD YOU EVEN DARE?!
YOU'RE SUCH A DISGUSTING LETCH!!

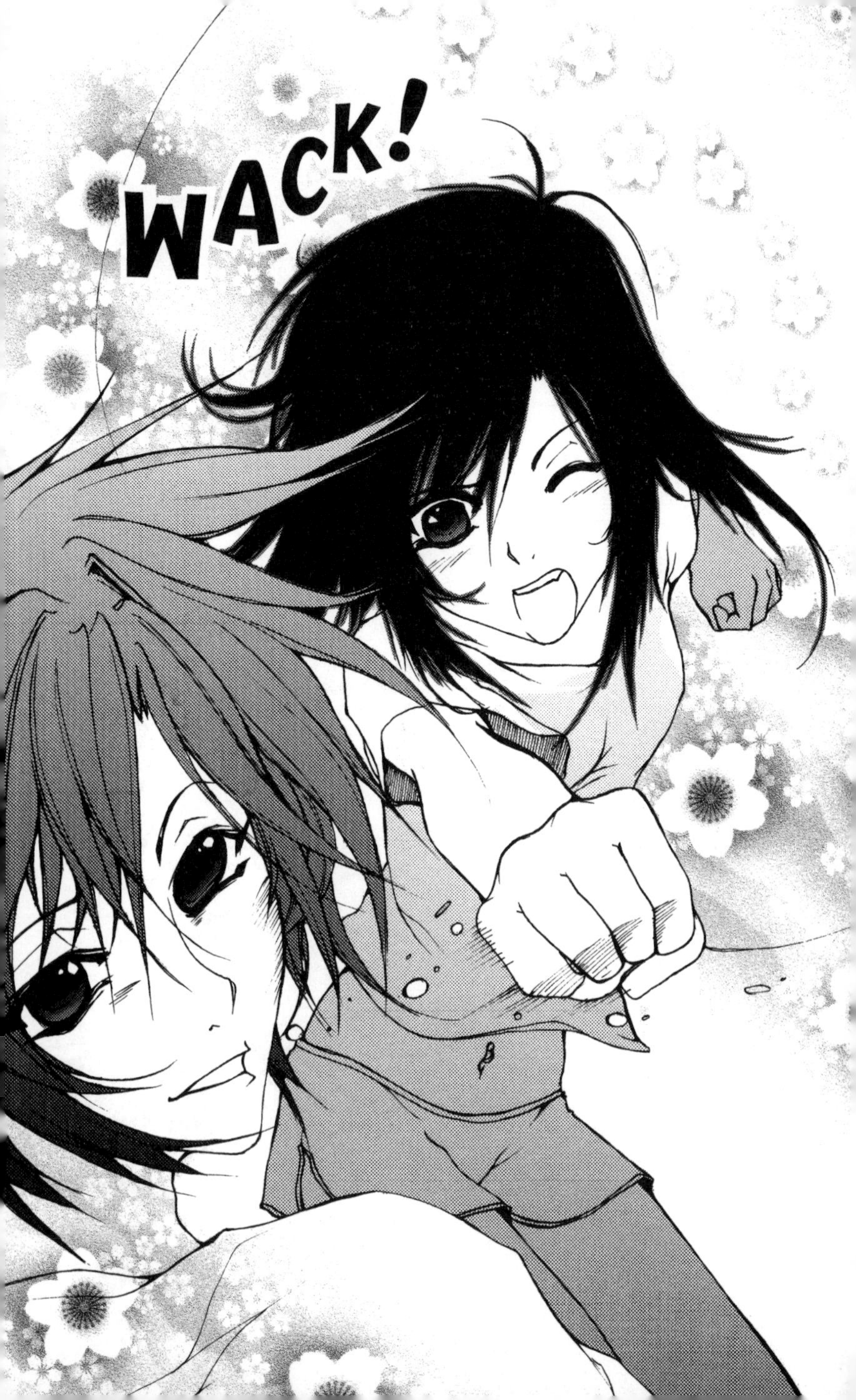
WACK!

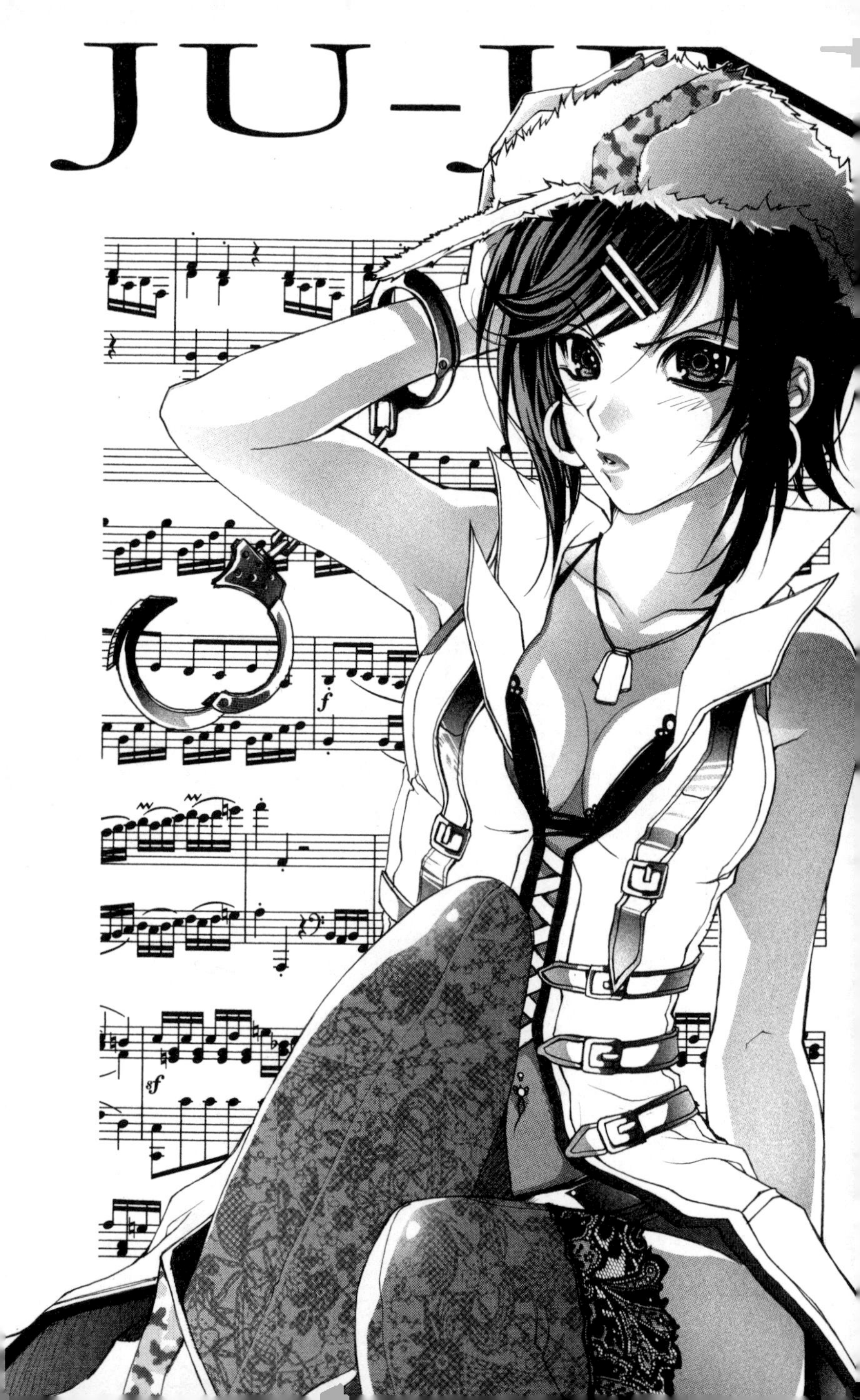
JU–

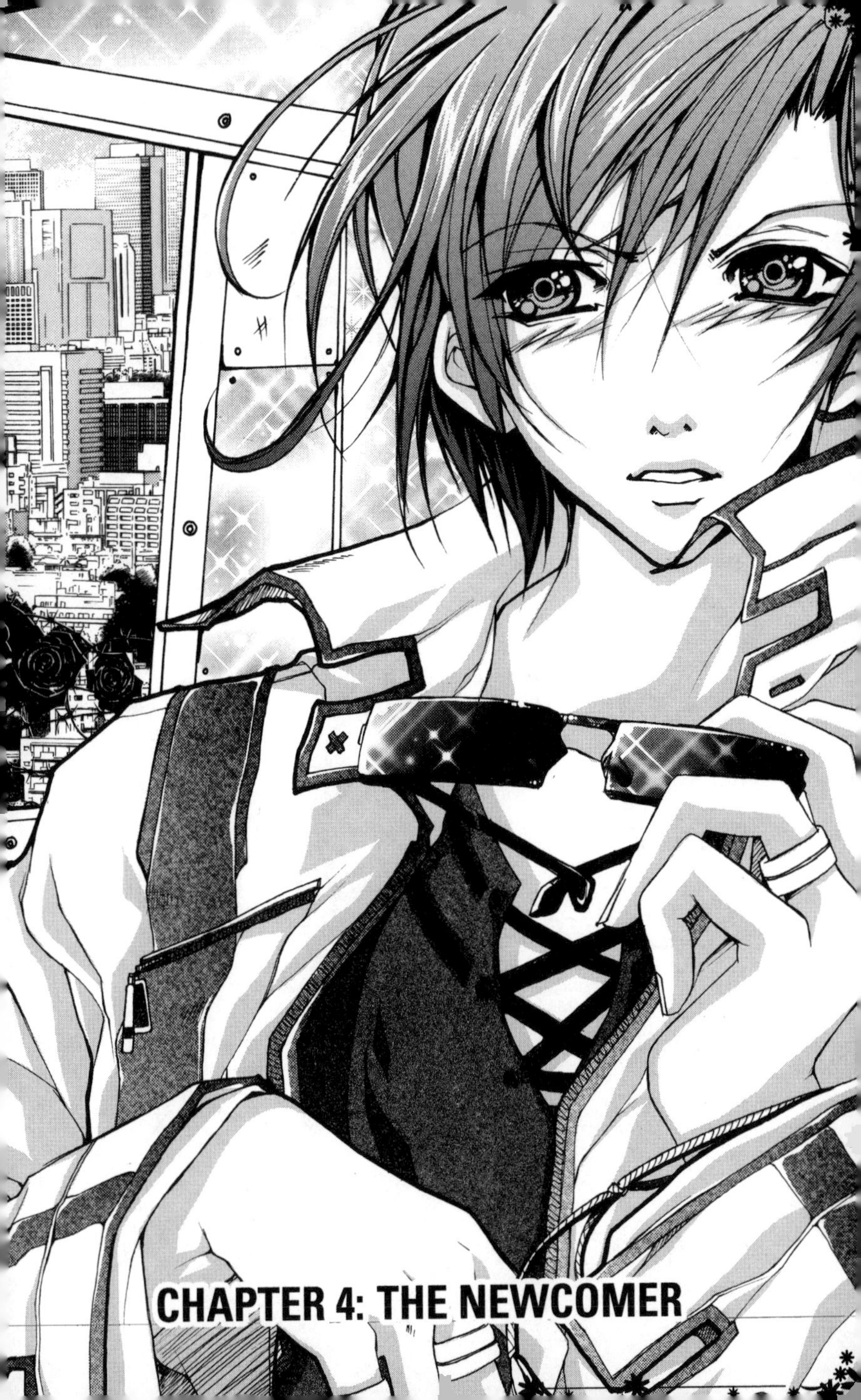
CHAPTER 4: THE NEWCOMER

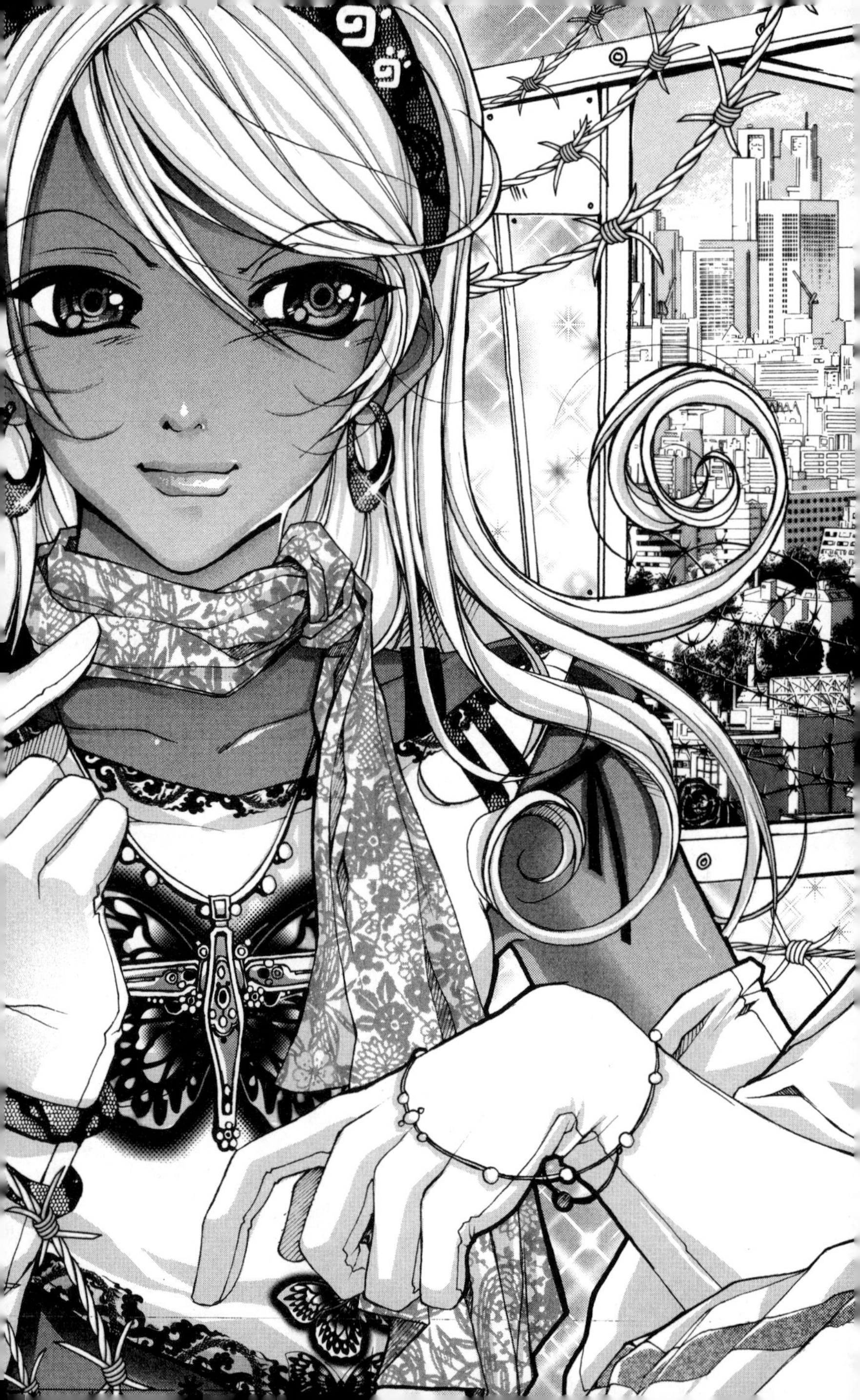

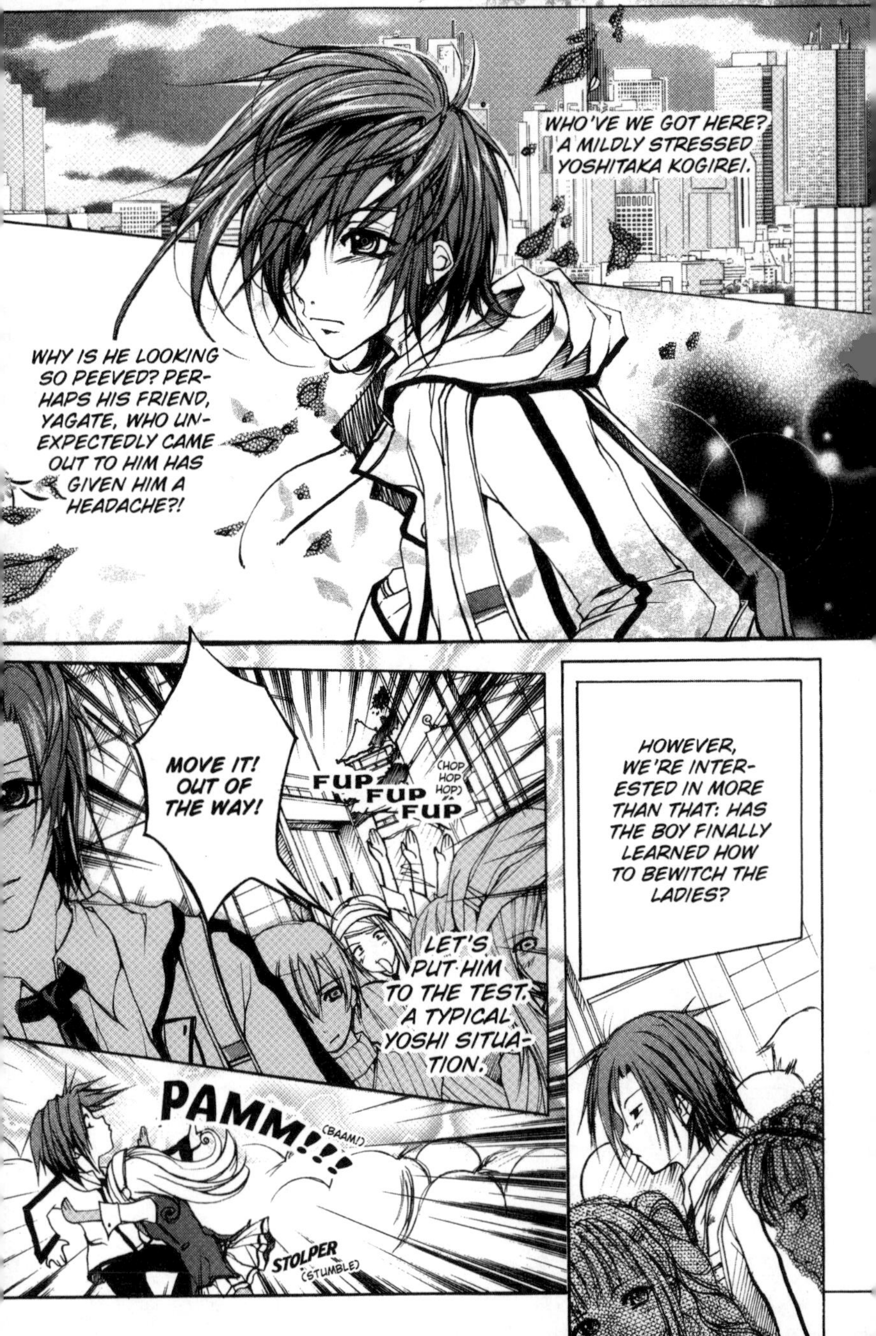
WHO'VE WE GOT HERE? A MILDLY STRESSED YOSHITAKA KOGIREI.
WHY IS HE LOOKING SO PEEVED? PER-HAPS HIS FRIEND, YAGATE, WHO UN-EXPECTEDLY CAME OUT TO HIM HAS GIVEN HIM A HEADACHE?!
HOWEVER, WE'RE INTER-ESTED IN MORE THAN THAT: HAS THE BOY FINALLY LEARNED HOW TO BEWITCH THE LADIES?
MOVE IT! OUT OF THE WAY!
FUP FUP FUP
(HOP HOP HOP)
LET'S PUT HIM TO THE TEST. A TYPICAL YOSHI SITUA-TION.
PAMM!!!
(BAAM!)
STOLPER
(STUMBLE)

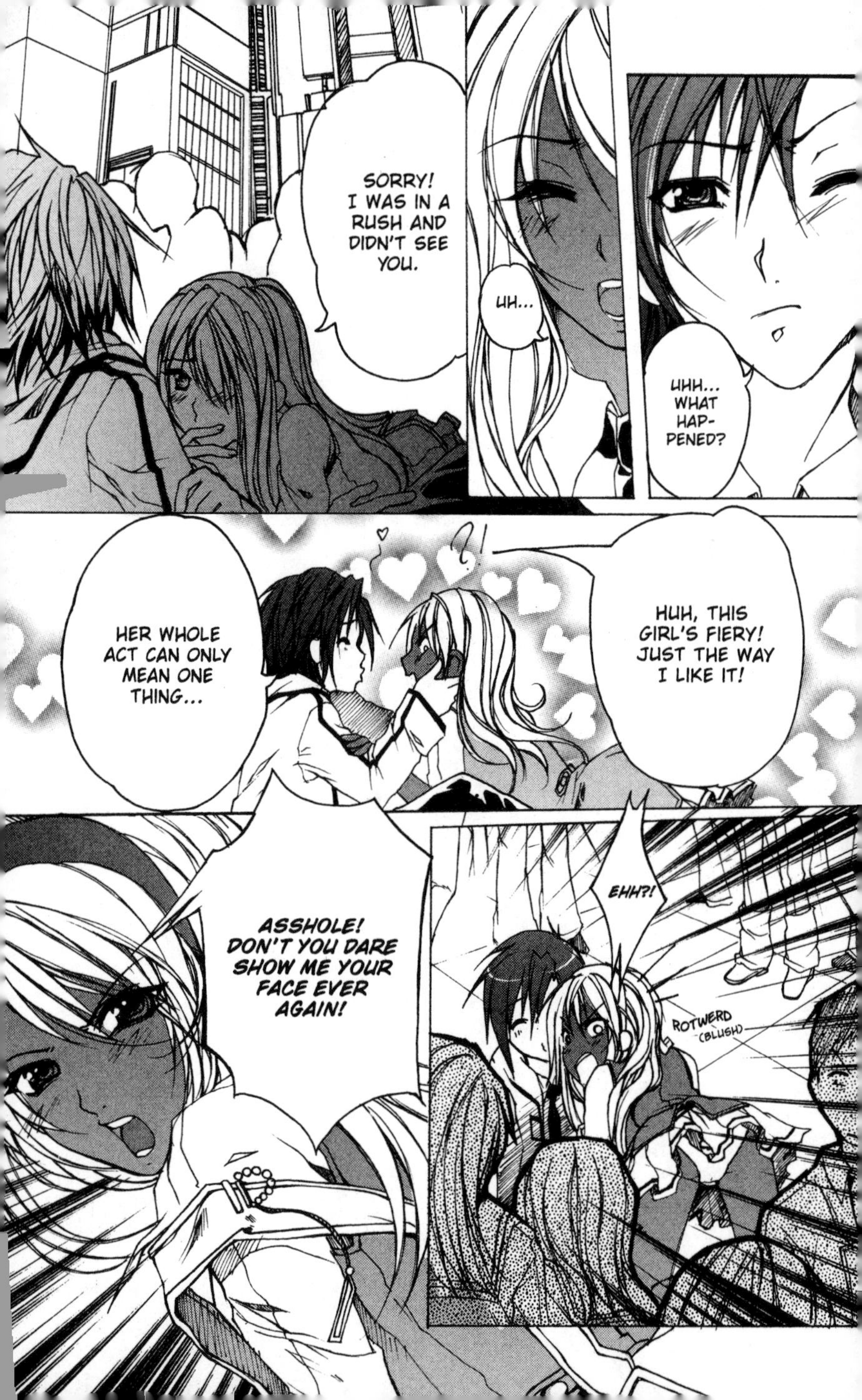
UHH... WHAT HAP-PENED?
UH...
SORRY! I WAS IN A RUSH AND DIDN'T SEE YOU.
HUH, THIS GIRL'S FIERY! JUST THE WAY I LIKE IT!
HER WHOLE ACT CAN ONLY MEAN ONE THING...
EHH?!
ROTWERD (BLUSH)
ASSHOLE! DON'T YOU DARE SHOW ME YOUR FACE EVER AGAIN!

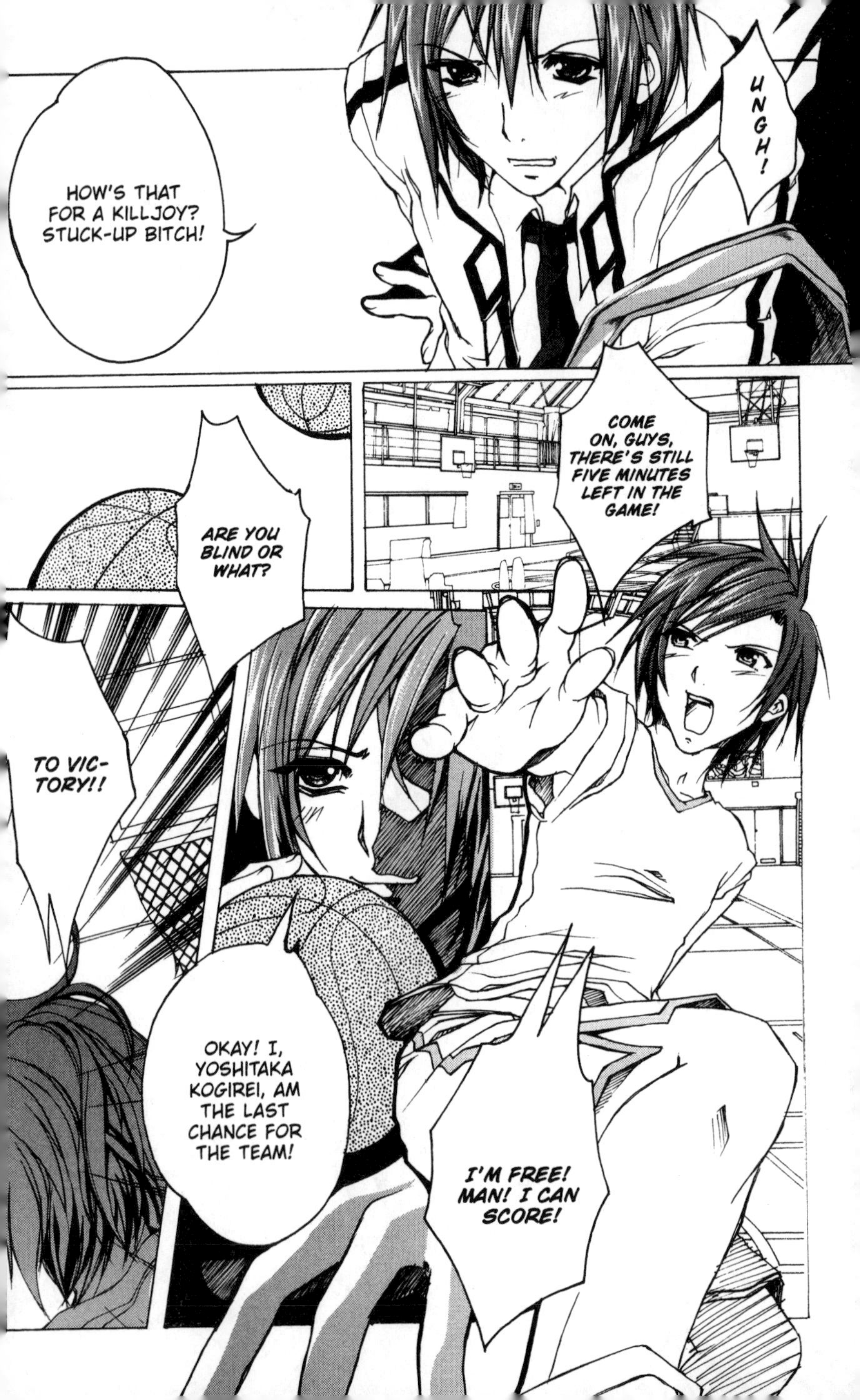
UNGH!
HOW'S THAT FOR A KILLJOY? STUCK-UP BITCH!
COME ON, GUYS, THERE'S STILL FIVE MINUTES LEFT IN THE GAME!
ARE YOU BLIND OR WHAT?
I'M FREE! MAN! I CAN SCORE!
OKAY! I, YOSHITAKA KOGIREI, AM THE LAST CHANCE FOR THE TEAM!
TO VIC-TORY!!

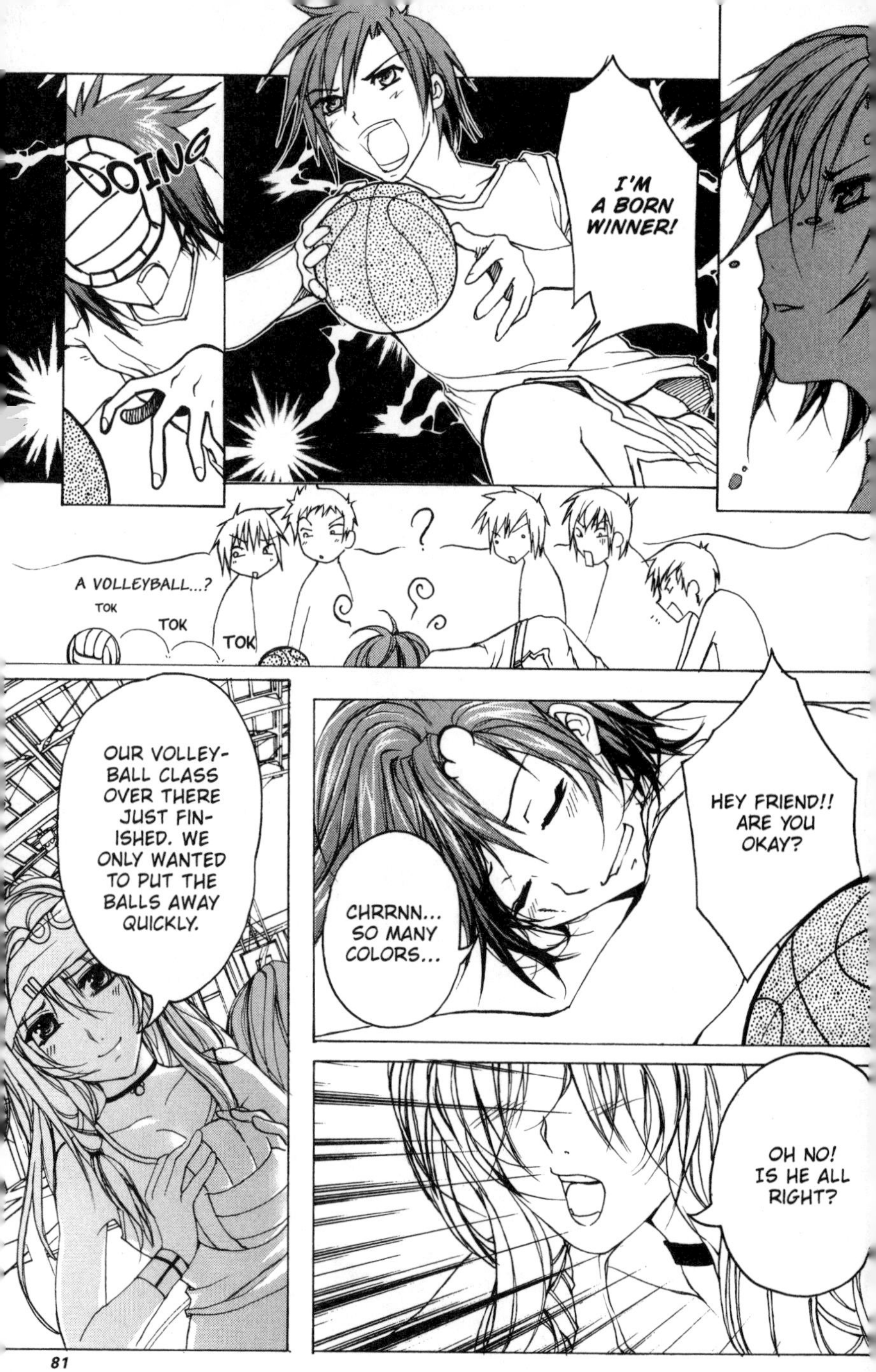
I'M A BORN WINNER!
DOING
A VOLLEYBALL...?
TOK
TOK
TOK
HEY FRIEND!! ARE YOU OKAY?
CHRRNN... SO MANY COLORS...
OH NO! IS HE ALL RIGHT?
OUR VOLLEY-BALL CLASS OVER THERE JUST FIN-ISHED. WE ONLY WANTED TO PUT THE BALLS AWAY QUICKLY.

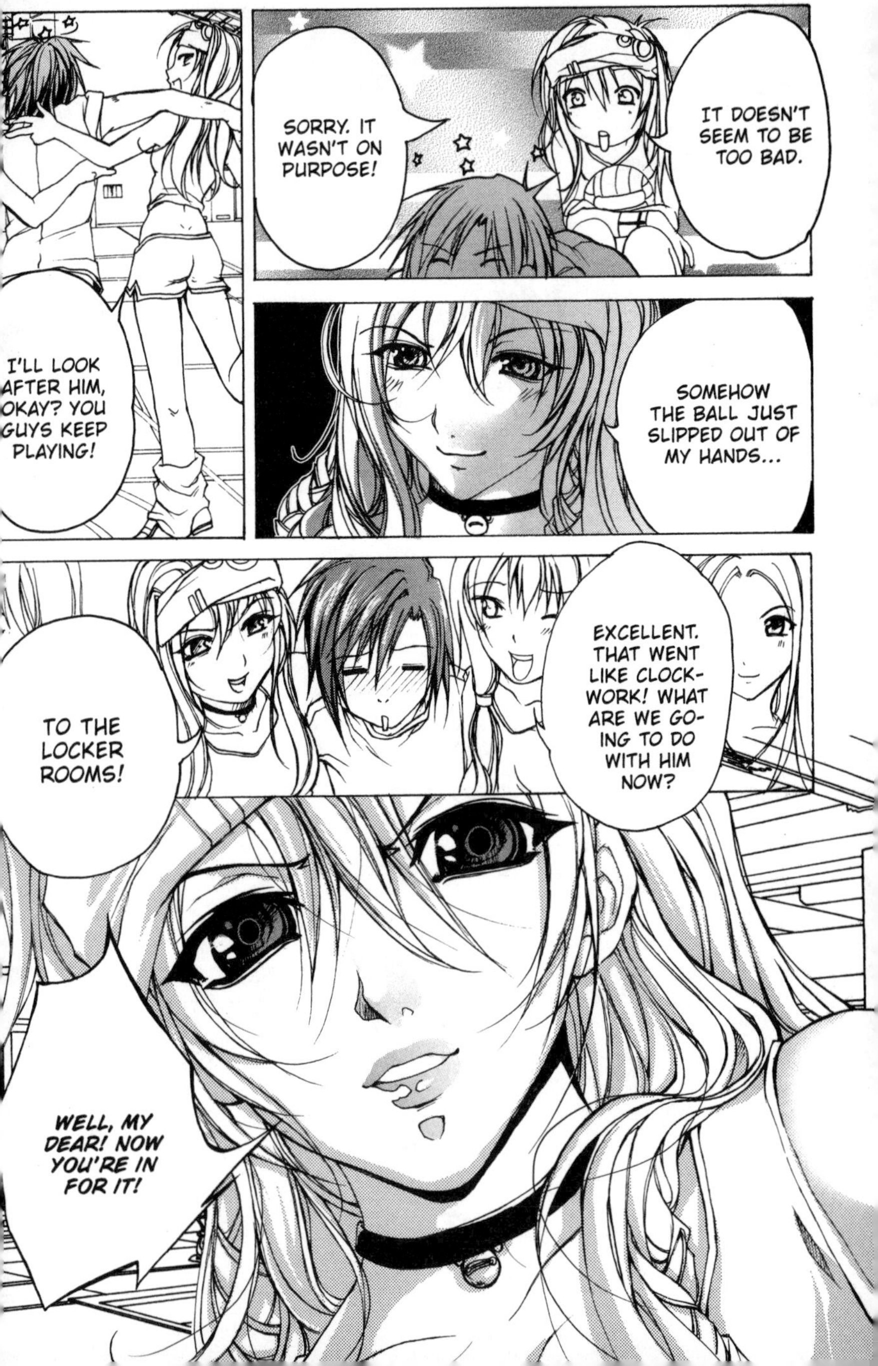
IT DOESN'T SEEM TO BE TOO BAD.
SORRY. IT WASN'T ON PURPOSE!
SOMEHOW THE BALL JUST SLIPPED OUT OF MY HANDS...
I'LL LOOK AFTER HIM, OKAY? YOU GUYS KEEP PLAYING!
EXCELLENT. THAT WENT LIKE CLOCK-WORK! WHAT ARE WE GO-ING TO DO WITH HIM NOW?
TO THE LOCKER ROOMS!
WELL, MY DEAR! NOW YOU'RE IN FOR IT!

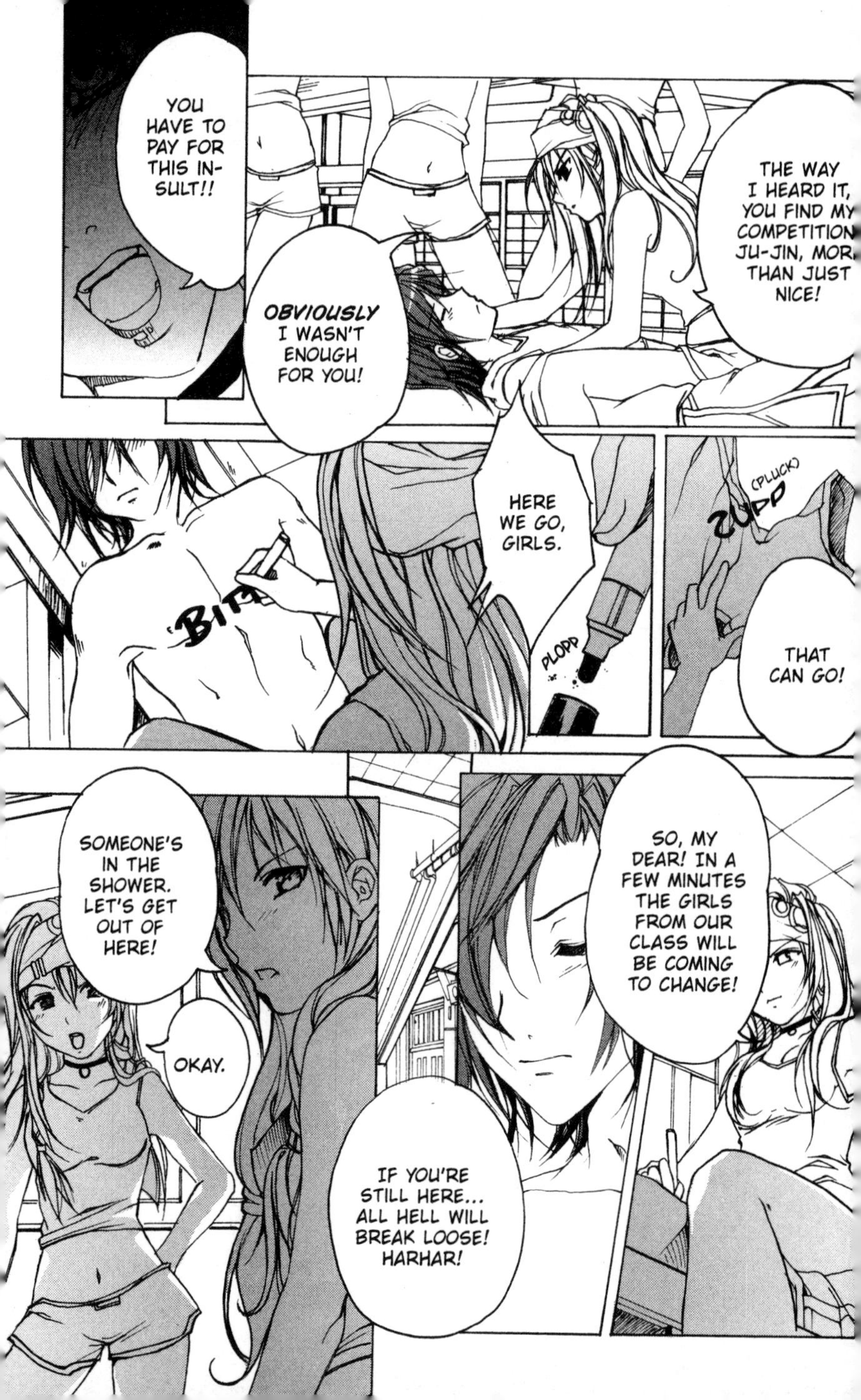
THE WAY I HEARD IT, YOU FIND MY COMPETITION JU-JIN, MOR THAN JUST NICE!
OBVIOUSLY I WASN'T ENOUGH FOR YOU!
YOU HAVE TO PAY FOR THIS IN-SULT!!
(PLUCK)
ZUPP
THAT CAN GO!
HERE WE GO, GIRLS.
PLOPP
SO, MY DEAR! IN A FEW MINUTES THE GIRLS FROM OUR CLASS WILL BE COMING TO CHANGE!
IF YOU'RE STILL HERE... ALL HELL WILL BREAK LOOSE! HARHAR!
SOMEONE'S IN THE SHOWER. LET'S GET OUT OF HERE!
OKAY.

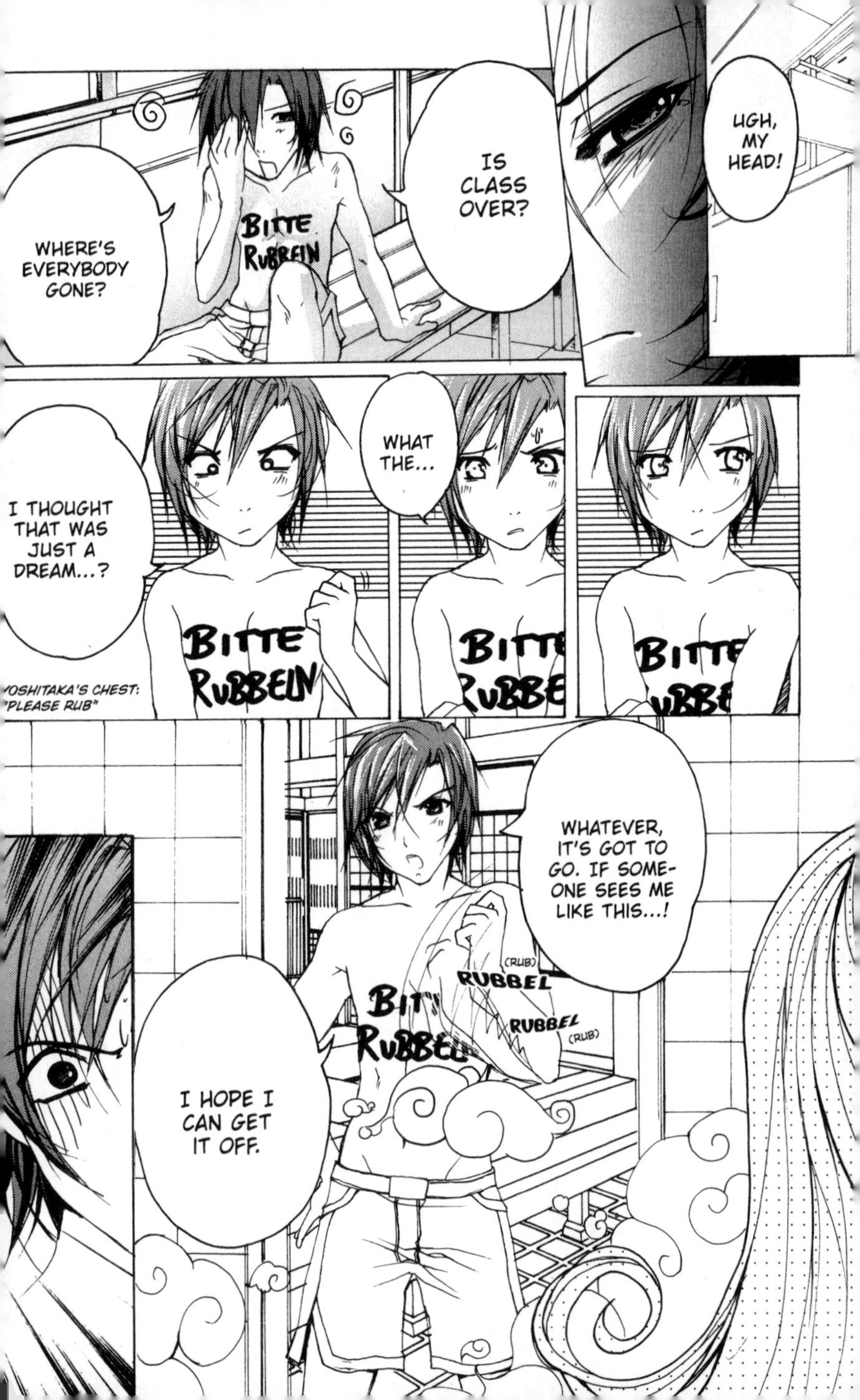
UGH, MY HEAD!
IS CLASS OVER?
WHERE'S EVERYBODY GONE?
BITTE RUBBEIN
WHAT THE...
I THOUGHT THAT WAS JUST A DREAM...?
BITTE RUBBELN
YOSHITAKA'S CHEST: "PLEASE RUB"
WHATEVER, IT'S GOT TO GO. IF SOME-ONE SEES ME LIKE THIS...!
RUBBEL (RUB)
RUBBEL (RUB)
BITTE RUBBELN
I HOPE I CAN GET IT OFF.

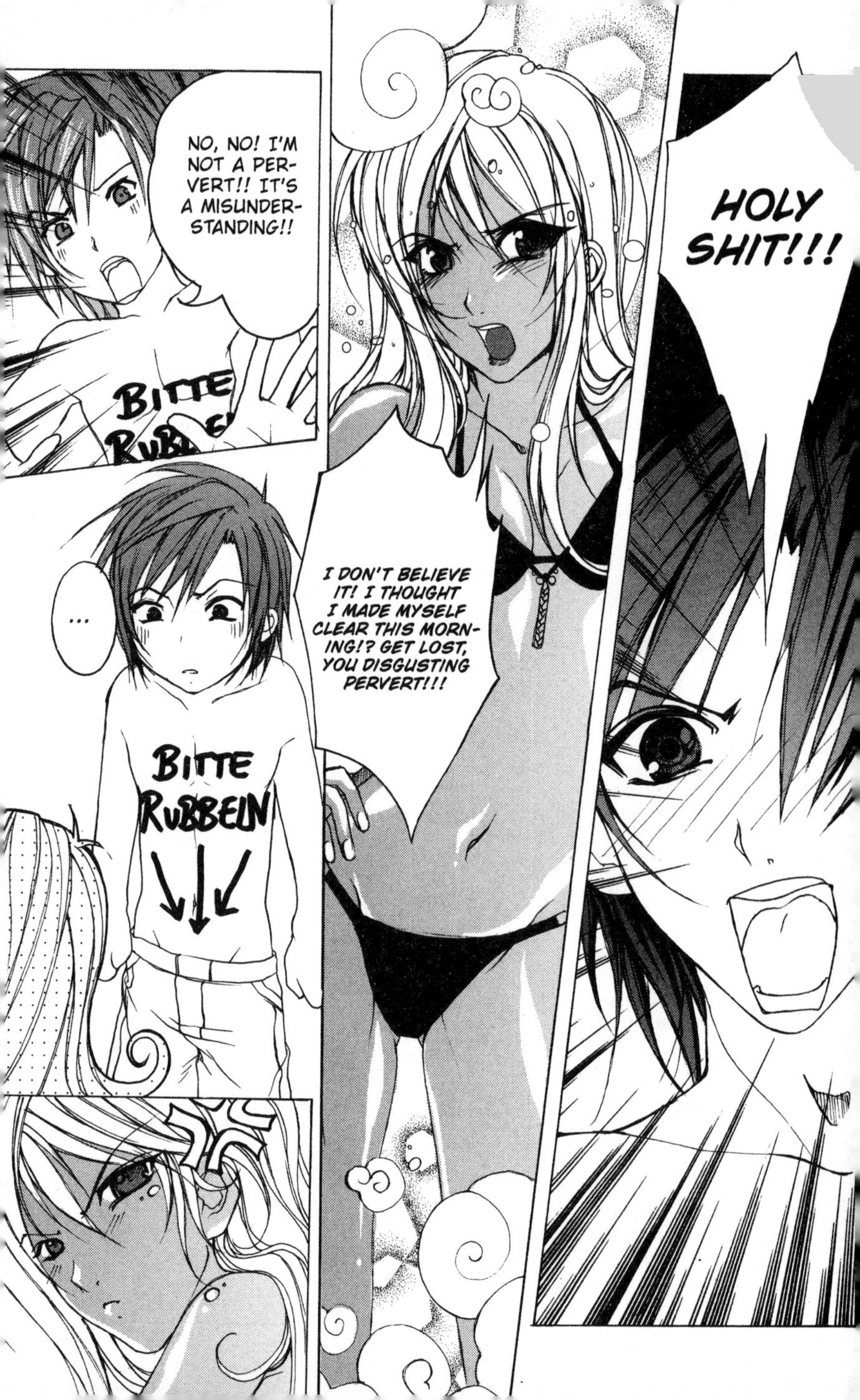
HOLY SHIT!!!
I DON'T BELIEVE IT! I THOUGHT I MADE MYSELF CLEAR THIS MORNING!? GET LOST, YOU DISGUSTING PERVERT!!!
NO, NO! I'M NOT A PERVERT!! IT'S A MISUNDERSTANDING!!
...
BITTE RUBBELN

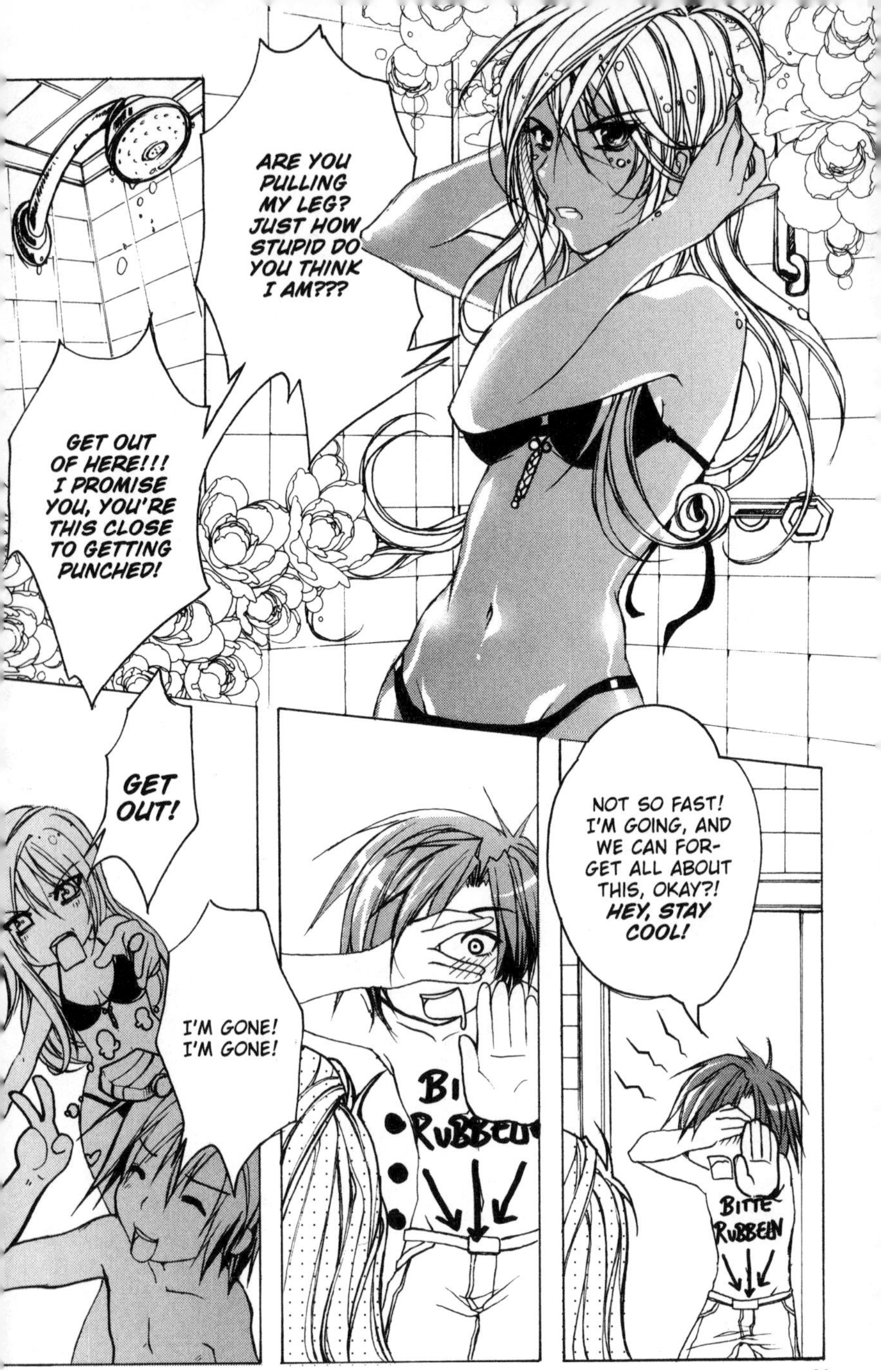
ARE YOU PULLING MY LEG? JUST HOW STUPID DO YOU THINK I AM???
GET OUT OF HERE!!! I PROMISE YOU, YOU'RE THIS CLOSE TO GETTING PUNCHED!
NOT SO FAST! I'M GOING, AND WE CAN FOR-GET ALL ABOUT THIS, OKAY?! HEY, STAY COOL!
BITTE RUBBELN
GET OUT!
I'M GONE! I'M GONE!

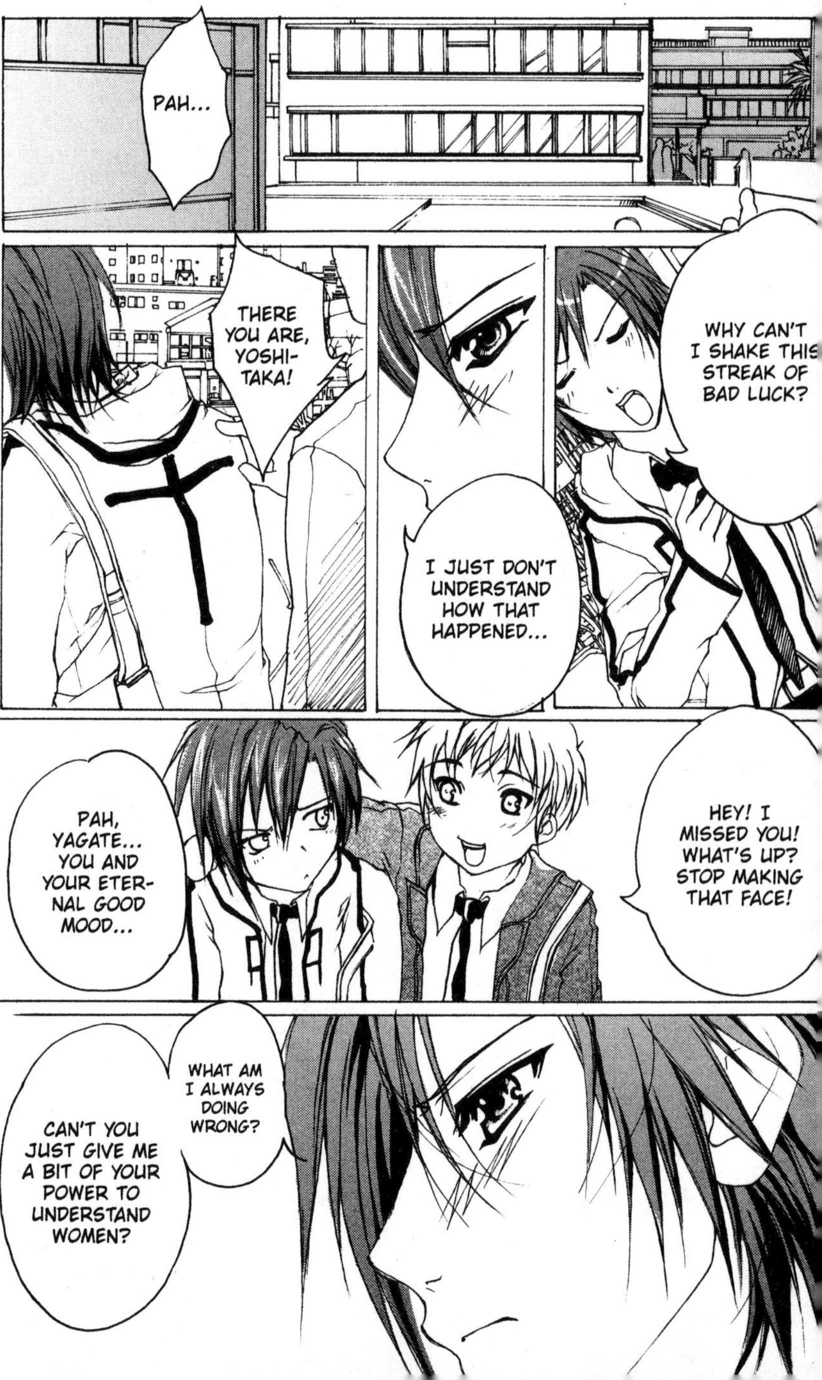
PAH...
WHY CAN'T I SHAKE THIS STREAK OF BAD LUCK?
I JUST DON'T UNDERSTAND HOW THAT HAPPENED...
THERE YOU ARE, YOSHI-TAKA!
HEY! I MISSED YOU! WHAT'S UP? STOP MAKING THAT FACE!
PAH, YAGATE... YOU AND YOUR ETER-NAL GOOD MOOD...
WHAT AM I ALWAYS DOING WRONG?
CAN'T YOU JUST GIVE ME A BIT OF YOUR POWER TO UNDERSTAND WOMEN?

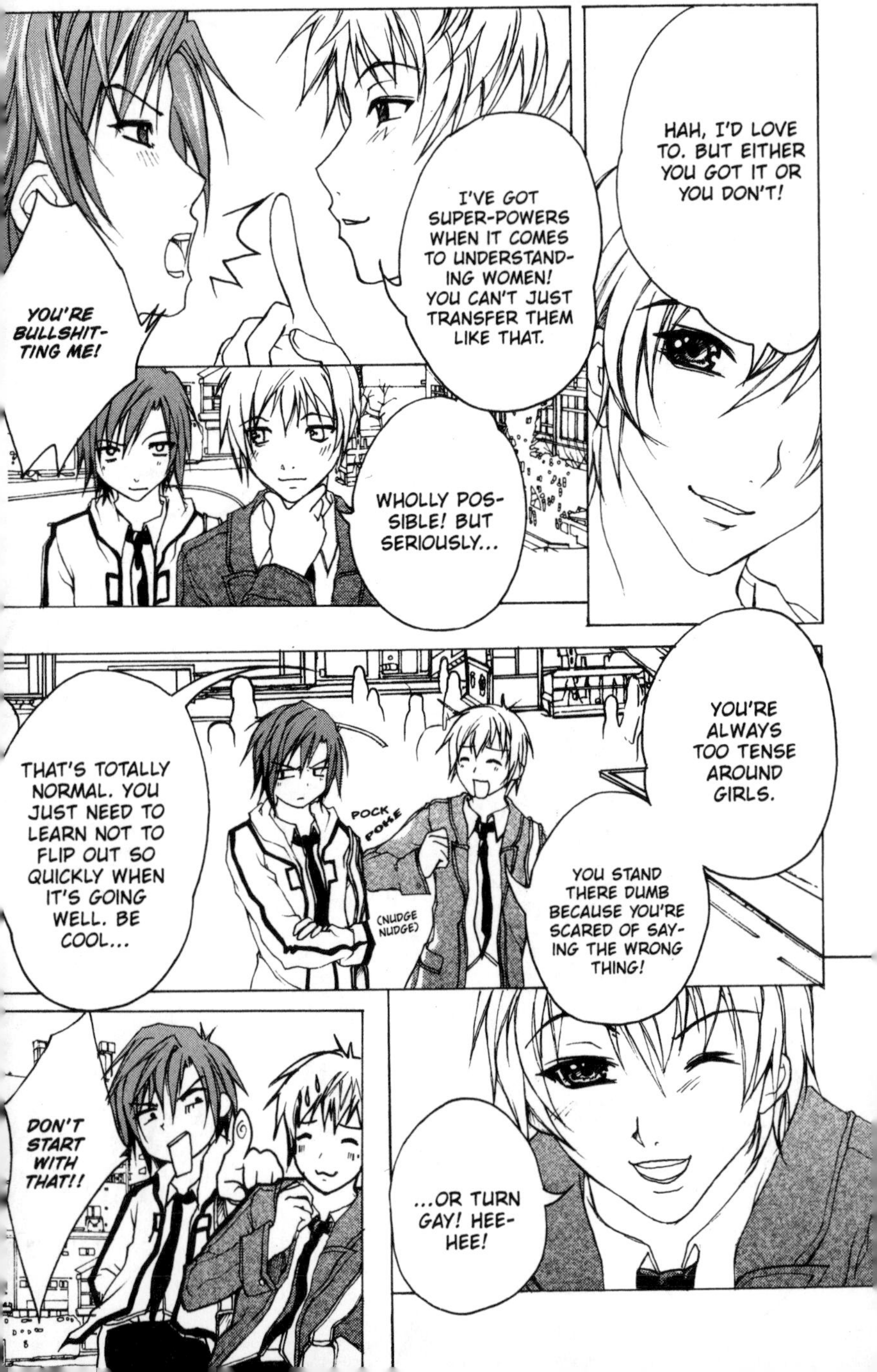
HAH, I'D LOVE TO. BUT EITHER YOU GOT IT OR YOU DON'T!
I'VE GOT SUPER-POWERS WHEN IT COMES TO UNDERSTANDING WOMEN! YOU CAN'T JUST TRANSFER THEM LIKE THAT.
YOU'RE BULLSHITTING ME!
WHOLLY POSSIBLE! BUT SERIOUSLY...
YOU'RE ALWAYS TOO TENSE AROUND GIRLS.
YOU STAND THERE DUMB BECAUSE YOU'RE SCARED OF SAYING THE WRONG THING!
POCK
POKE
(NUDGE NUDGE)
THAT'S TOTALLY NORMAL. YOU JUST NEED TO LEARN NOT TO FLIP OUT SO QUICKLY WHEN IT'S GOING WELL. BE COOL...
...OR TURN GAY! HEE-HEE!
DON'T START WITH THAT!!

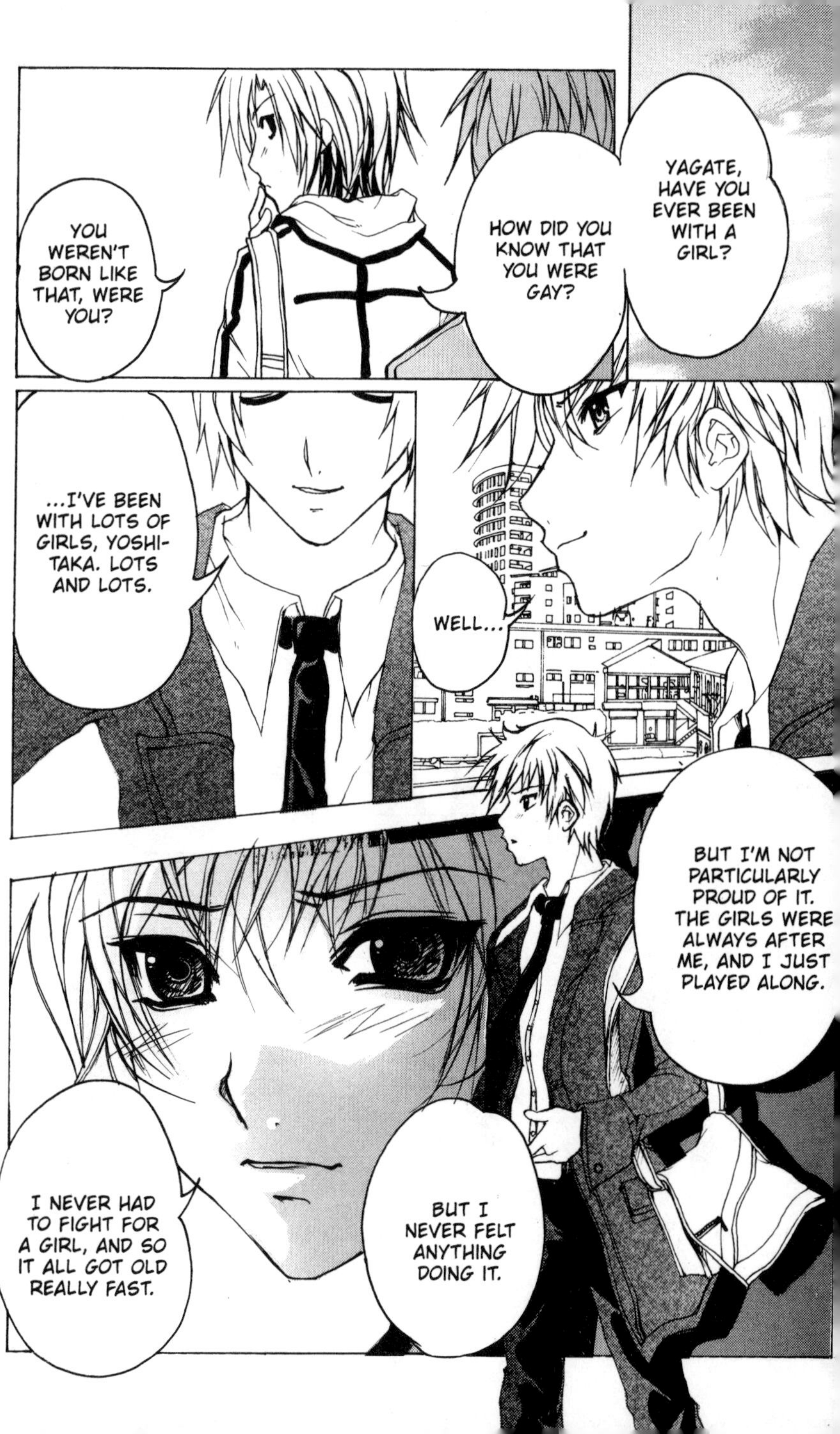
YAGATE, HAVE YOU EVER BEEN WITH A GIRL?
HOW DID YOU KNOW THAT YOU WERE GAY?
YOU WEREN'T BORN LIKE THAT, WERE YOU?
WELL...
...I'VE BEEN WITH LOTS OF GIRLS, YOSHI-TAKA. LOTS AND LOTS.
BUT I'M NOT PARTICULARLY PROUD OF IT. THE GIRLS WERE ALWAYS AFTER ME, AND I JUST PLAYED ALONG.
BUT I NEVER FELT ANYTHING DOING IT.
I NEVER HAD TO FIGHT FOR A GIRL, AND SO IT ALL GOT OLD REALLY FAST.

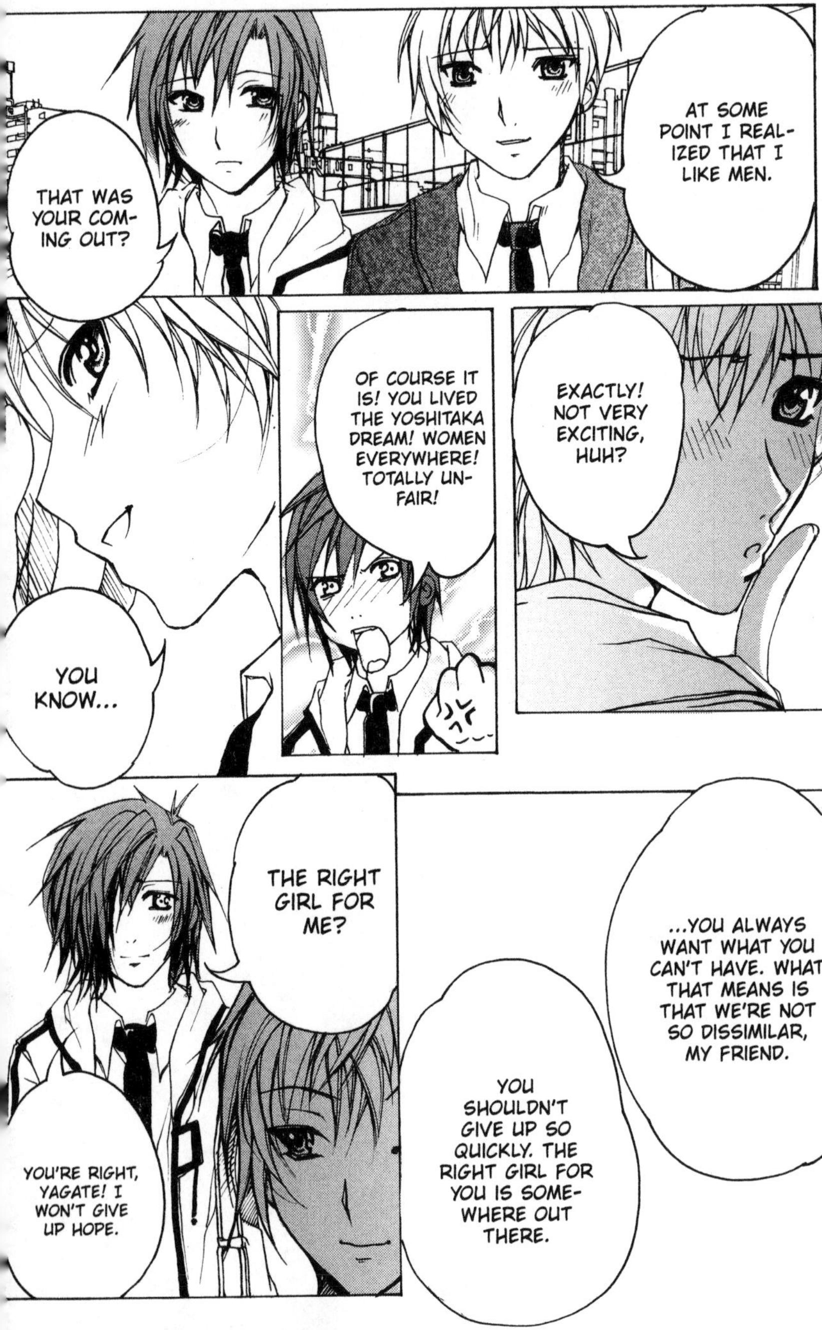
AT SOME POINT I REALIZED THAT I LIKE MEN.
THAT WAS YOUR COMING OUT?
EXACTLY! NOT VERY EXCITING, HUH?
OF COURSE IT IS! YOU LIVED THE YOSHITAKA DREAM! WOMEN EVERYWHERE! TOTALLY UNFAIR!
YOU KNOW...
...YOU ALWAYS WANT WHAT YOU CAN'T HAVE. WHAT THAT MEANS IS THAT WE'RE NOT SO DISSIMILAR, MY FRIEND.
YOU SHOULDN'T GIVE UP SO QUICKLY. THE RIGHT GIRL FOR YOU IS SOMEWHERE OUT THERE.
THE RIGHT GIRL FOR ME?
YOU'RE RIGHT, YAGATE! I WON'T GIVE UP HOPE.

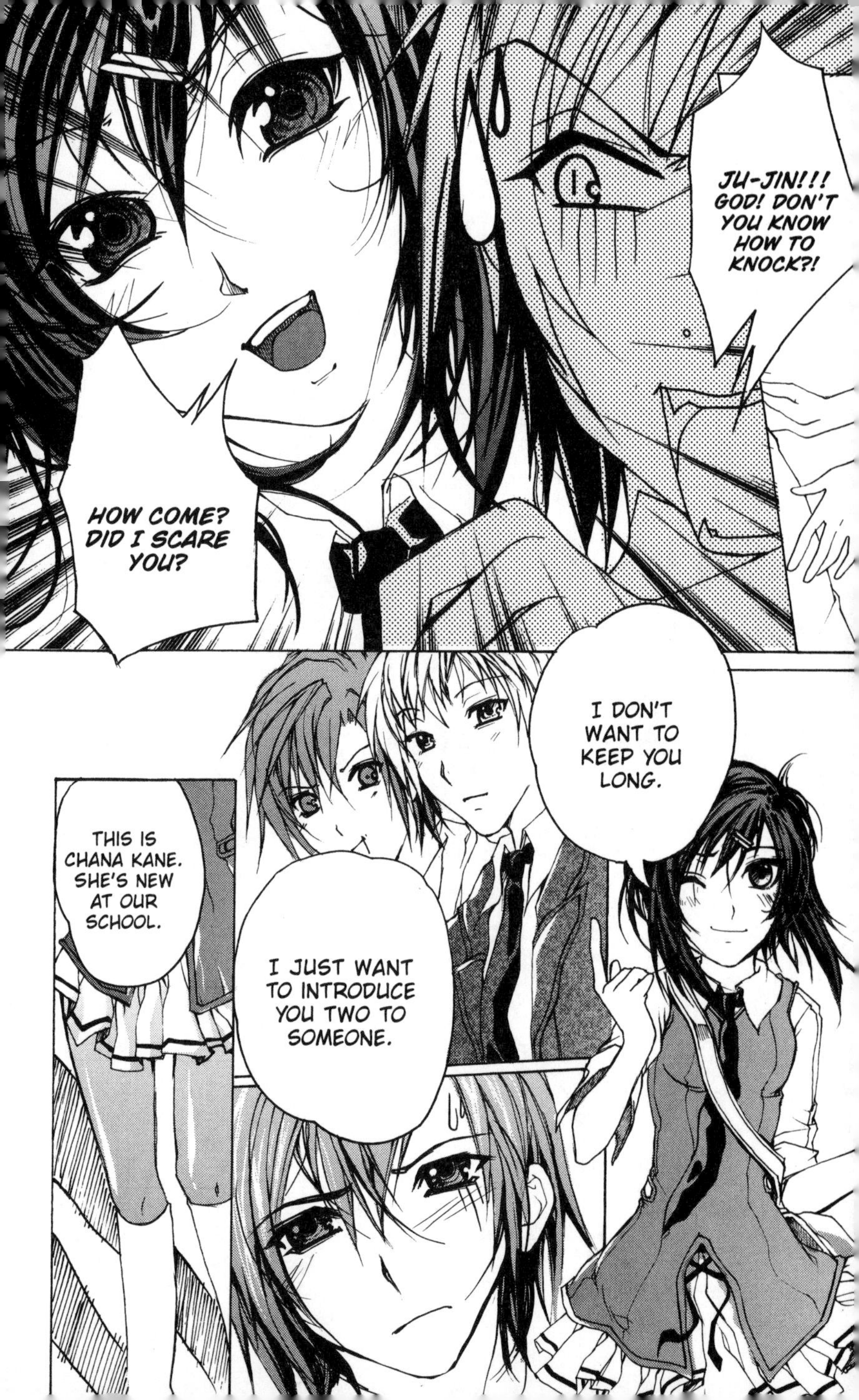
JU-JIN!!! GOD! DON'T YOU KNOW HOW TO KNOCK?!
HOW COME? DID I SCARE YOU?
I DON'T WANT TO KEEP YOU LONG.
I JUST WANT TO INTRODUCE YOU TWO TO SOMEONE.
THIS IS CHANA KANE. SHE'S NEW AT OUR SCHOOL.

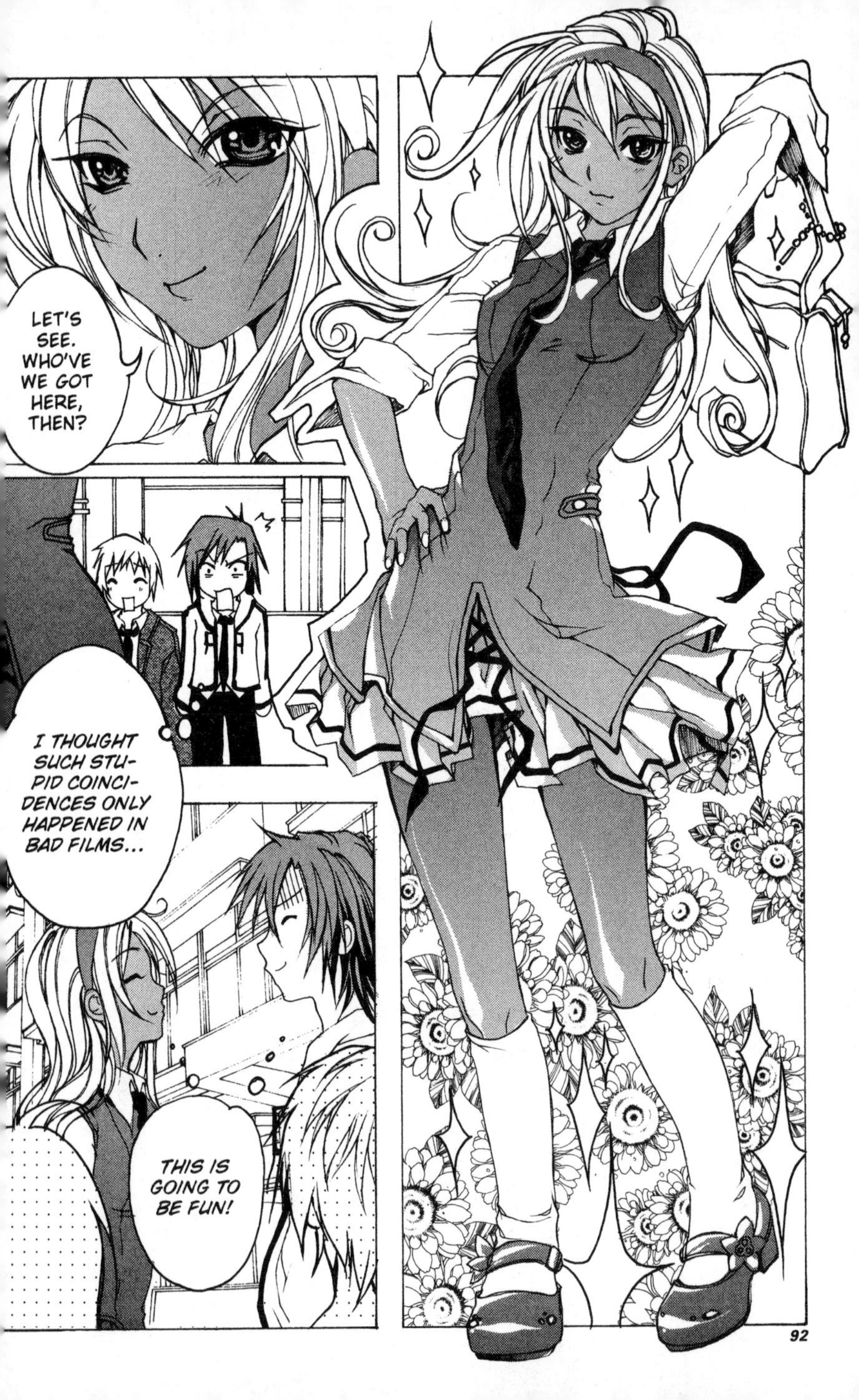
LET'S SEE. WHO'VE WE GOT HERE, THEN?
I THOUGHT SUCH STUPID COINCIDENCES ONLY HAPPENED IN BAD FILMS...
THIS IS GOING TO BE FUN!

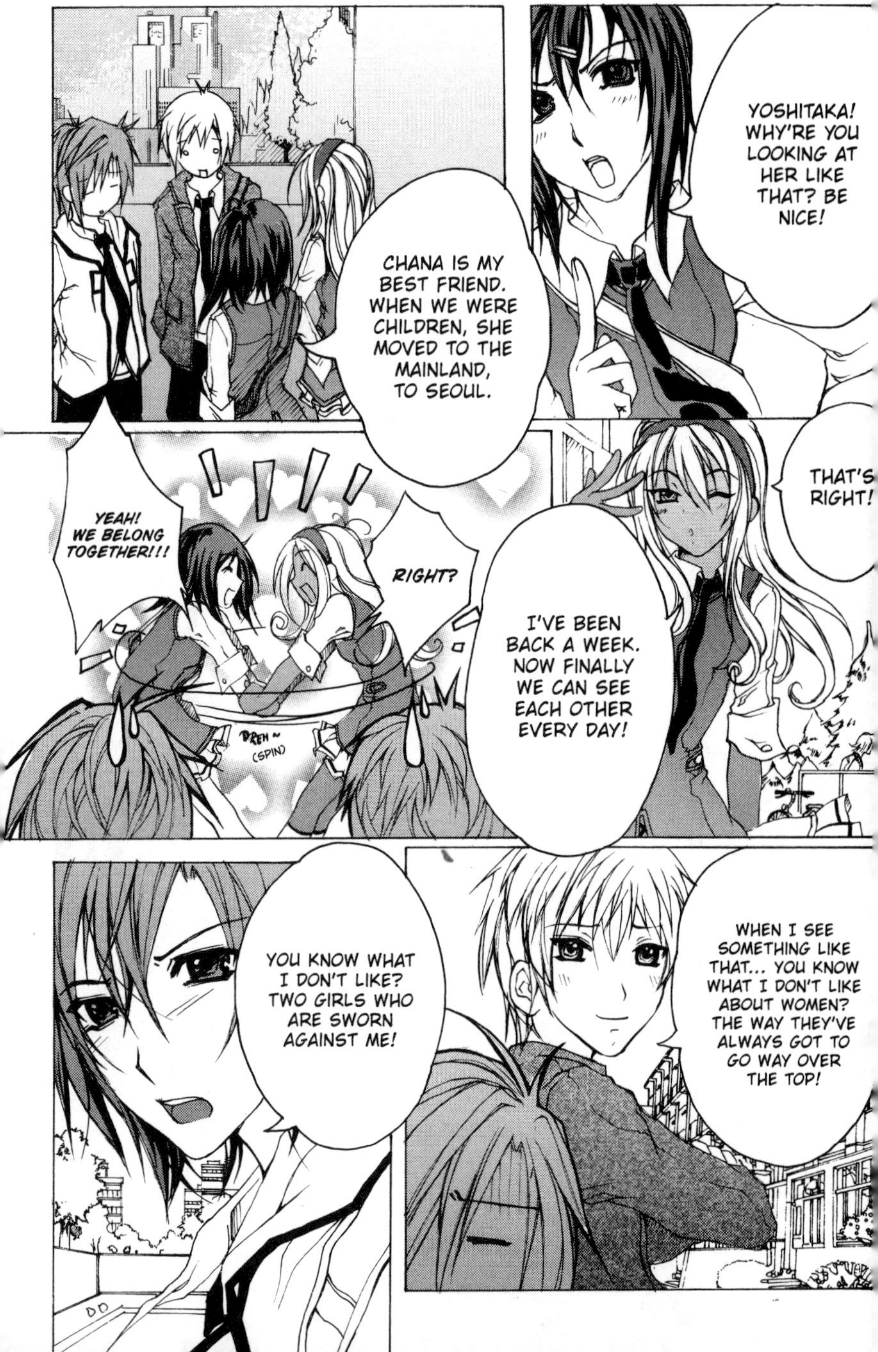
YOSHITAKA! WHY'RE YOU LOOKING AT HER LIKE THAT? BE NICE!
CHANA IS MY BEST FRIEND. WHEN WE WERE CHILDREN, SHE MOVED TO THE MAINLAND, TO SEOUL.
THAT'S RIGHT!
I'VE BEEN BACK A WEEK. NOW FINALLY WE CAN SEE EACH OTHER EVERY DAY!
RIGHT?
YEAH! WE BELONG TOGETHER!!!
DREH~
(SPIN)
WHEN I SEE SOMETHING LIKE THAT... YOU KNOW WHAT I DON'T LIKE ABOUT WOMEN? THE WAY THEY'VE ALWAYS GOT TO GO WAY OVER THE TOP!
YOU KNOW WHAT I DON'T LIKE? TWO GIRLS WHO ARE SWORN AGAINST ME!

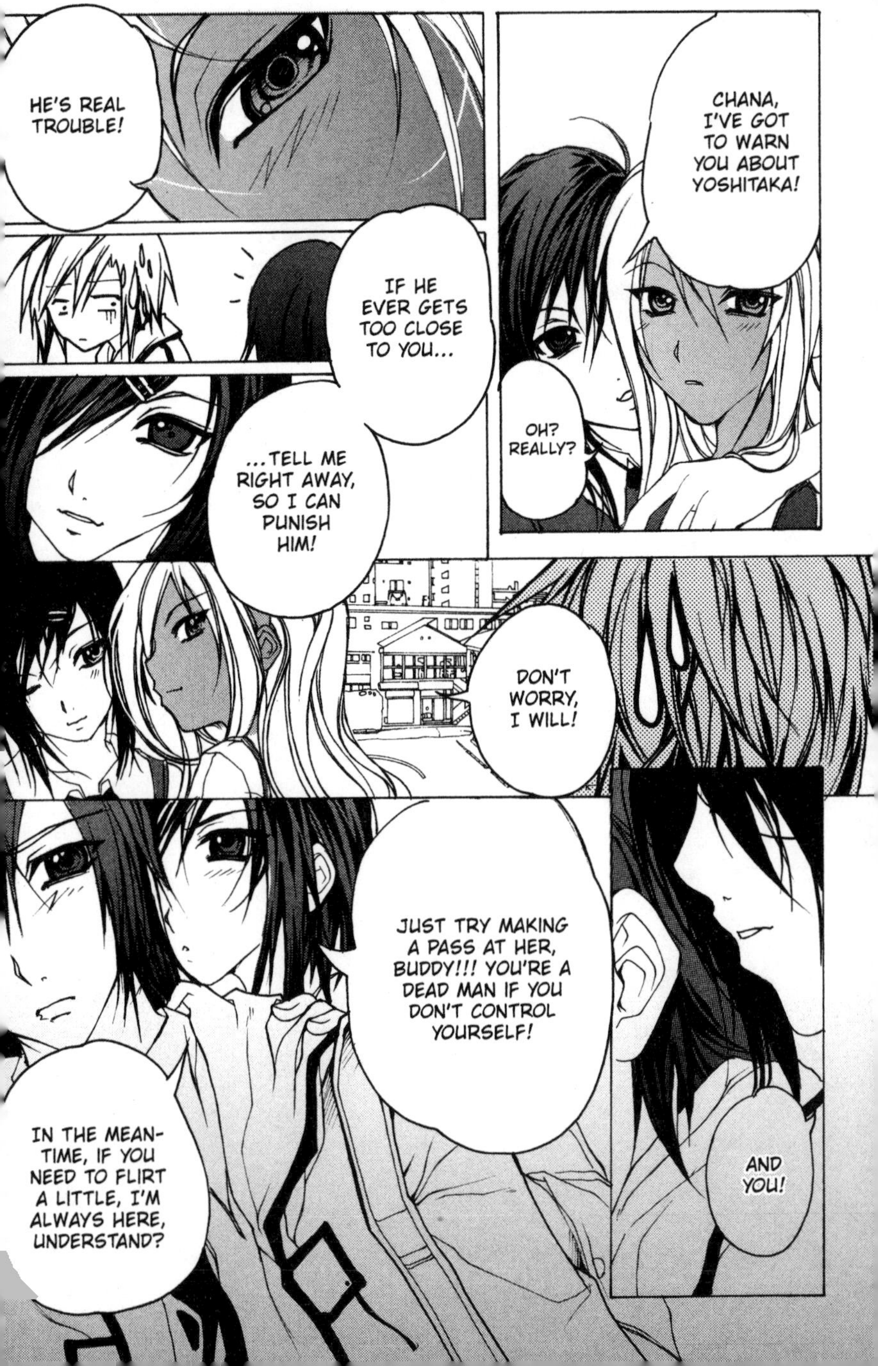
CHANA, I'VE GOT TO WARN YOU ABOUT YOSHITAKA!
OH? REALLY?
HE'S REAL TROUBLE!
IF HE EVER GETS TOO CLOSE TO YOU...
...TELL ME RIGHT AWAY, SO I CAN PUNISH HIM!
DON'T WORRY, I WILL!
AND YOU!
JUST TRY MAKING A PASS AT HER, BUDDY!!! YOU'RE A DEAD MAN IF YOU DON'T CONTROL YOURSELF!
IN THE MEAN-TIME, IF YOU NEED TO FLIRT A LITTLE, I'M ALWAYS HERE, UNDERSTAND?

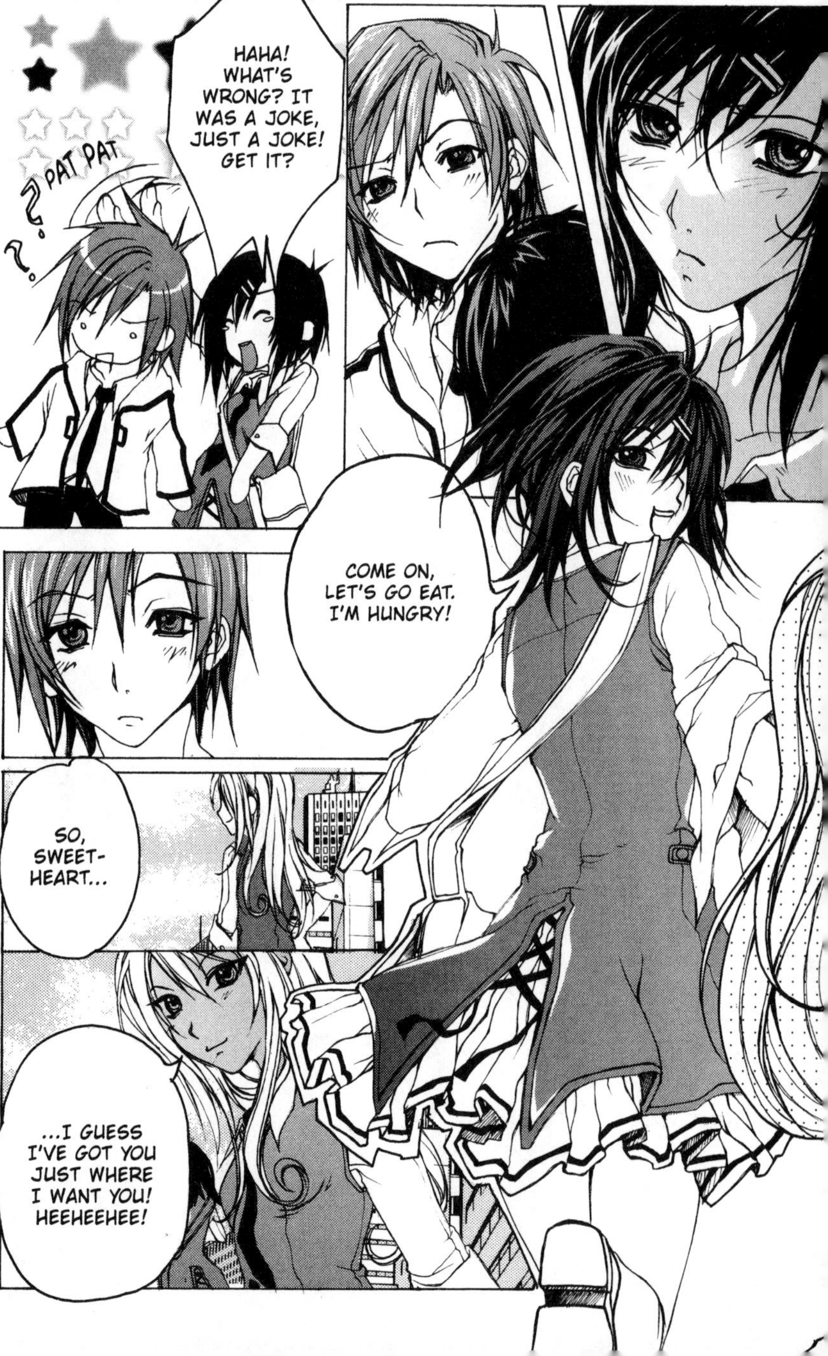
HAHA! WHAT'S WRONG? IT WAS A JOKE, JUST A JOKE! GET IT?
PAT PAT
COME ON, LET'S GO EAT. I'M HUNGRY!
SO, SWEET-HEART...
...I GUESS I'VE GOT YOU JUST WHERE I WANT YOU! HEEHEEHEE!

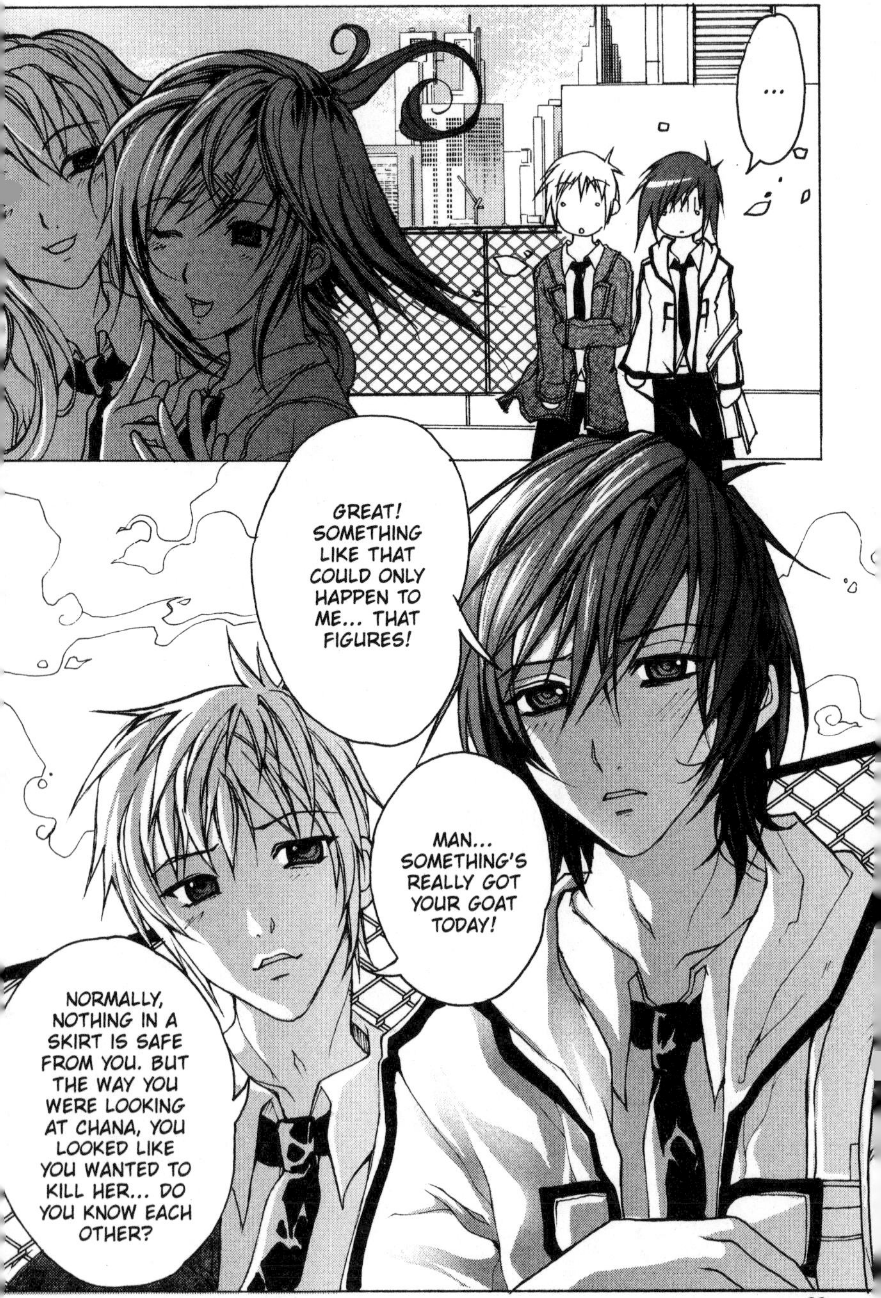
...
GREAT! SOMETHING LIKE THAT COULD ONLY HAPPEN TO ME... THAT FIGURES!
MAN... SOMETHING'S REALLY GOT YOUR GOAT TODAY!
NORMALLY, NOTHING IN A SKIRT IS SAFE FROM YOU. BUT THE WAY YOU WERE LOOKING AT CHANA, YOU LOOKED LIKE YOU WANTED TO KILL HER... DO YOU KNOW EACH OTHER?

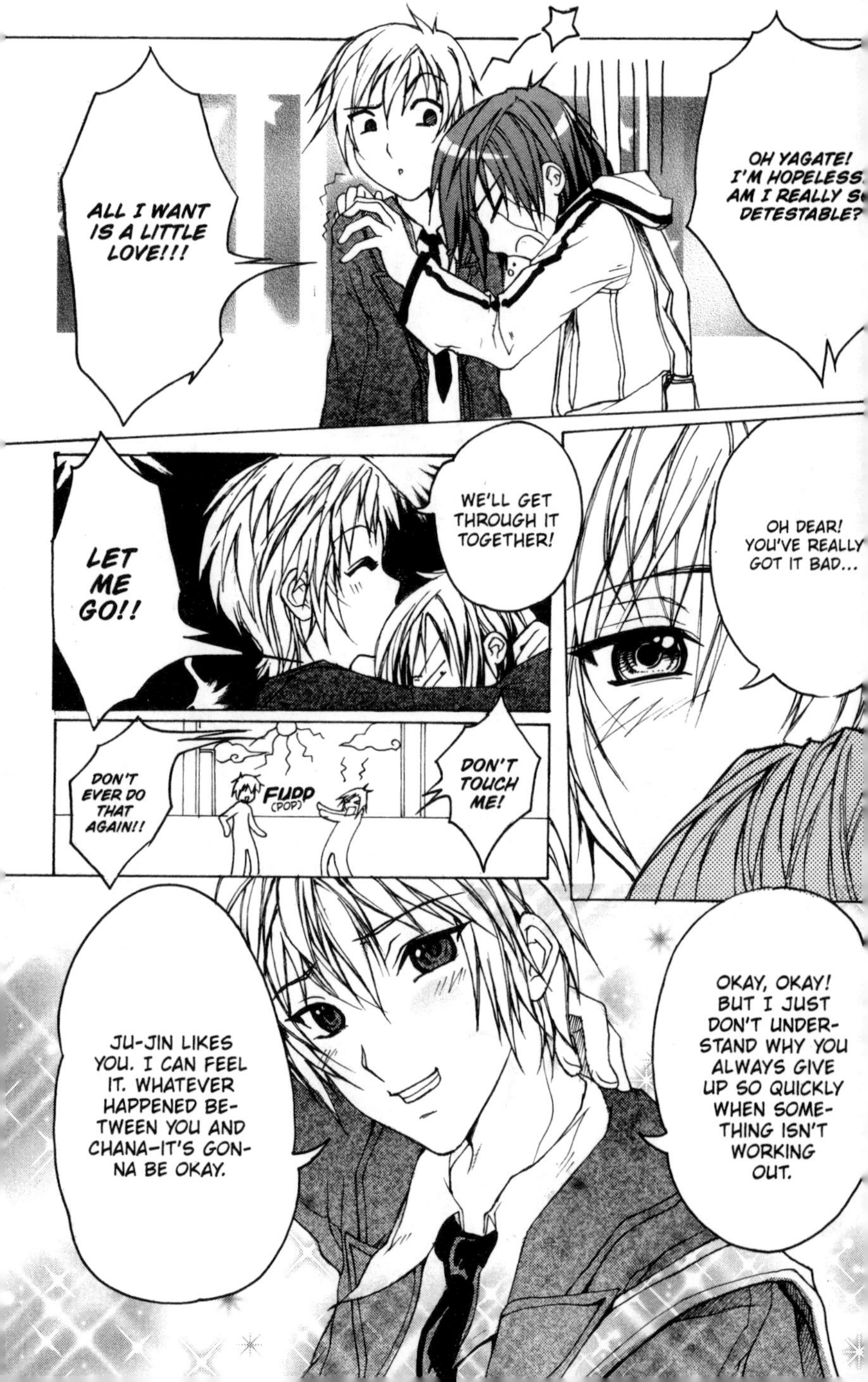
OH YAGATE! I'M HOPELESS AM I REALLY S DETESTABLE?
ALL I WANT IS A LITTLE LOVE!!!
OH DEAR! YOU'VE REALLY GOT IT BAD...
WE'LL GET THROUGH IT TOGETHER!
LET ME GO!!
DON'T TOUCH ME!
FUPP (POP)
DON'T EVER DO THAT AGAIN!!
OKAY, OKAY! BUT I JUST DON'T UNDER-STAND WHY YOU ALWAYS GIVE UP SO QUICKLY WHEN SOME-THING ISN'T WORKING OUT.
JU-JIN LIKES YOU. I CAN FEEL IT. WHATEVER HAPPENED BE-TWEEN YOU AND CHANA–IT'S GON-NA BE OKAY.

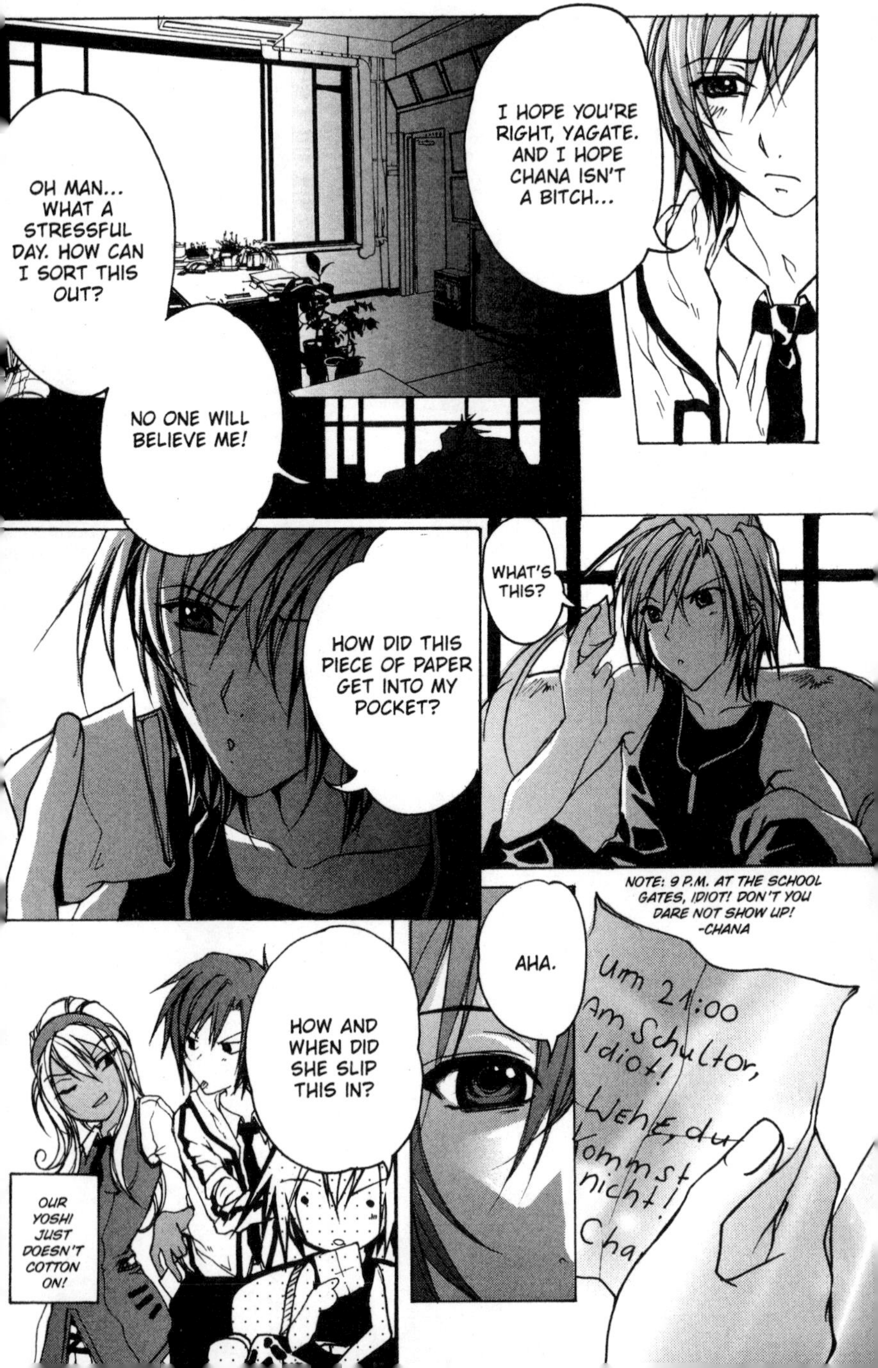
I HOPE YOU'RE RIGHT, YAGATE. AND I HOPE CHANA ISN'T A BITCH...
OH MAN... WHAT A STRESSFUL DAY. HOW CAN I SORT THIS OUT?
NO ONE WILL BELIEVE ME!
WHAT'S THIS?
HOW DID THIS PIECE OF PAPER GET INTO MY POCKET?
NOTE: 9 P.M. AT THE SCHOOL GATES, IDIOT! DON'T YOU DARE NOT SHOW UP! -CHANA
AHA.
Um 21:00 Am Schultor, Idiot! Wehe, du kommst nicht! Cha
HOW AND WHEN DID SHE SLIP THIS IN?
OUR YOSHI JUST DOESN'T COTTON ON!

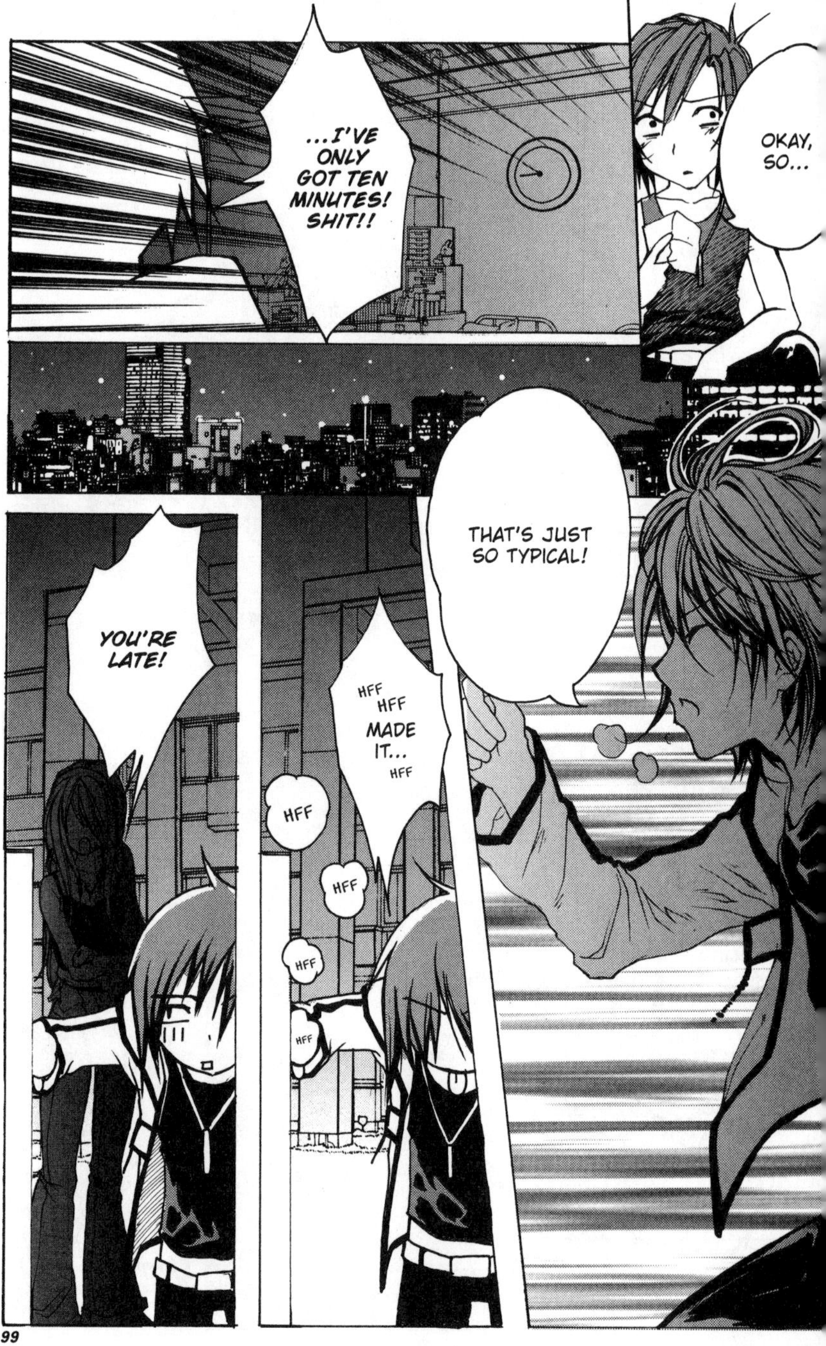
OKAY, SO...
...I'VE ONLY GOT TEN MINUTES! SHIT!!
THAT'S JUST SO TYPICAL!
HFF HFF MADE IT... HFF
HFF
HFF
HFF
HFF
YOU'RE LATE!

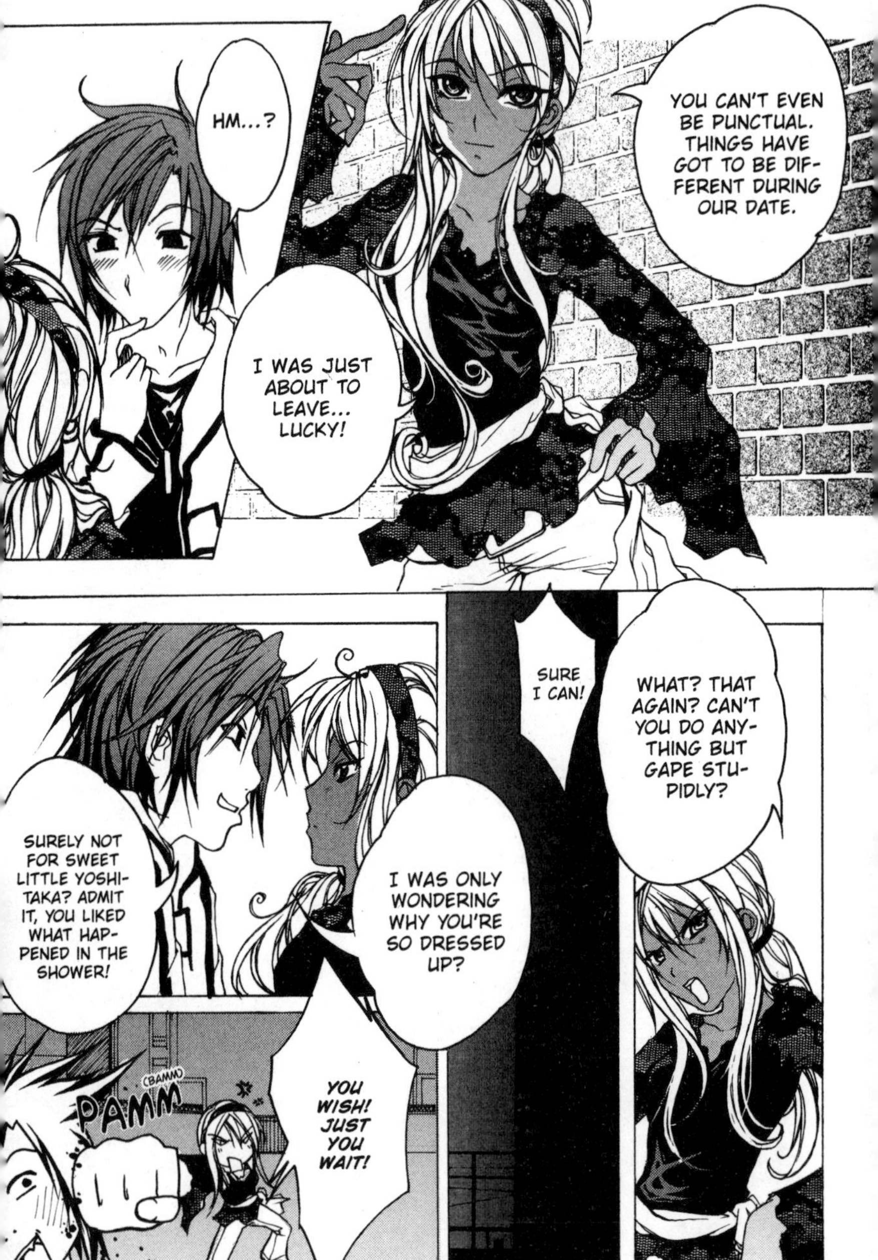
YOU CAN'T EVEN BE PUNCTUAL. THINGS HAVE GOT TO BE DIF-FERENT DURING OUR DATE.
I WAS JUST ABOUT TO LEAVE... LUCKY!
HM...?
WHAT? THAT AGAIN? CAN'T YOU DO ANY-THING BUT GAPE STU-PIDLY?
SURE I CAN!
I WAS ONLY WONDERING WHY YOU'RE SO DRESSED UP?
SURELY NOT FOR SWEET LITTLE YOSHI-TAKA? ADMIT IT, YOU LIKED WHAT HAP-PENED IN THE SHOWER!
YOU WISH! JUST YOU WAIT!
PAMM
(BAMM)

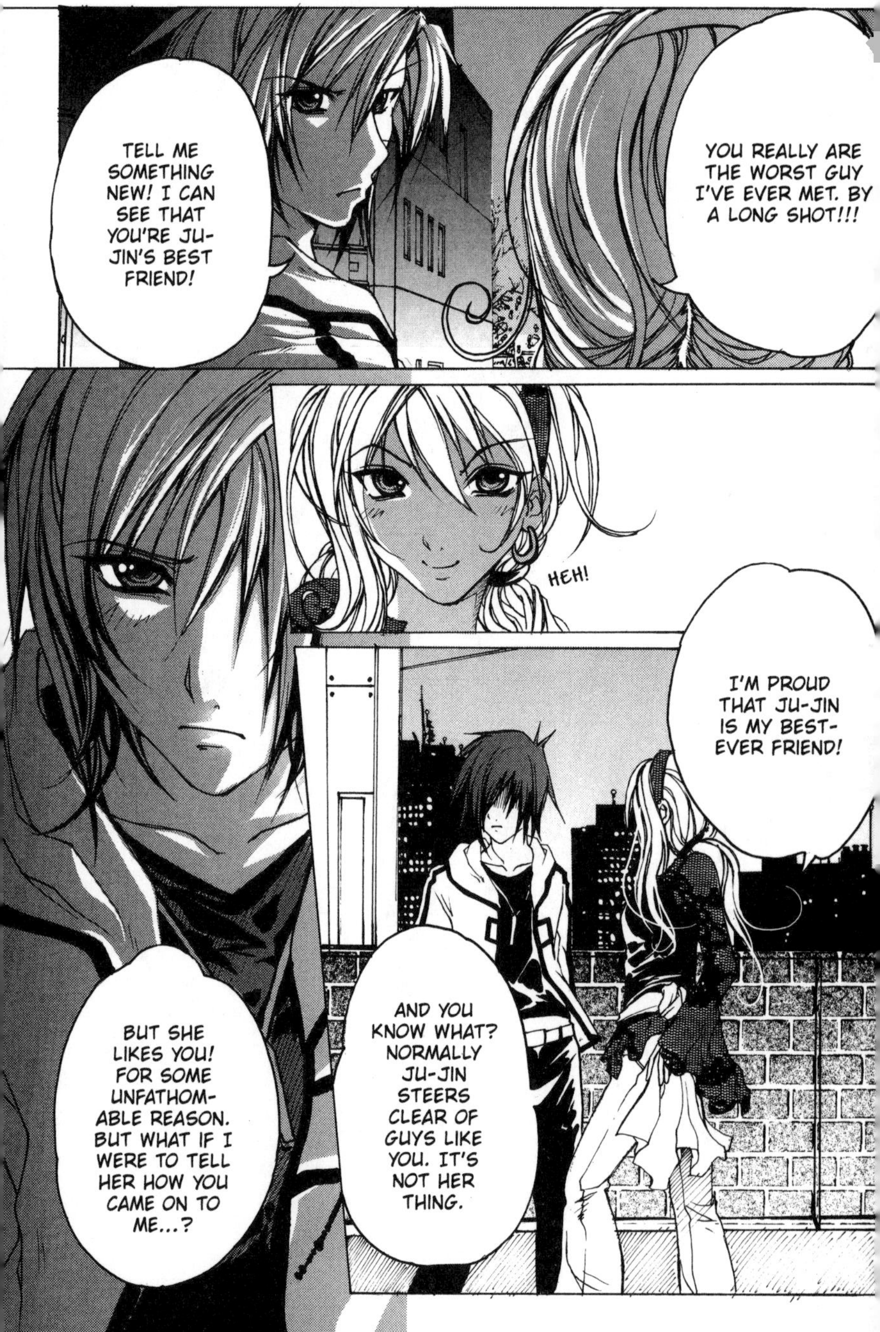
YOU REALLY ARE THE WORST GUY I'VE EVER MET. BY A LONG SHOT!!!
TELL ME SOMETHING NEW! I CAN SEE THAT YOU'RE JU-JIN'S BEST FRIEND!
HEH!
I'M PROUD THAT JU-JIN IS MY BEST-EVER FRIEND!
AND YOU KNOW WHAT? NORMALLY JU-JIN STEERS CLEAR OF GUYS LIKE YOU. IT'S NOT HER THING.
BUT SHE LIKES YOU! FOR SOME UNFATHOM-ABLE REASON. BUT WHAT IF I WERE TO TELL HER HOW YOU CAME ON TO ME...?

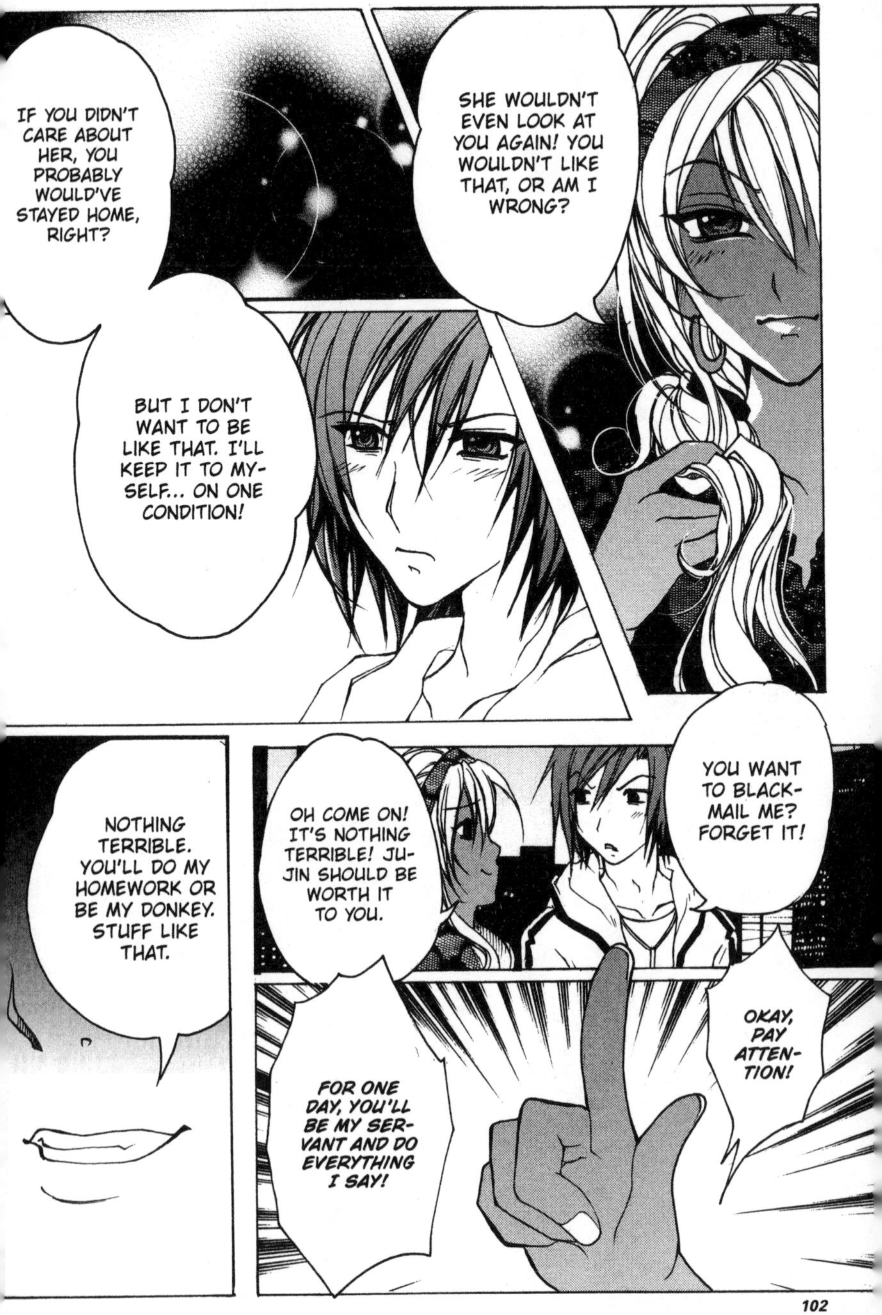
SHE WOULDN'T EVEN LOOK AT YOU AGAIN! YOU WOULDN'T LIKE THAT, OR AM I WRONG?
IF YOU DIDN'T CARE ABOUT HER, YOU PROBABLY WOULD'VE STAYED HOME, RIGHT?
BUT I DON'T WANT TO BE LIKE THAT. I'LL KEEP IT TO MY-SELF... ON ONE CONDITION!
YOU WANT TO BLACK-MAIL ME? FORGET IT!
OH COME ON! IT'S NOTHING TERRIBLE! JU-JIN SHOULD BE WORTH IT TO YOU.
OKAY, PAY ATTEN-TION!
FOR ONE DAY, YOU'LL BE MY SER-VANT AND DO EVERYTHING I SAY!
NOTHING TERRIBLE. YOU'LL DO MY HOMEWORK OR BE MY DONKEY. STUFF LIKE THAT.

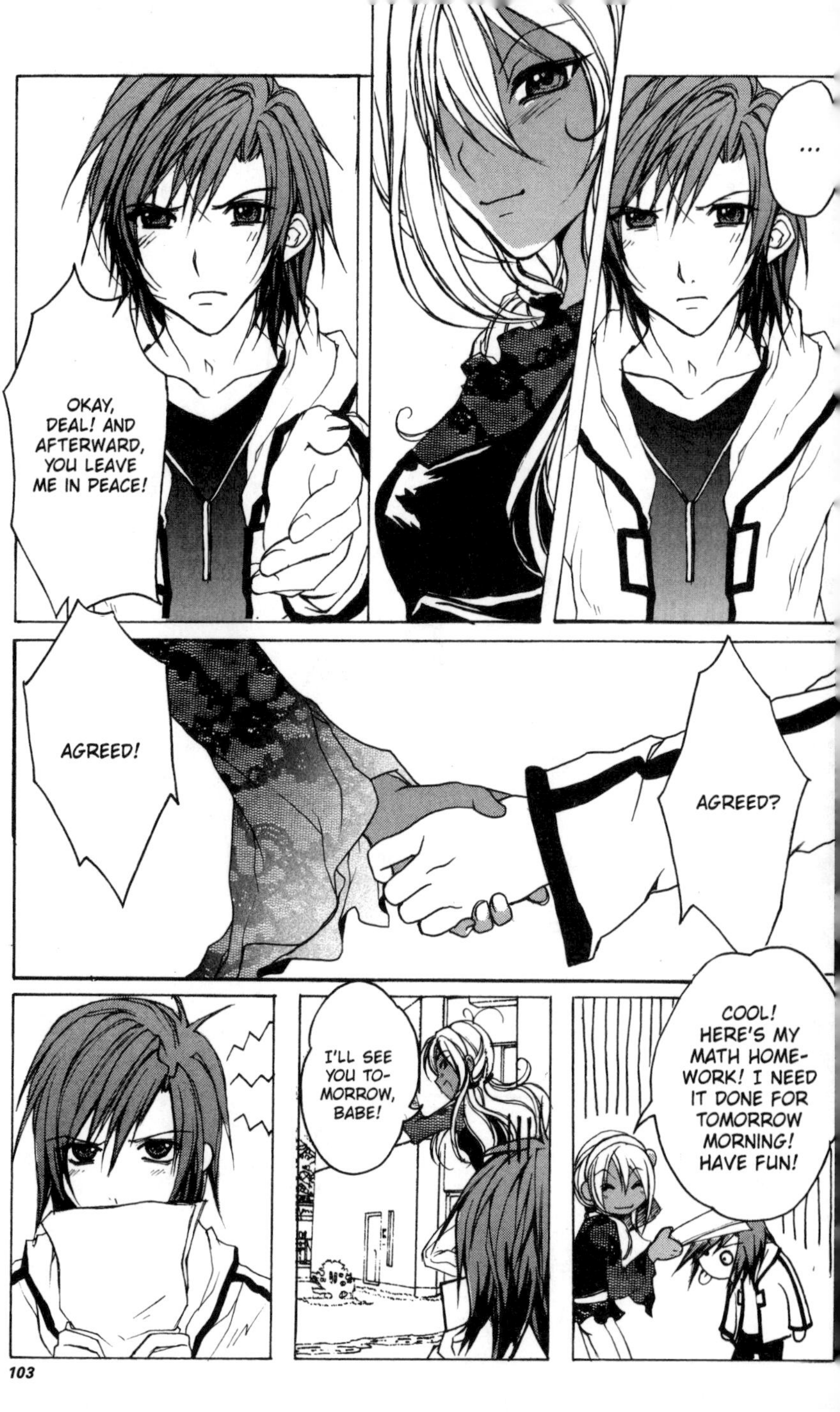
...
OKAY, DEAL! AND AFTERWARD, YOU LEAVE ME IN PEACE!
AGREED?
AGREED!
COOL! HERE'S MY MATH HOME-WORK! I NEED IT DONE FOR TOMORROW MORNING! HAVE FUN!
I'LL SEE YOU TO-MORROW, BABE!

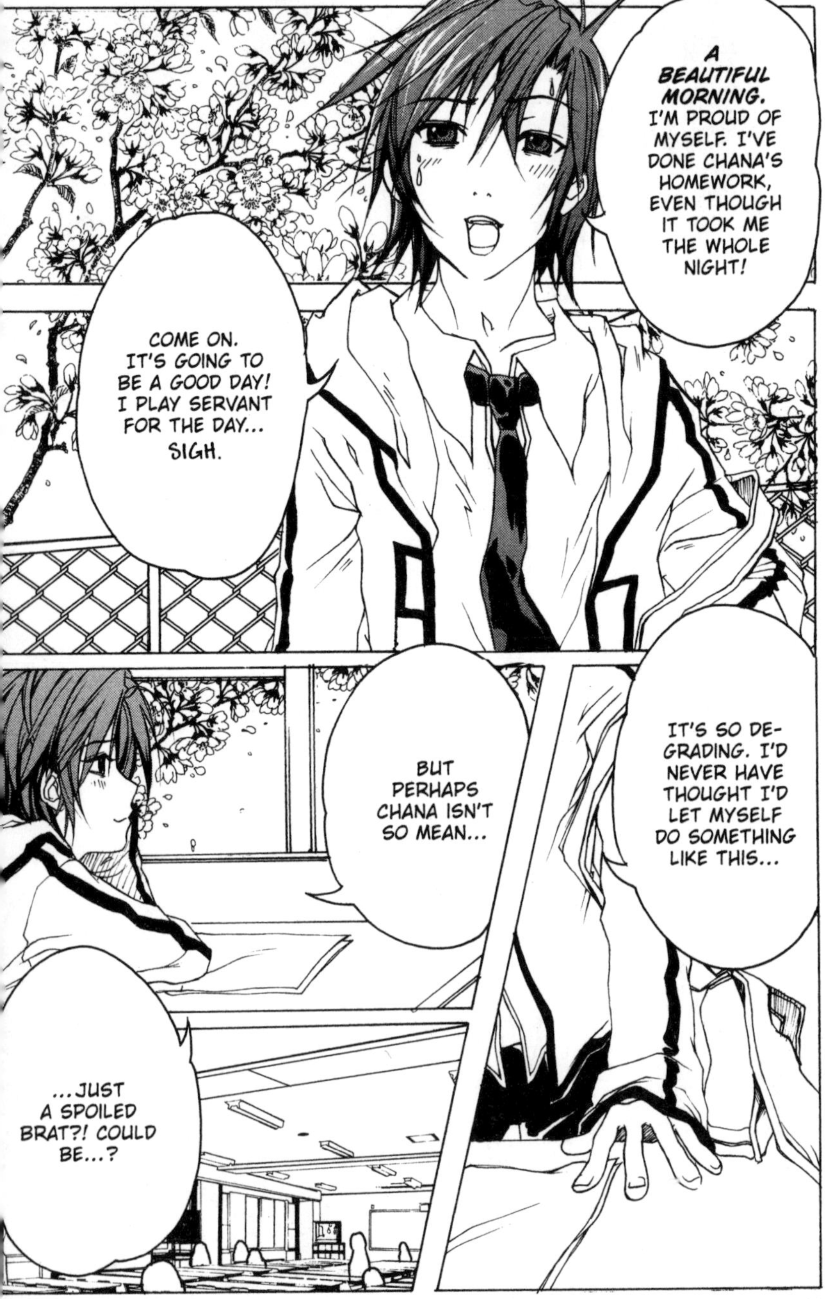
A BEAUTIFUL MORNING. I'M PROUD OF MYSELF. I'VE DONE CHANA'S HOMEWORK, EVEN THOUGH IT TOOK ME THE WHOLE NIGHT!
COME ON. IT'S GOING TO BE A GOOD DAY! I PLAY SERVANT FOR THE DAY... SIGH.
IT'S SO DE-GRADING. I'D NEVER HAVE THOUGHT I'D LET MYSELF DO SOMETHING LIKE THIS...
BUT PERHAPS CHANA ISN'T SO MEAN...
...JUST A SPOILED BRAT?! COULD BE...?

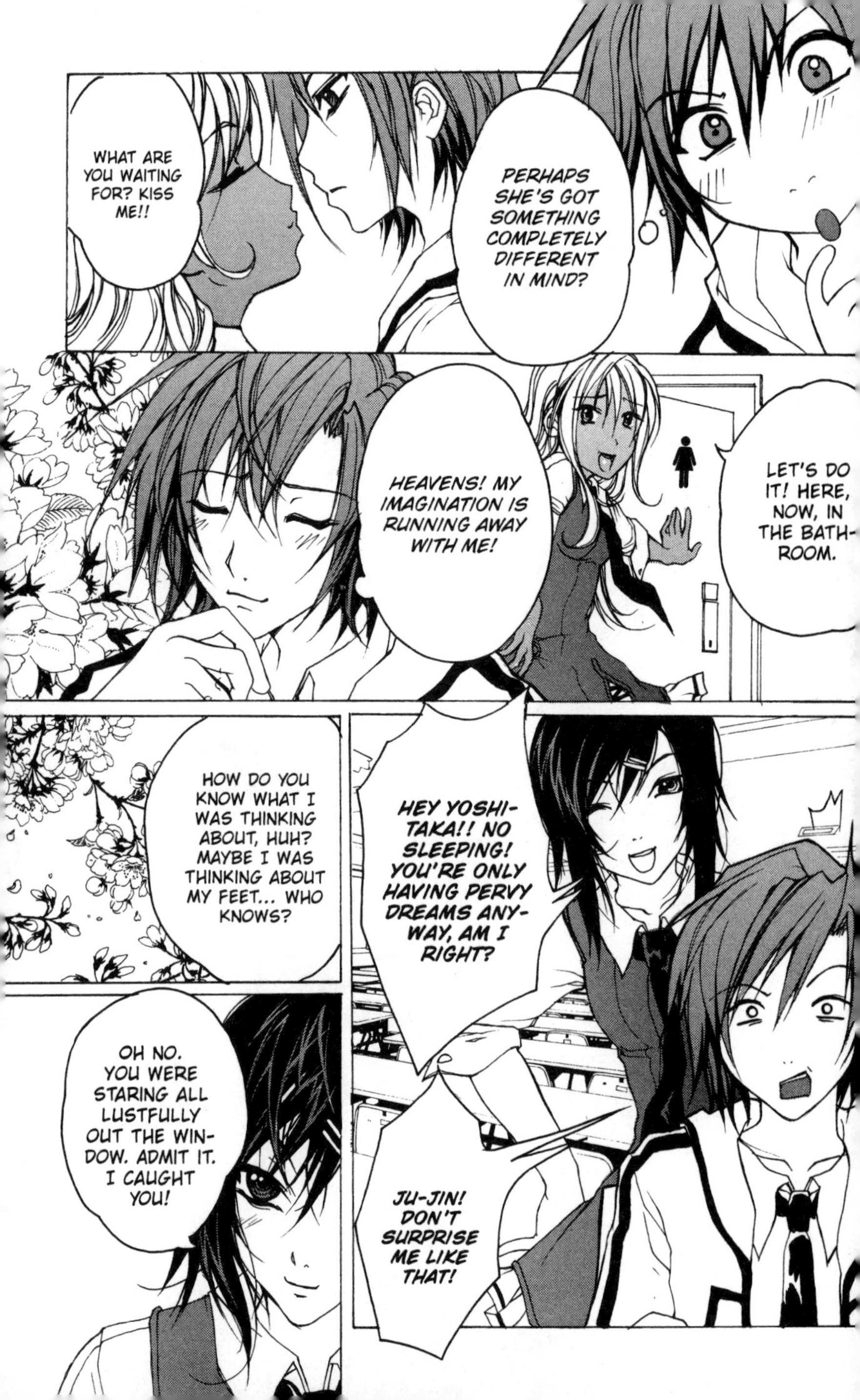
PERHAPS SHE'S GOT SOMETHING COMPLETELY DIFFERENT IN MIND?
WHAT ARE YOU WAITING FOR? KISS ME!!
LET'S DO IT! HERE, NOW, IN THE BATH-ROOM.
HEAVENS! MY IMAGINATION IS RUNNING AWAY WITH ME!
HEY YOSHI-TAKA!! NO SLEEPING! YOU'RE ONLY HAVING PERVY DREAMS ANY-WAY, AM I RIGHT?
JU-JIN! DON'T SURPRISE ME LIKE THAT!
HOW DO YOU KNOW WHAT I WAS THINKING ABOUT, HUH? MAYBE I WAS THINKING ABOUT MY FEET... WHO KNOWS?
OH NO. YOU WERE STARING ALL LUSTFULLY OUT THE WIN-DOW. ADMIT IT. I CAUGHT YOU!

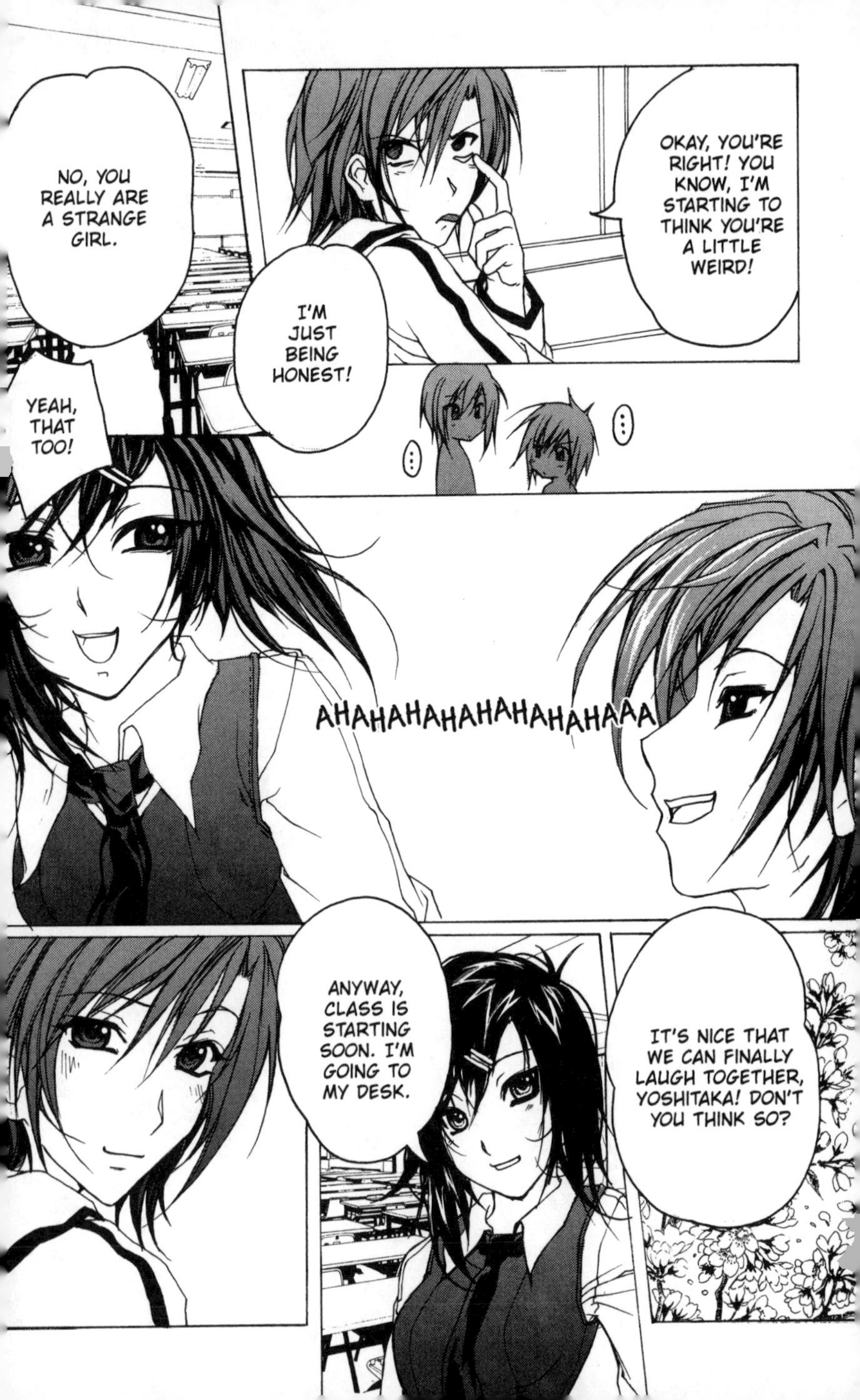
OKAY, YOU'RE RIGHT! YOU KNOW, I'M STARTING TO THINK YOU'RE A LITTLE WEIRD!
I'M JUST BEING HONEST!
NO, YOU REALLY ARE A STRANGE GIRL.
YEAH, THAT TOO!
...
...
AHAHAHAHAHAHAHAHAHAAA
IT'S NICE THAT WE CAN FINALLY LAUGH TOGETHER, YOSHITAKA! DON'T YOU THINK SO?
ANYWAY, CLASS IS STARTING SOON. I'M GOING TO MY DESK.

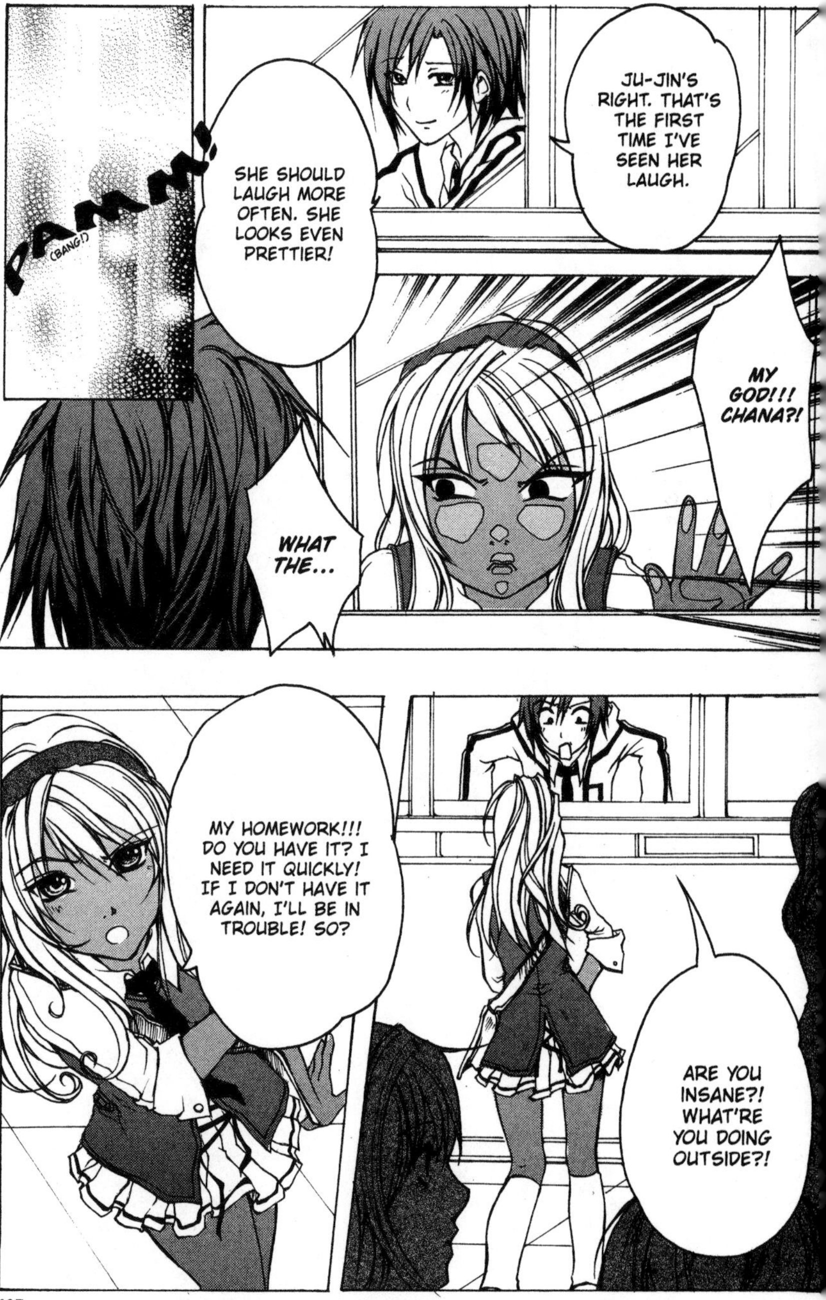
JU-JIN'S RIGHT. THAT'S THE FIRST TIME I'VE SEEN HER LAUGH.
SHE SHOULD LAUGH MORE OFTEN. SHE LOOKS EVEN PRETTIER!
PAMM! (BANG!)
MY GOD!!! CHANA?!
WHAT THE...
ARE YOU INSANE?! WHAT'RE YOU DOING OUTSIDE?!
MY HOMEWORK!!! DO YOU HAVE IT? I NEED IT QUICKLY! IF I DON'T HAVE IT AGAIN, I'LL BE IN TROUBLE! SO?

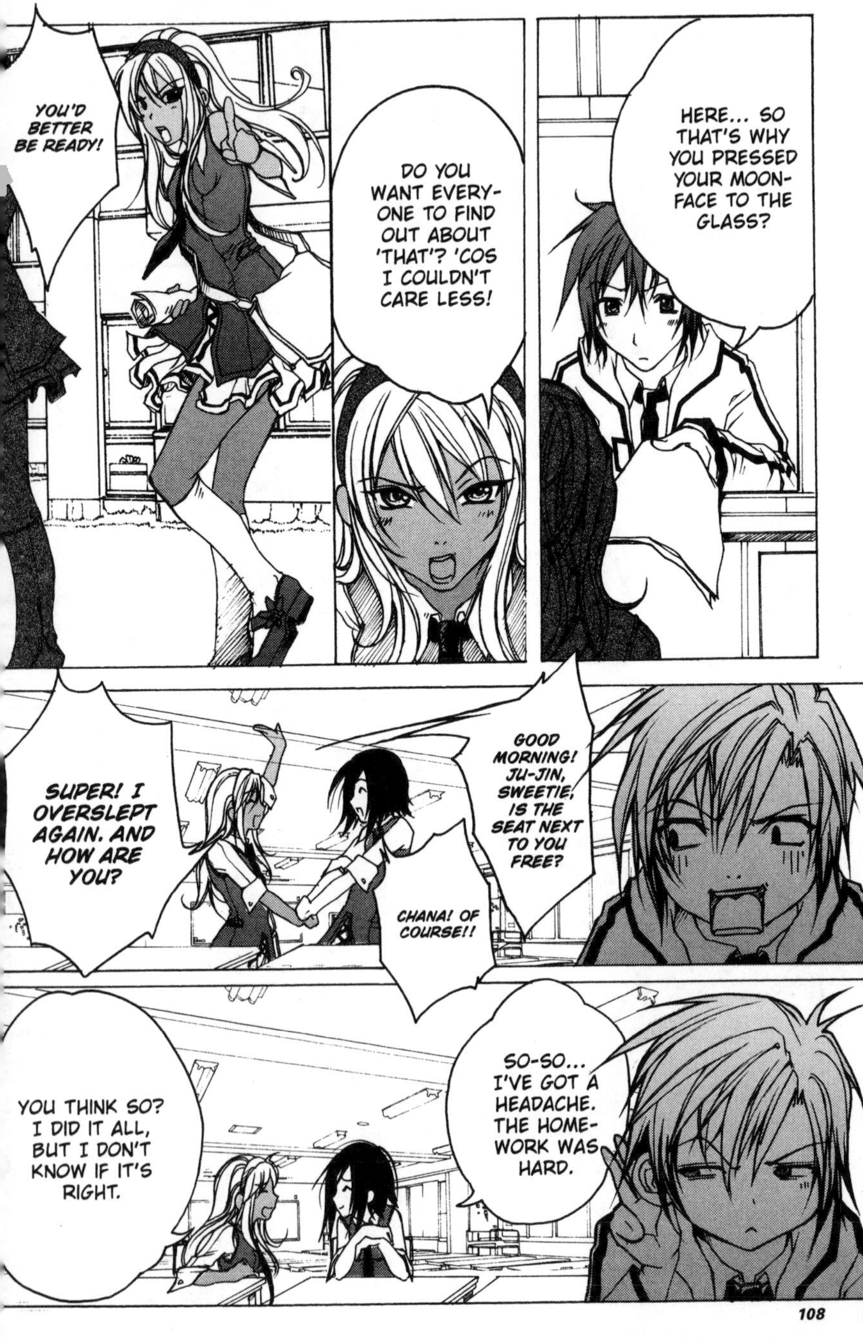
HERE... SO THAT'S WHY YOU PRESSED YOUR MOON-FACE TO THE GLASS?
DO YOU WANT EVERY-ONE TO FIND OUT ABOUT 'THAT'? 'COS I COULDN'T CARE LESS!
YOU'D BETTER BE READY!
GOOD MORNING! JU-JIN, SWEETIE, IS THE SEAT NEXT TO YOU FREE?
CHANA! OF COURSE!!
SUPER! I OVERSLEPT AGAIN. AND HOW ARE YOU?
SO-SO... I'VE GOT A HEADACHE. THE HOME-WORK WAS HARD.
YOU THINK SO? I DID IT ALL, BUT I DON'T KNOW IF IT'S RIGHT.

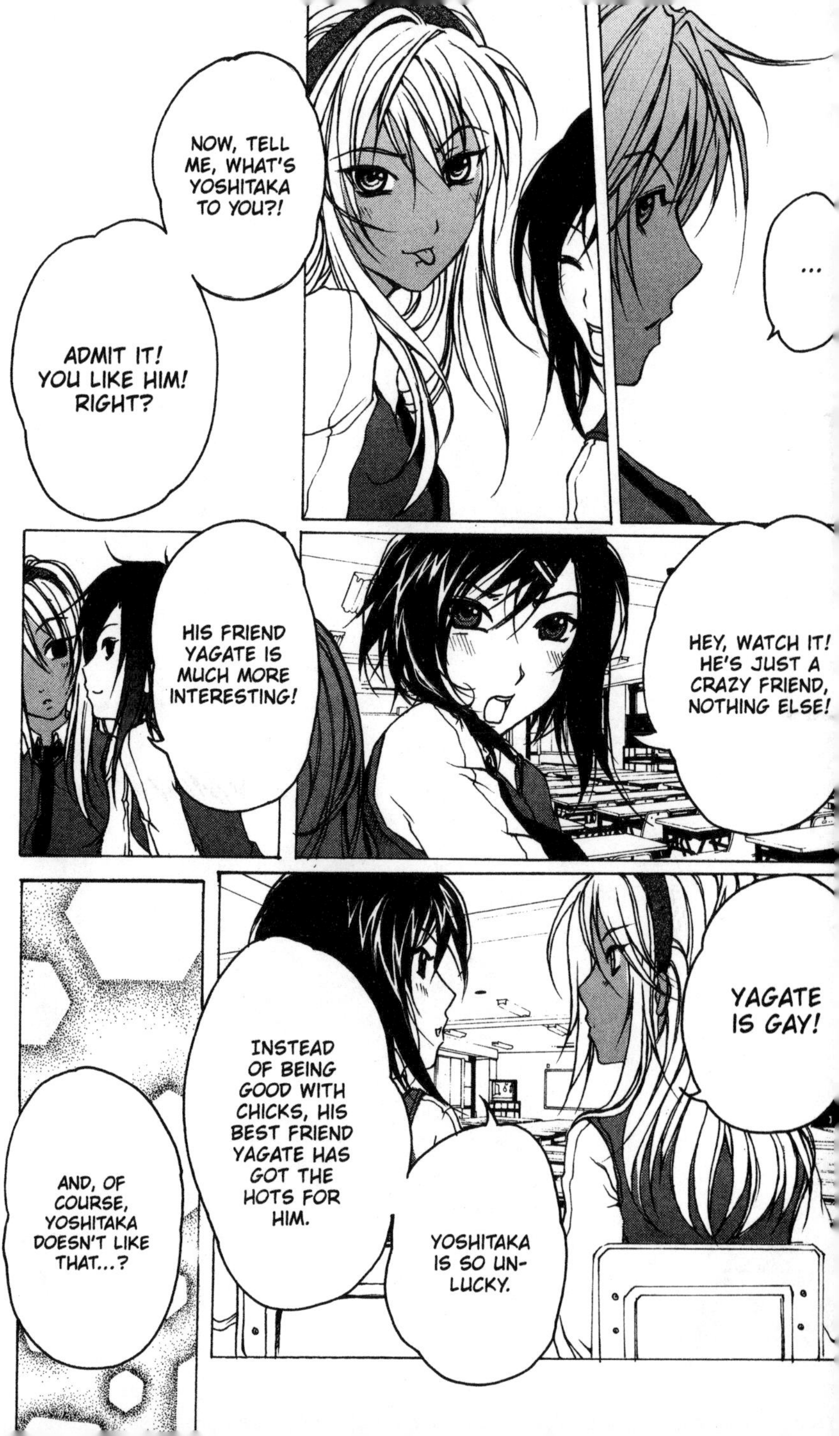
...
NOW, TELL ME, WHAT'S YOSHITAKA TO YOU?!
ADMIT IT! YOU LIKE HIM! RIGHT?
HEY, WATCH IT! HE'S JUST A CRAZY FRIEND, NOTHING ELSE!
HIS FRIEND YAGATE IS MUCH MORE INTERESTING!
YAGATE IS GAY!
INSTEAD OF BEING GOOD WITH CHICKS, HIS BEST FRIEND YAGATE HAS GOT THE HOTS FOR HIM.
YOSHITAKA IS SO UN-LUCKY.
AND, OF COURSE, YOSHITAKA DOESN'T LIKE THAT...?

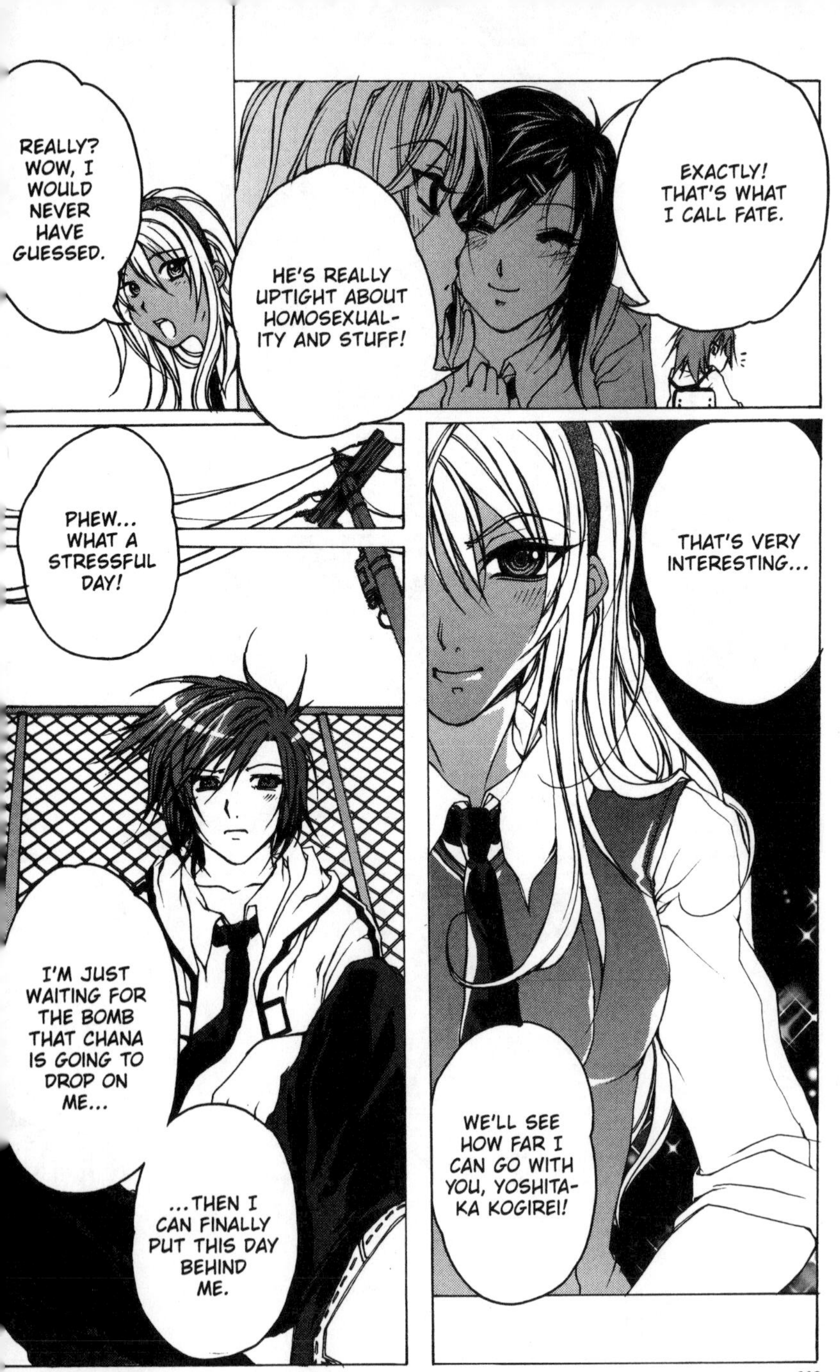
EXACTLY! THAT'S WHAT I CALL FATE.
HE'S REALLY UPTIGHT ABOUT HOMOSEXUAL-ITY AND STUFF!
REALLY? WOW, I WOULD NEVER HAVE GUESSED.
THAT'S VERY INTERESTING...
WE'LL SEE HOW FAR I CAN GO WITH YOU, YOSHITA-KA KOGIREI!
PHEW... WHAT A STRESSFUL DAY!
I'M JUST WAITING FOR THE BOMB THAT CHANA IS GOING TO DROP ON ME...
...THEN I CAN FINALLY PUT THIS DAY BEHIND ME.

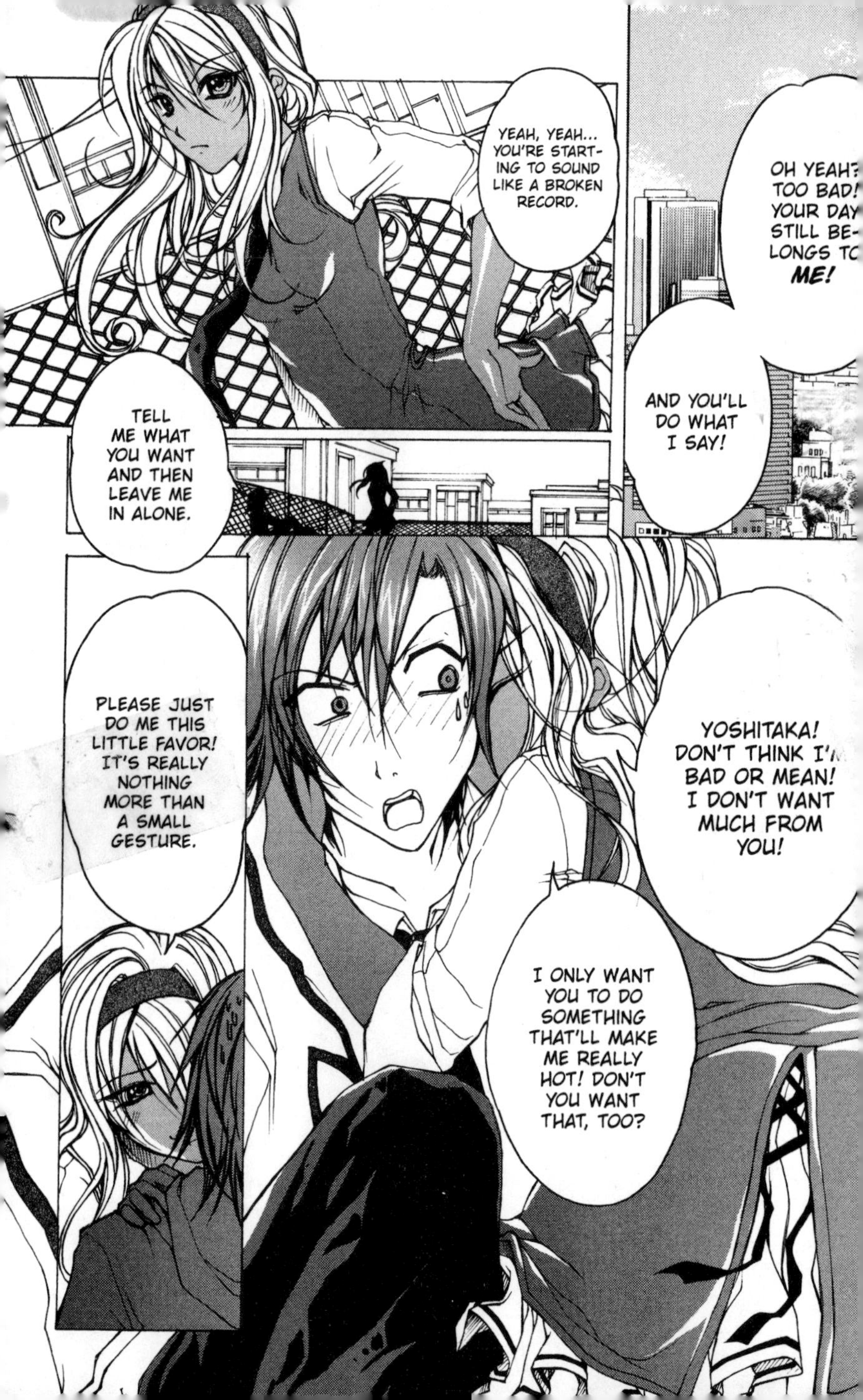
OH YEAH? TOO BAD! YOUR DAY STILL BE-LONGS TO ME!
AND YOU'LL DO WHAT I SAY!
YEAH, YEAH... YOU'RE START-ING TO SOUND LIKE A BROKEN RECORD.
TELL ME WHAT YOU WANT AND THEN LEAVE ME IN ALONE.
YOSHITAKA! DON'T THINK I'M BAD OR MEAN! I DON'T WANT MUCH FROM YOU!
I ONLY WANT YOU TO DO SOMETHING THAT'LL MAKE ME REALLY HOT! DON'T YOU WANT THAT, TOO?
PLEASE JUST DO ME THIS LITTLE FAVOR! IT'S REALLY NOTHING MORE THAN A SMALL GESTURE.

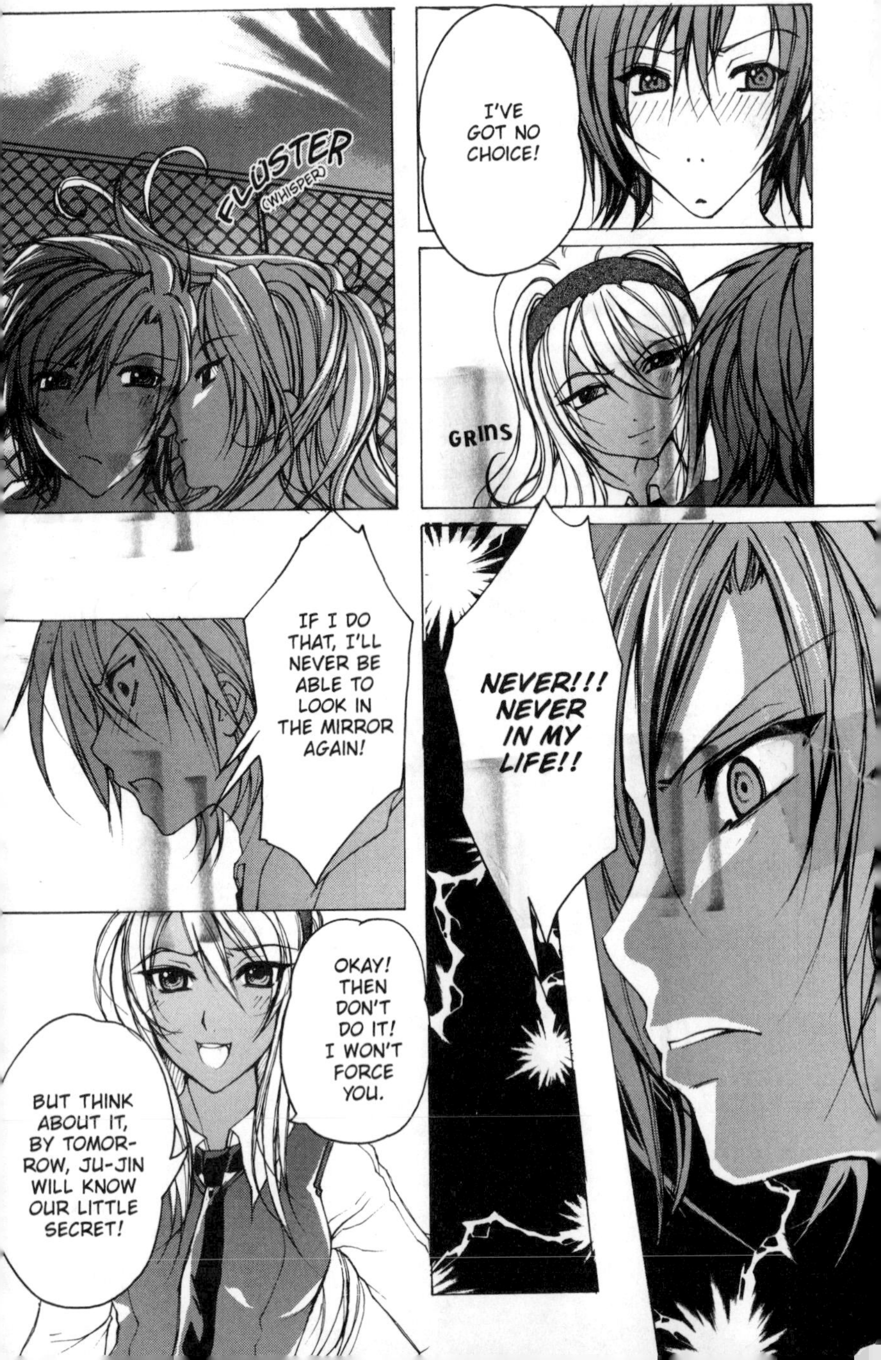
I'VE GOT NO CHOICE!
GRINS
FLUSTER
(WHISPER)
NEVER!!! NEVER IN MY LIFE!!
IF I DO THAT, I'LL NEVER BE ABLE TO LOOK IN THE MIRROR AGAIN!
OKAY! THEN DON'T DO IT! I WON'T FORCE YOU.
BUT THINK ABOUT IT, BY TOMOR-ROW, JU-JIN WILL KNOW OUR LITTLE SECRET!

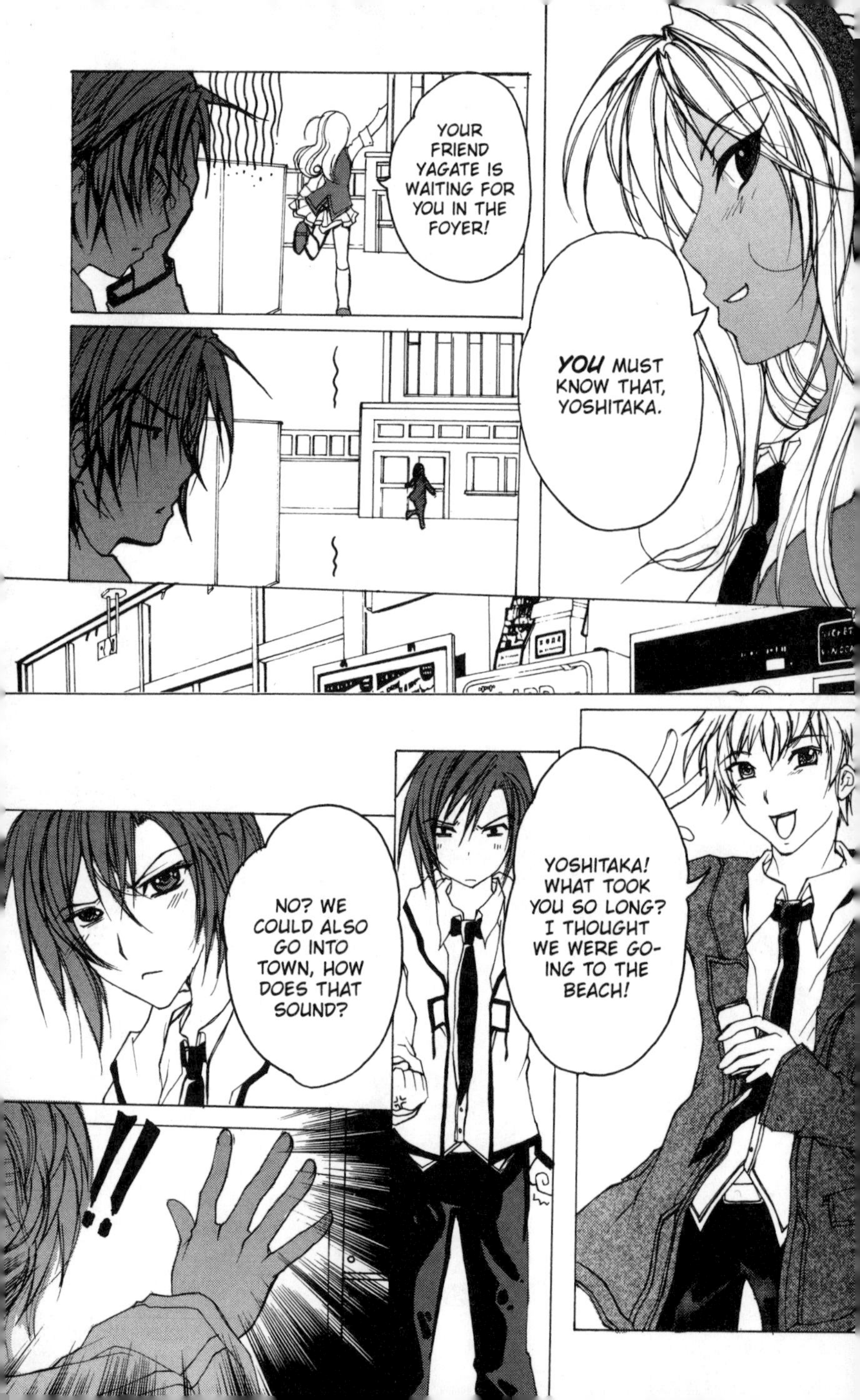
YOUR FRIEND YAGATE IS WAITING FOR YOU IN THE FOYER!
YOU MUST KNOW THAT, YOSHITAKA.
YOSHITAKA! WHAT TOOK YOU SO LONG? I THOUGHT WE WERE GO-ING TO THE BEACH!
NO? WE COULD ALSO GO INTO TOWN, HOW DOES THAT SOUND?

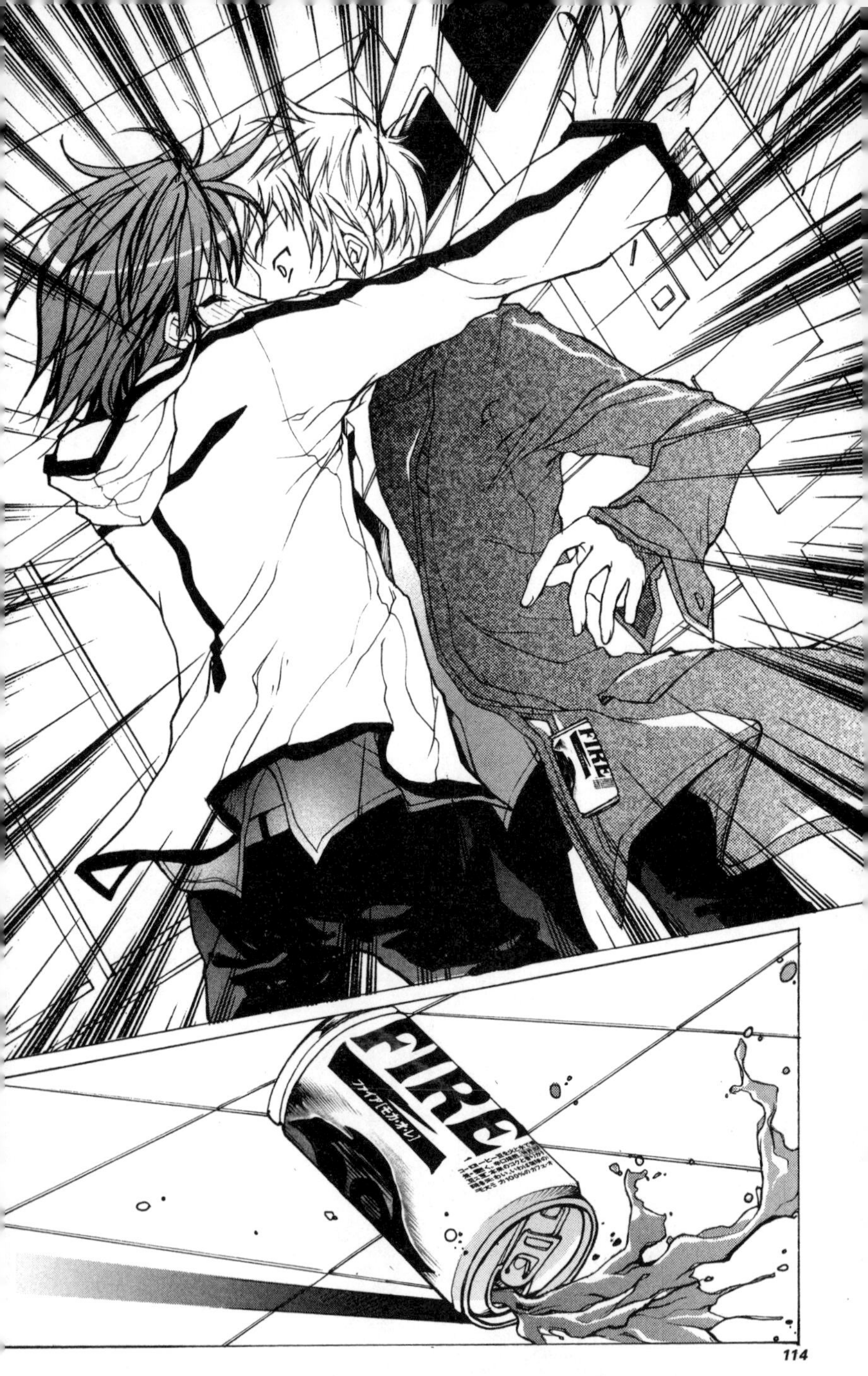
FIRE

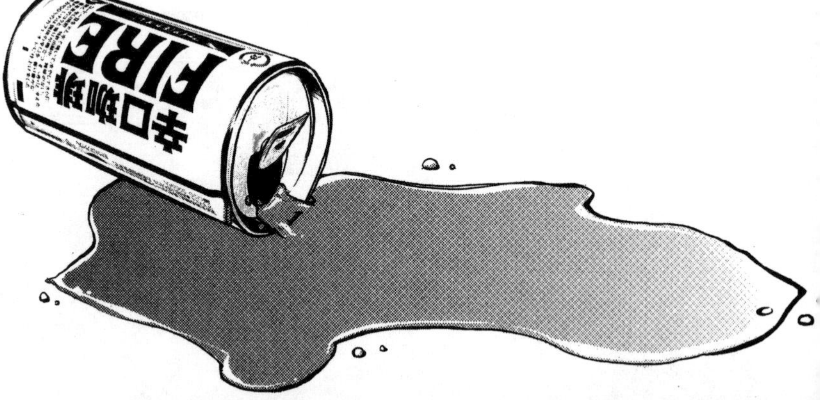
辛口珈琲
FIRE

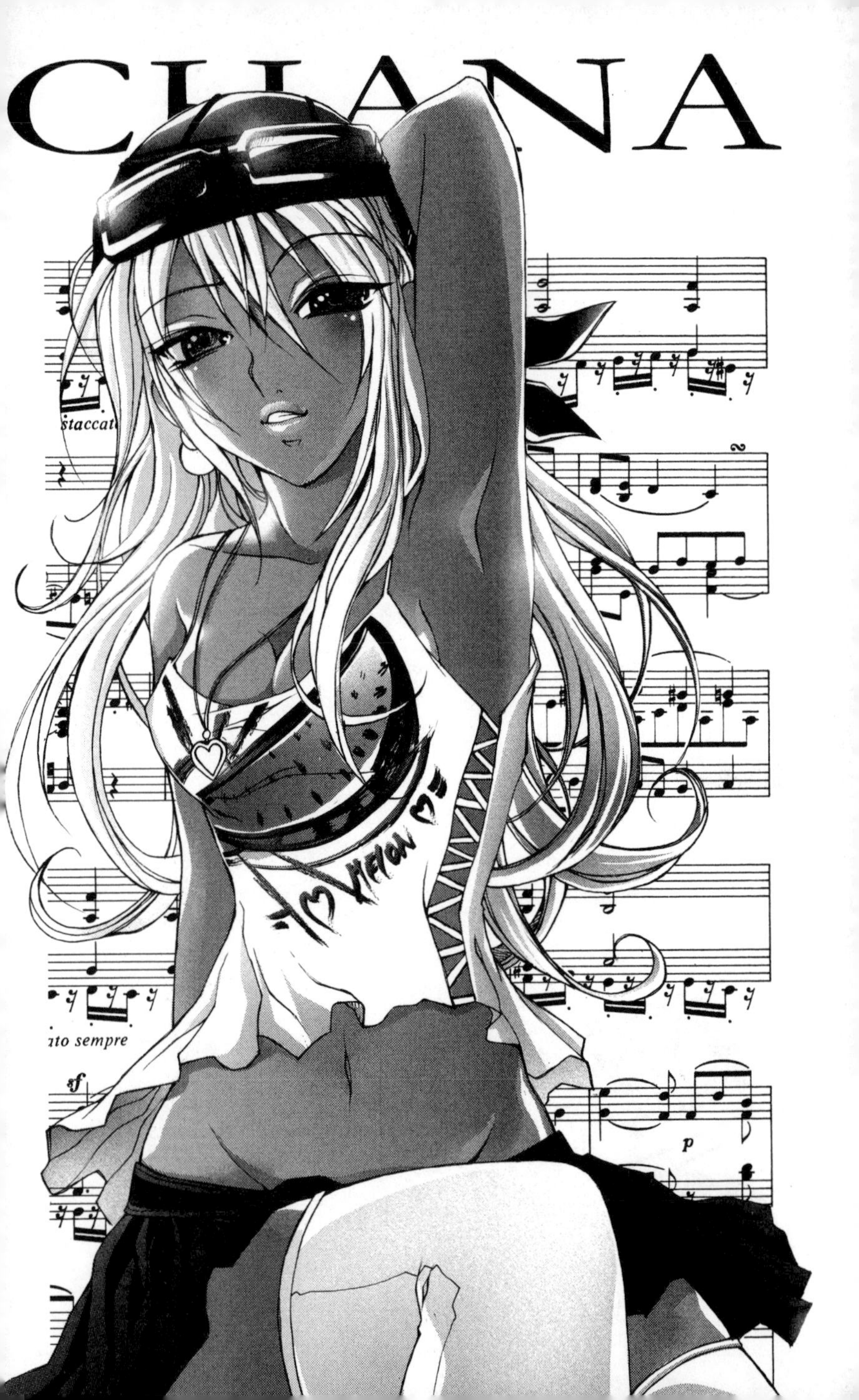
CHANA
staccat
ato sempre
sf
p

CHAPTER 5: CONVERSATION

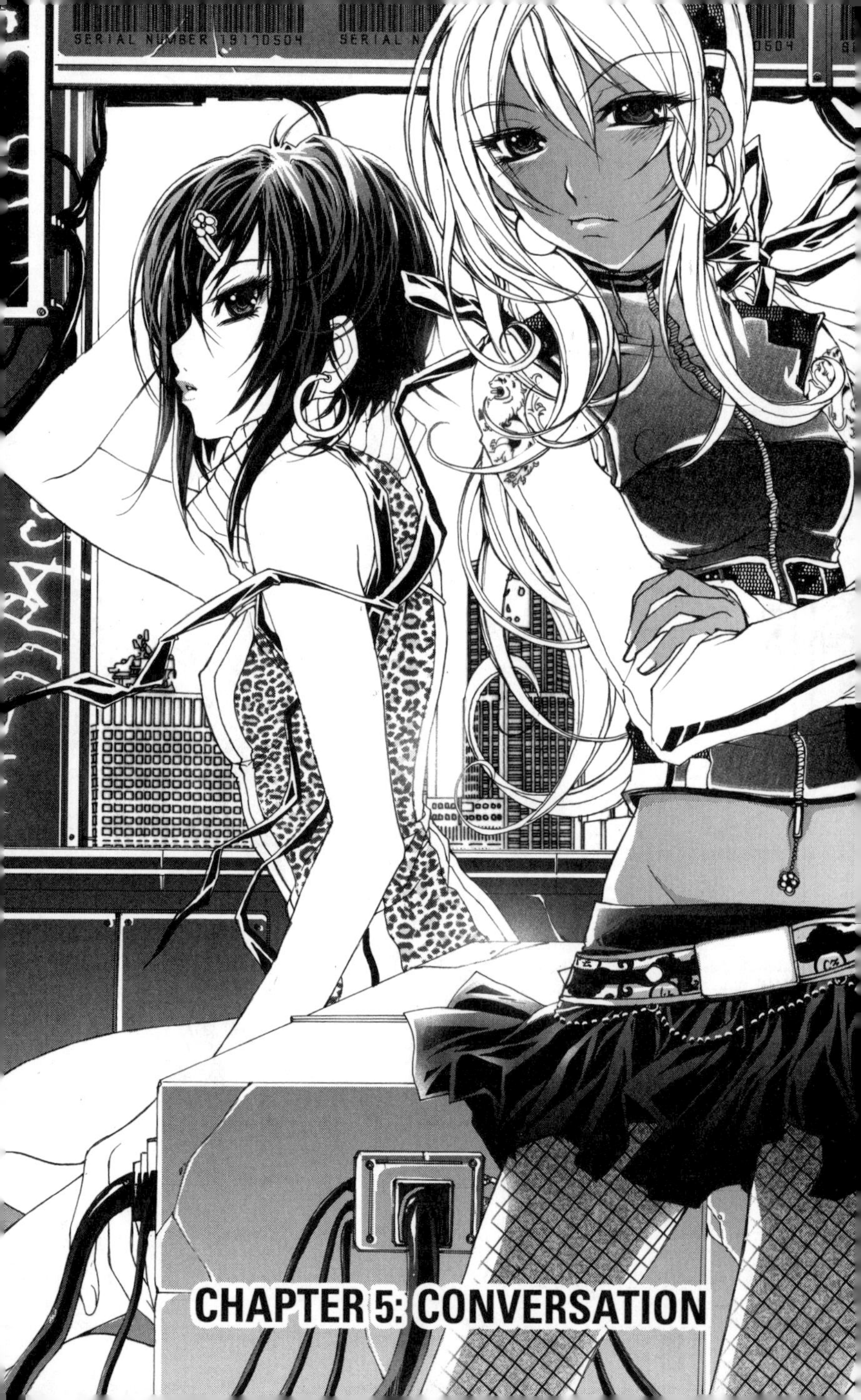
SERIAL NUMBER 19170504

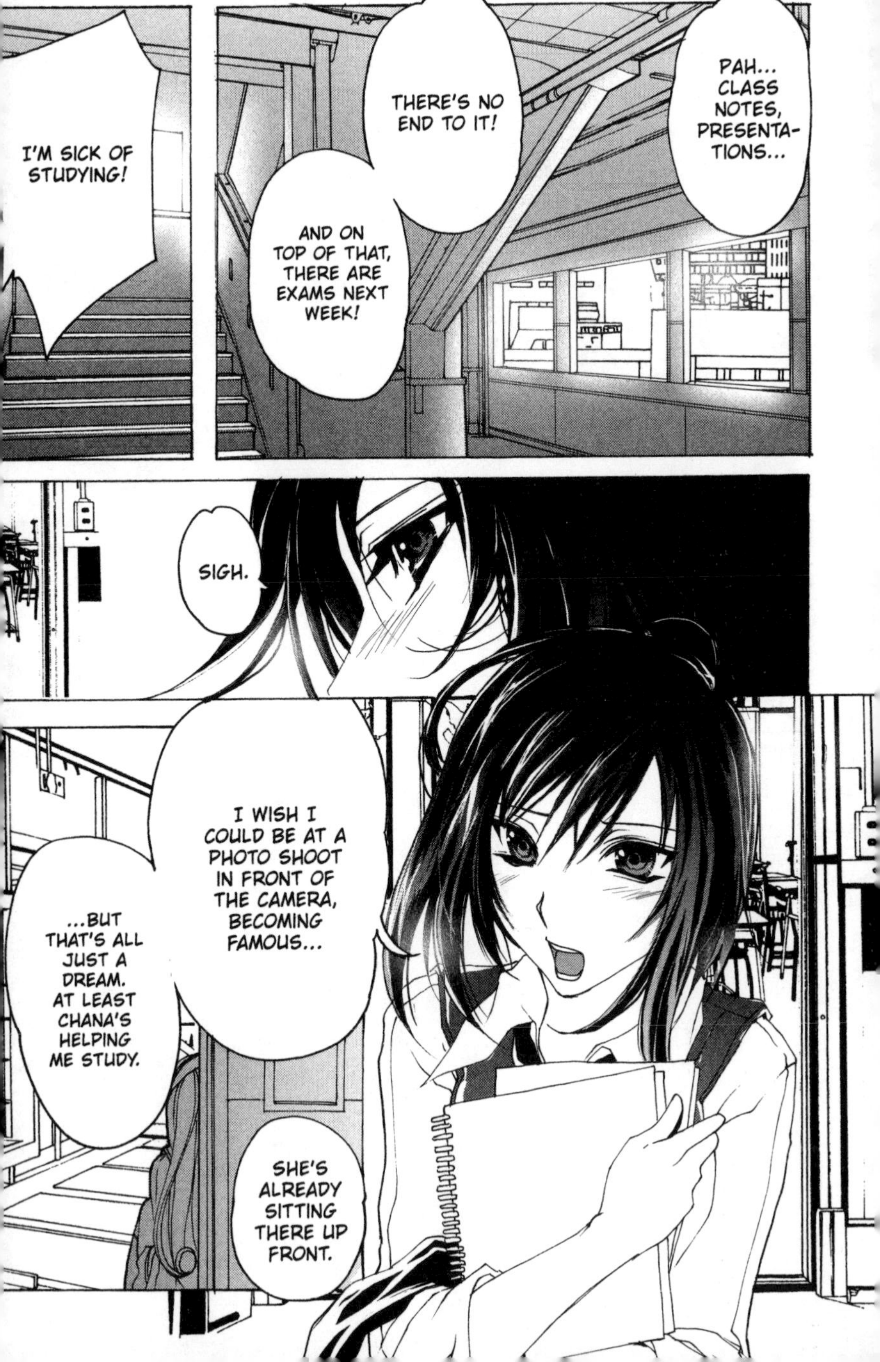
PAH... CLASS NOTES, PRESENTA- TIONS...
THERE'S NO END TO IT!
AND ON TOP OF THAT, THERE ARE EXAMS NEXT WEEK!
I'M SICK OF STUDYING!
SIGH.
I WISH I COULD BE AT A PHOTO SHOOT IN FRONT OF THE CAMERA, BECOMING FAMOUS...
...BUT THAT'S ALL JUST A DREAM. AT LEAST CHANA'S HELPING ME STUDY.
SHE'S ALREADY SITTING THERE UP FRONT.

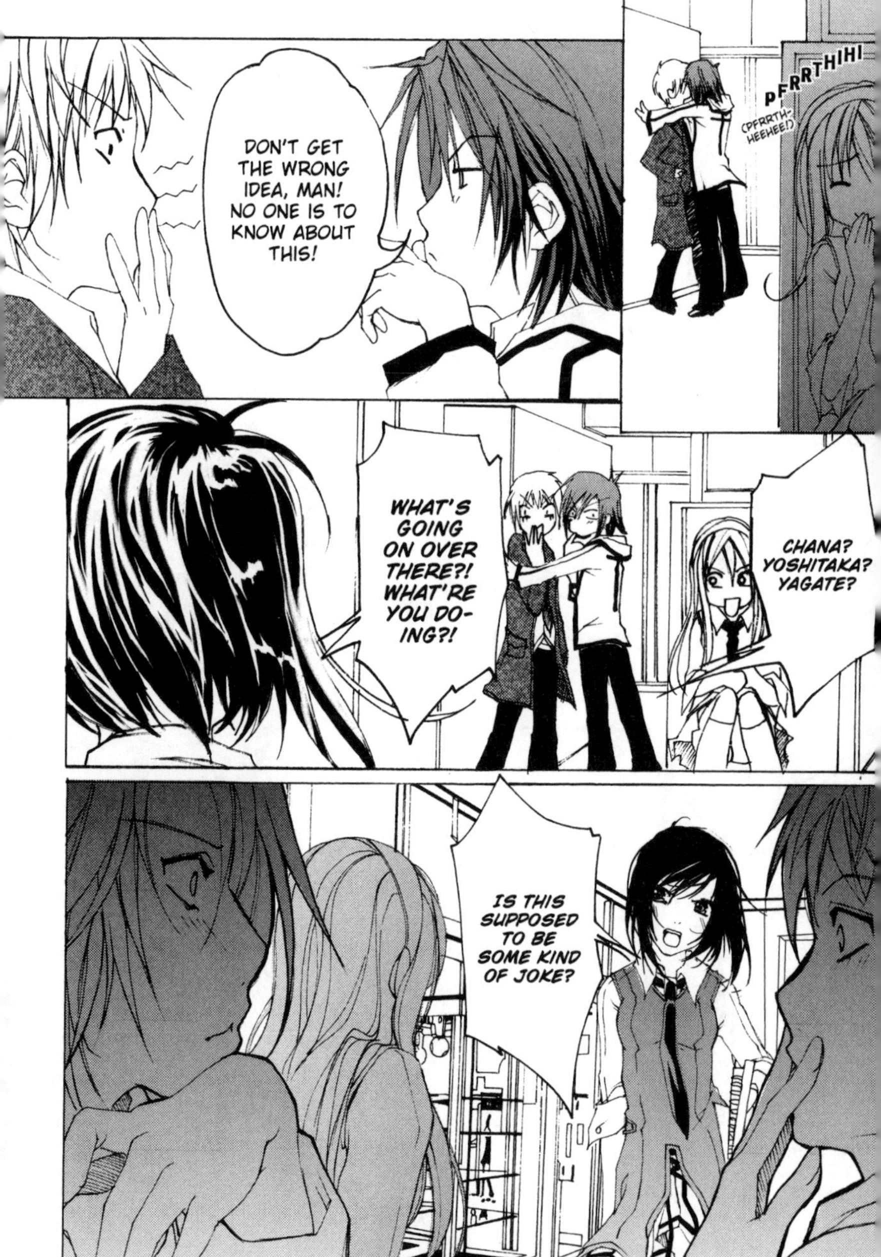
PFRRTHIHI
(PFRRTH-HEEHEE!)
DON'T GET THE WRONG IDEA, MAN! NO ONE IS TO KNOW ABOUT THIS!
CHANA? YOSHITAKA? YAGATE?
WHAT'S GOING ON OVER THERE?! WHAT'RE YOU DO-ING?!
IS THIS SUPPOSED TO BE SOME KIND OF JOKE?

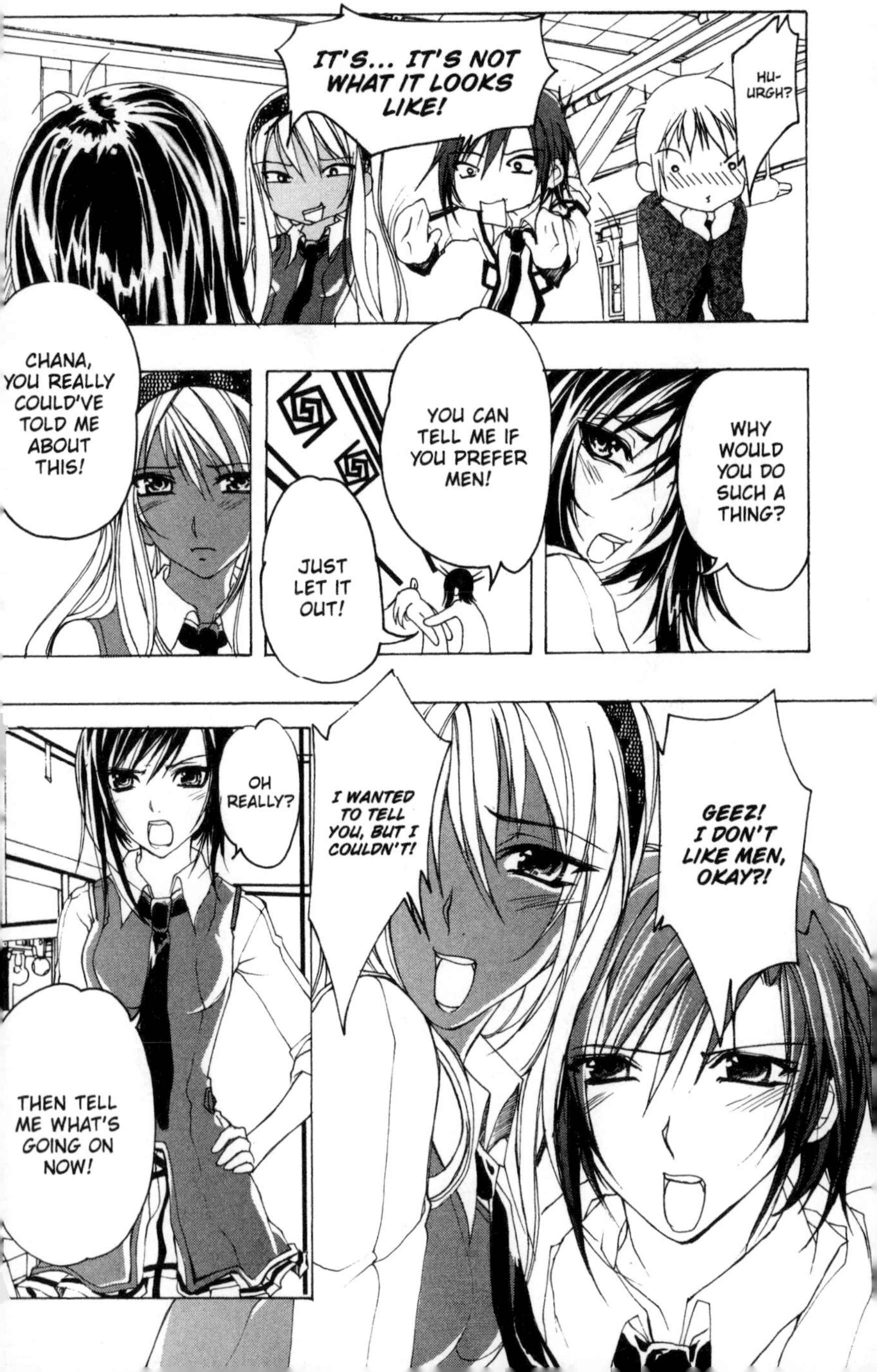
HU-URGH?
IT'S... IT'S NOT WHAT IT LOOKS LIKE!
WHY WOULD YOU DO SUCH A THING?
YOU CAN TELL ME IF YOU PREFER MEN!
JUST LET IT OUT!
CHANA, YOU REALLY COULD'VE TOLD ME ABOUT THIS!
GEEZ! I DON'T LIKE MEN, OKAY?!
I WANTED TO TELL YOU, BUT I COULDN'T!
OH REALLY?
THEN TELL ME WHAT'S GOING ON NOW!

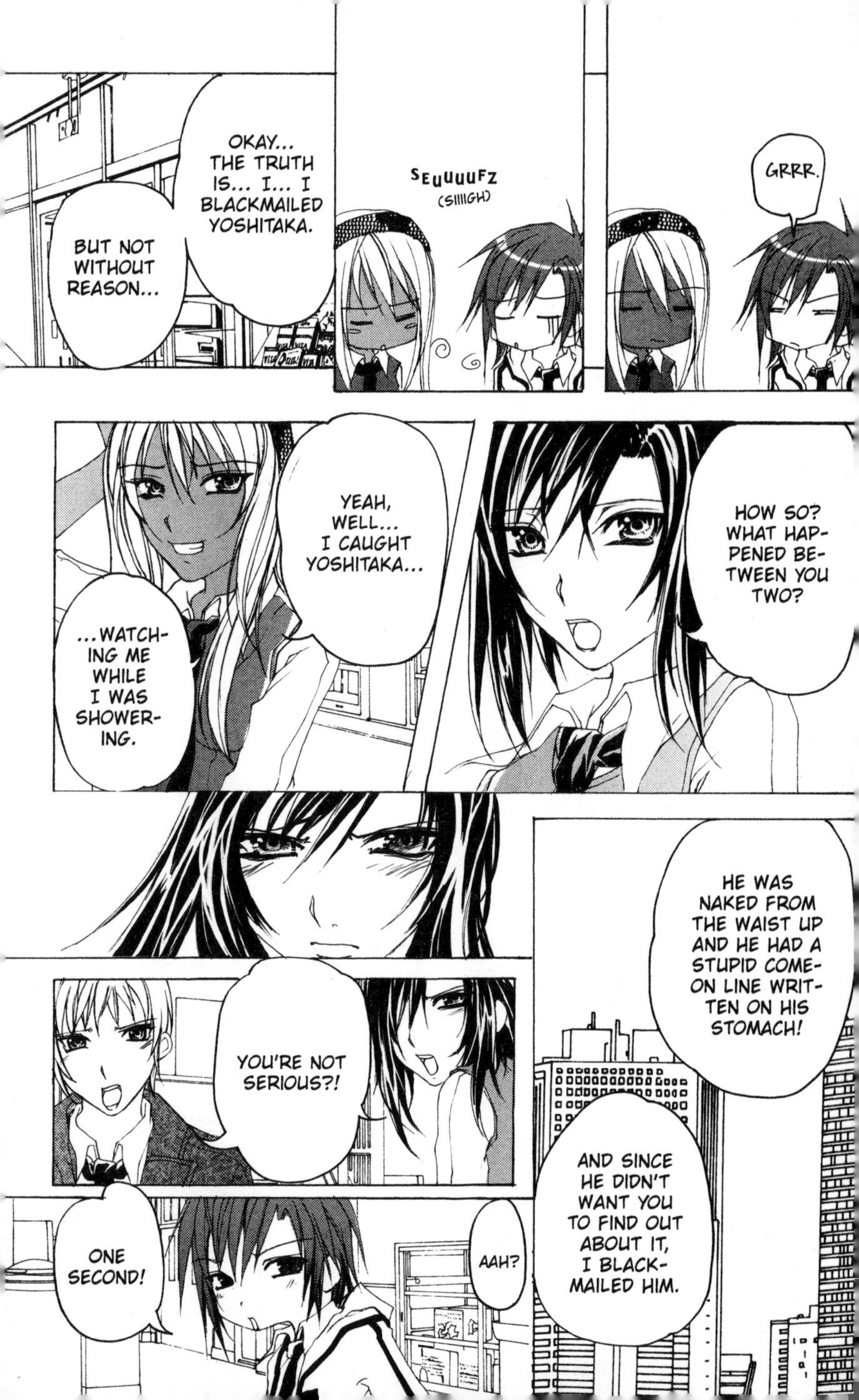
GRRR.
SEUUUUFZ
(SIIIIGH)
OKAY... THE TRUTH IS... I... I BLACKMAILED YOSHITAKA.
BUT NOT WITHOUT REASON...
HOW SO? WHAT HAP-PENED BE-TWEEN YOU TWO?
YEAH, WELL... I CAUGHT YOSHITAKA...
...WATCH-ING ME WHILE I WAS SHOWER-ING.
HE WAS NAKED FROM THE WAIST UP AND HE HAD A STUPID COME-ON LINE WRIT-TEN ON HIS STOMACH!
AND SINCE HE DIDN'T WANT YOU TO FIND OUT ABOUT IT, I BLACK-MAILED HIM.
YOU'RE NOT SERIOUS?!
AAH?
ONE SECOND!

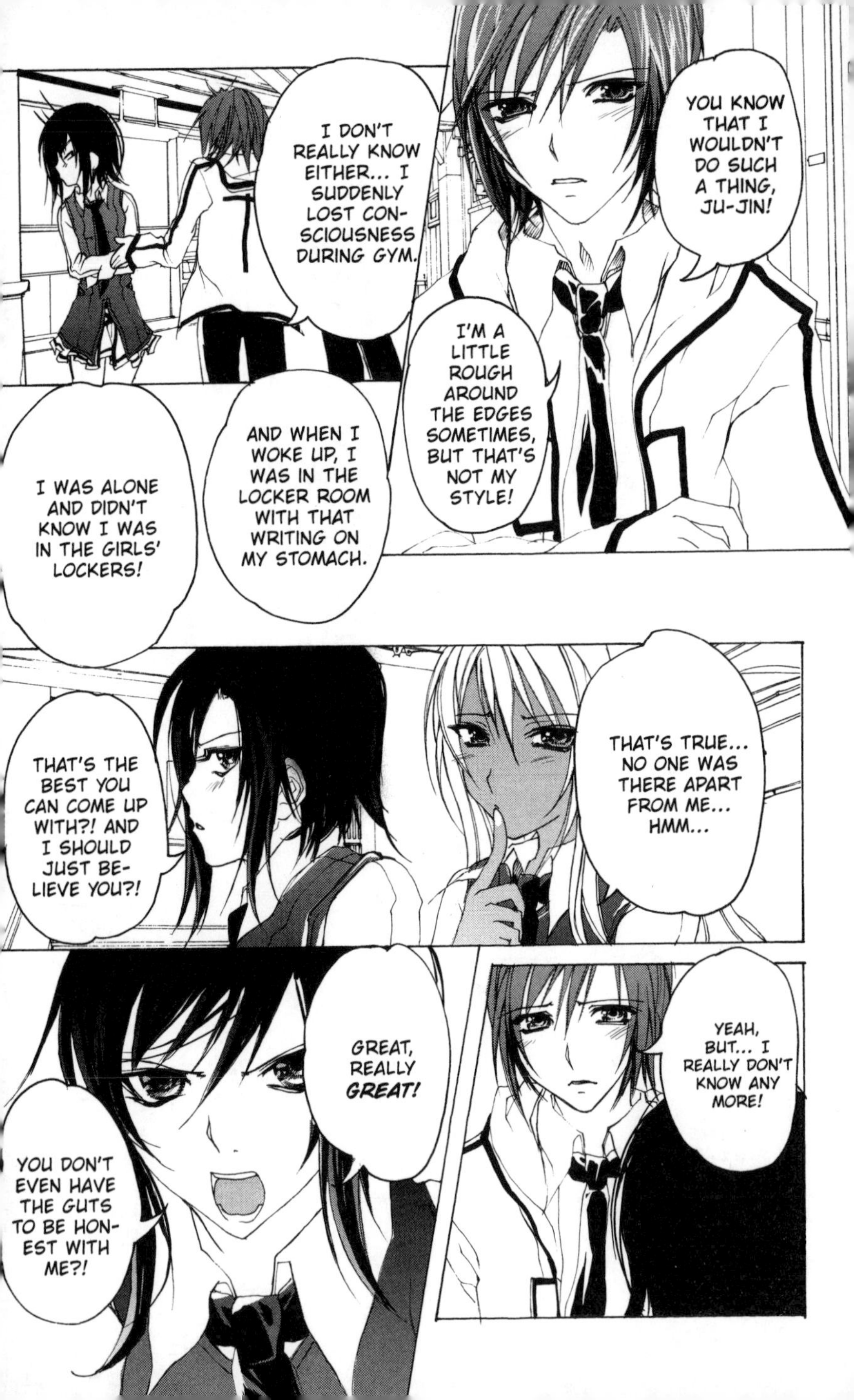
YOU KNOW THAT I WOULDN'T DO SUCH A THING, JU-JIN!
I'M A LITTLE ROUGH AROUND THE EDGES SOMETIMES, BUT THAT'S NOT MY STYLE!
I DON'T REALLY KNOW EITHER... I SUDDENLY LOST CON-SCIOUSNESS DURING GYM.
AND WHEN I WOKE UP, I WAS IN THE LOCKER ROOM WITH THAT WRITING ON MY STOMACH.
I WAS ALONE AND DIDN'T KNOW I WAS IN THE GIRLS' LOCKERS!
THAT'S TRUE... NO ONE WAS THERE APART FROM ME... HMM...
THAT'S THE BEST YOU CAN COME UP WITH?! AND I SHOULD JUST BE-LIEVE YOU?!
YEAH, BUT... I REALLY DON'T KNOW ANY MORE!
GREAT, REALLY ***GREAT!***
YOU DON'T EVEN HAVE THE GUTS TO BE HON-EST WITH ME?!

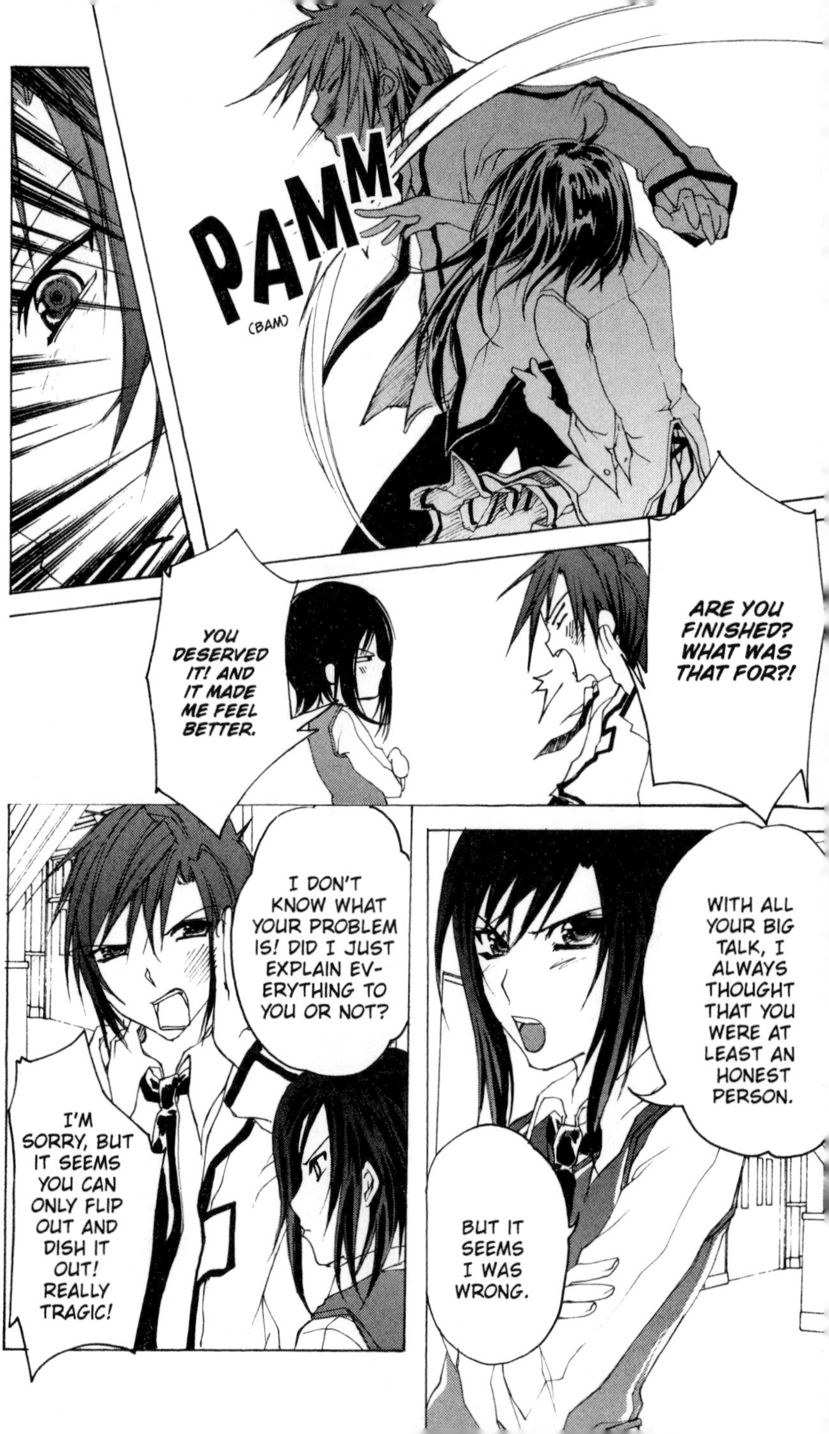
PAMM
(BAM)
ARE YOU FINISHED? WHAT WAS THAT FOR?!
YOU DESERVED IT! AND IT MADE ME FEEL BETTER.
WITH ALL YOUR BIG TALK, I ALWAYS THOUGHT THAT YOU WERE AT LEAST AN HONEST PERSON.
BUT IT SEEMS I WAS WRONG.
I DON'T KNOW WHAT YOUR PROBLEM IS! DID I JUST EXPLAIN EV-ERYTHING TO YOU OR NOT?
I'M SORRY, BUT IT SEEMS YOU CAN ONLY FLIP OUT AND DISH IT OUT! REALLY TRAGIC!

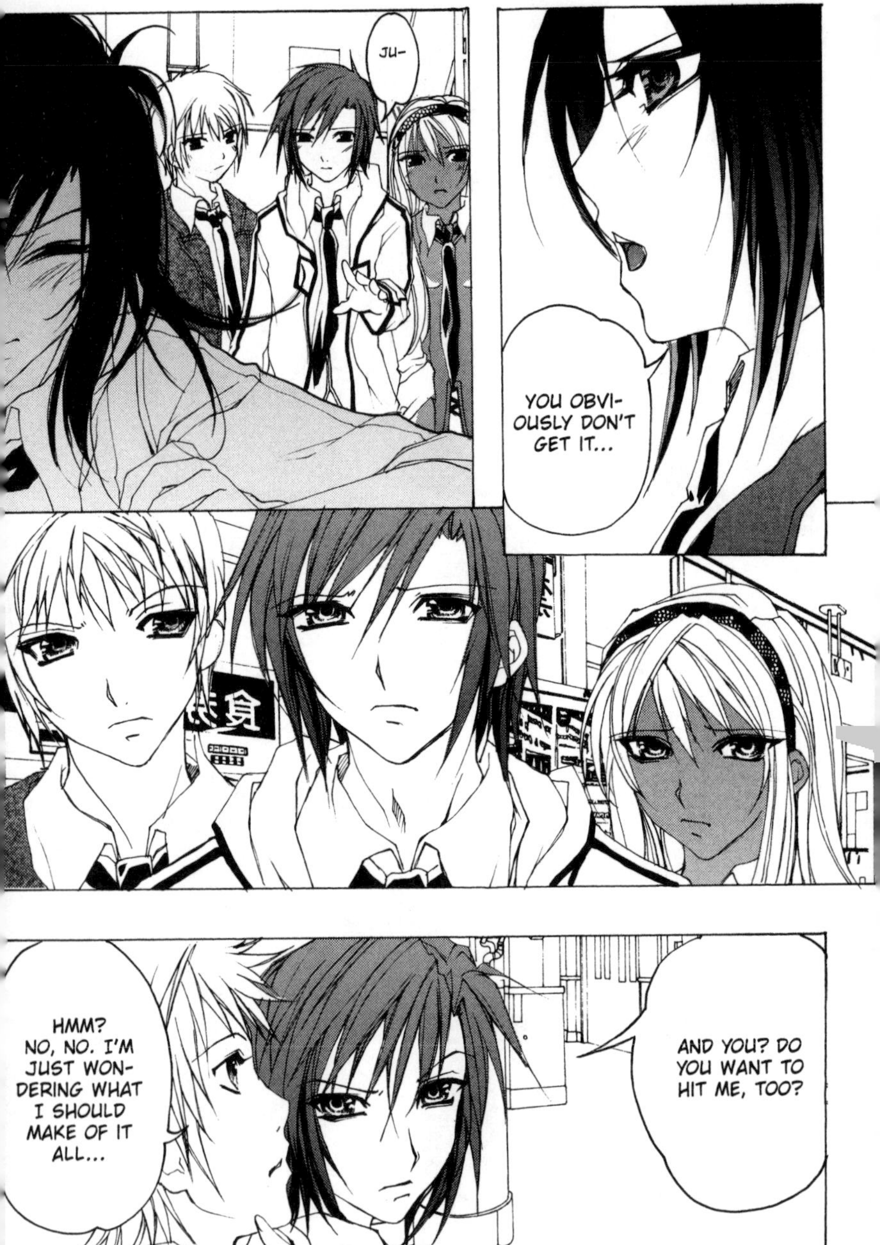
YOU OBVI-OUSLY DON'T GET IT...
JU-
AND YOU? DO YOU WANT TO HIT ME, TOO?
HMM? NO, NO. I'M JUST WON-DERING WHAT I SHOULD MAKE OF IT ALL...

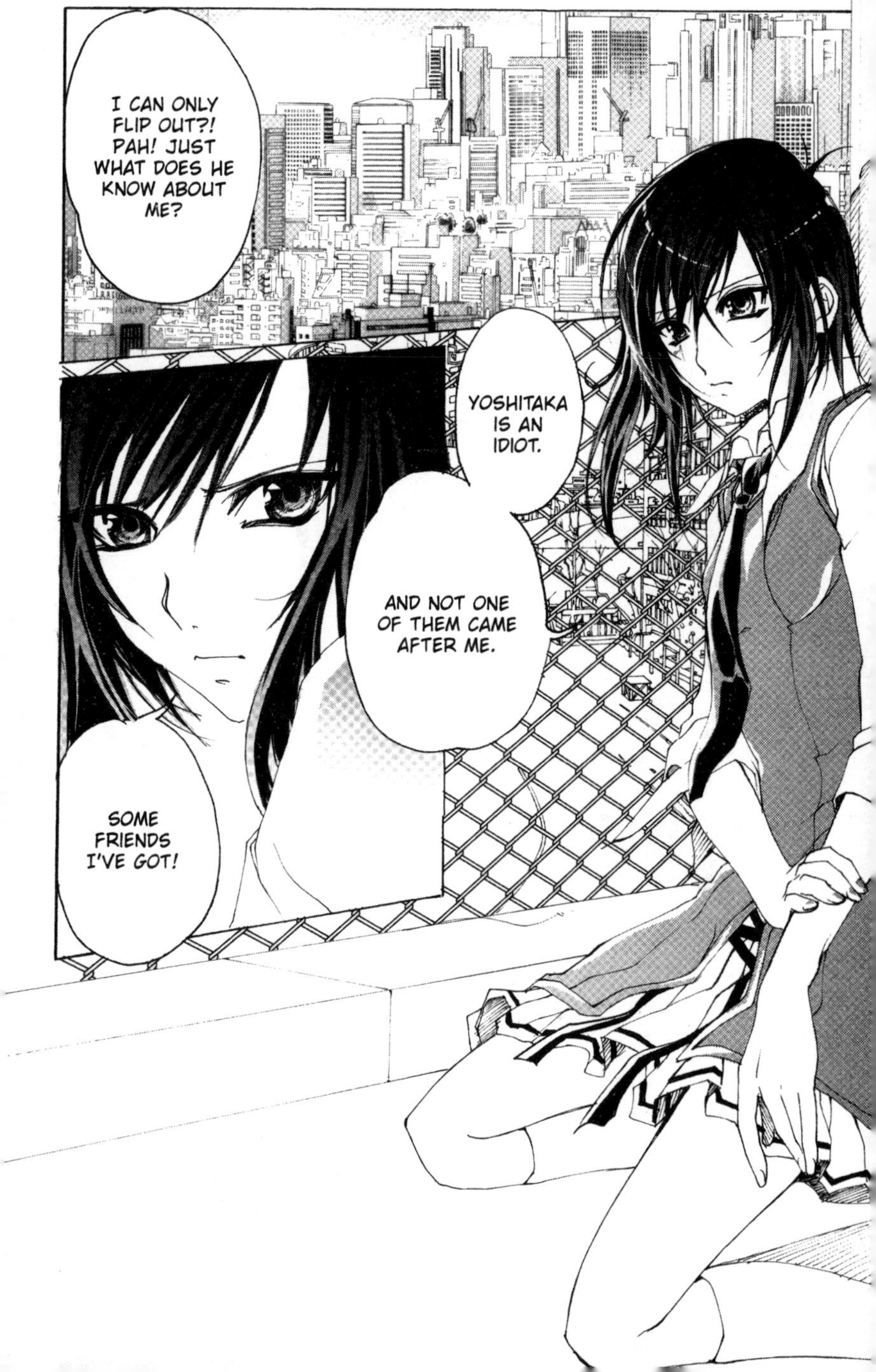
I CAN ONLY FLIP OUT?! PAH! JUST WHAT DOES HE KNOW ABOUT ME?
YOSHITAKA IS AN IDIOT.
AND NOT ONE OF THEM CAME AFTER ME.
SOME FRIENDS I'VE GOT!

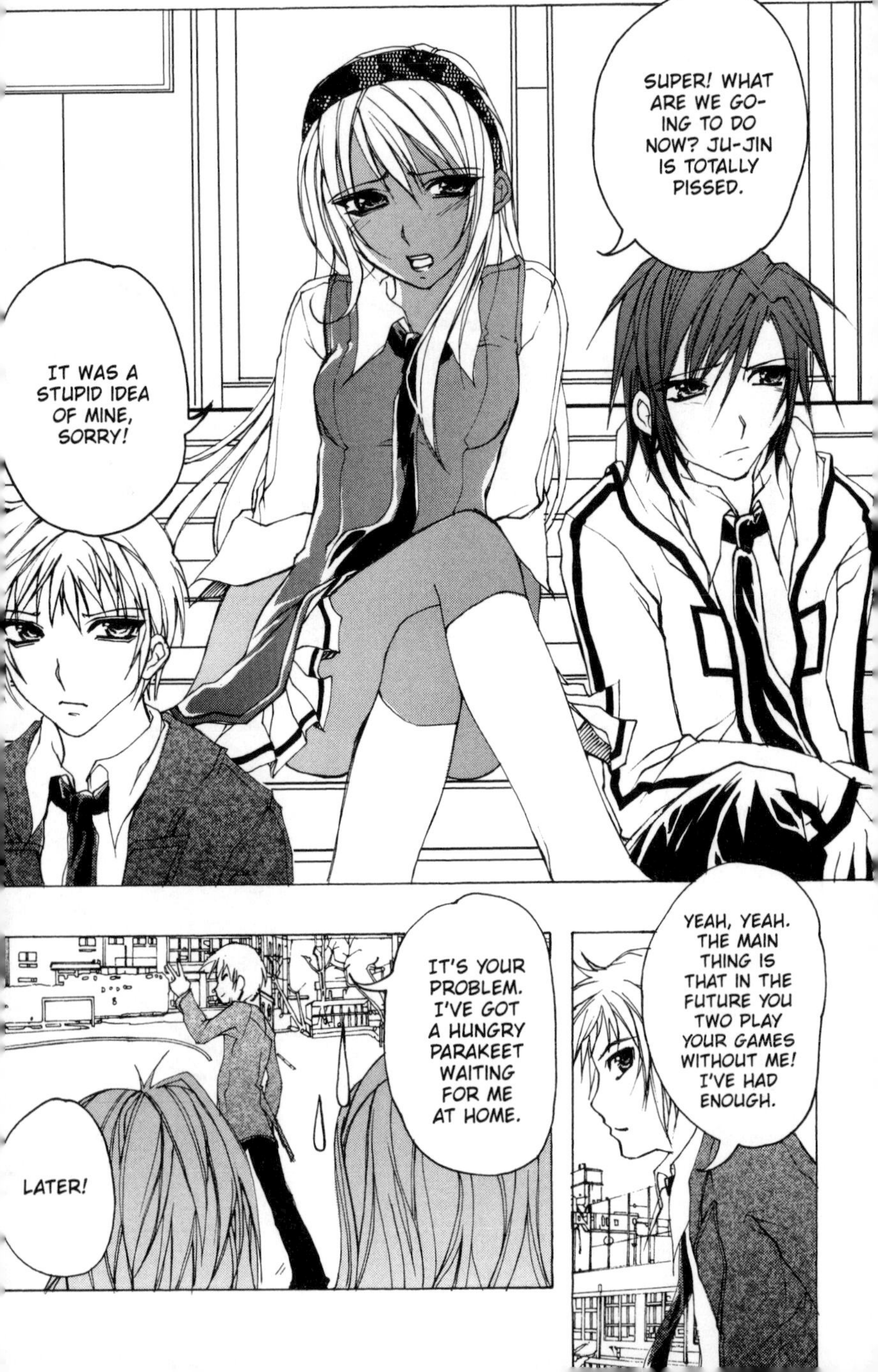
SUPER! WHAT ARE WE GO-ING TO DO NOW? JU-JIN IS TOTALLY PISSED.
IT WAS A STUPID IDEA OF MINE, SORRY!
YEAH, YEAH. THE MAIN THING IS THAT IN THE FUTURE YOU TWO PLAY YOUR GAMES WITHOUT ME! I'VE HAD ENOUGH.
IT'S YOUR PROBLEM. I'VE GOT A HUNGRY PARAKEET WAITING FOR ME AT HOME.
LATER!

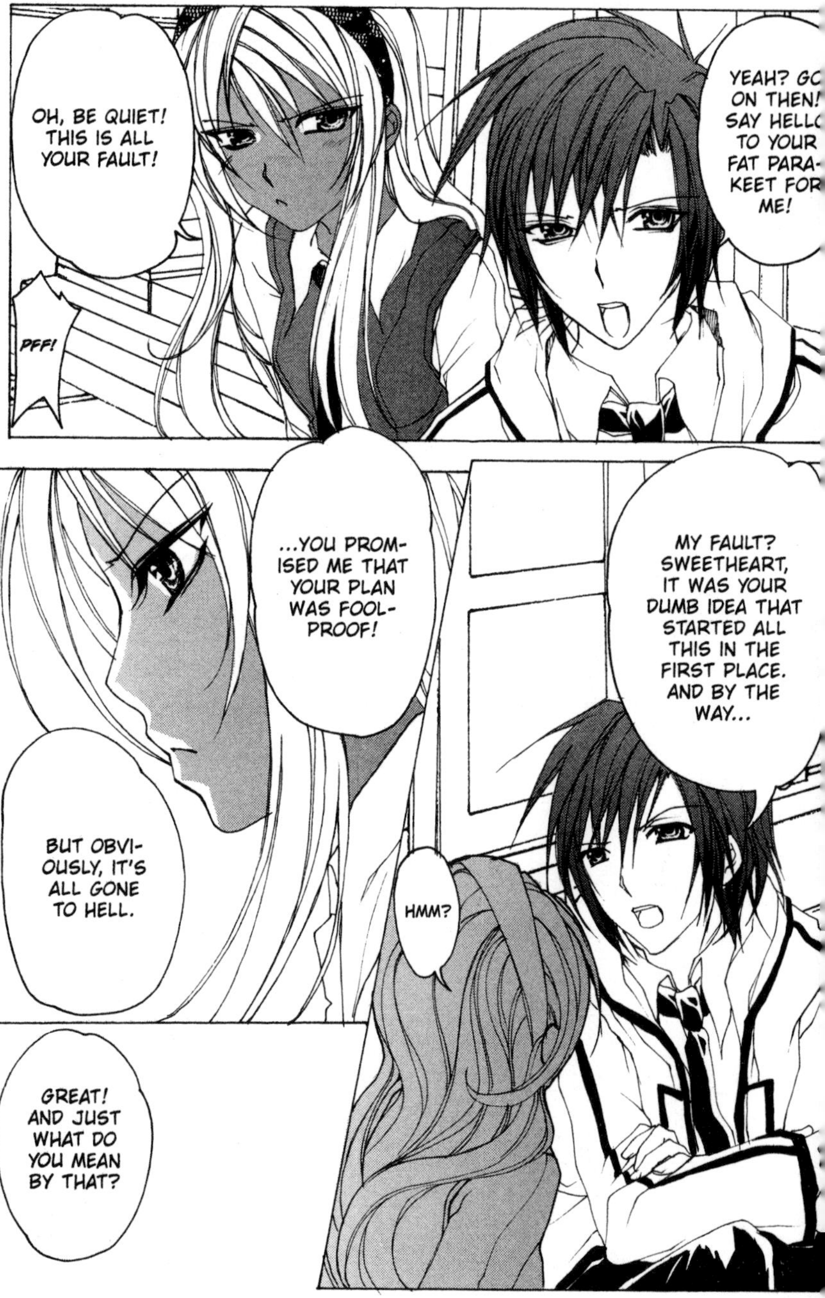
YEAH? GO ON THEN! SAY HELLO TO YOUR FAT PARA-KEET FOR ME!
OH, BE QUIET! THIS IS ALL YOUR FAULT!
PFF!
MY FAULT? SWEETHEART, IT WAS YOUR DUMB IDEA THAT STARTED ALL THIS IN THE FIRST PLACE. AND BY THE WAY...
HMM?
...YOU PROM-ISED ME THAT YOUR PLAN WAS FOOL-PROOF!
BUT OBVI-OUSLY, IT'S ALL GONE TO HELL.
GREAT! AND JUST WHAT DO YOU MEAN BY THAT?

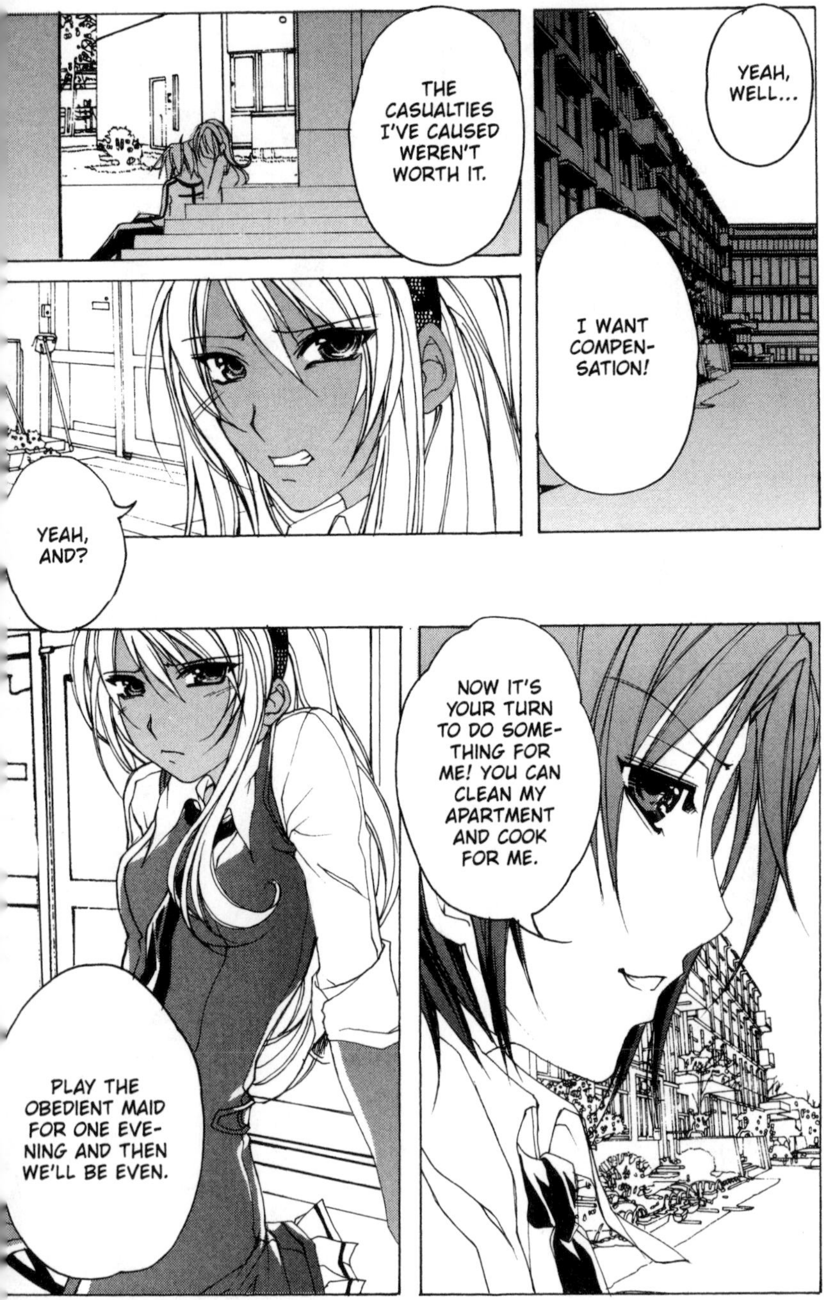
YEAH, WELL...
I WANT COMPEN-SATION!
THE CASUALTIES I'VE CAUSED WEREN'T WORTH IT.
YEAH, AND?
NOW IT'S YOUR TURN TO DO SOME-THING FOR ME! YOU CAN CLEAN MY APARTMENT AND COOK FOR ME.
PLAY THE OBEDIENT MAID FOR ONE EVE-NING AND THEN WE'LL BE EVEN.

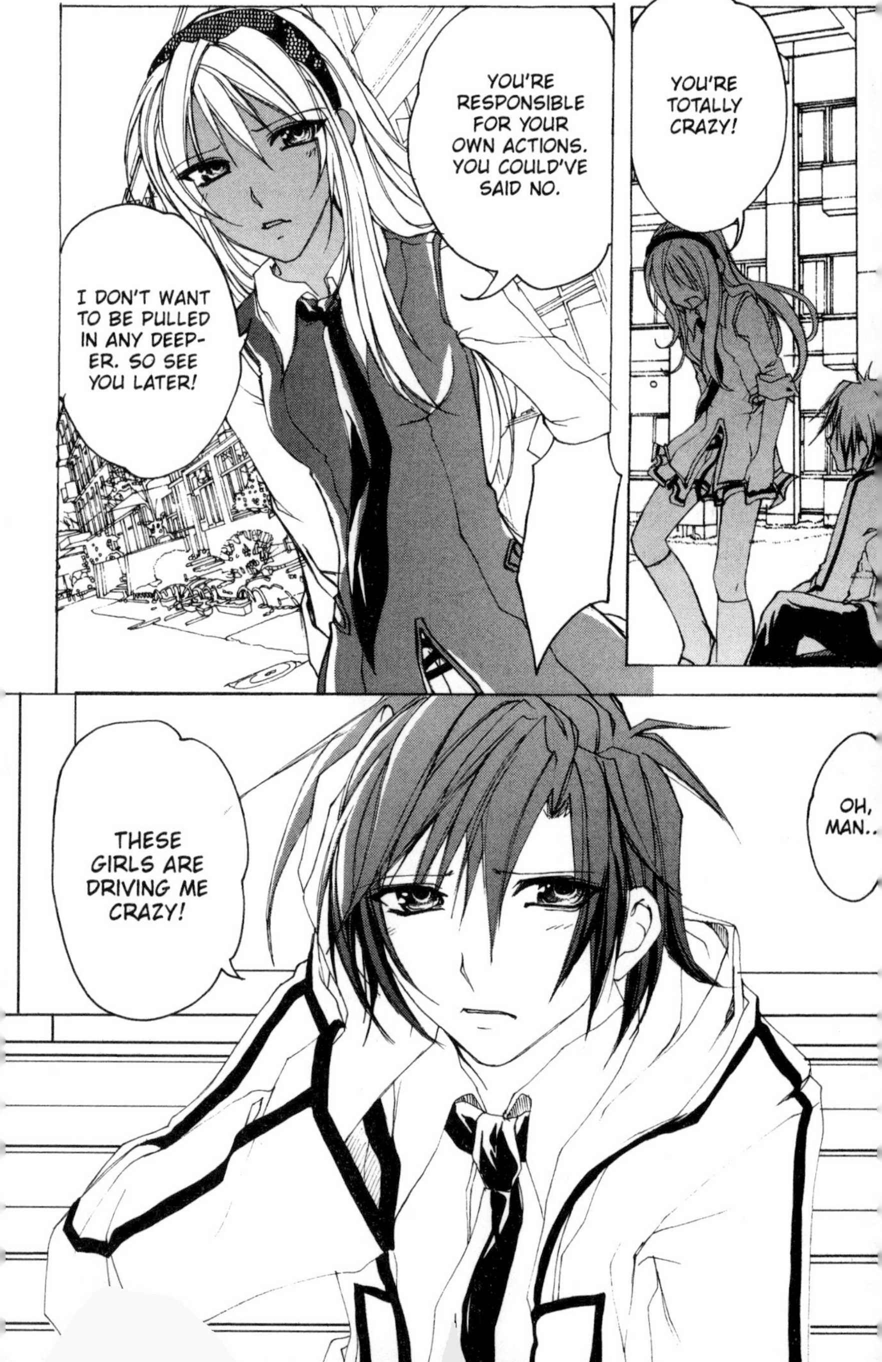
YOU'RE TOTALLY CRAZY!
YOU'RE RESPONSIBLE FOR YOUR OWN ACTIONS. YOU COULD'VE SAID NO.
I DON'T WANT TO BE PULLED IN ANY DEEPER. SO SEE YOU LATER!
OH, MAN..
THESE GIRLS ARE DRIVING ME CRAZY!

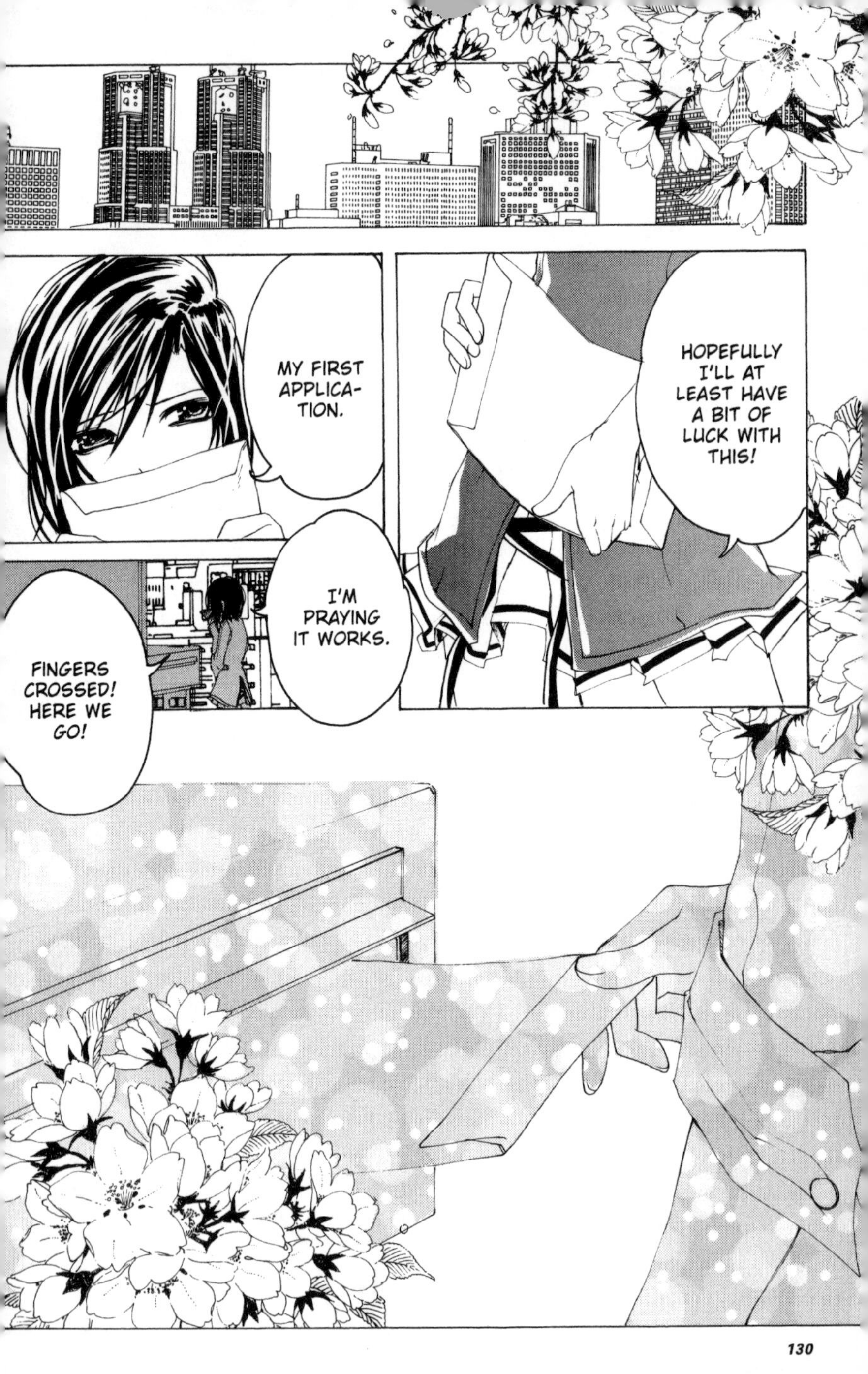
HOPEFULLY I'LL AT LEAST HAVE A BIT OF LUCK WITH THIS!
MY FIRST APPLICATION.
I'M PRAYING IT WORKS.
FINGERS CROSSED! HERE WE GO!

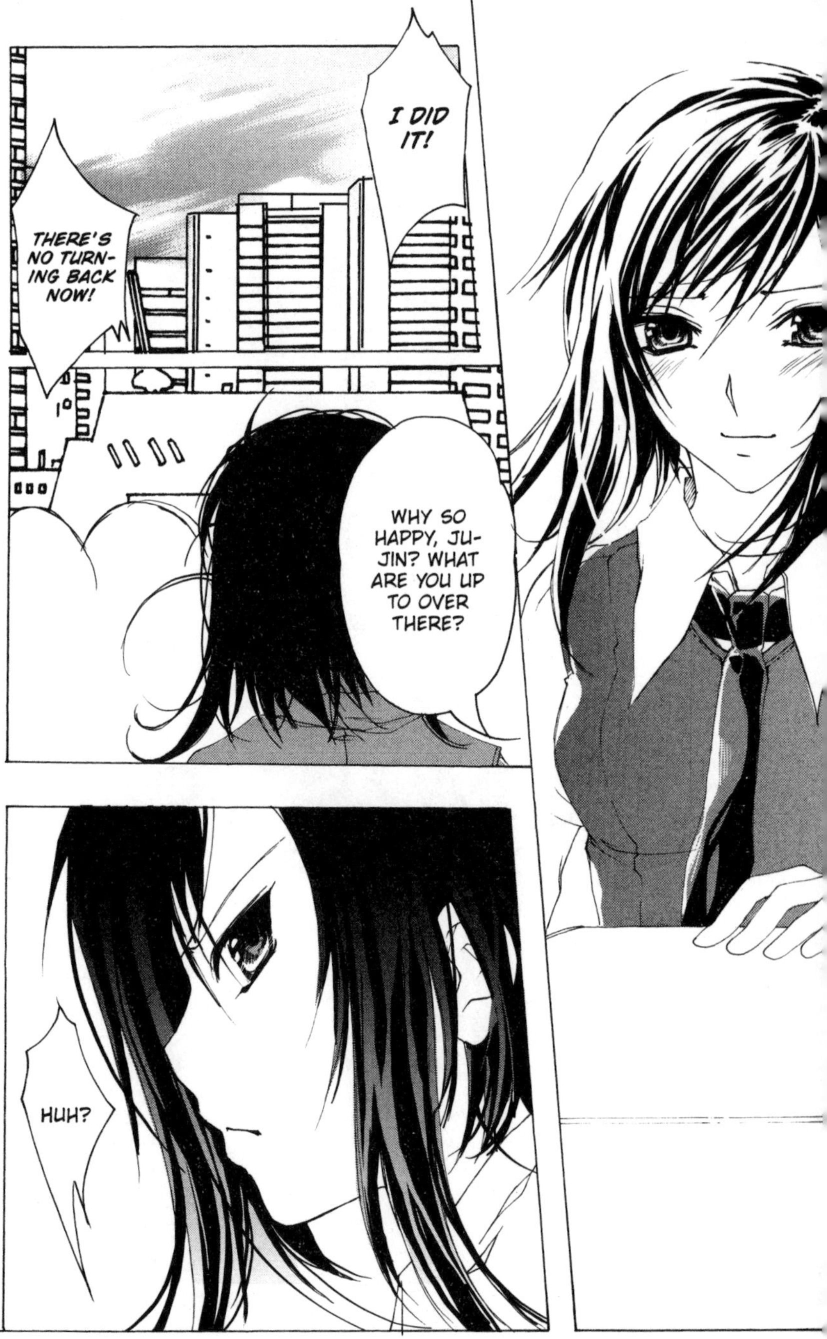
I DID IT!
THERE'S NO TURNING-ING BACK NOW!
WHY SO HAPPY, JU-JIN? WHAT ARE YOU UP TO OVER THERE?
HUH?

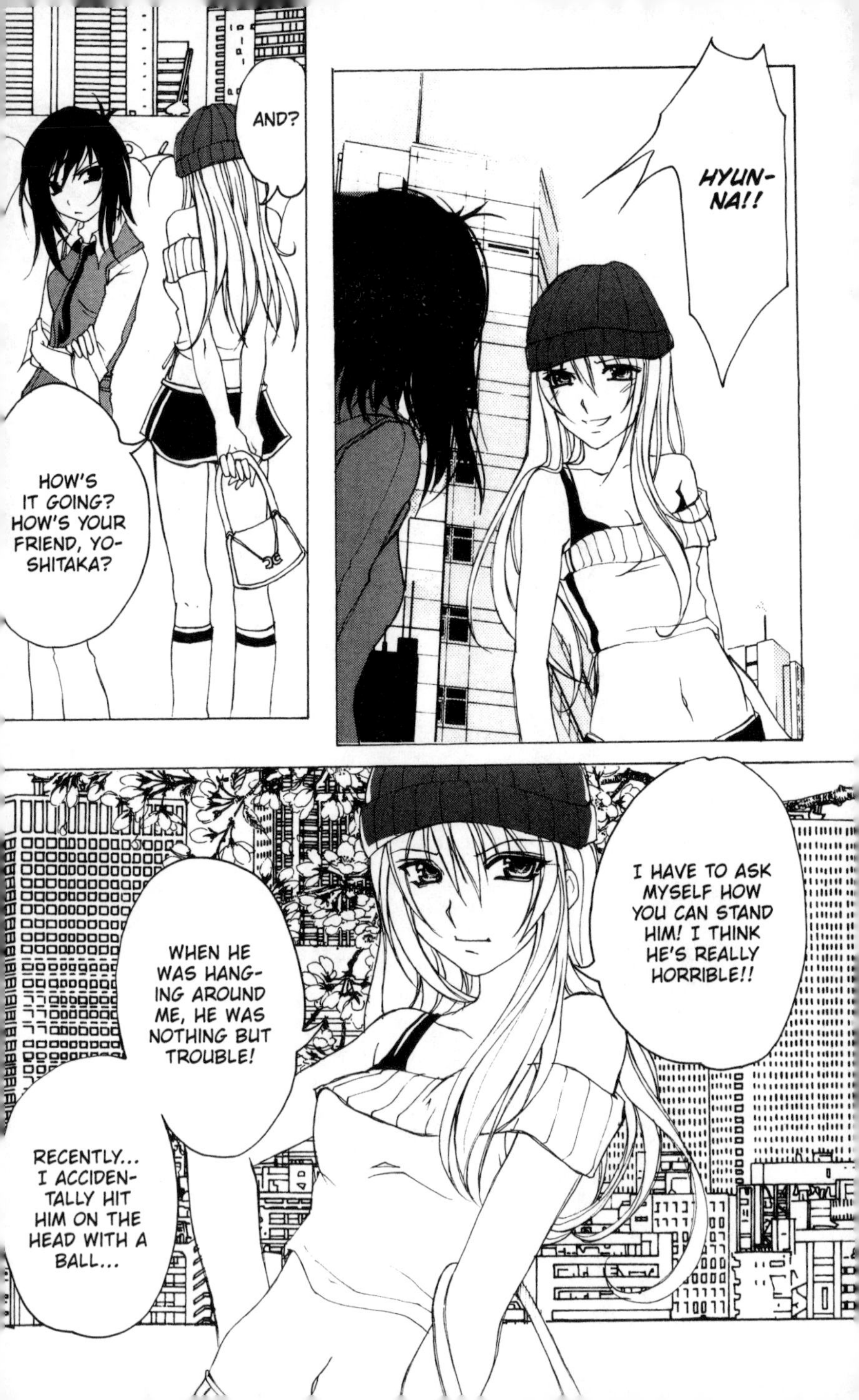
HYUN-NA!!
AND?
HOW'S IT GOING? HOW'S YOUR FRIEND, YO-SHITAKA?
I HAVE TO ASK MYSELF HOW YOU CAN STAND HIM! I THINK HE'S REALLY HORRIBLE!!
WHEN HE WAS HANG-ING AROUND ME, HE WAS NOTHING BUT TROUBLE!
RECENTLY... I ACCIDEN-TALLY HIT HIM ON THE HEAD WITH A BALL...

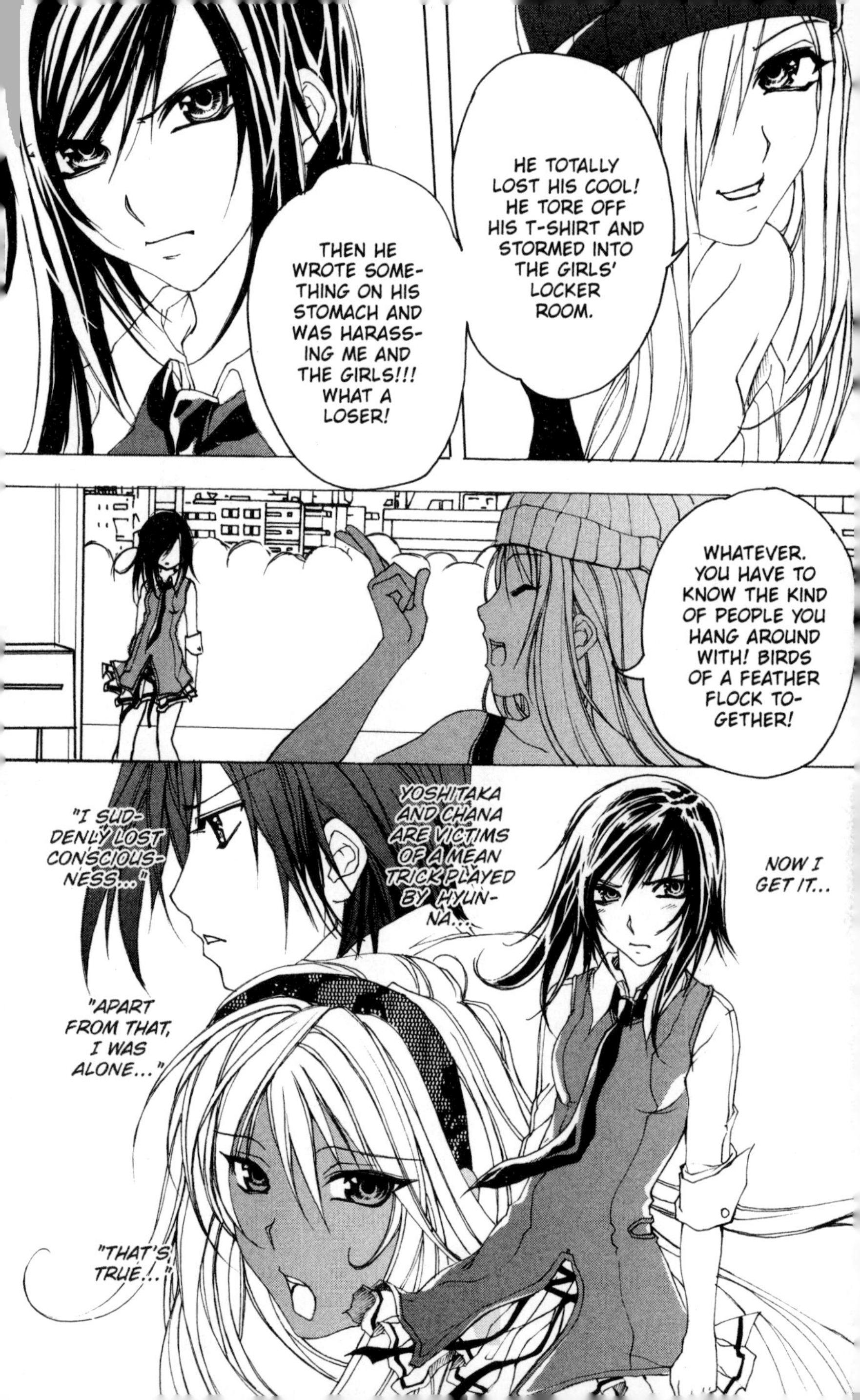
HE TOTALLY LOST HIS COOL! HE TORE OFF HIS T-SHIRT AND STORMED INTO THE GIRLS' LOCKER ROOM.
THEN HE WROTE SOME-THING ON HIS STOMACH AND WAS HARASS-ING ME AND THE GIRLS!!! WHAT A LOSER!
WHATEVER. YOU HAVE TO KNOW THE KIND OF PEOPLE YOU HANG AROUND WITH! BIRDS OF A FEATHER FLOCK TO-GETHER!
NOW I GET IT...
YOSHITAKA AND CHANA ARE VICTIMS OF A MEAN TRICK PLAYED BY HYUN-NA...
"I SUD-DENLY LOST CONSCIOUS-NESS..."
"APART FROM THAT, I WAS ALONE..."
"THAT'S TRUE..."

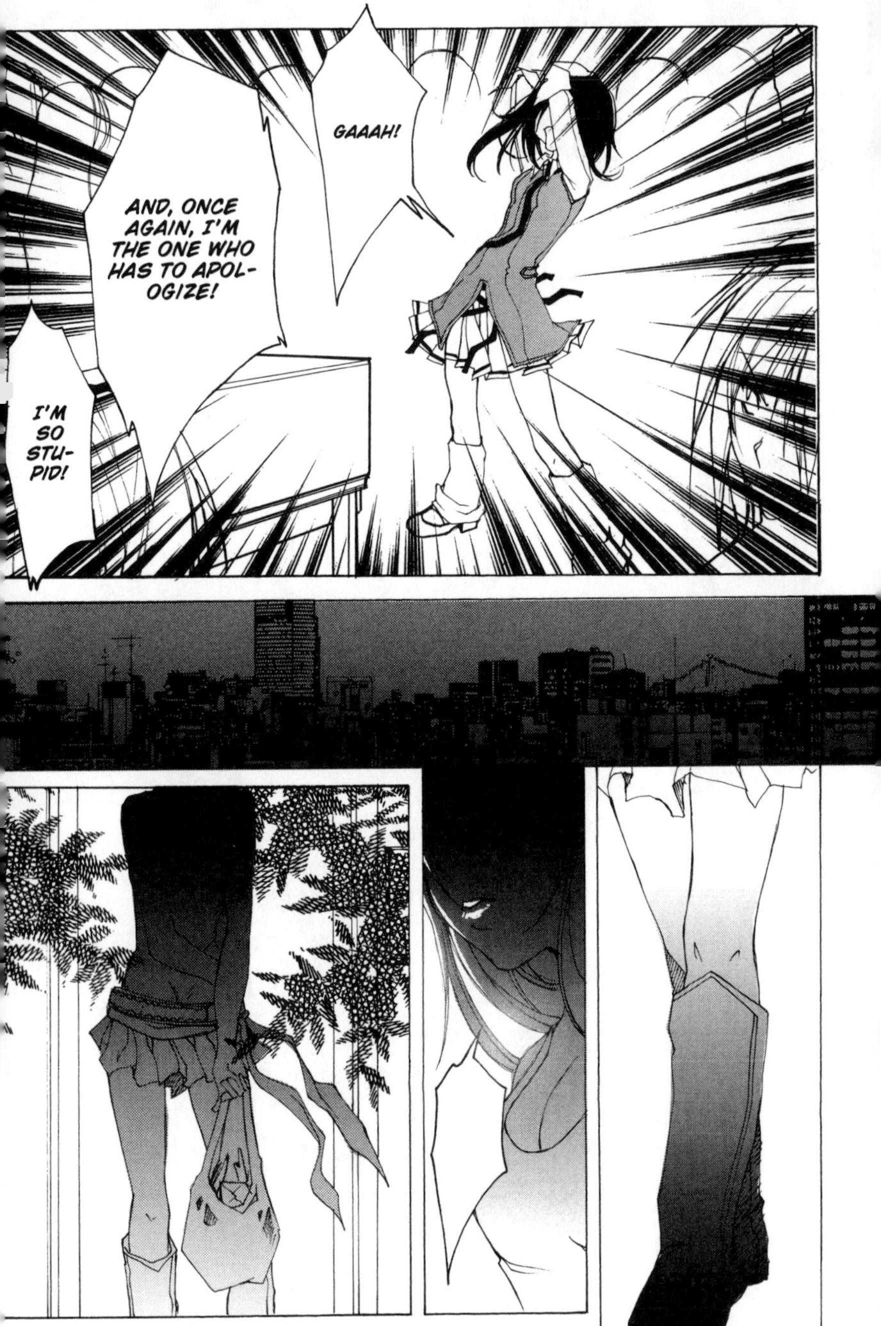
GAAAH!
AND, ONCE AGAIN, I'M THE ONE WHO HAS TO APOLOGIZE!
I'M SO STUPID!

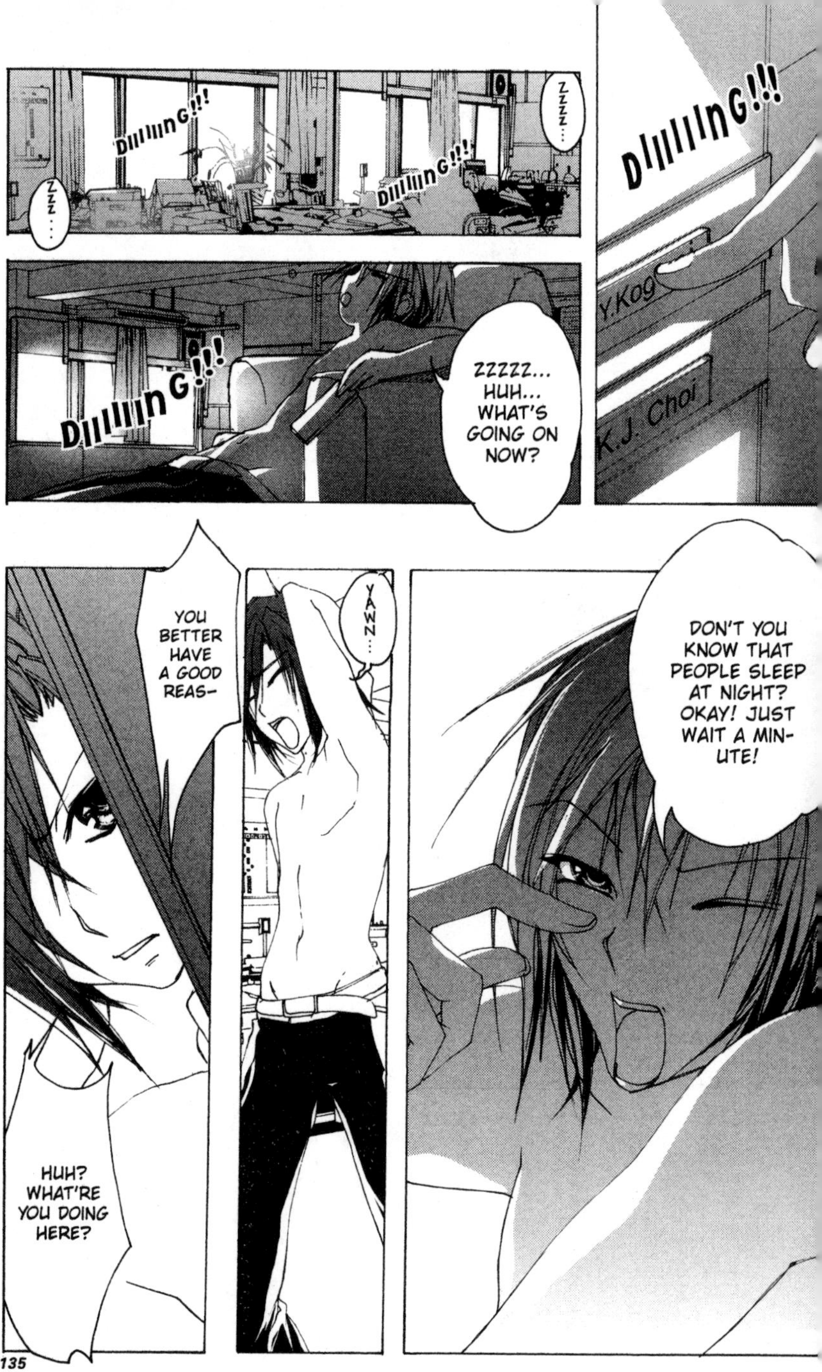
DIIIIING!!!
ZZZZ...
DIIIING!!!
DIIIING!!!
ZZZ...
DIIIIING!!!
ZZZZZ... HUH... WHAT'S GOING ON NOW?
DON'T YOU KNOW THAT PEOPLE SLEEP AT NIGHT? OKAY! JUST WAIT A MIN-UTE!
YAWN...
YOU BETTER HAVE A GOOD REAS-
HUH? WHAT'RE YOU DOING HERE?

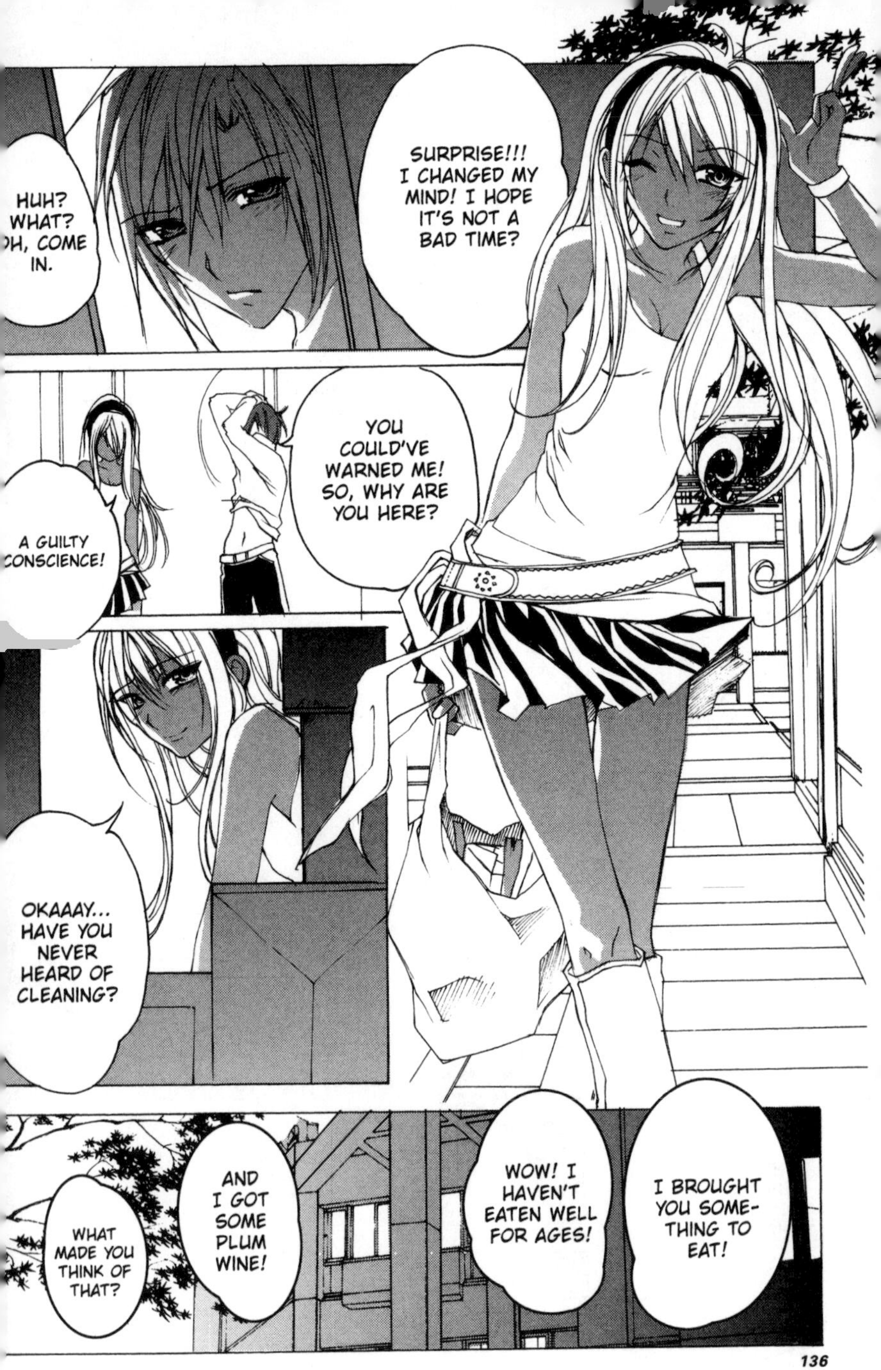
SURPRISE!!! I CHANGED MY MIND! I HOPE IT'S NOT A BAD TIME?
HUH? WHAT? H, COME IN.
YOU COULD'VE WARNED ME! SO, WHY ARE YOU HERE?
A GUILTY ONSCIENCE!
OKAAAY... HAVE YOU NEVER HEARD OF CLEANING?
I BROUGHT YOU SOME-THING TO EAT!
WOW! I HAVEN'T EATEN WELL FOR AGES!
AND I GOT SOME PLUM WINE!
WHAT MADE YOU THINK OF THAT?

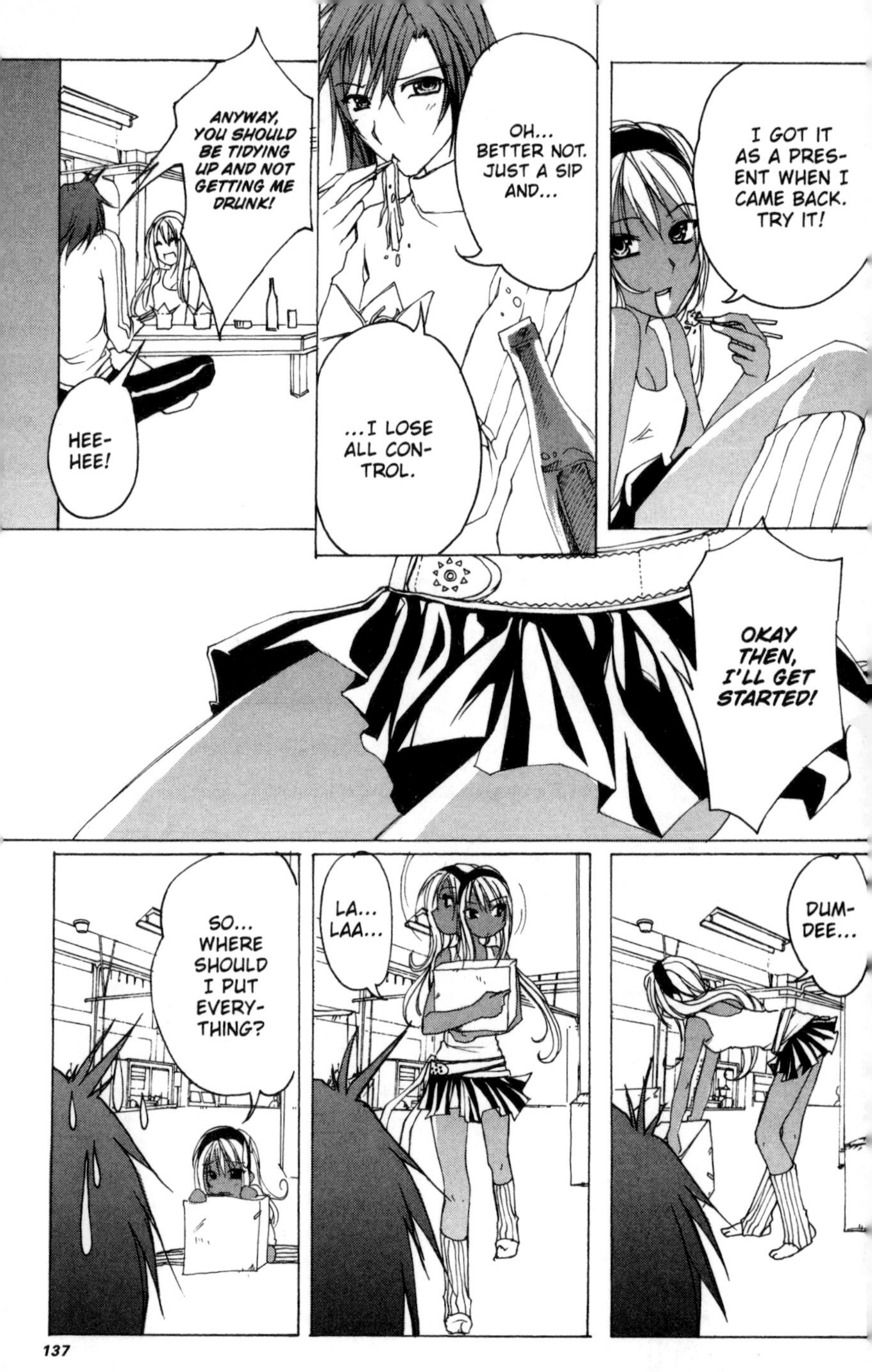
I GOT IT AS A PRESENT WHEN I CAME BACK. TRY IT!
OH... BETTER NOT. JUST A SIP AND...
...I LOSE ALL CONTROL.
ANYWAY, YOU SHOULD BE TIDYING UP AND NOT GETTING ME DRUNK!
HEE-HEE!
OKAY THEN, I'LL GET STARTED!
DUM-DEE...
LA... LAA...
SO... WHERE SHOULD I PUT EVERYTHING?

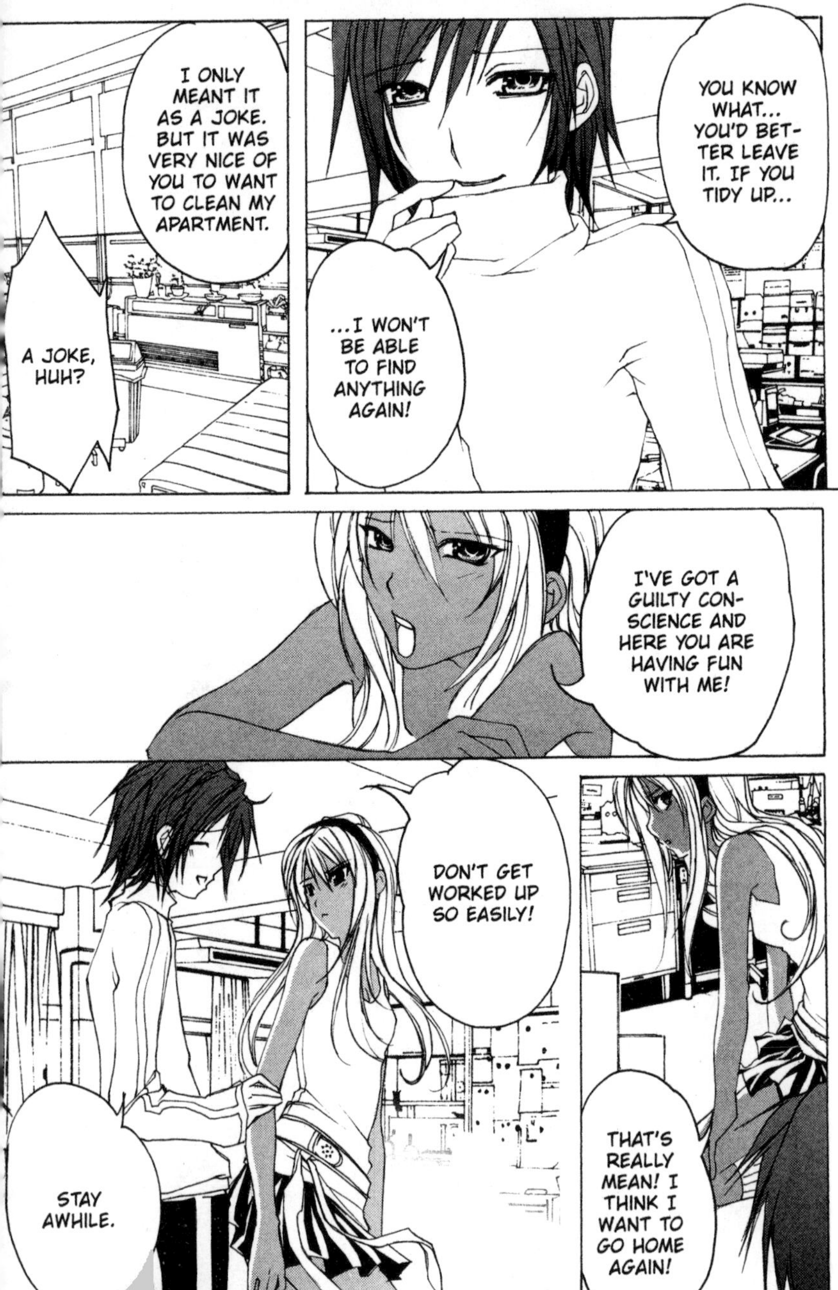
YOU KNOW WHAT... YOU'D BETTER LEAVE IT. IF YOU TIDY UP...
...I WON'T BE ABLE TO FIND ANYTHING AGAIN!
I ONLY MEANT IT AS A JOKE. BUT IT WAS VERY NICE OF YOU TO WANT TO CLEAN MY APARTMENT.
A JOKE, HUH?
I'VE GOT A GUILTY CONSCIENCE AND HERE YOU ARE HAVING FUN WITH ME!
THAT'S REALLY MEAN! I THINK I WANT TO GO HOME AGAIN!
DON'T GET WORKED UP SO EASILY!
STAY AWHILE.

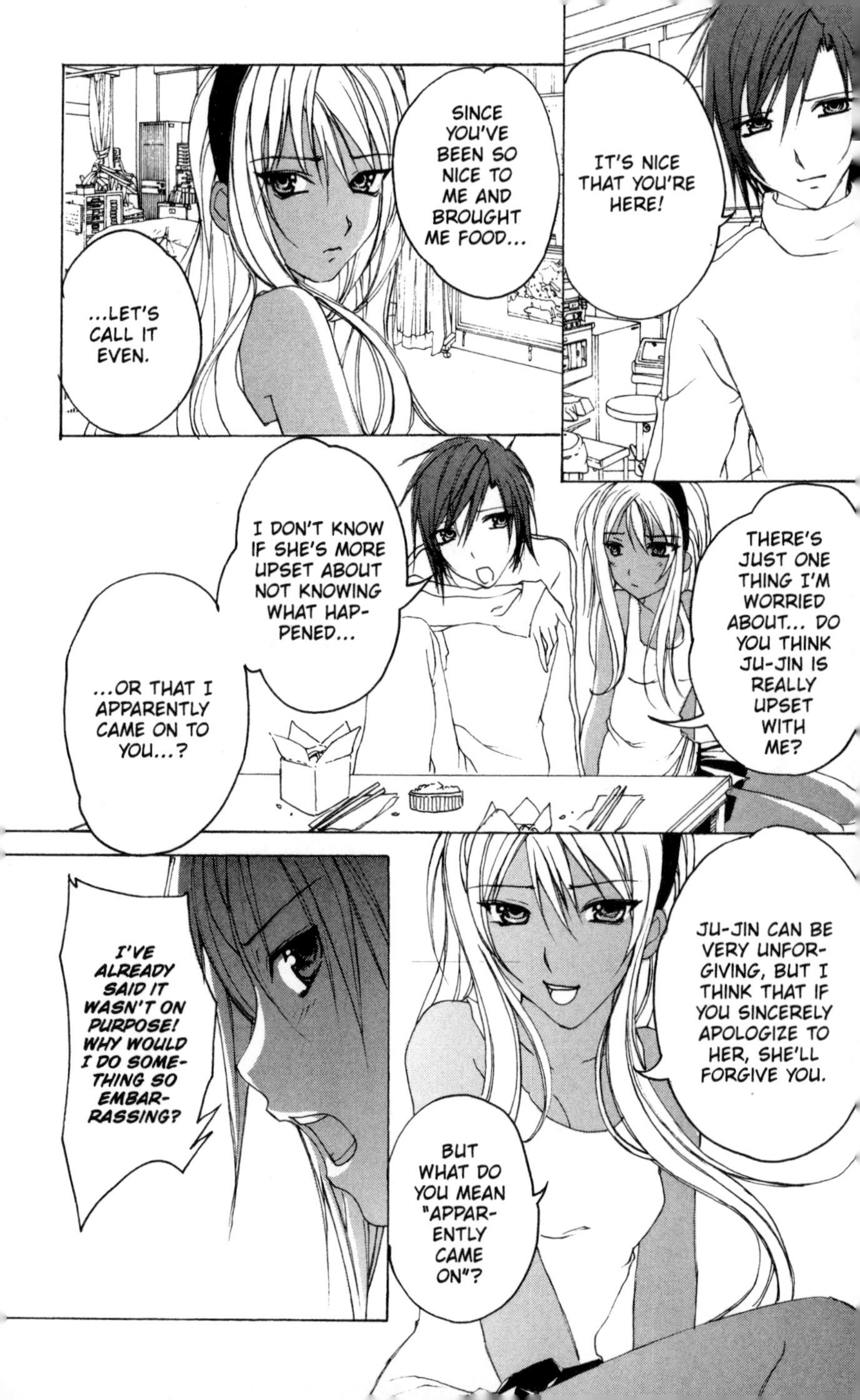
IT'S NICE THAT YOU'RE HERE!
SINCE YOU'VE BEEN SO NICE TO ME AND BROUGHT ME FOOD...
...LET'S CALL IT EVEN.
THERE'S JUST ONE THING I'M WORRIED ABOUT... DO YOU THINK JU-JIN IS REALLY UPSET WITH ME?
I DON'T KNOW IF SHE'S MORE UPSET ABOUT NOT KNOWING WHAT HAP-PENED...
...OR THAT I APPARENTLY CAME ON TO YOU...?
JU-JIN CAN BE VERY UNFOR-GIVING, BUT I THINK THAT IF YOU SINCERELY APOLOGIZE TO HER, SHE'LL FORGIVE YOU.
BUT WHAT DO YOU MEAN "APPAR-ENTLY CAME ON"?
I'VE ALREADY SAID IT WASN'T ON PURPOSE! WHY WOULD I DO SOME-THING SO EMBAR-RASSING?

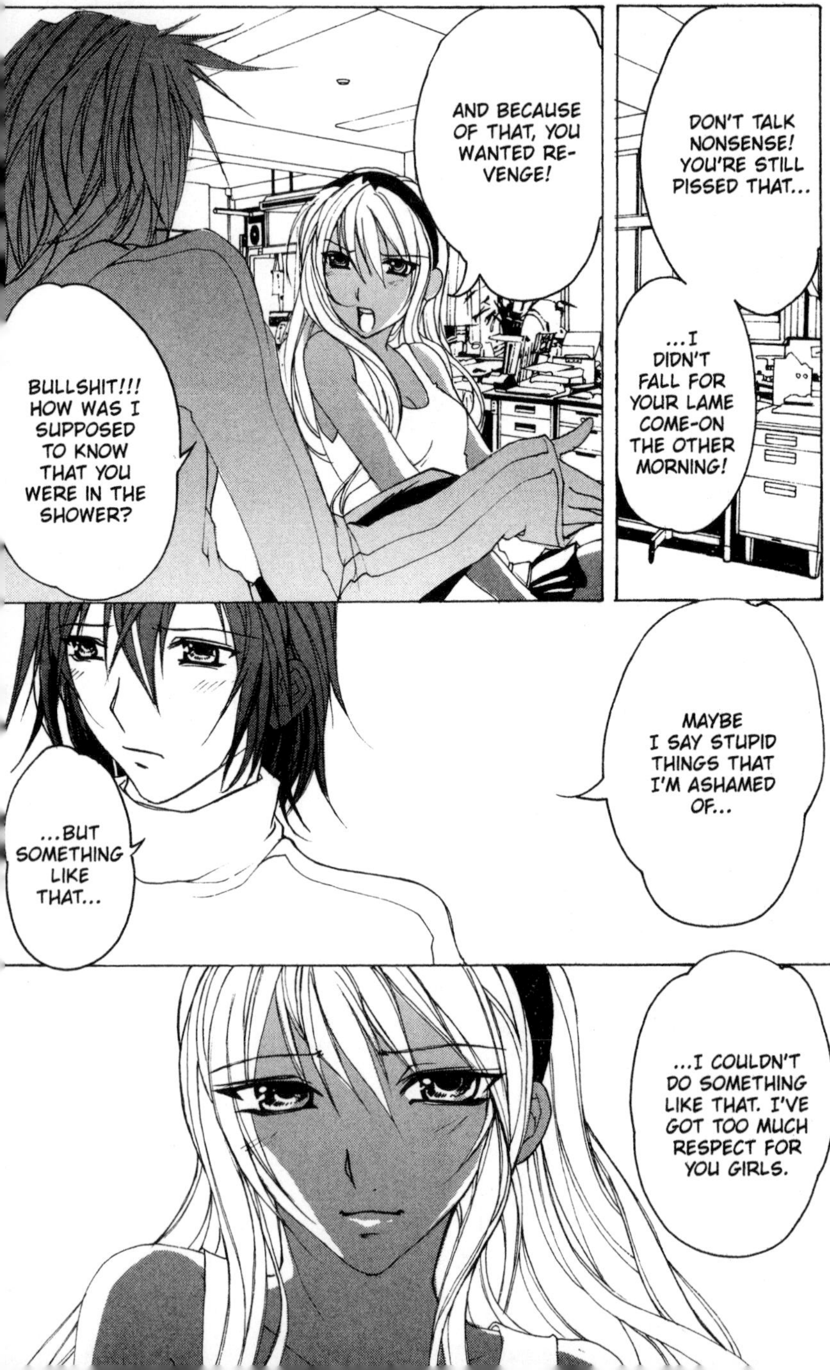
DON'T TALK NONSENSE! YOU'RE STILL PISSED THAT...
...I DIDN'T FALL FOR YOUR LAME COME-ON THE OTHER MORNING!
AND BECAUSE OF THAT, YOU WANTED RE-VENGE!
BULLSHIT!!! HOW WAS I SUPPOSED TO KNOW THAT YOU WERE IN THE SHOWER?
MAYBE I SAY STUPID THINGS THAT I'M ASHAMED OF...
...BUT SOMETHING LIKE THAT...
...I COULDN'T DO SOMETHING LIKE THAT. I'VE GOT TOO MUCH RESPECT FOR YOU GIRLS.

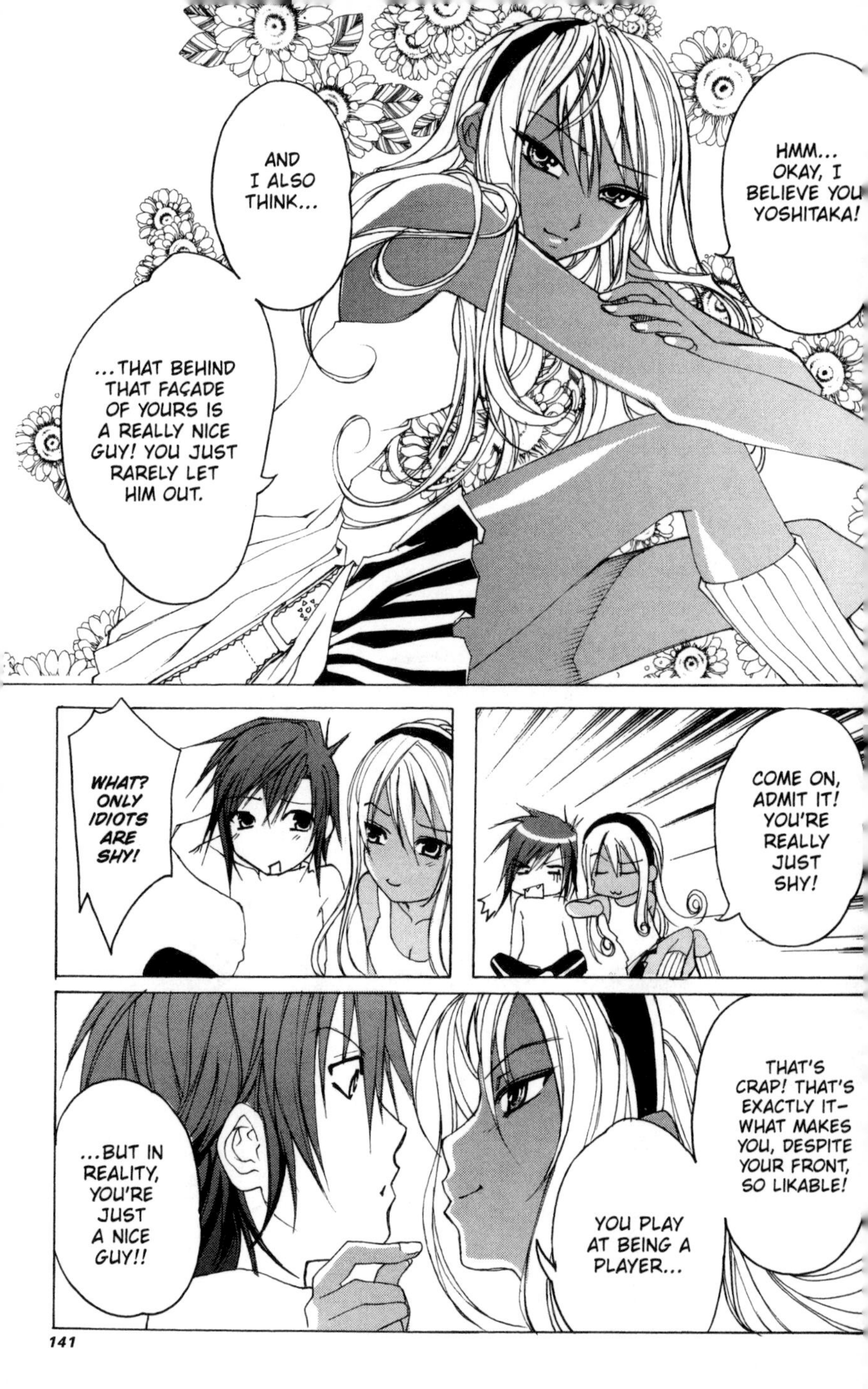
HMM... OKAY, I BELIEVE YOU YOSHITAKA!
AND I ALSO THINK...
...THAT BEHIND THAT FAÇADE OF YOURS IS A REALLY NICE GUY! YOU JUST RARELY LET HIM OUT.
COME ON, ADMIT IT! YOU'RE REALLY JUST SHY!
WHAT? ONLY IDIOTS ARE SHY!
THAT'S CRAP! THAT'S EXACTLY IT- WHAT MAKES YOU, DESPITE YOUR FRONT, SO LIKABLE!
YOU PLAY AT BEING A PLAYER...
...BUT IN REALITY, YOU'RE JUST A NICE GUY!!

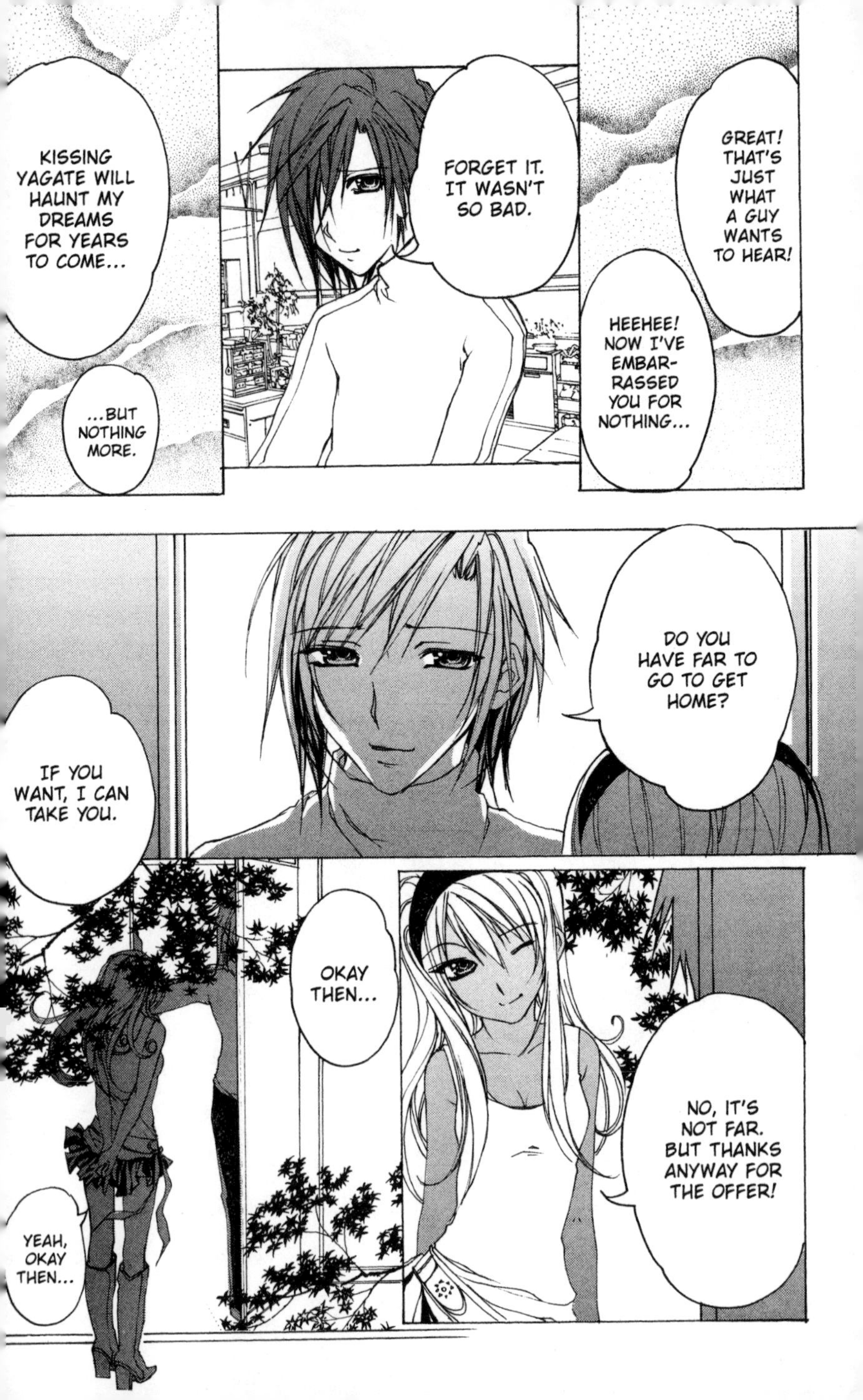
GREAT! THAT'S JUST WHAT A GUY WANTS TO HEAR!
HEEHEE! NOW I'VE EMBARRASSED YOU FOR NOTHING...
FORGET IT. IT WASN'T SO BAD.
KISSING YAGATE WILL HAUNT MY DREAMS FOR YEARS TO COME...
...BUT NOTHING MORE.
DO YOU HAVE FAR TO GO TO GET HOME?
IF YOU WANT, I CAN TAKE YOU.
NO, IT'S NOT FAR. BUT THANKS ANYWAY FOR THE OFFER!
OKAY THEN...
YEAH, OKAY THEN...

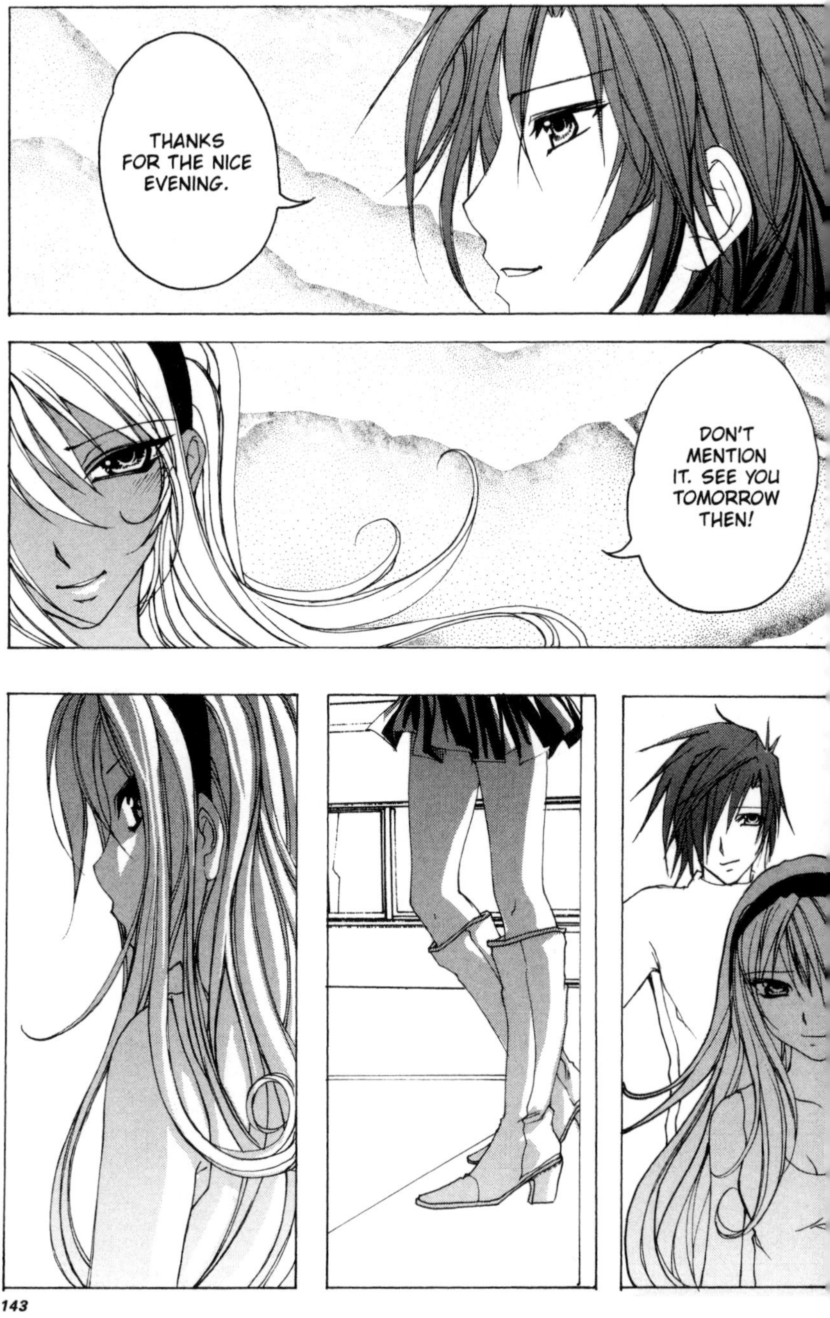
THANKS FOR THE NICE EVENING.
DON'T MENTION IT. SEE YOU TOMORROW THEN!

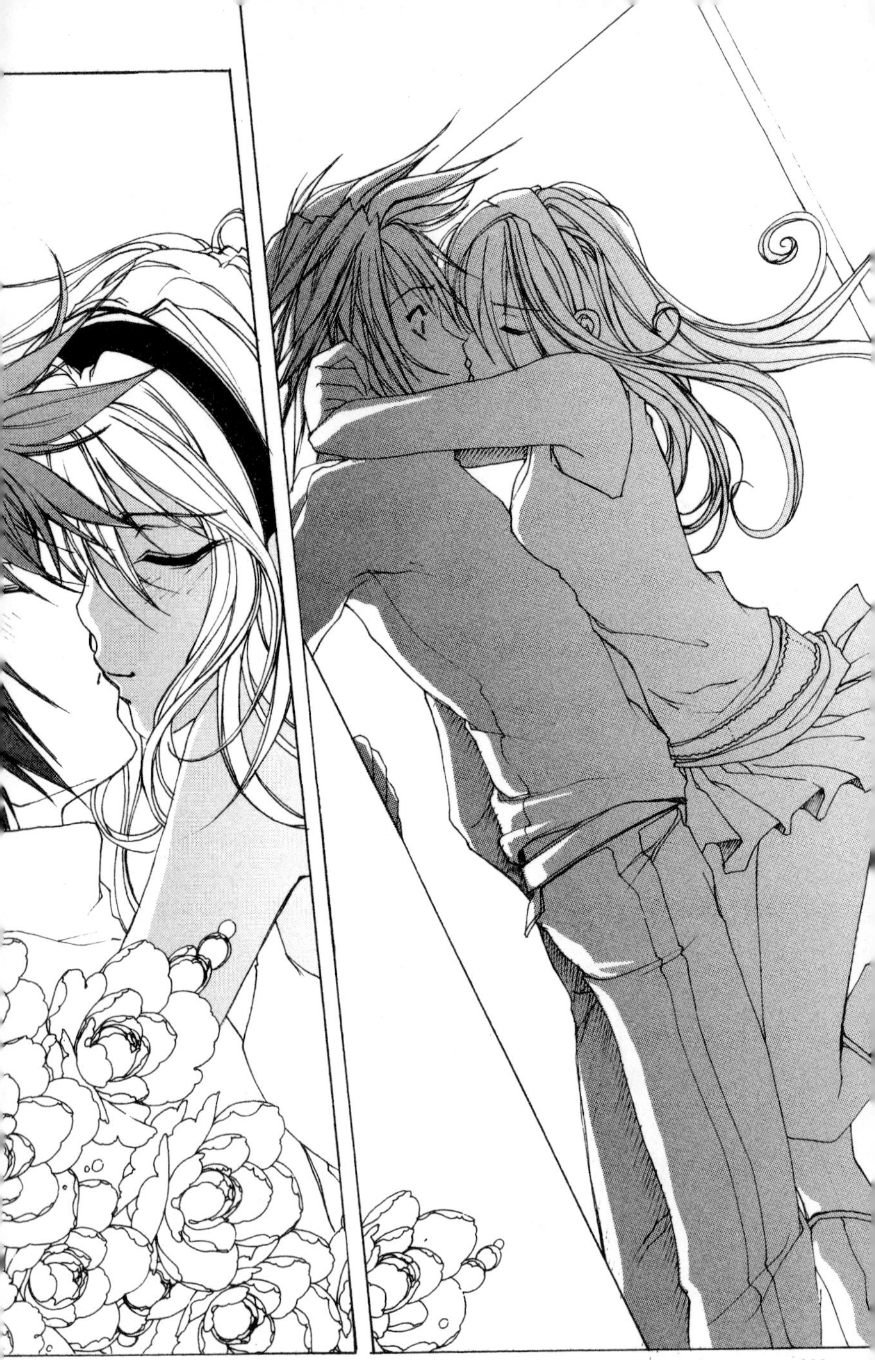

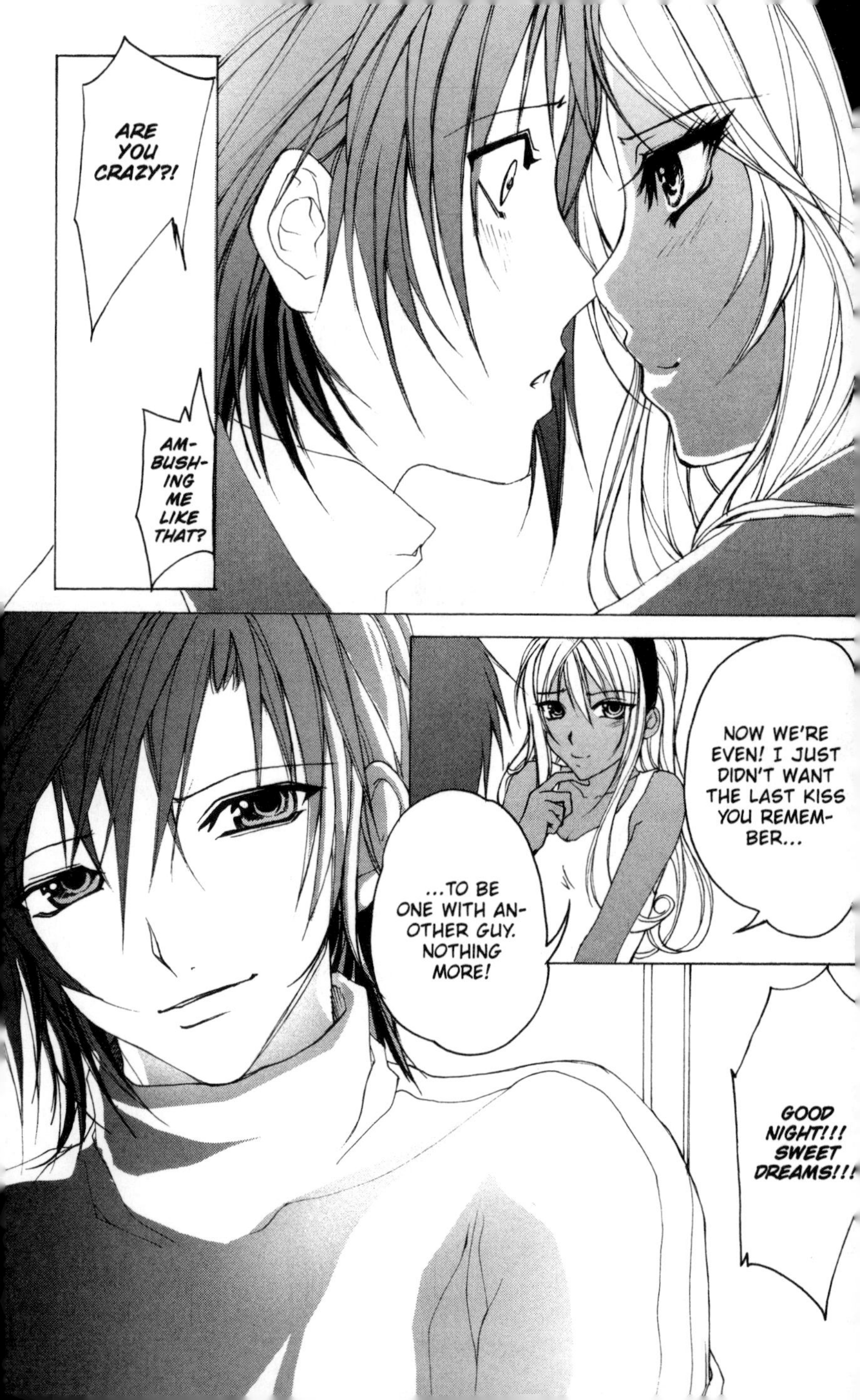
ARE YOU CRAZY?!
AM-BUSH-ING ME LIKE THAT?
NOW WE'RE EVEN! I JUST DIDN'T WANT THE LAST KISS YOU REMEM-BER...
...TO BE ONE WITH AN-OTHER GUY. NOTHING MORE!
GOOD NIGHT!!! SWEET DREAMS!!!

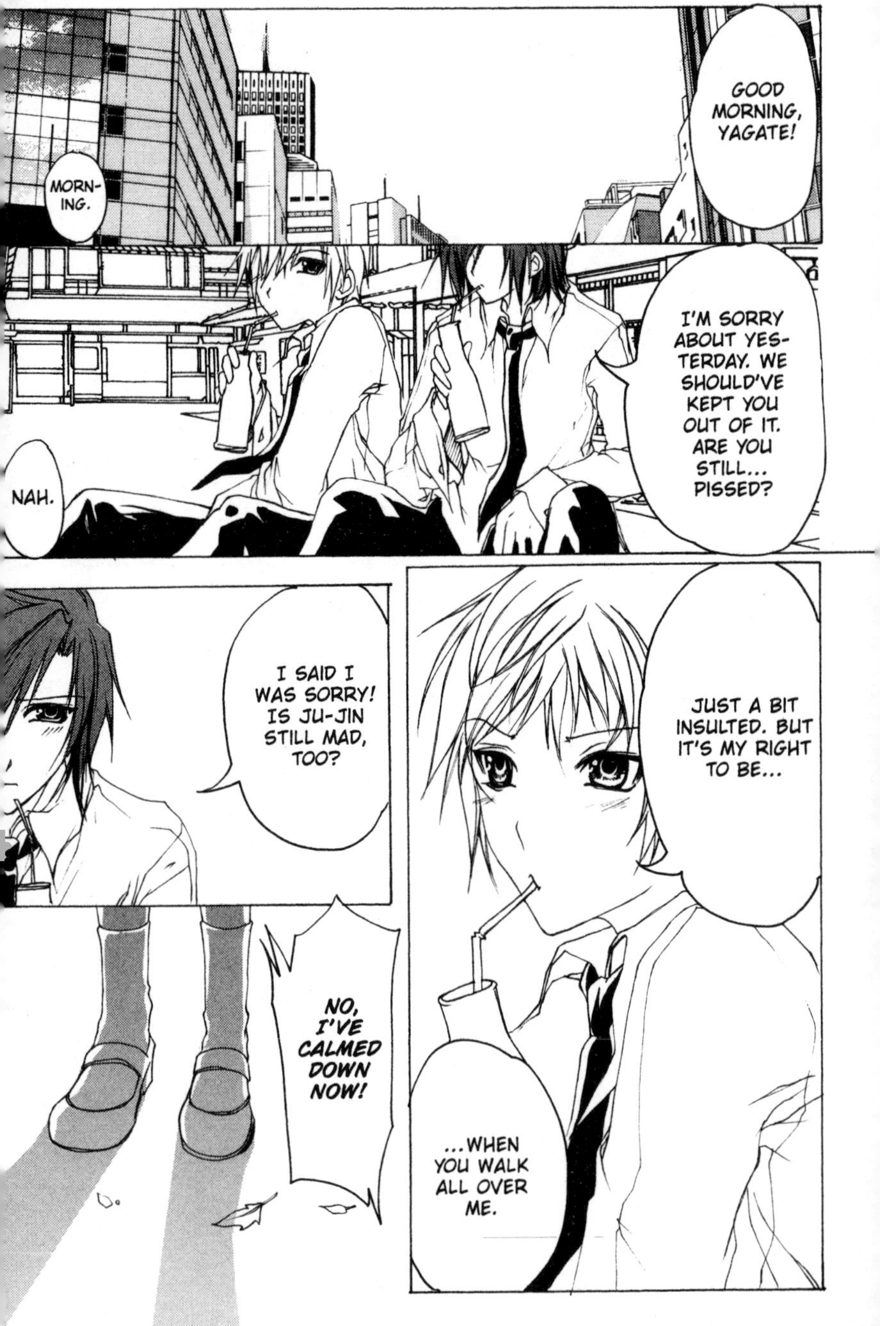
GOOD MORNING, YAGATE!
MORN-ING.
I'M SORRY ABOUT YES-TERDAY. WE SHOULD'VE KEPT YOU OUT OF IT. ARE YOU STILL... PISSED?
NAH.
JUST A BIT INSULTED. BUT IT'S MY RIGHT TO BE...
...WHEN YOU WALK ALL OVER ME.
I SAID I WAS SORRY! IS JU-JIN STILL MAD, TOO?
NO, I'VE CALMED DOWN NOW!

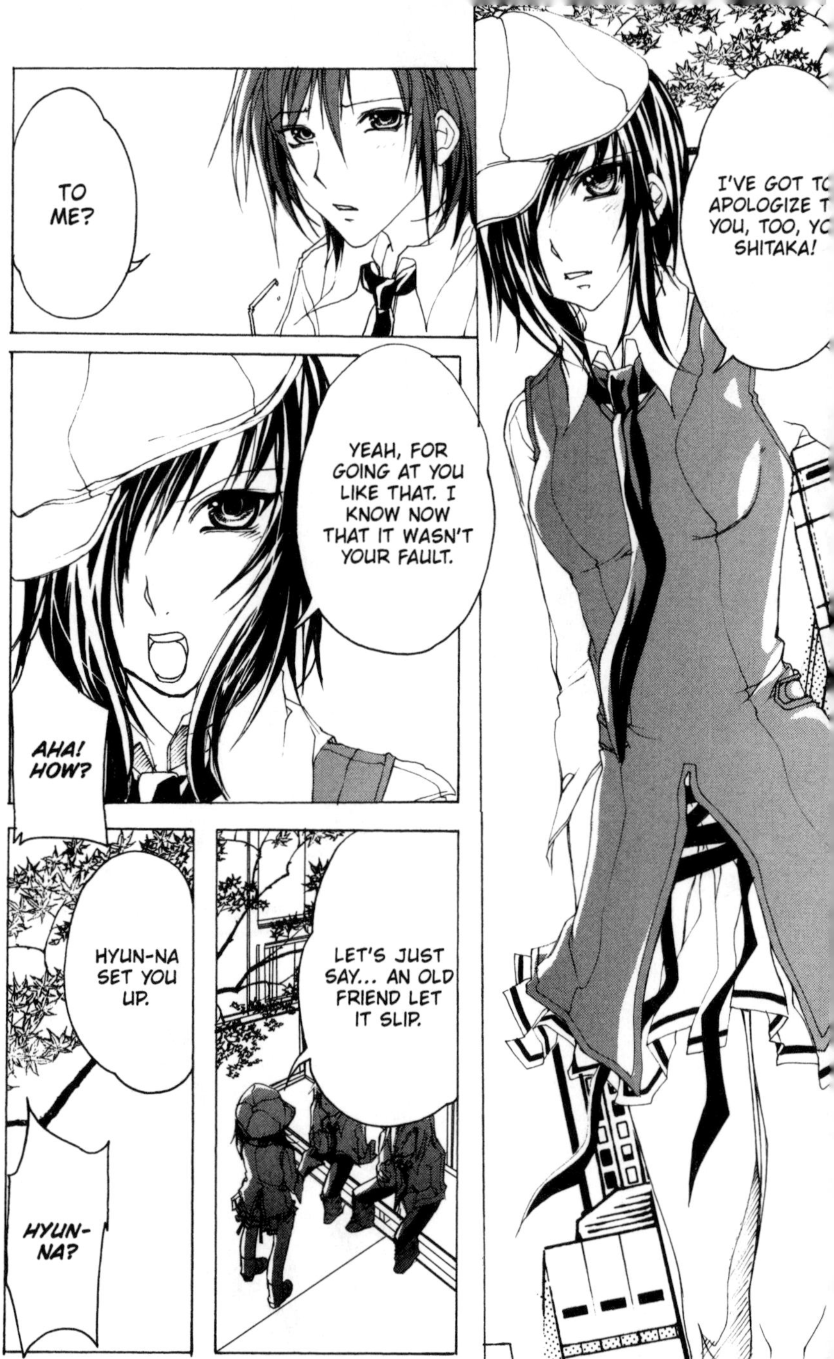
I'VE GOT TO APOLOGIZE T YOU, TOO, YO SHITAKA!
TO ME?
YEAH, FOR GOING AT YOU LIKE THAT. I KNOW NOW THAT IT WASN'T YOUR FAULT.
AHA! HOW?
LET'S JUST SAY... AN OLD FRIEND LET IT SLIP.
HYUN-NA SET YOU UP.
HYUN-NA?

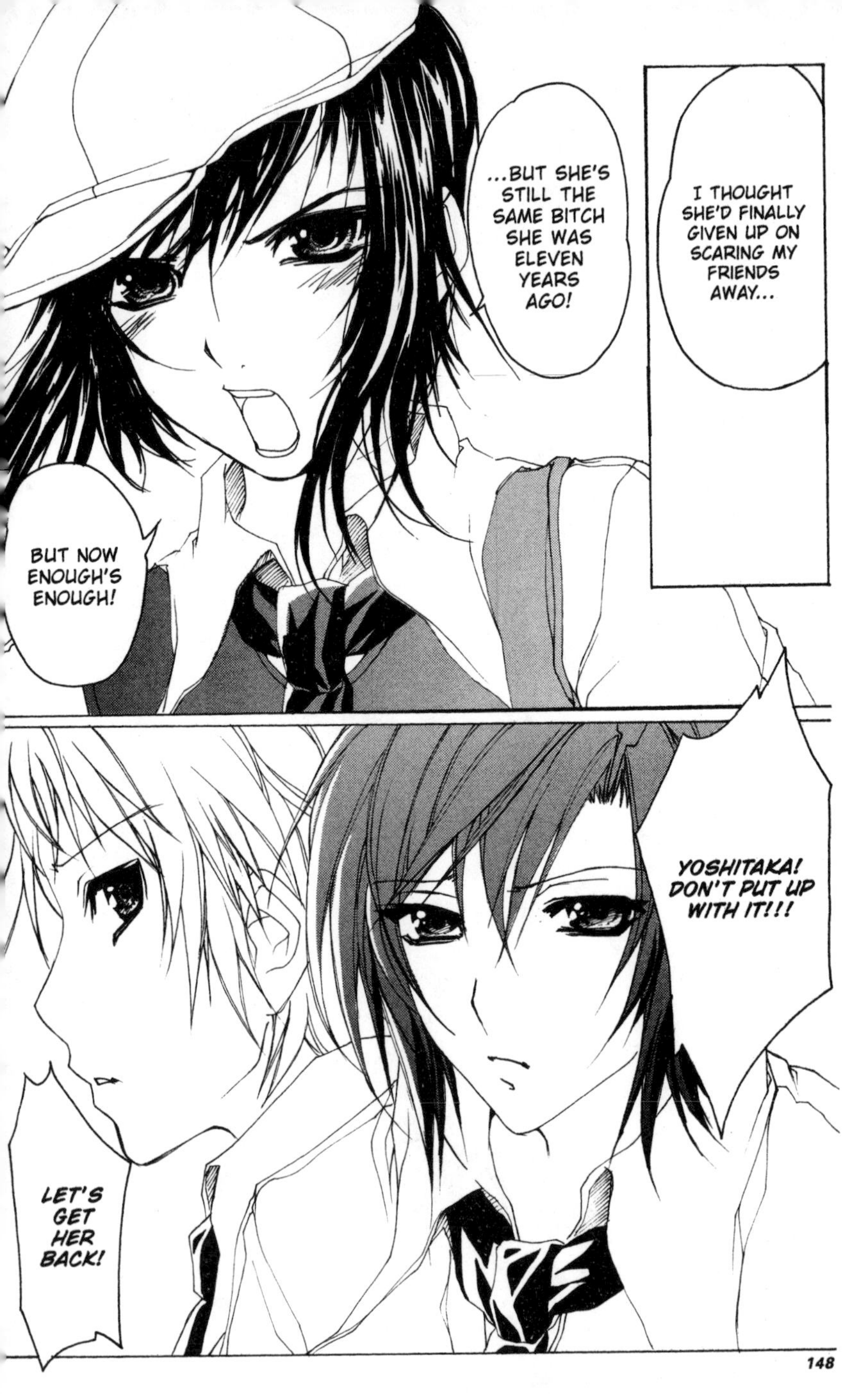
I THOUGHT SHE'D FINALLY GIVEN UP ON SCARING MY FRIENDS AWAY...
...BUT SHE'S STILL THE SAME BITCH SHE WAS ELEVEN YEARS AGO!
BUT NOW ENOUGH'S ENOUGH!
YOSHITAKA! DON'T PUT UP WITH IT!!!
LET'S GET HER BACK!

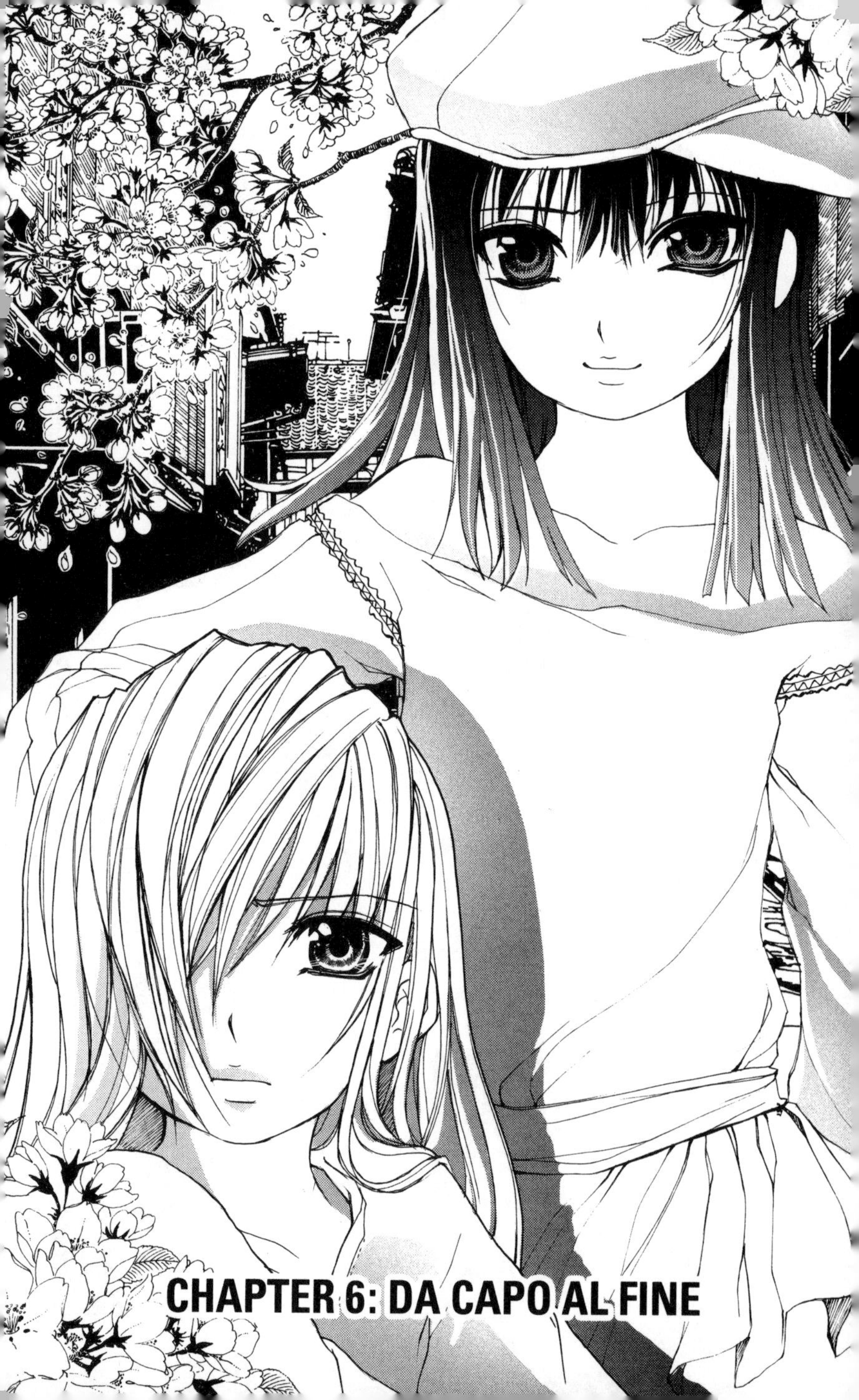

CHAPTER 6: DA CAPO AL FINE

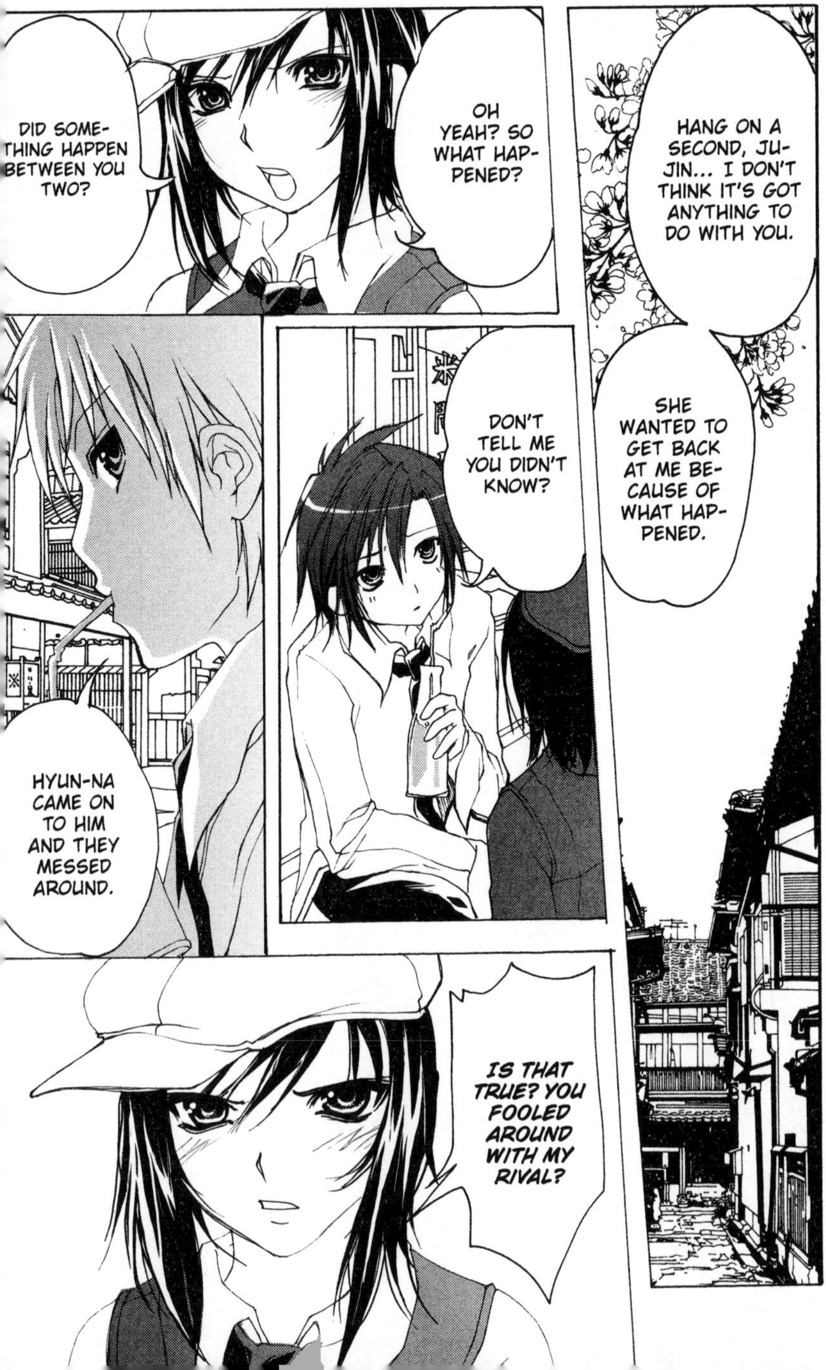
HANG ON A SECOND, JU-JIN... I DON'T THINK IT'S GOT ANYTHING TO DO WITH YOU.
SHE WANTED TO GET BACK AT ME BE-CAUSE OF WHAT HAP-PENED.
OH YEAH? SO WHAT HAP-PENED?
DID SOME-THING HAPPEN BETWEEN YOU TWO?
DON'T TELL ME YOU DIDN'T KNOW?
HYUN-NA CAME ON TO HIM AND THEY MESSED AROUND.
IS THAT TRUE? YOU FOOLED AROUND WITH MY RIVAL?

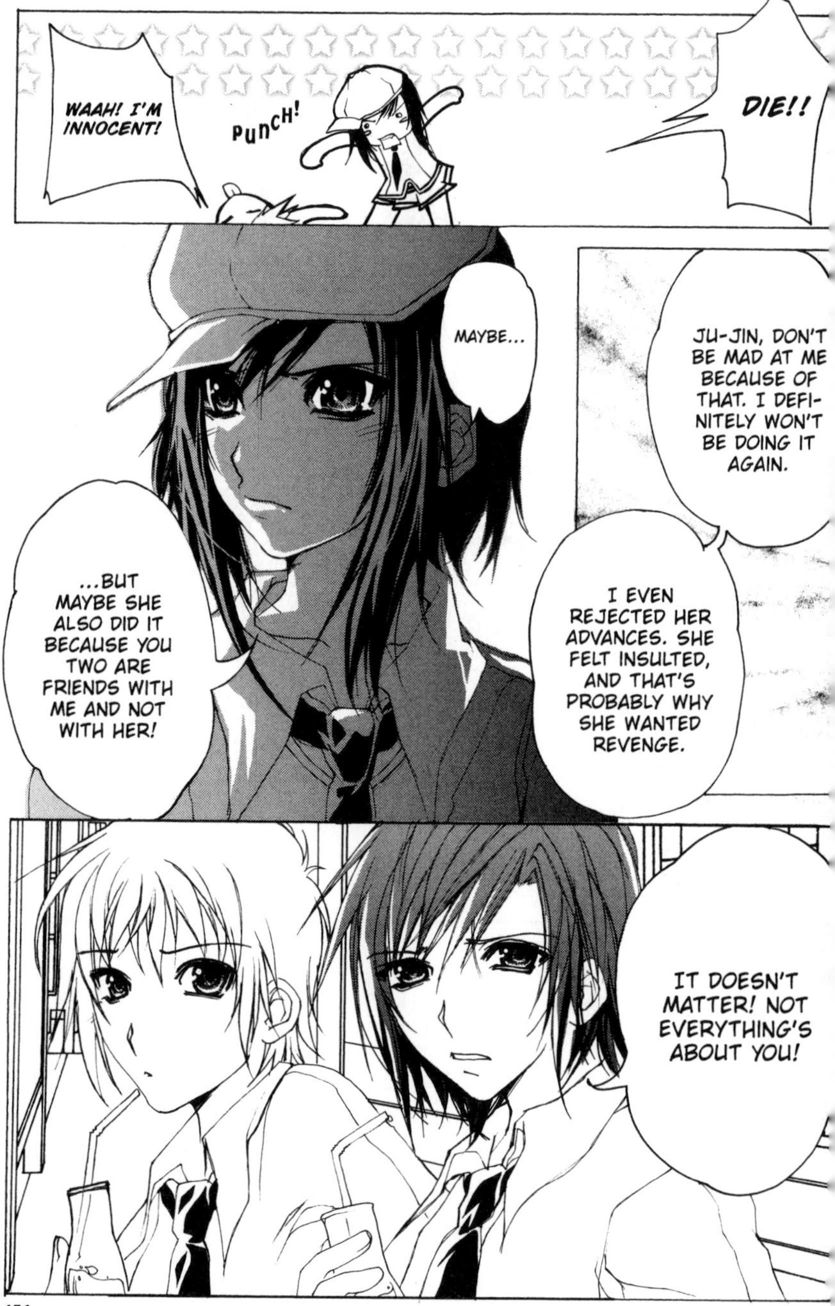
DIE!!
PUNCH!
WAAH! I'M INNOCENT!
JU-JIN, DON'T BE MAD AT ME BECAUSE OF THAT. I DEFINITELY WON'T BE DOING IT AGAIN.
I EVEN REJECTED HER ADVANCES. SHE FELT INSULTED, AND THAT'S PROBABLY WHY SHE WANTED REVENGE.
MAYBE...
...BUT MAYBE SHE ALSO DID IT BECAUSE YOU TWO ARE FRIENDS WITH ME AND NOT WITH HER!
IT DOESN'T MATTER! NOT EVERYTHING'S ABOUT YOU!

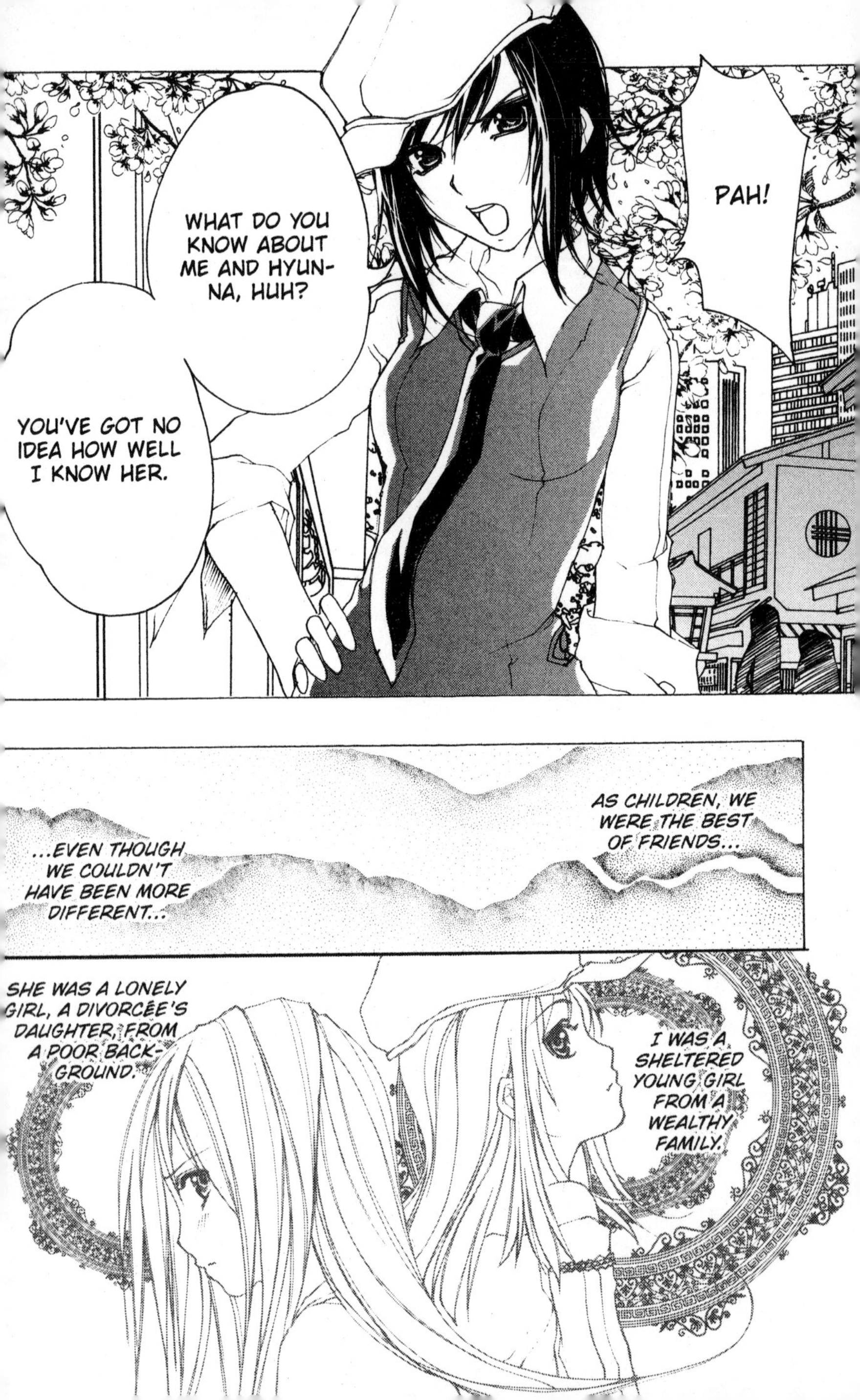
PAH!
WHAT DO YOU KNOW ABOUT ME AND HYUN-NA, HUH?
YOU'VE GOT NO IDEA HOW WELL I KNOW HER.
AS CHILDREN, WE WERE THE BEST OF FRIENDS...
...EVEN THOUGH WE COULDN'T HAVE BEEN MORE DIFFERENT...
I WAS A SHELTERED YOUNG GIRL FROM A WEALTHY FAMILY.
SHE WAS A LONELY GIRL, A DIVORCÉE'S DAUGHTER, FROM A POOR BACK-GROUND.

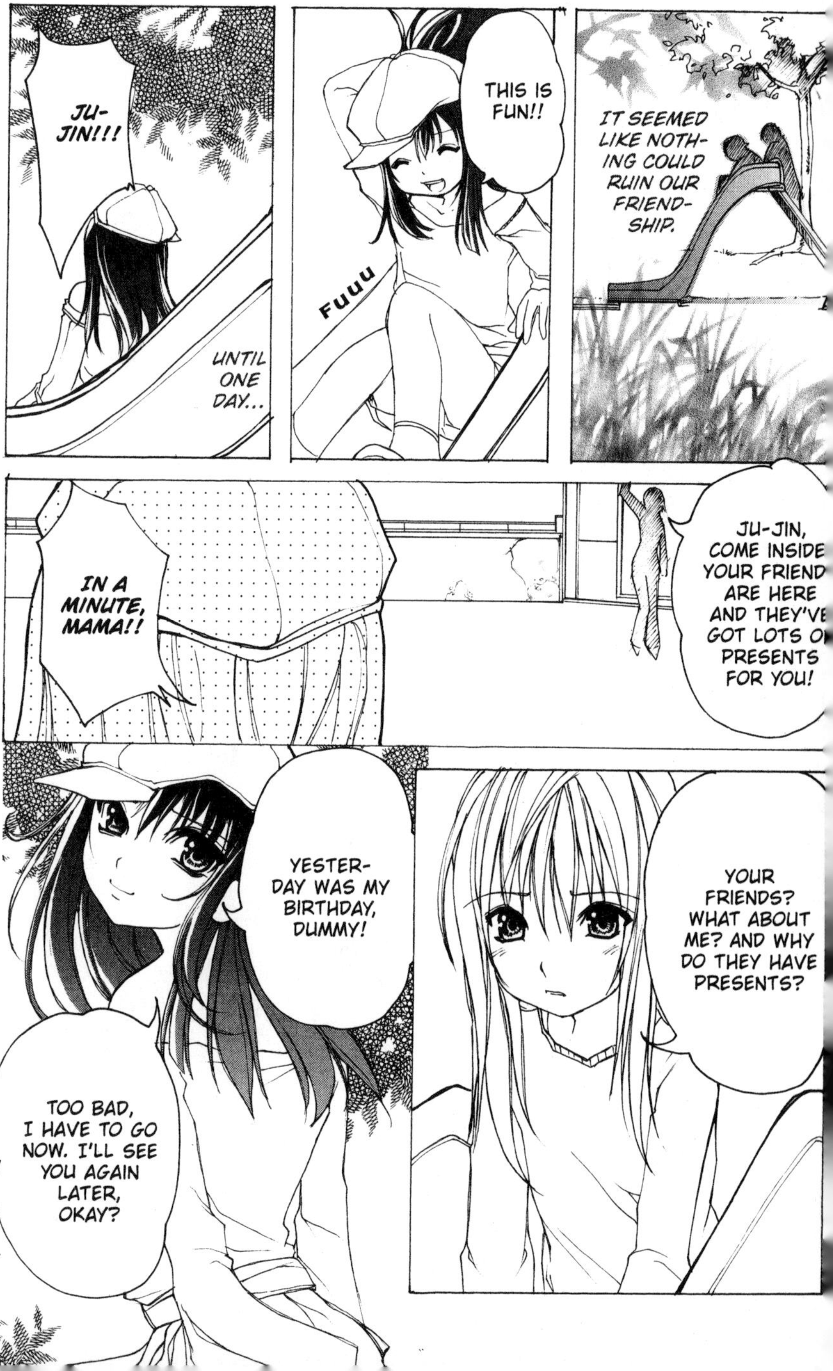
IT SEEMED LIKE NOTHING COULD RUIN OUR FRIENDSHIP.
THIS IS FUN!!
FUUU
JU-JIN!!!
UNTIL ONE DAY...
JU-JIN, COME INSIDE YOUR FRIEND ARE HERE AND THEY'VE GOT LOTS O PRESENTS FOR YOU!
IN A MINUTE, MAMA!!
YOUR FRIENDS? WHAT ABOUT ME? AND WHY DO THEY HAVE PRESENTS?
YESTERDAY WAS MY BIRTHDAY, DUMMY!
TOO BAD, I HAVE TO GO NOW. I'LL SEE YOU AGAIN LATER, OKAY?

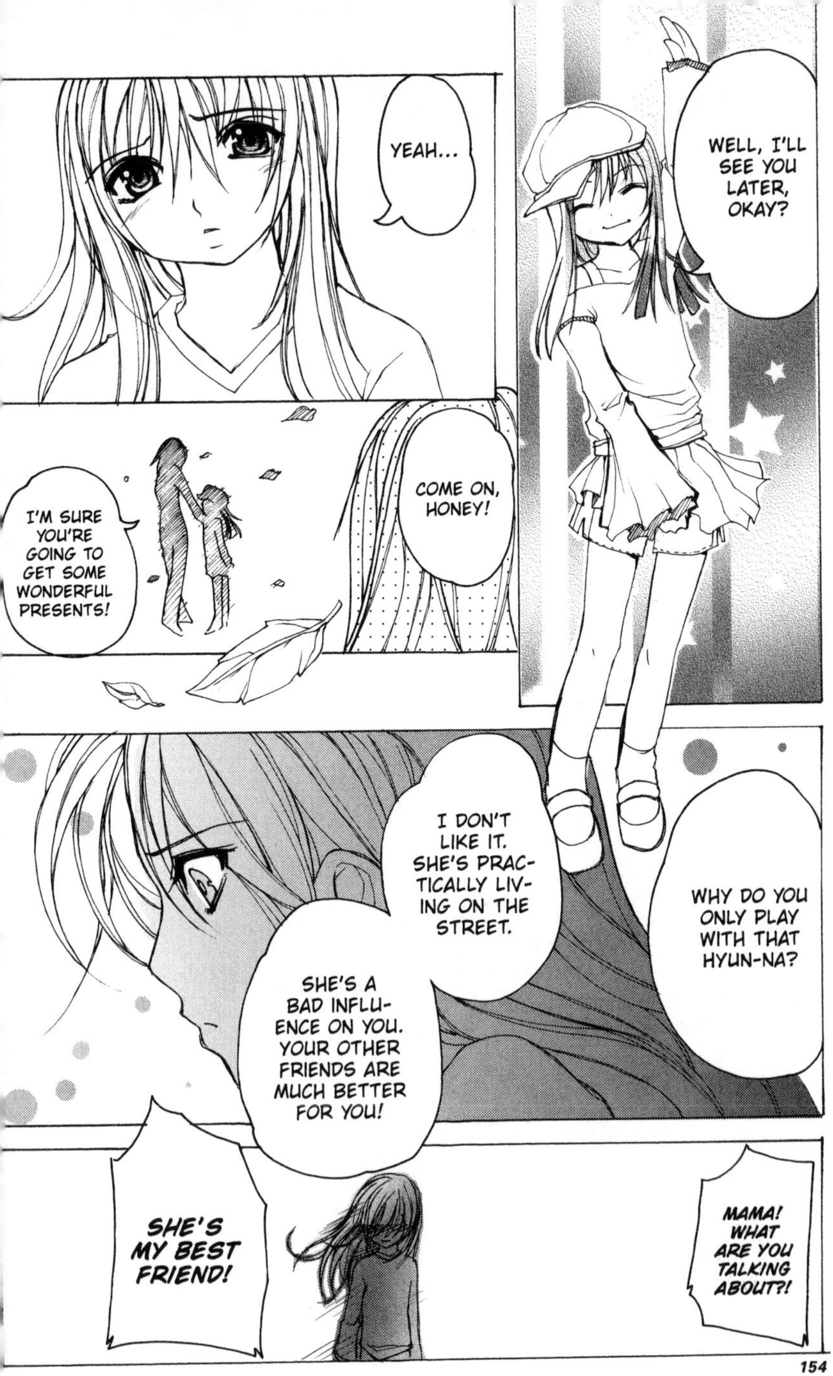
WELL, I'LL SEE YOU LATER, OKAY?
YEAH...
COME ON, HONEY!
I'M SURE YOU'RE GOING TO GET SOME WONDERFUL PRESENTS!
WHY DO YOU ONLY PLAY WITH THAT HYUN-NA?
I DON'T LIKE IT. SHE'S PRACTICALLY LIVING ON THE STREET.
SHE'S A BAD INFLUENCE ON YOU. YOUR OTHER FRIENDS ARE MUCH BETTER FOR YOU!
MAMA! WHAT ARE YOU TALKING ABOUT?!
SHE'S MY BEST FRIEND!

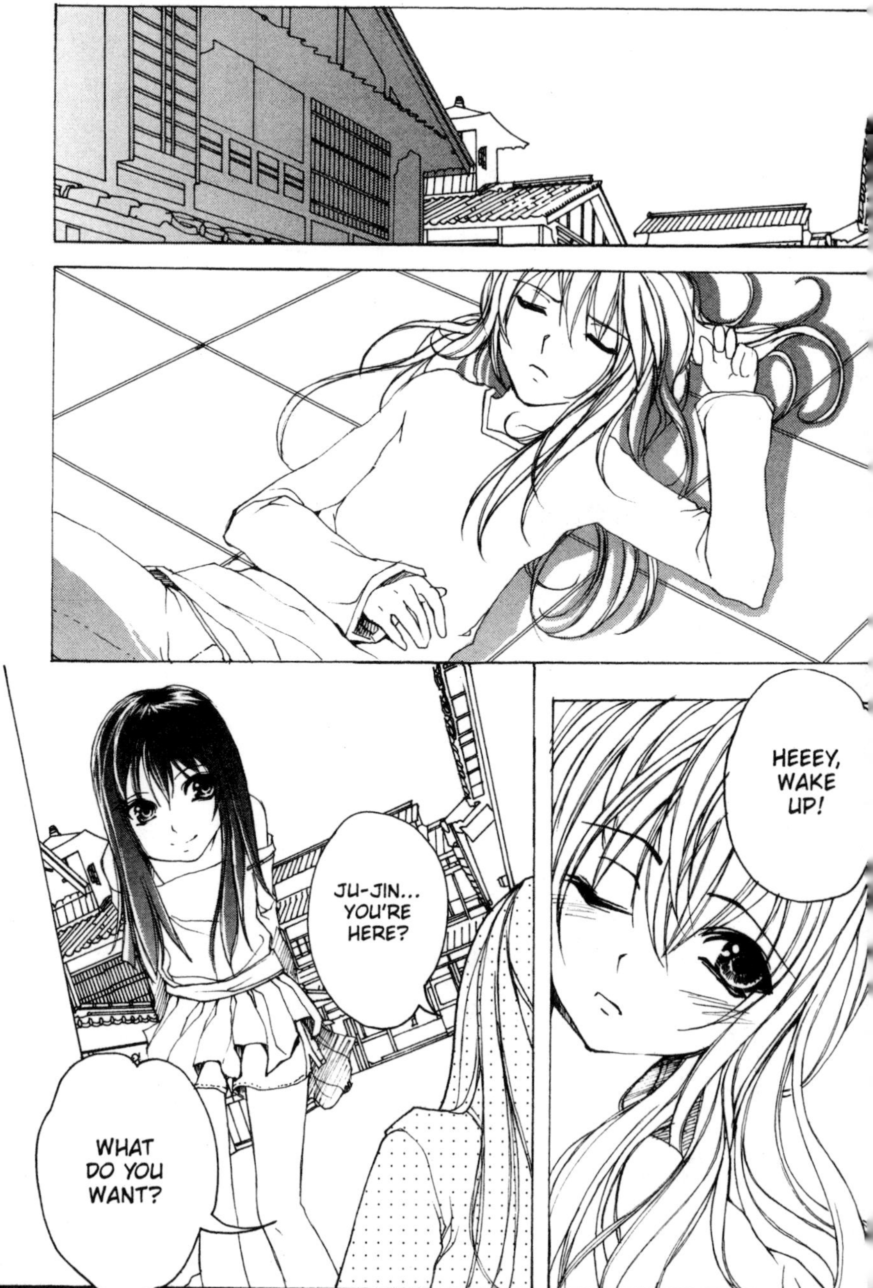
HEEEY, WAKE UP!
JU-JIN... YOU'RE HERE?
WHAT DO YOU WANT?

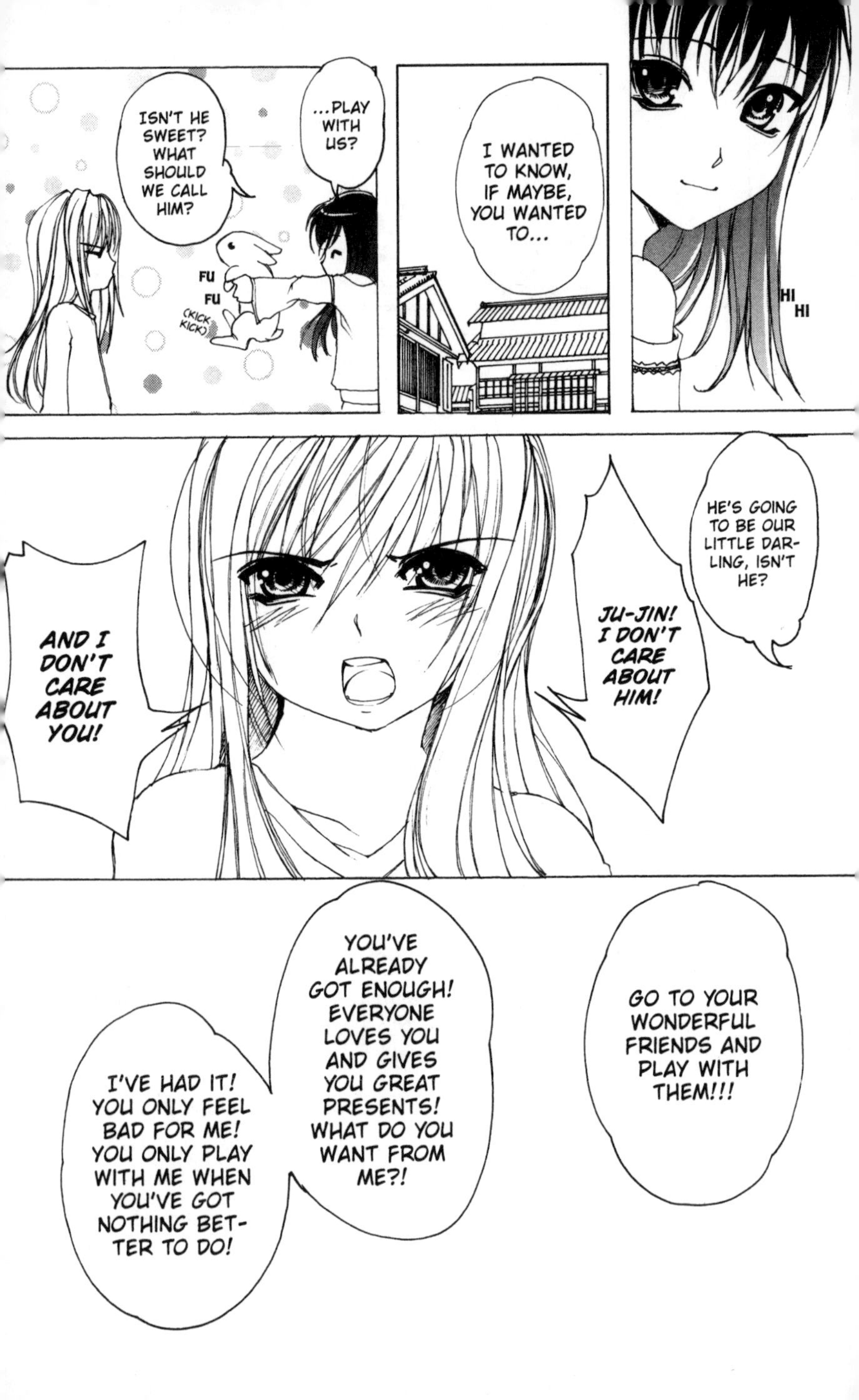
HI HI
I WANTED TO KNOW, IF MAYBE, YOU WANTED TO...
...PLAY WITH US?
ISN'T HE SWEET? WHAT SHOULD WE CALL HIM?
FU FU
(KICK KICK)
HE'S GOING TO BE OUR LITTLE DARLING, ISN'T HE?
JU-JIN! I DON'T CARE ABOUT HIM!
AND I DON'T CARE ABOUT YOU!
GO TO YOUR WONDERFUL FRIENDS AND PLAY WITH THEM!!!
YOU'VE ALREADY GOT ENOUGH! EVERYONE LOVES YOU AND GIVES YOU GREAT PRESENTS! WHAT DO YOU WANT FROM ME?!
I'VE HAD IT! YOU ONLY FEEL BAD FOR ME! YOU ONLY PLAY WITH ME WHEN YOU'VE GOT NOTHING BETTER TO DO!

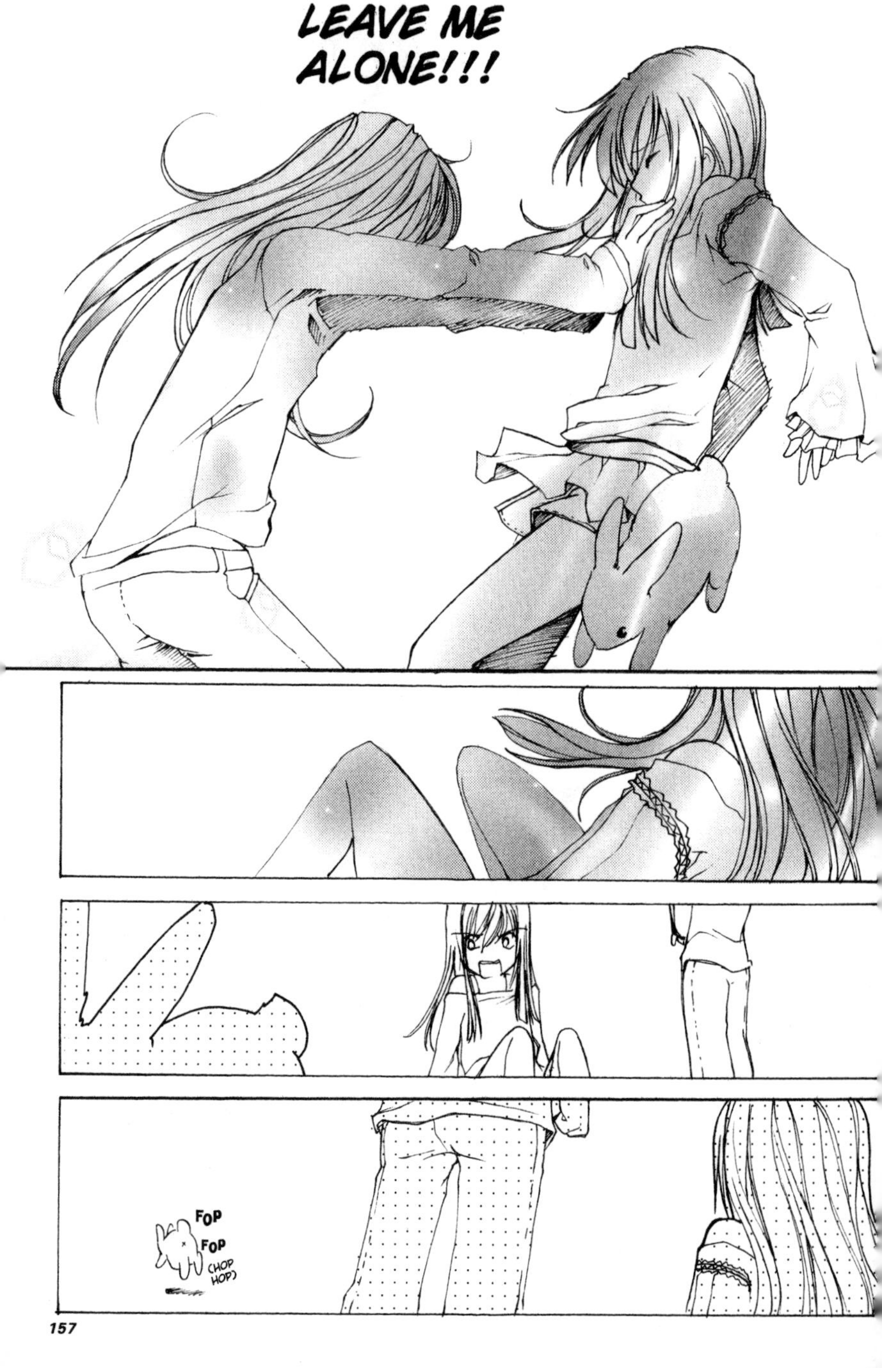
LEAVE ME ALONE!!!
FOP FOP
(HOP HOP)

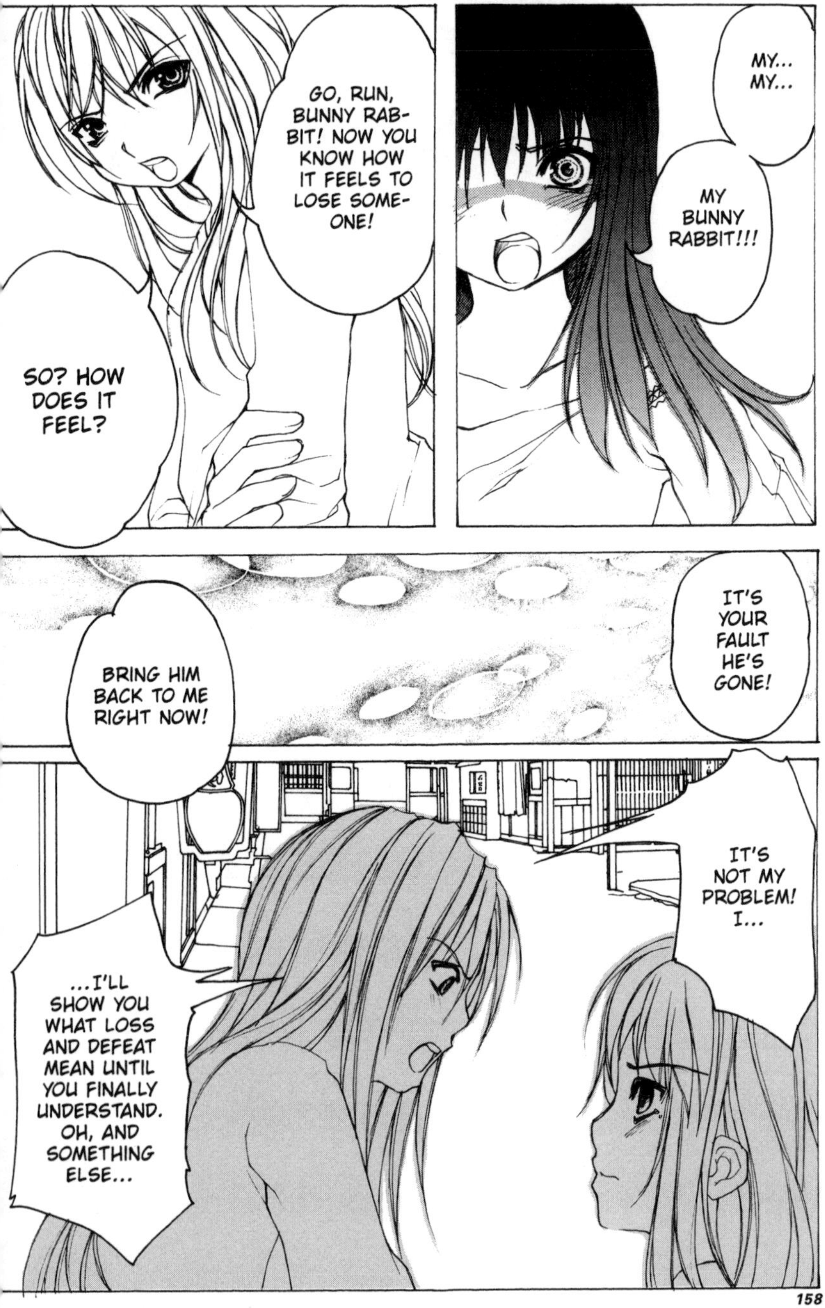
MY... MY...
MY BUNNY RABBIT!!!
GO, RUN, BUNNY RABBIT! NOW YOU KNOW HOW IT FEELS TO LOSE SOMEONE!
SO? HOW DOES IT FEEL?
IT'S YOUR FAULT HE'S GONE!
BRING HIM BACK TO ME RIGHT NOW!
IT'S NOT MY PROBLEM! I...
...I'LL SHOW YOU WHAT LOSS AND DEFEAT MEAN UNTIL YOU FINALLY UNDERSTAND. OH, AND SOMETHING ELSE...

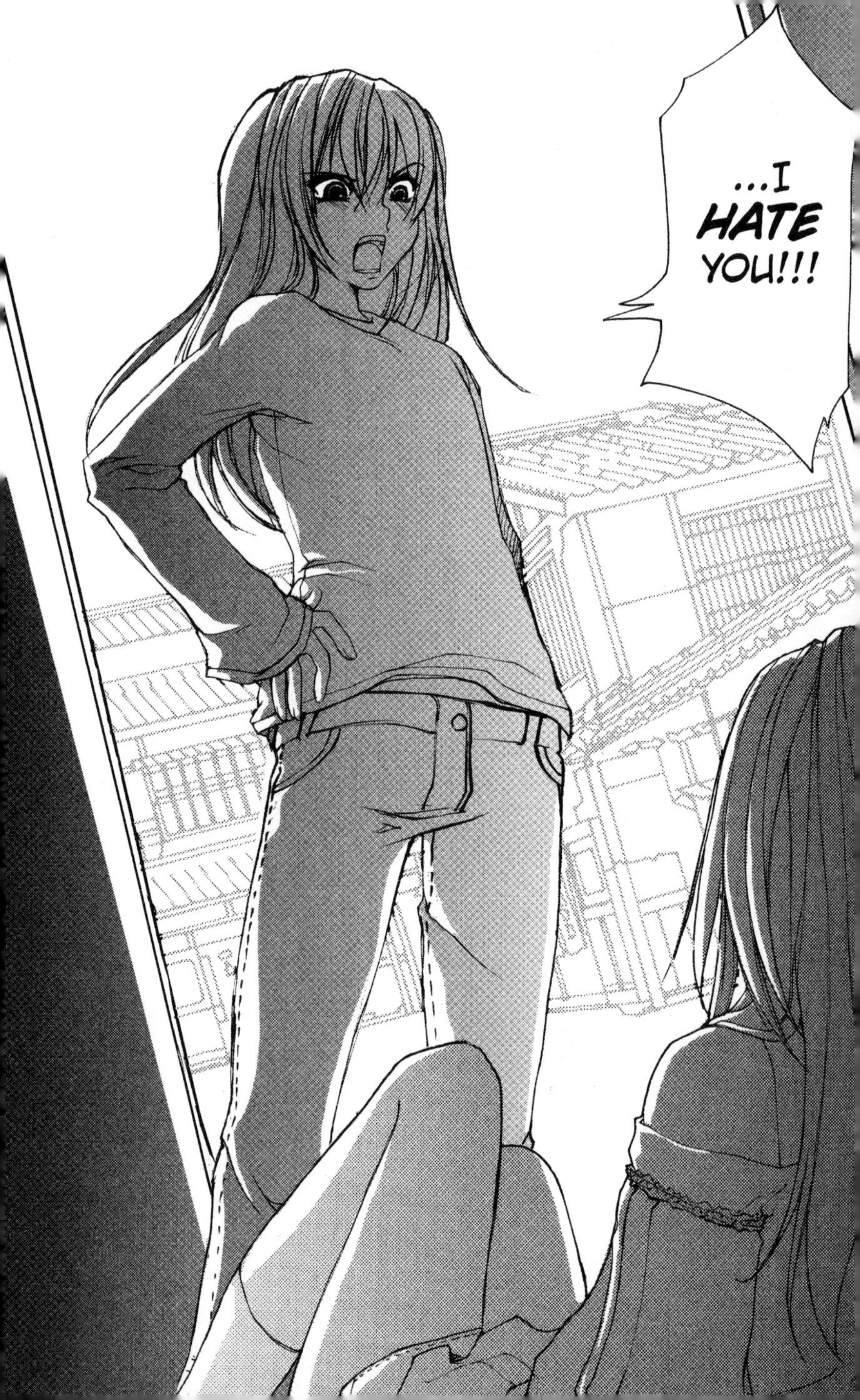
...I **HATE** YOU!!!

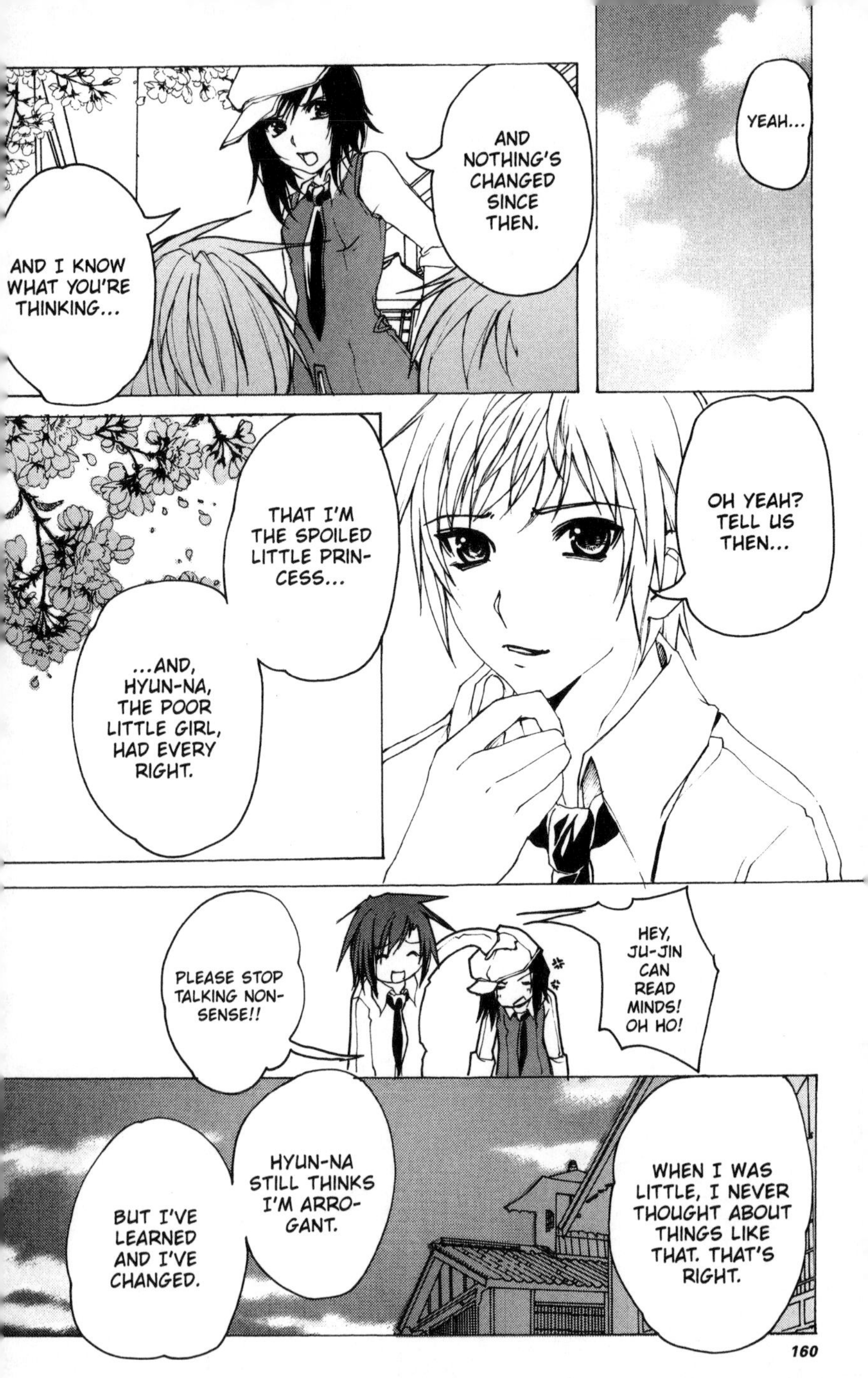
YEAH...
AND NOTHING'S CHANGED SINCE THEN.
AND I KNOW WHAT YOU'RE THINKING...
OH YEAH? TELL US THEN...
THAT I'M THE SPOILED LITTLE PRIN-CESS...
...AND, HYUN-NA, THE POOR LITTLE GIRL, HAD EVERY RIGHT.
HEY, JU-JIN CAN READ MINDS! OH HO!
PLEASE STOP TALKING NON-SENSE!!
WHEN I WAS LITTLE, I NEVER THOUGHT ABOUT THINGS LIKE THAT. THAT'S RIGHT.
HYUN-NA STILL THINKS I'M ARRO-GANT.
BUT I'VE LEARNED AND I'VE CHANGED.

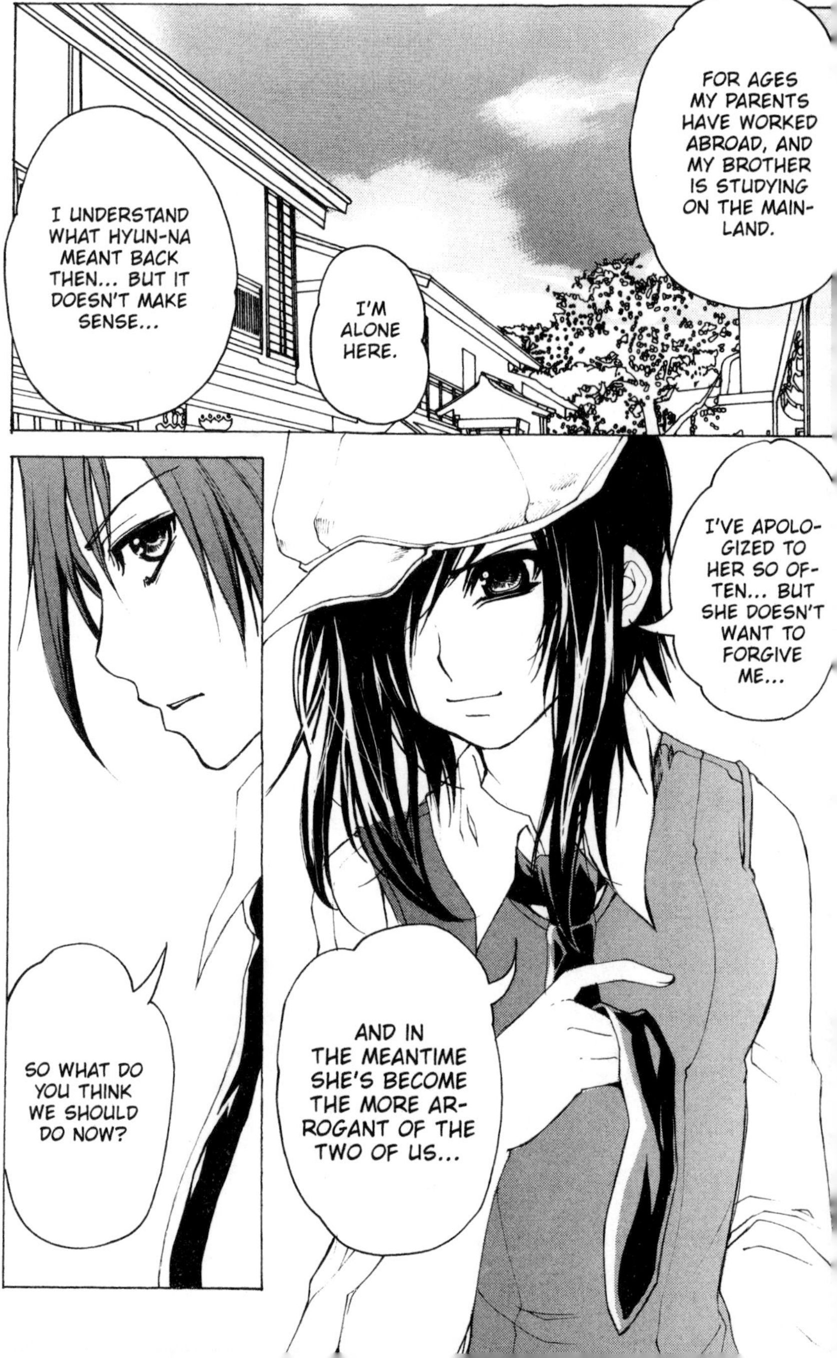
FOR AGES MY PARENTS HAVE WORKED ABROAD, AND MY BROTHER IS STUDYING ON THE MAIN-LAND.
I'M ALONE HERE.
I UNDERSTAND WHAT HYUN-NA MEANT BACK THEN... BUT IT DOESN'T MAKE SENSE...
I'VE APOLO-GIZED TO HER SO OF-TEN... BUT SHE DOESN'T WANT TO FORGIVE ME...
AND IN THE MEANTIME SHE'S BECOME THE MORE AR-ROGANT OF THE TWO OF US...
SO WHAT DO YOU THINK WE SHOULD DO NOW?

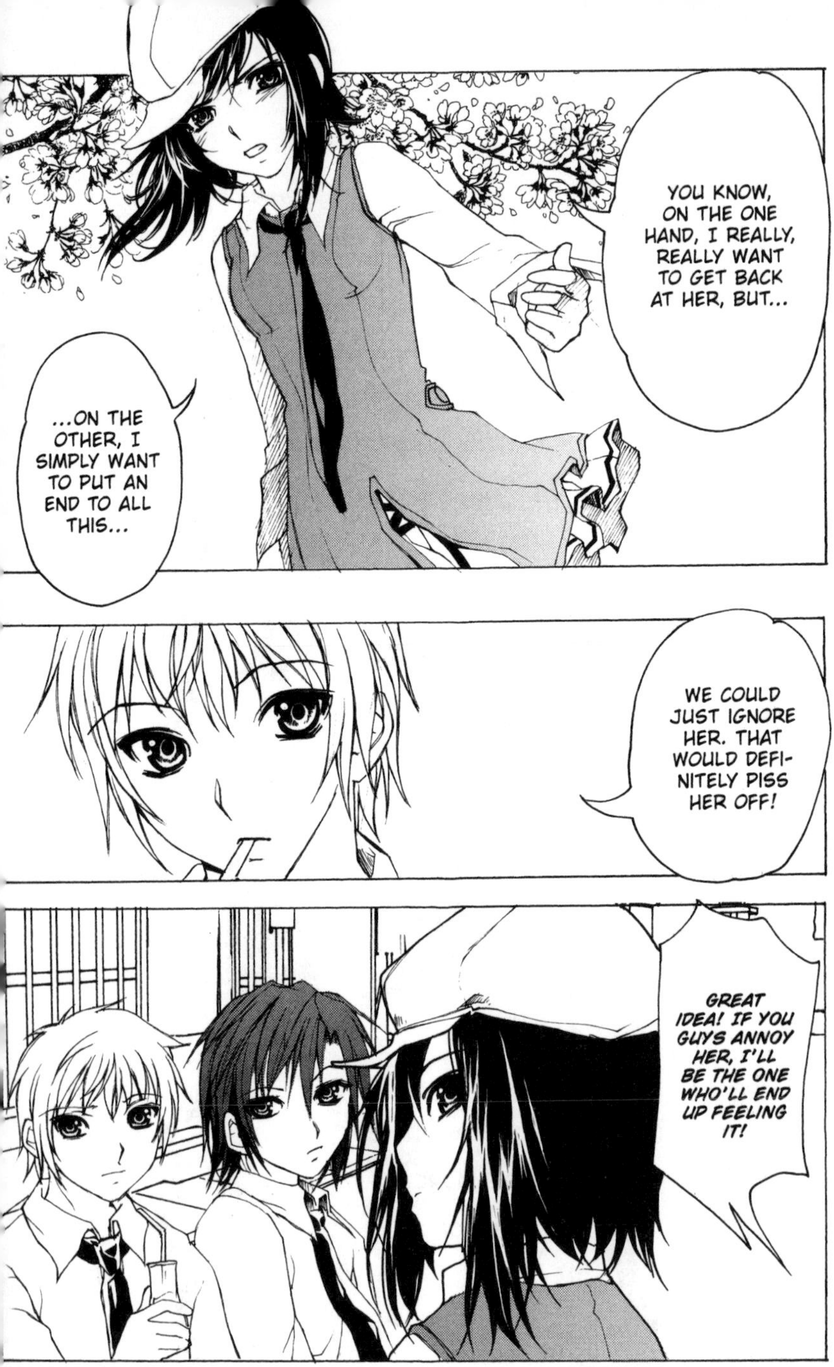
YOU KNOW, ON THE ONE HAND, I REALLY, REALLY WANT TO GET BACK AT HER, BUT...
...ON THE OTHER, I SIMPLY WANT TO PUT AN END TO ALL THIS...
WE COULD JUST IGNORE HER. THAT WOULD DEFI-NITELY PISS HER OFF!
GREAT IDEA! IF YOU GUYS ANNOY HER, I'LL BE THE ONE WHO'LL END UP FEELING IT!

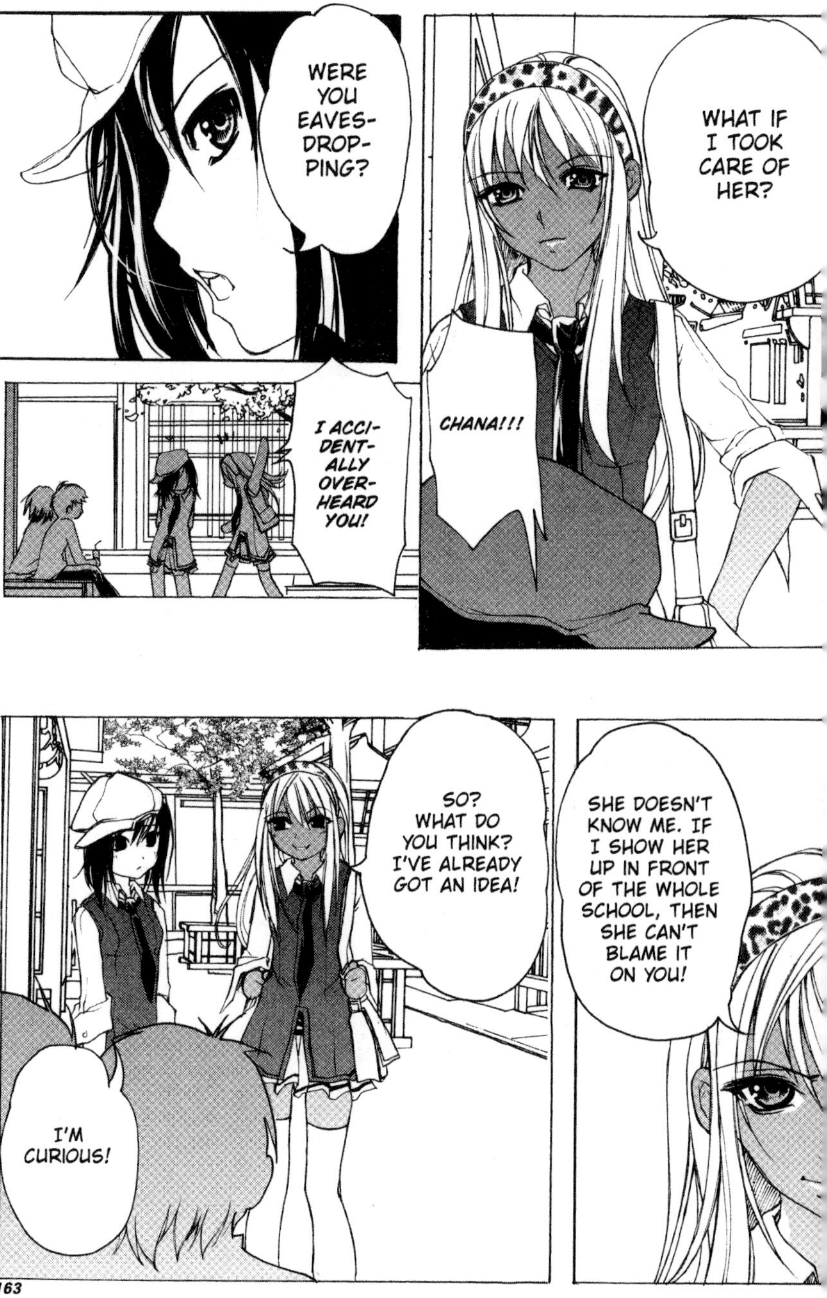
WHAT IF I TOOK CARE OF HER?
CHANA!!!
WERE YOU EAVES-DROP-PING?
I ACCI-DENT-ALLY OVER-HEARD YOU!
SHE DOESN'T KNOW ME. IF I SHOW HER UP IN FRONT OF THE WHOLE SCHOOL, THEN SHE CAN'T BLAME IT ON YOU!
SO? WHAT DO YOU THINK? I'VE ALREADY GOT AN IDEA!
I'M CURIOUS!

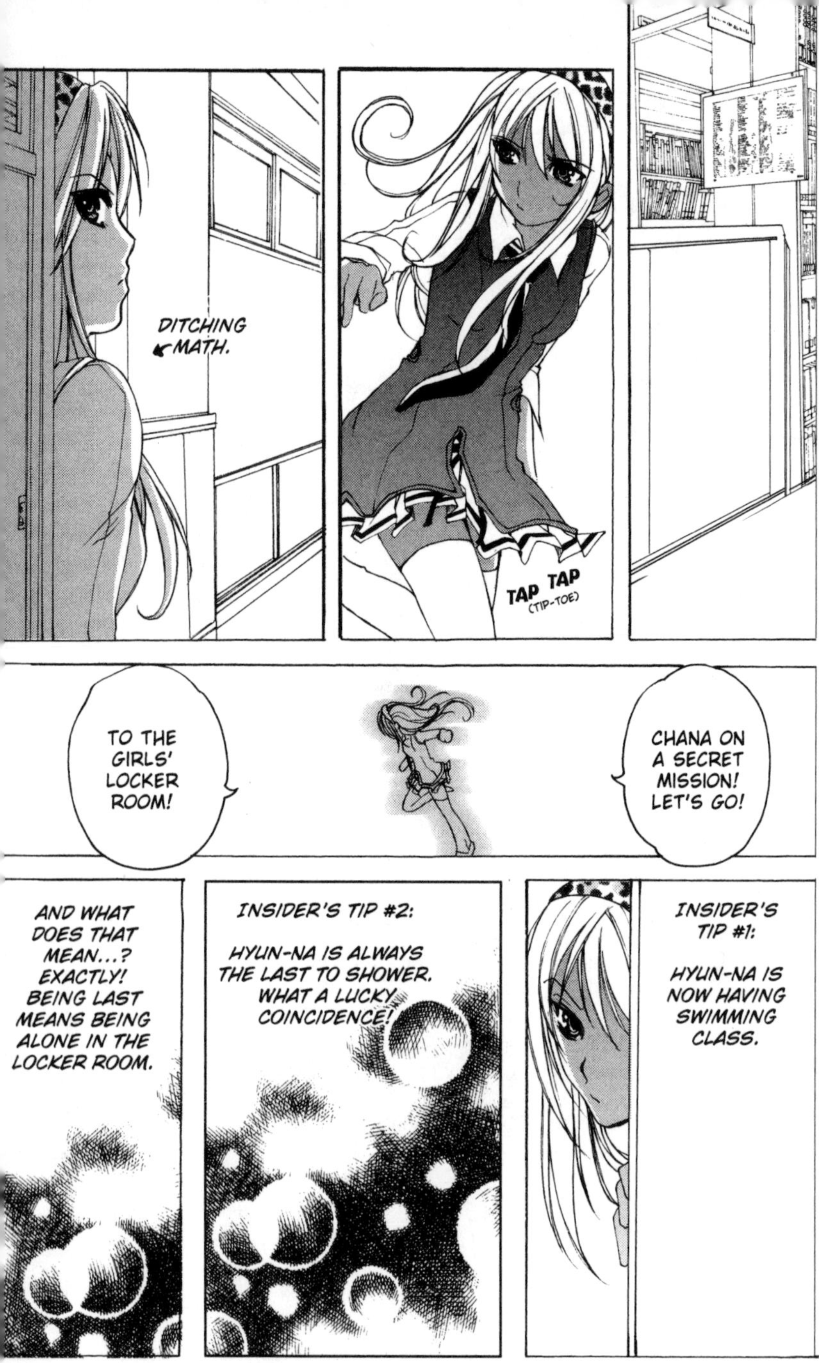
TAP TAP
(TIP-TOE)
DITCHING MATH.
CHANA ON A SECRET MISSION! LET'S GO!
TO THE GIRLS' LOCKER ROOM!
INSIDER'S TIP #1:
HYUN-NA IS NOW HAVING SWIMMING CLASS.
INSIDER'S TIP #2:
HYUN-NA IS ALWAYS THE LAST TO SHOWER. WHAT A LUCKY COINCIDENCE!
AND WHAT DOES THAT MEAN...? EXACTLY! BEING LAST MEANS BEING ALONE IN THE LOCKER ROOM.

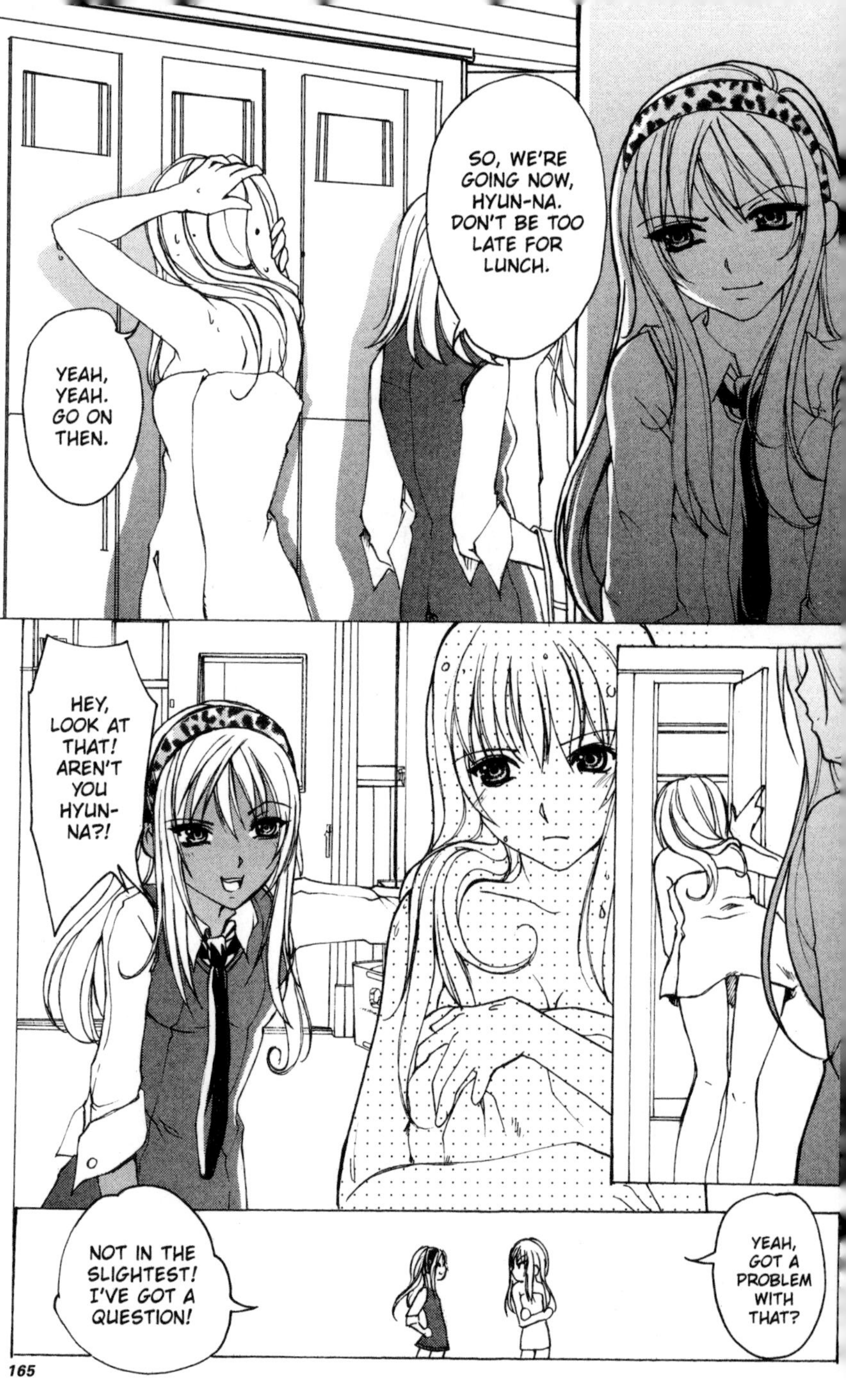
SO, WE'RE GOING NOW, HYUN-NA. DON'T BE TOO LATE FOR LUNCH.
YEAH, YEAH. GO ON THEN.
HEY, LOOK AT THAT! AREN'T YOU HYUN-NA?!
YEAH, GOT A PROBLEM WITH THAT?
NOT IN THE SLIGHTEST! I'VE GOT A QUESTION!

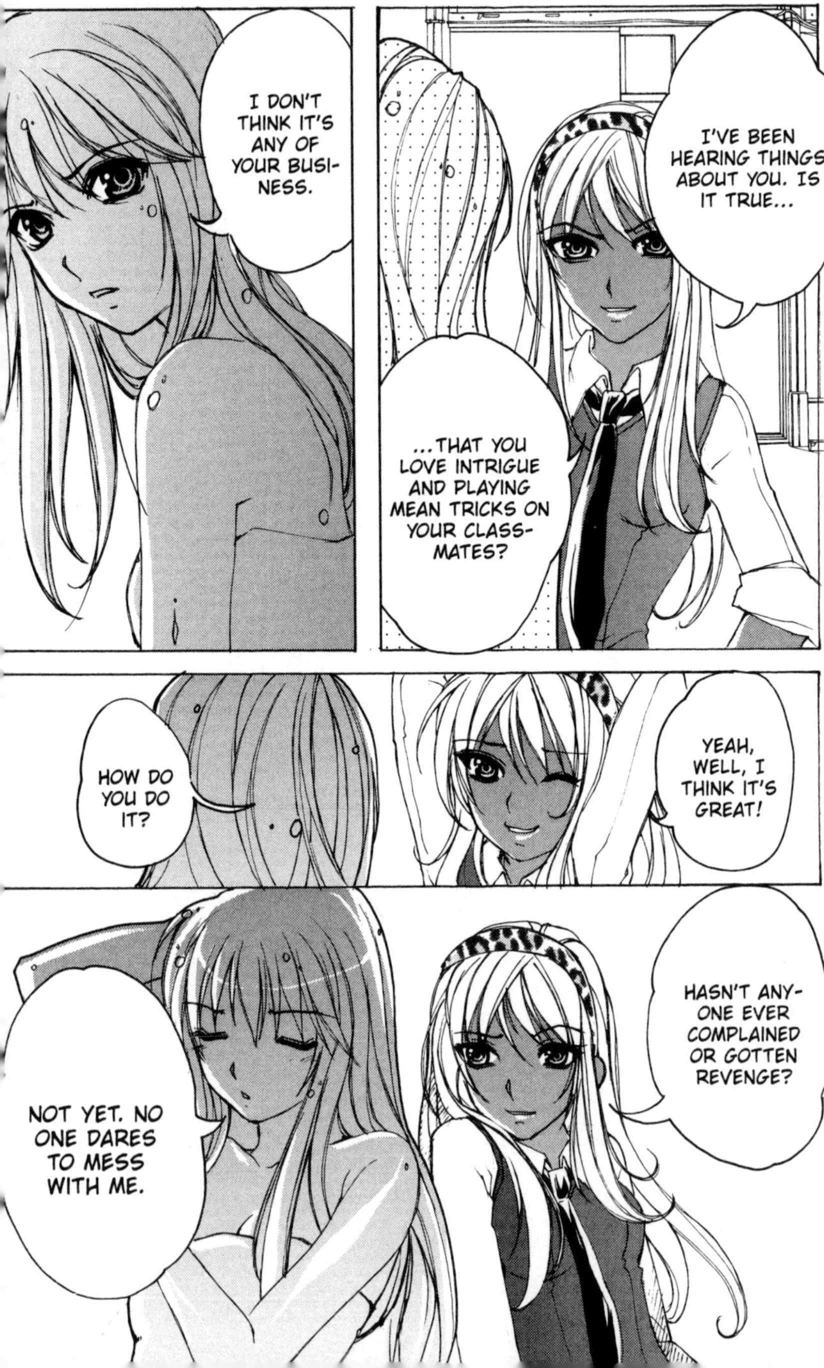
I'VE BEEN HEARING THINGS ABOUT YOU. IS IT TRUE...
...THAT YOU LOVE INTRIGUE AND PLAYING MEAN TRICKS ON YOUR CLASS-MATES?
I DON'T THINK IT'S ANY OF YOUR BUSI-NESS.
YEAH, WELL, I THINK IT'S GREAT!
HOW DO YOU DO IT?
HASN'T ANY-ONE EVER COMPLAINED OR GOTTEN REVENGE?
NOT YET. NO ONE DARES TO MESS WITH ME.

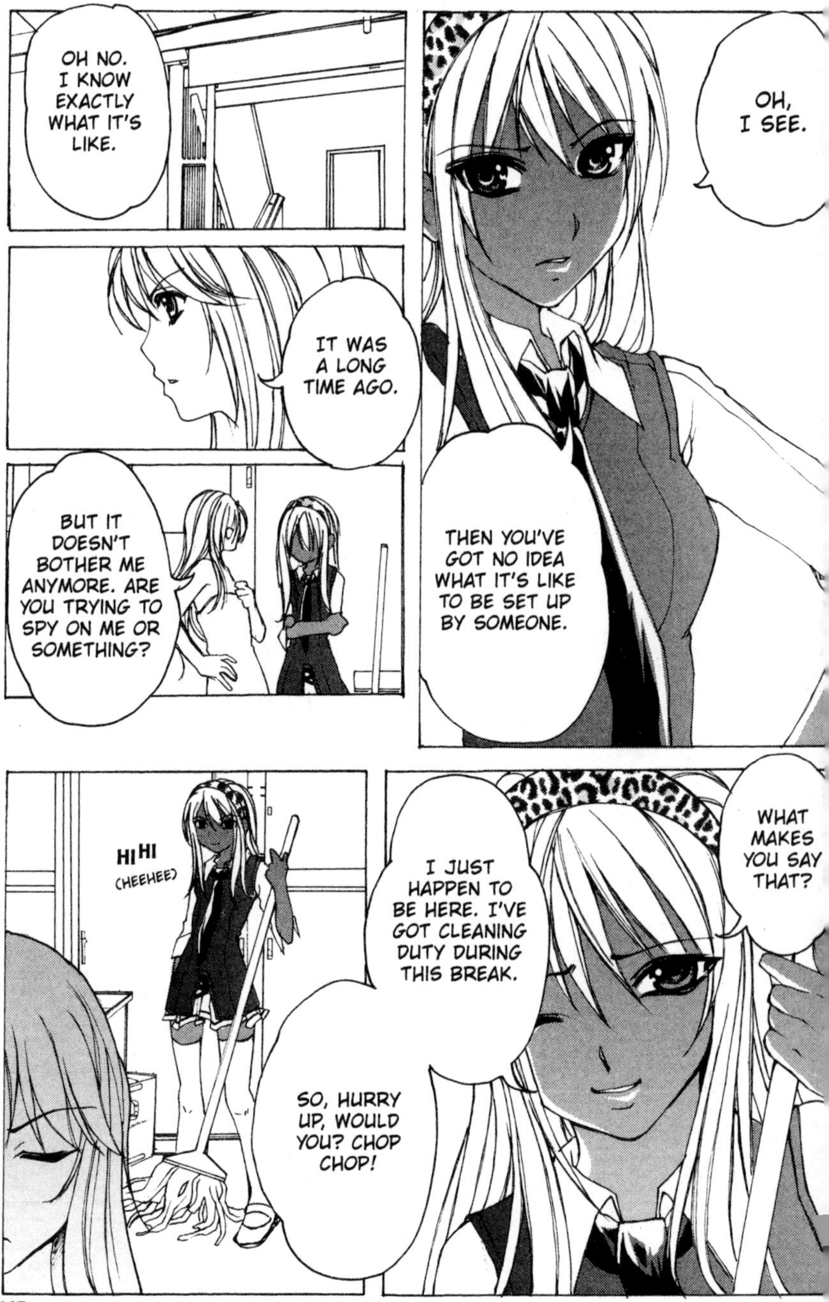
OH, I SEE.
THEN YOU'VE GOT NO IDEA WHAT IT'S LIKE TO BE SET UP BY SOMEONE.
OH NO. I KNOW EXACTLY WHAT IT'S LIKE.
IT WAS A LONG TIME AGO.
BUT IT DOESN'T BOTHER ME ANYMORE. ARE YOU TRYING TO SPY ON ME OR SOMETHING?
WHAT MAKES YOU SAY THAT?
I JUST HAPPEN TO BE HERE. I'VE GOT CLEANING DUTY DURING THIS BREAK.
SO, HURRY UP, WOULD YOU? CHOP CHOP!
HI HI
(CHEEHEE)

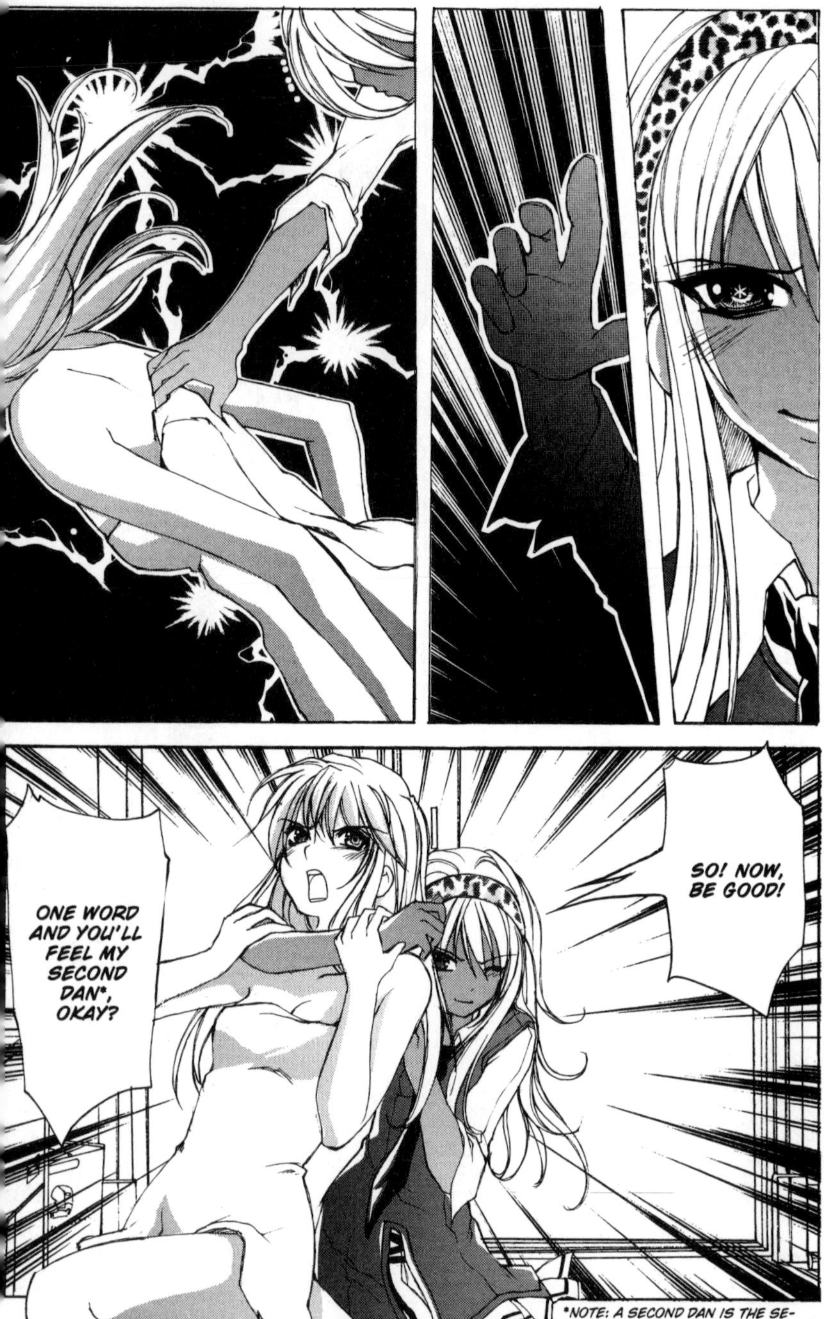
SO! NOW, BE GOOD!
ONE WORD AND YOU'LL FEEL MY SECOND DAN*, OKAY?

*NOTE: A SECOND DAN IS THE SECOND BLACK BELT IN TAE KWON DO.

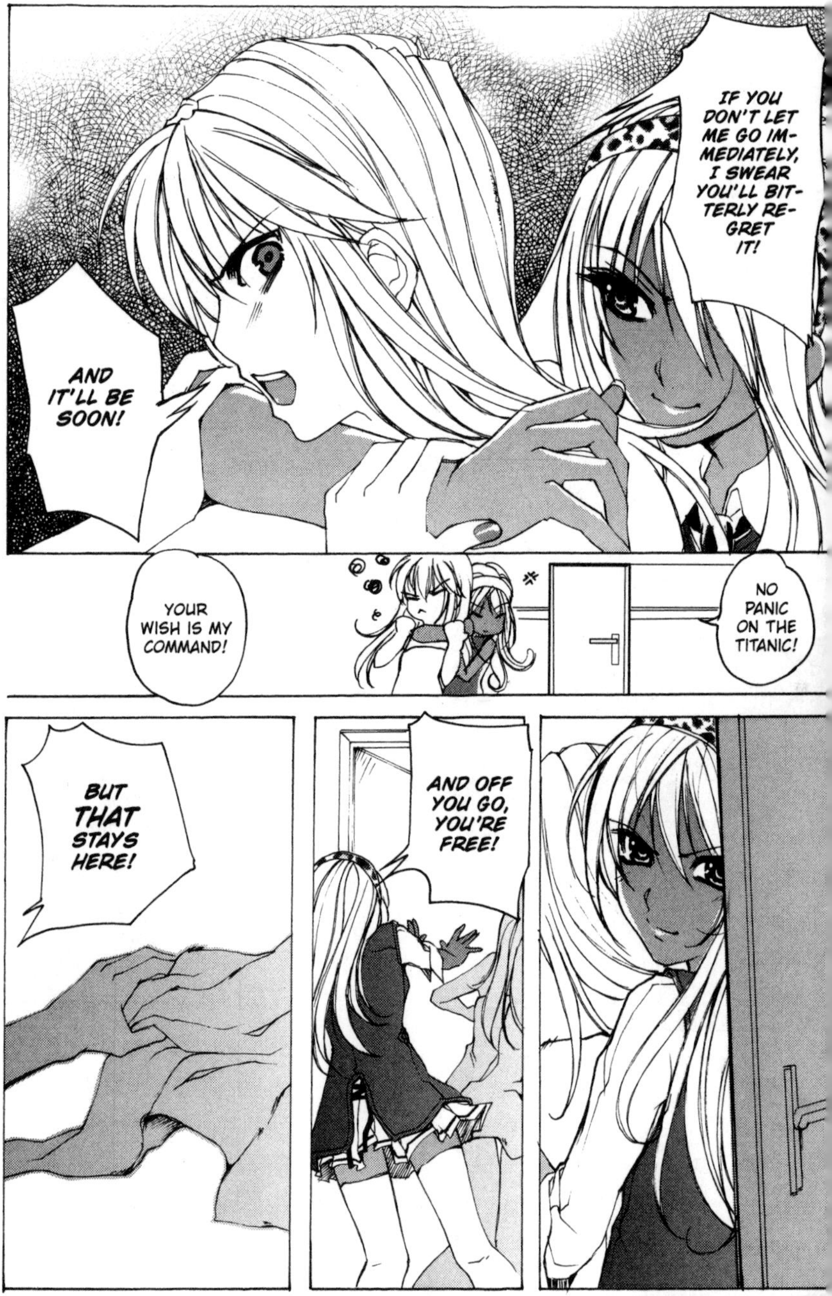
IF YOU DON'T LET ME GO IMMEDIATELY, I SWEAR YOU'LL BITTERLY REGRET IT!
AND IT'LL BE SOON!
NO PANIC ON THE TITANIC!
YOUR WISH IS MY COMMAND!
AND OFF YOU GO, YOU'RE FREE!
BUT THAT STAYS HERE!

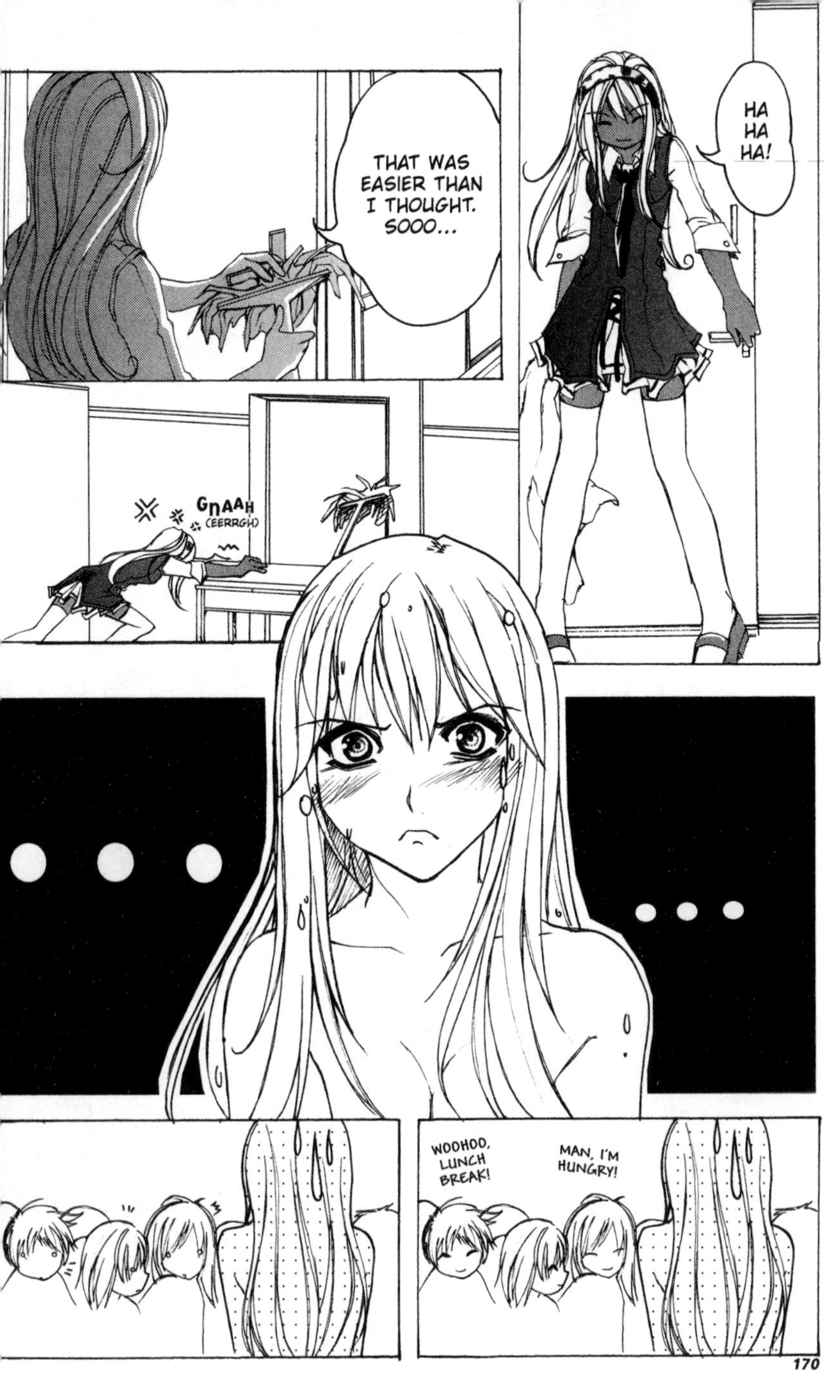
HA HA HA!
THAT WAS EASIER THAN I THOUGHT. SOOO...
GNAAH (EERRGH)
...
...
MAN, I'M HUNGRY!
WOOHOO, LUNCH BREAK!

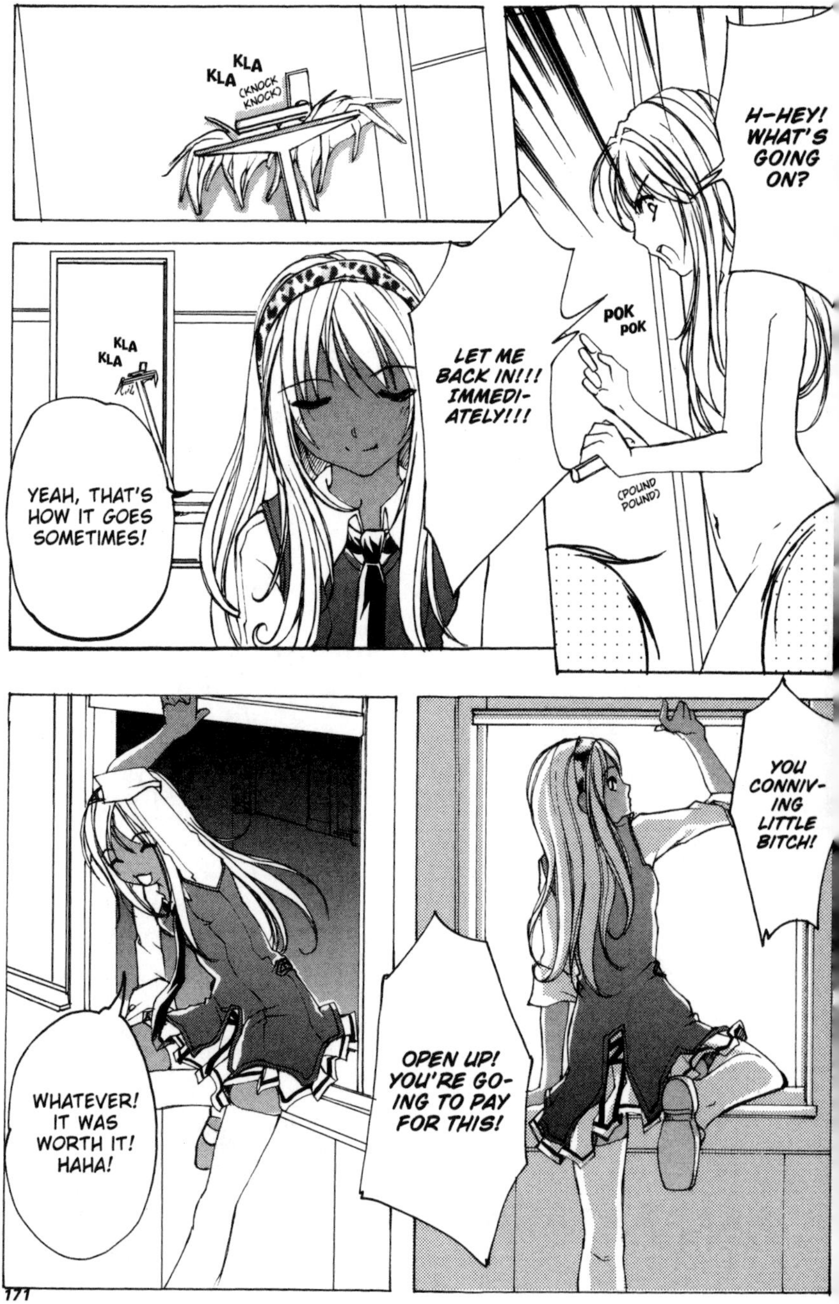
H-HEY! WHAT'S GOING ON?
LET ME BACK IN!!! IMMEDI-ATELY!!!
POK POK
(POUND POUND)
KLA KLA
(KNOCK KNOCK)
KLA KLA
YEAH, THAT'S HOW IT GOES SOMETIMES!
YOU CONNIV-ING LITTLE BITCH!
OPEN UP! YOU'RE GO-ING TO PAY FOR THIS!
WHATEVER! IT WAS WORTH IT! HAHA!

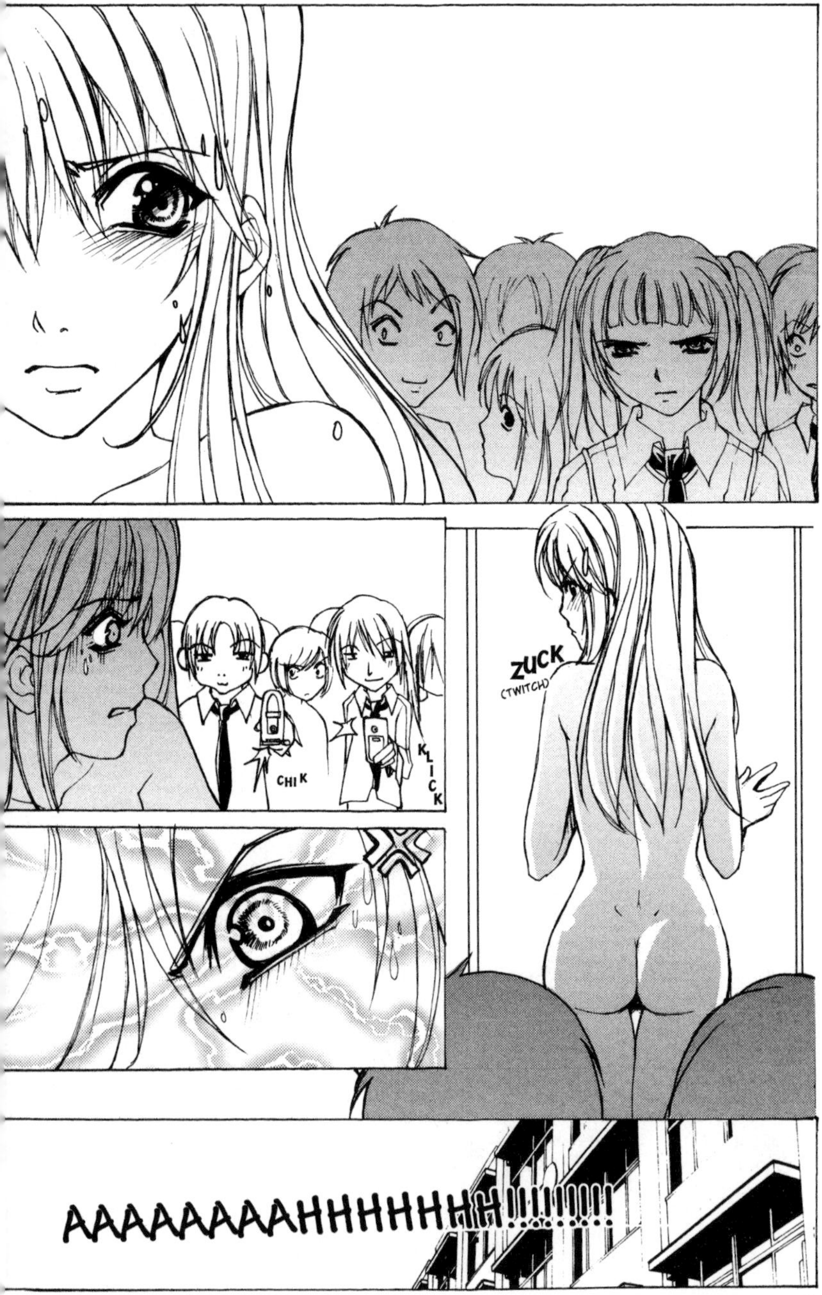
ZUCK
(TWITCH)
KLICK
CHIK
AAAAAAAAHHHHHHH!!!!!!!!

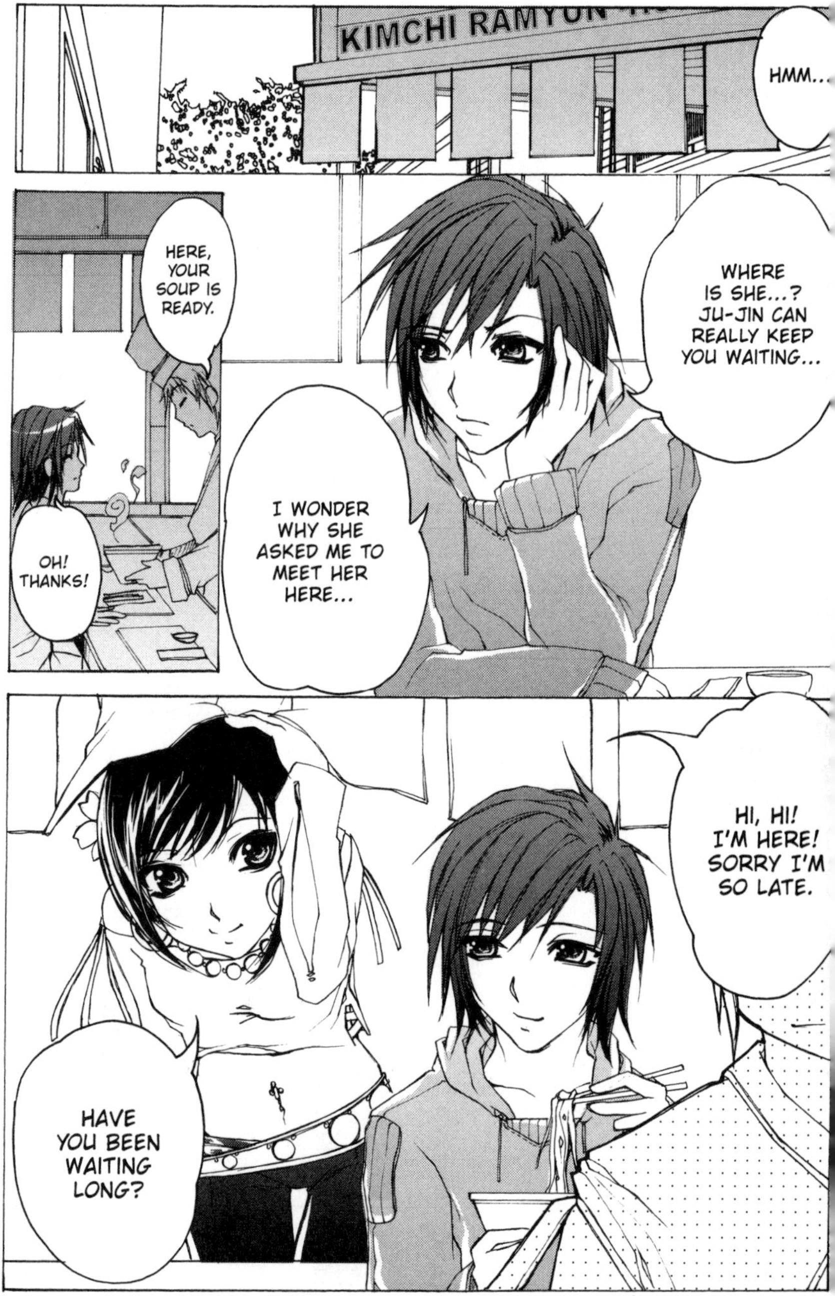
KIMCHI RAMYUN
HMM...
WHERE IS SHE...? JU-JIN CAN REALLY KEEP YOU WAITING...
I WONDER WHY SHE ASKED ME TO MEET HER HERE...
HERE, YOUR SOUP IS READY.
OH! THANKS!
HI, HI! I'M HERE! SORRY I'M SO LATE.
HAVE YOU BEEN WAITING LONG?

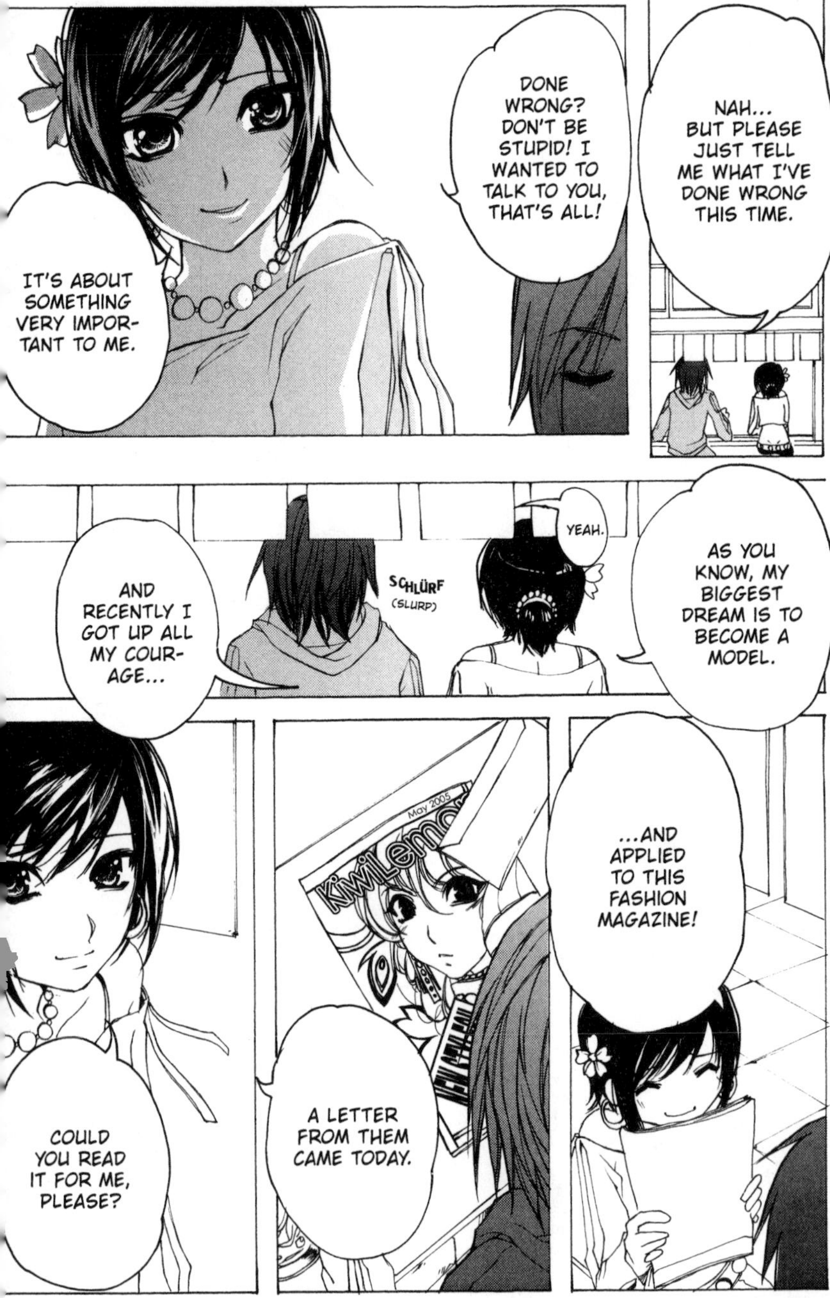
NAH... BUT PLEASE JUST TELL ME WHAT I'VE DONE WRONG THIS TIME.
DONE WRONG? DON'T BE STUPID! I WANTED TO TALK TO YOU, THAT'S ALL!
IT'S ABOUT SOMETHING VERY IMPORTANT TO ME.
AS YOU KNOW, MY BIGGEST DREAM IS TO BECOME A MODEL.
YEAH.
SCHLÜRF
(SLURP)
AND RECENTLY I GOT UP ALL MY COURAGE...
...AND APPLIED TO THIS FASHION MAGAZINE!
May 2005
A LETTER FROM THEM CAME TODAY.
COULD YOU READ IT FOR ME, PLEASE?

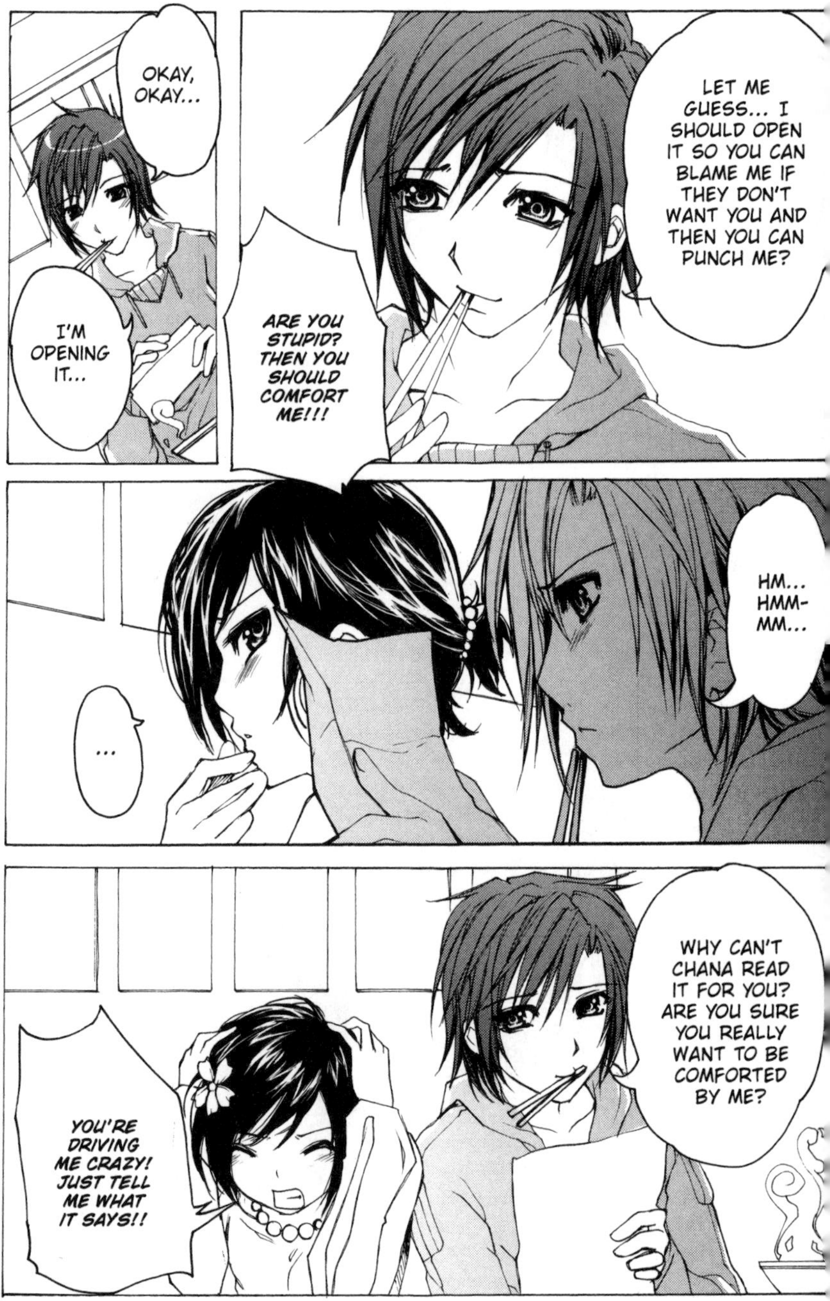
LET ME GUESS... I SHOULD OPEN IT SO YOU CAN BLAME ME IF THEY DON'T WANT YOU AND THEN YOU CAN PUNCH ME?
ARE YOU STUPID? THEN YOU SHOULD COMFORT ME!!!
OKAY, OKAY...
I'M OPENING IT...
HM... HMM-MM...
...
WHY CAN'T CHANA READ IT FOR YOU? ARE YOU SURE YOU REALLY WANT TO BE COMFORTED BY ME?
YOU'RE DRIVING ME CRAZY! JUST TELL ME WHAT IT SAYS!!

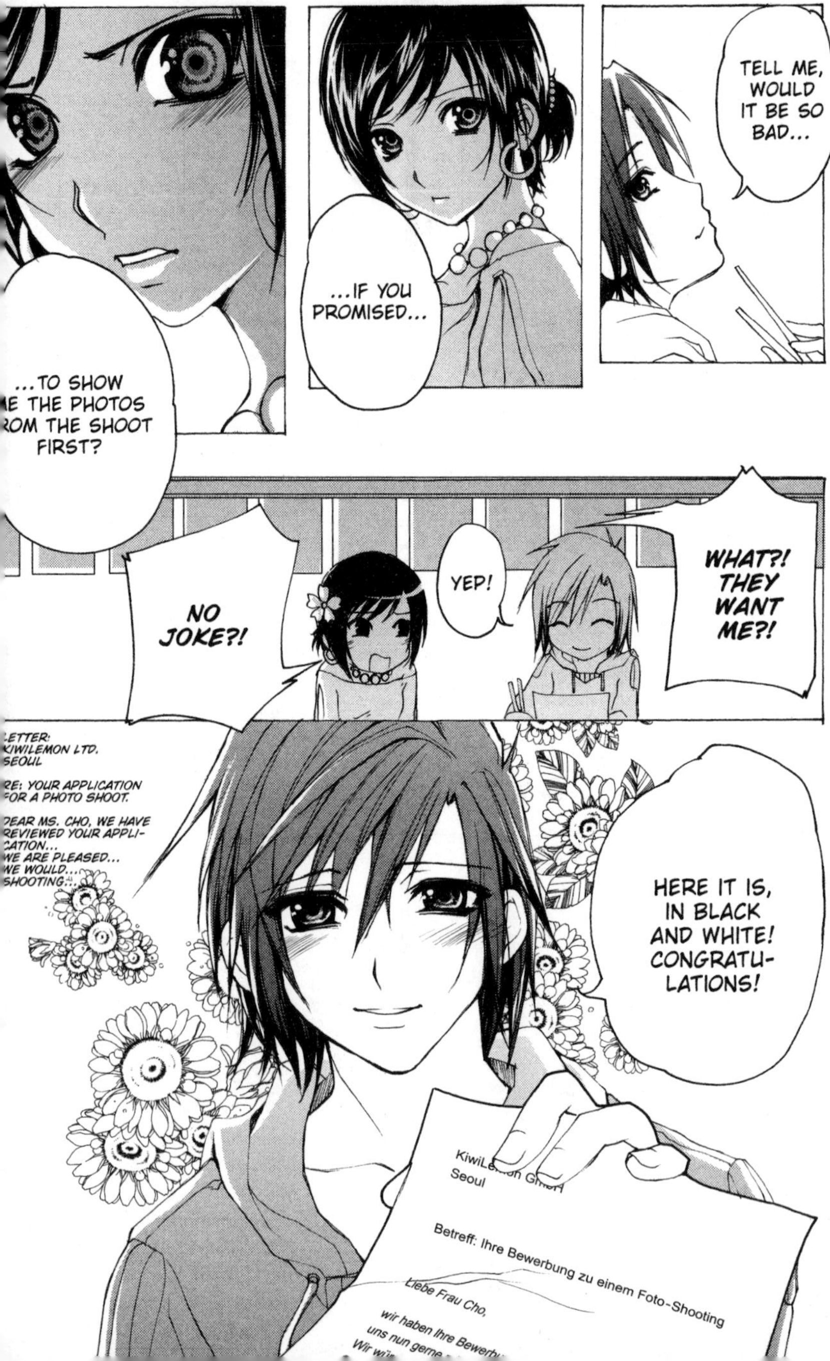
TELL ME, WOULD IT BE SO BAD...
...IF YOU PROMISED...
...TO SHOW E THE PHOTOS ROM THE SHOOT FIRST?
WHAT?! THEY WANT ME?!
YEP!
NO JOKE?!
HERE IT IS, IN BLACK AND WHITE! CONGRATULATIONS!
ETTER: KIWILEMON LTD. SEOUL
RE: YOUR APPLICATION OR A PHOTO SHOOT.
EAR MS. CHO, WE HAVE REVIEWED YOUR APPLI-CATION... WE ARE PLEASED... WE WOULD... SHOOTING...
KiwiLe
Seoul
Betreff: Ihre Bewerbung zu einem Foto-Shooting
Liebe Frau Cho,
wir haben Ihre Bewerbu
uns nun gerne

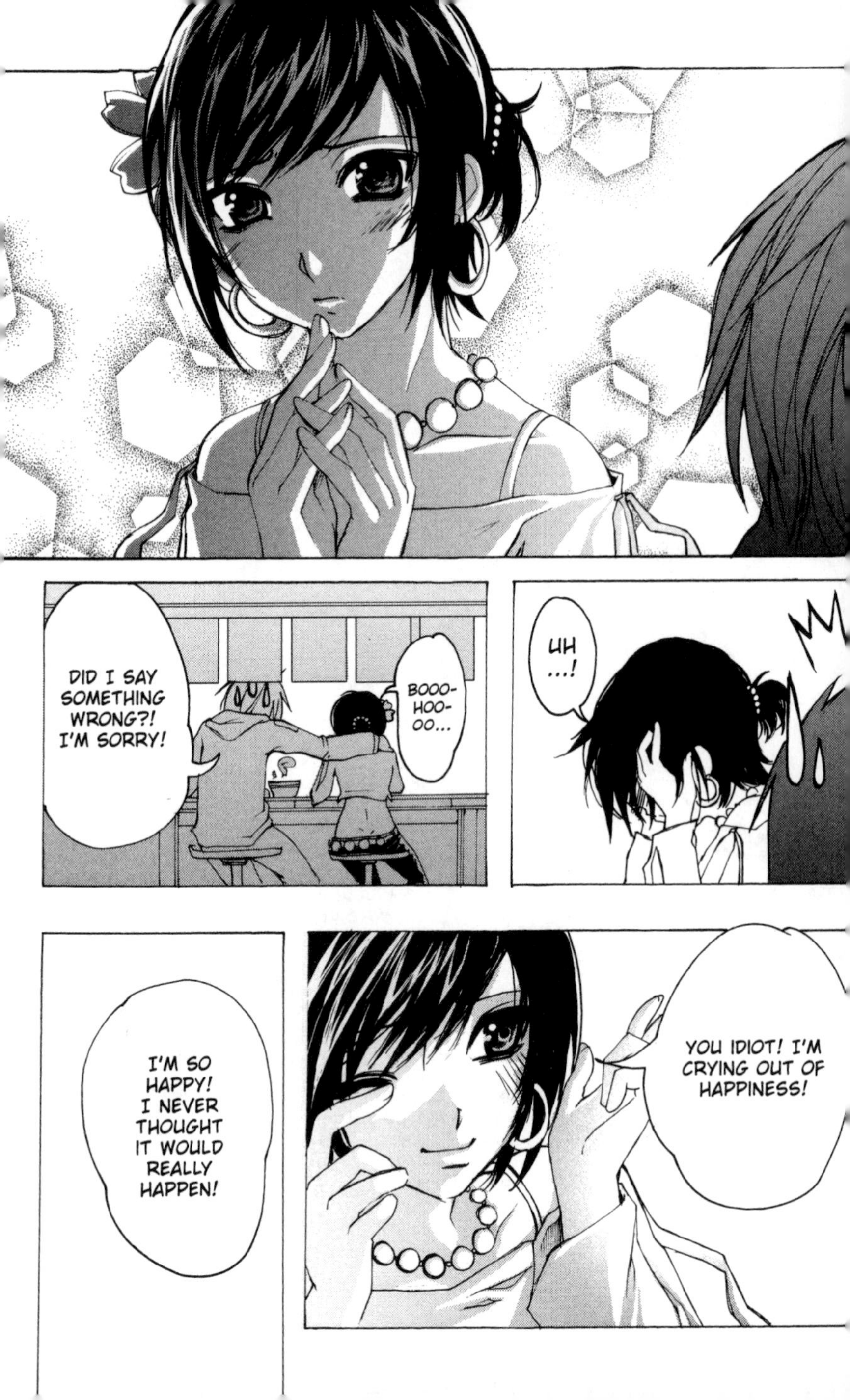
UH ...!
BOOO-HOO-OO...
DID I SAY SOMETHING WRONG?! I'M SORRY!
YOU IDIOT! I'M CRYING OUT OF HAPPINESS!
I'M SO HAPPY! I NEVER THOUGHT IT WOULD REALLY HAPPEN!

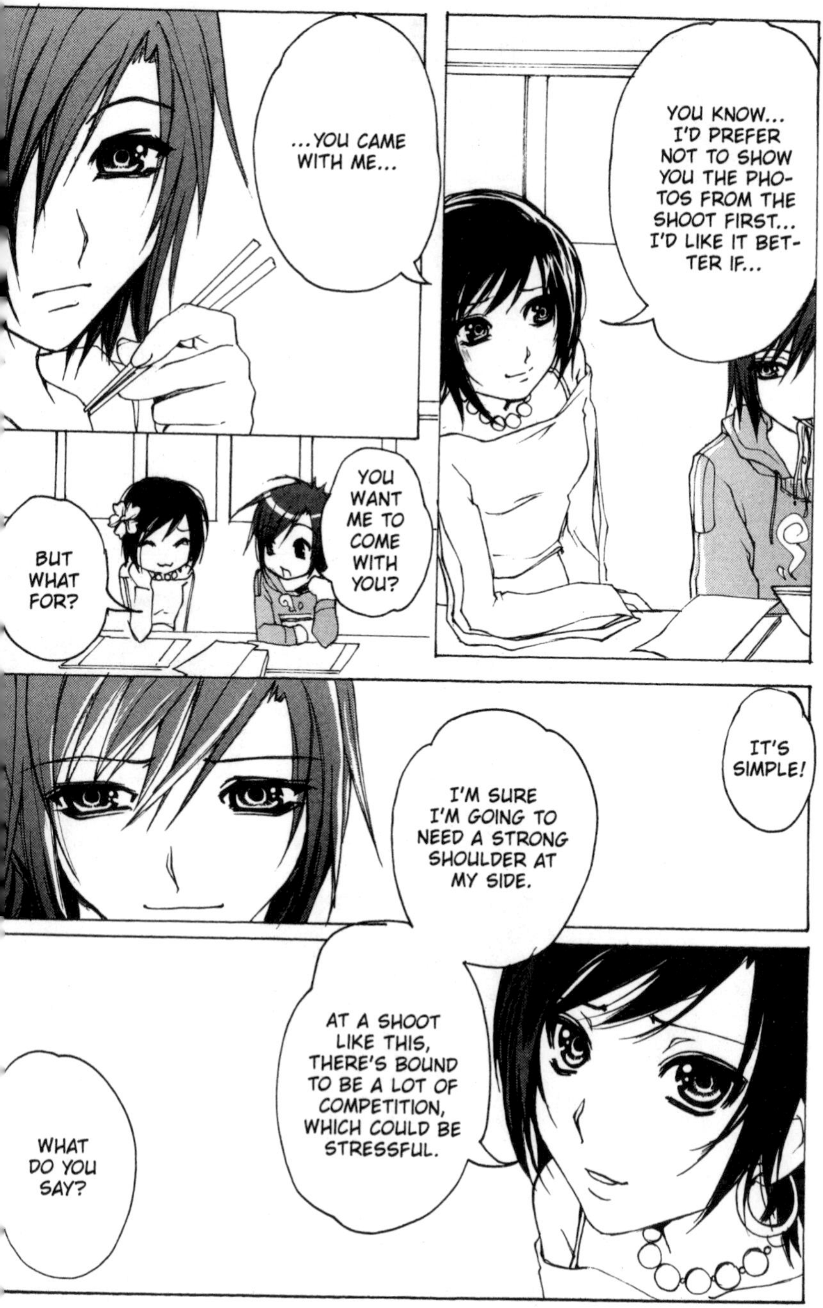
YOU KNOW... I'D PREFER NOT TO SHOW YOU THE PHOTOS FROM THE SHOOT FIRST... I'D LIKE IT BETTER IF...
...YOU CAME WITH ME...
YOU WANT ME TO COME WITH YOU?
BUT WHAT FOR?
IT'S SIMPLE!
I'M SURE I'M GOING TO NEED A STRONG SHOULDER AT MY SIDE.
AT A SHOOT LIKE THIS, THERE'S BOUND TO BE A LOT OF COMPETITION, WHICH COULD BE STRESSFUL.
WHAT DO YOU SAY?

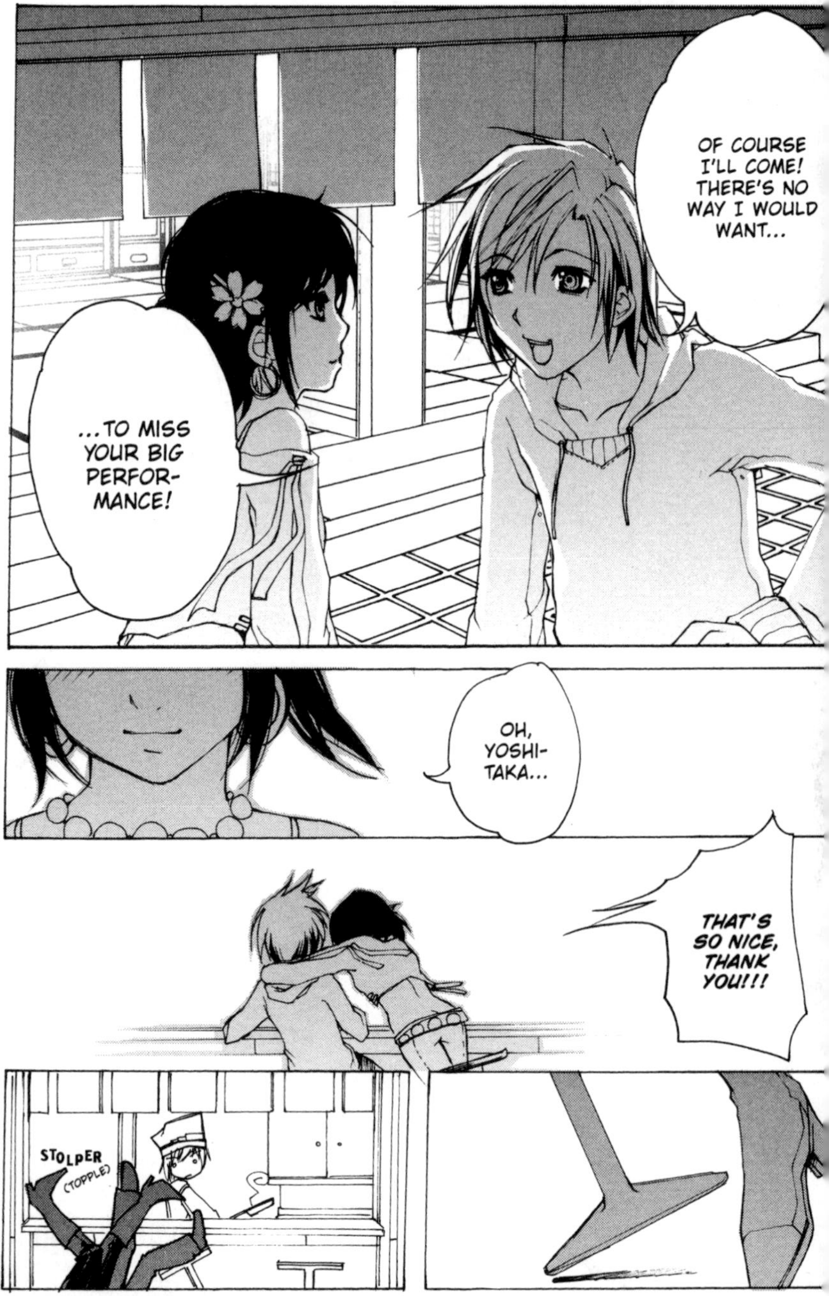
OF COURSE I'LL COME! THERE'S NO WAY I WOULD WANT...
...TO MISS YOUR BIG PERFORMANCE!
OH, YOSHI-TAKA...
THAT'S SO NICE, THANK YOU!!!
STOLPER
(TOPPLE)

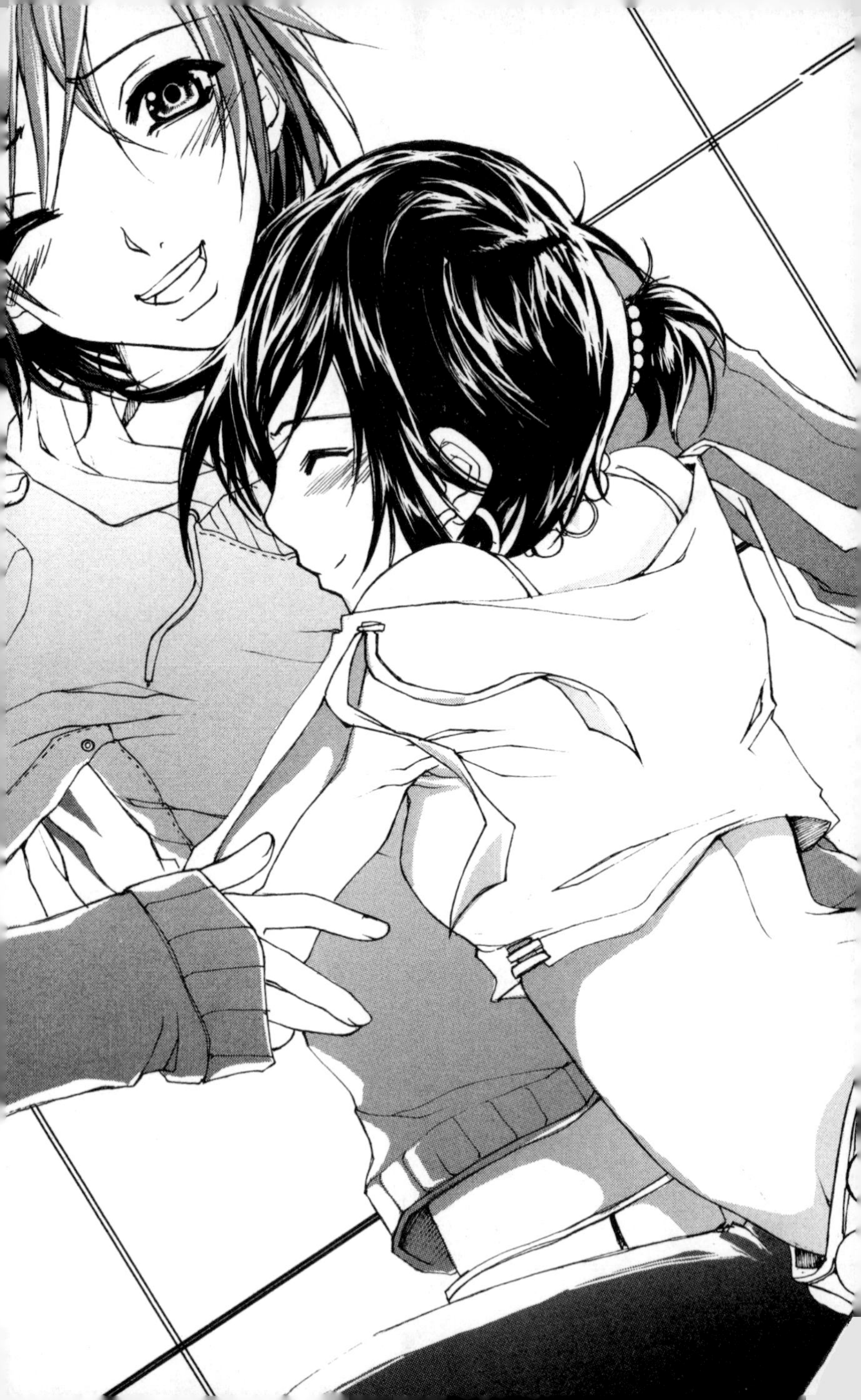

CAST & CREW

Name: Yoshitaka Kogirei
Age: 18
Birthday: April 17
Blood type: AB

Origins: Japan
Hair color: Dark blond
Eye color: Blue
Height: 6'

Name: Yagate Sotogawa
Age: 17
Birthday: August 9
Blood type: O

Origins: Japan
Hair color: Light blond
Eye color: Brown
Height: 5' 10"

Name: Ju-Jin Cho
Age: 16
Birthday: November 11
Blood type: B

Origins: South Korea
Hair color: Black
Eye color: Brown
Height: 5' 3"

Name: Chana Kane
Age: 17
Birthday: December 10
Blood type: O

Origins: Brazil
Hair color: Blonde (dyed)
Eye color: Brown
Height: 5' 6"

Name: Judith Park
Age: 21
Birthday: May 19
Blood type: O

Origins: South Korea
Hair color: Brown (dyed)
Eye color: Brown
Height: 5' 5"

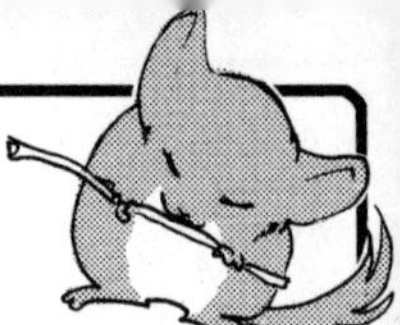

Hello, dear reader!

Phew! I really managed it and introduced you all to **Y Square**!

I'm just a little **proud** of myself that I really got through it all. At points it was very stressful to meet the deadlines and it also cost me a number of **sleepless nights**. I'm glad that my best friends were so understanding and supportive when I would lock myself away for weeks on end, showing no signs of life.

Even though I often moaned a lot, I mustn't forget to say that it really was a lot of **fun** for me and that I always particularly enjoy going to the big **book fairs**, which give me the opportunity to meet the readers.

Unfortunately, I already see that I have again made many drawing **blunders** and **mistakes**, for which I must deeply **apologize**. Many of the mistakes I made without knowing, mistakes that occurred because of haste, and mistakes that happened because I was testing out new techniques.

Therefore, I hope you can **forgive** me for the untidy, lopsided (etc. :P) parts. I also promise that in the **future**, I'll try harder in order to one day become a **good** cartoonist. ^_^

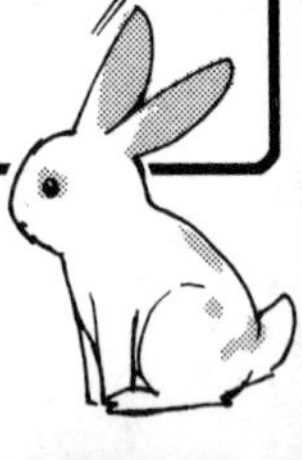

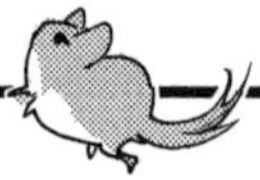

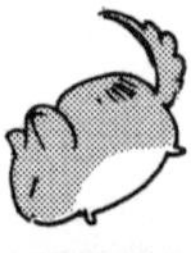

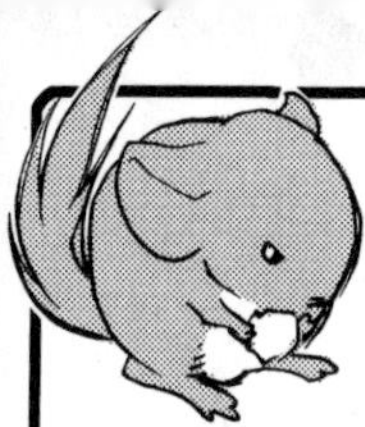

By the way, I'm often asked how you should pronounce **Y Square** and I've heard every possible variation: (HEEHEE)

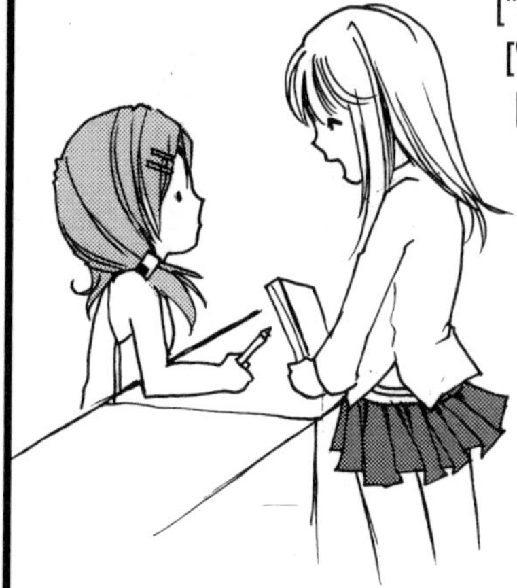

["Upsilon Skwaar"?]
["Why to the Square"?]
["Epsilon Skuar"?]

Okay, I always pronounce it in English, which is [Why Skwair]. ^_^

At this point, I would like to thank, with all my heart, Rob, who helped me in the beginning by correcting and improving my text and who gave me the courage to be more relaxed in my writing.

I really hope that you will also continue to support me and perhaps visit me at a book fair. It would make me very happy!

Thank you for reading, and until next time!

–*Judith*

HTTP://WWW.JUDITHPARK.COM

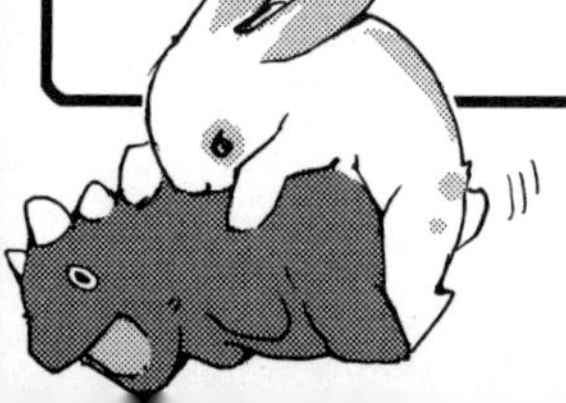

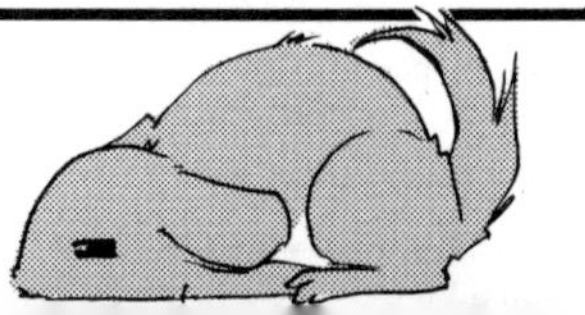

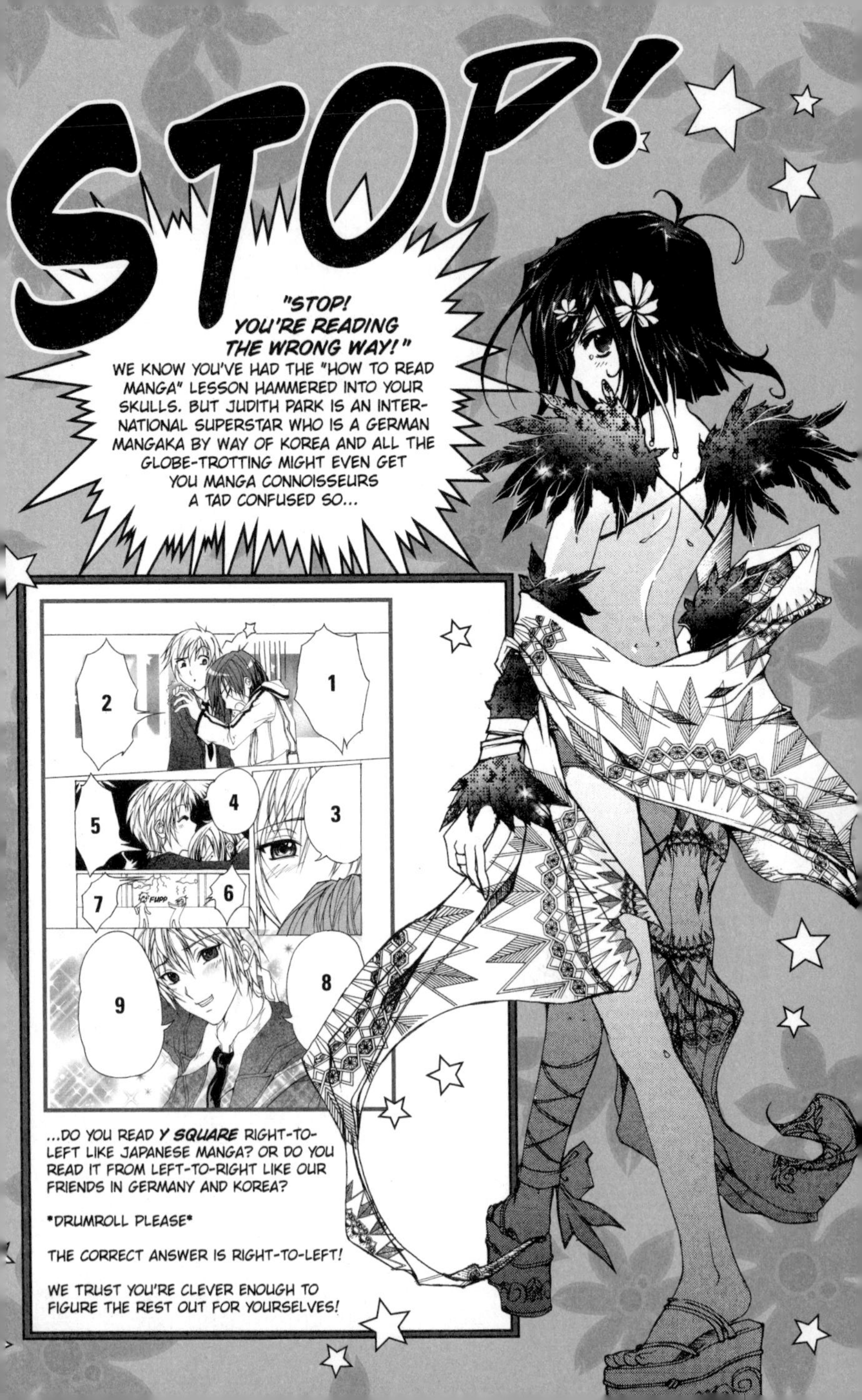
STOP!
"STOP! YOU'RE READING THE WRONG WAY!"
WE KNOW YOU'VE HAD THE "HOW TO READ MANGA" LESSON HAMMERED INTO YOUR SKULLS. BUT JUDITH PARK IS AN INTERNATIONAL SUPERSTAR WHO IS A GERMAN MANGAKA BY WAY OF KOREA AND ALL THE GLOBE-TROTTING MIGHT EVEN GET YOU MANGA CONNOISSEURS A TAD CONFUSED SO...
1
2
3
4
5
6
FUPP
7
8
9
...DO YOU READ Y SQUARE RIGHT-TO-LEFT LIKE JAPANESE MANGA? OR DO YOU READ IT FROM LEFT-TO-RIGHT LIKE OUR FRIENDS IN GERMANY AND KOREA?
DRUMROLL PLEASE
THE CORRECT ANSWER IS RIGHT-TO-LEFT!
WE TRUST YOU'RE CLEVER ENOUGH TO FIGURE THE REST OUT FOR YOURSELVES!